Global Logistics

Global Logistics

Nitin Johari

RANDOM PUBLICATIONS
NEW DELHI (INDIA)

Global Logistics

ISBN 978-93-5111-225-9

Published in 2014 in India by

Reprint 2020

RANDOM PUBLICATIONS

4376-A/4B, Gali Murari Lal, Ansari Road
New Delhi-110 002
Phone : +91-11-43580356, +91-11-23289044
e-mail: randomexports@gmail.com, sales@randompublications.com, info@randompublications.com

Type Setting by : Keystoneprintads, Delhi-110051
Printed at : Mehra Printers, Delhi-110 092

Preface

Logistics is the management of the flow of resources between the point of origin and the point of consumption in order to meet some requirements, for example, of customers or corporations. The resources managed in logistics can include physical items, such as food, materials, equipment, liquids, and staff, as well as abstract items, such as time, information, particles, and energy. The logistics of physical items usually involves the integration of information flow, material handling, production, packaging, inventory, transportation, warehousing, and often security. The complexity of logistics can be modeled, analyzed, visualized, and optimized by dedicated simulation software. The minimization of the use of resources is a common motivation logistics for import and export

The prevalent view is that term logistics comes from the late 19th century: from French logistique. However, the New Oxford American Dictionary defines logistics as "the detailed coordination of a complex operation involving many people, facilities, or supplies". As such, logistics is commonly seen as a branch of engineering that creates "people systems" rather than "machine systems". According to the Council of Logistics Management, logistics includes the integrated planning, control, realization, and monitoring of all internal and network-wide material, part, and product flow, including the necessary information flow, industrial and trading companies along the complete value-added chain for the purpose of conforming to customer requirements. Logistics is the process of planning, implementing, and controlling the effective and efficient flow of goods and services from the point of origin to the point of consumption

Inbounding logistics is one of the primary processes of logistics, concentrating on purchasing and arranging the inbound movement of materials, parts, and/or finished inventory from suppliers to manufacturing or assembly plants, warehouses, or retail stores. Outbound logistics is the process related to the storage and movement of the final product and the related information flows from the end of the production line to the end user. Global Logistics provides a wealth of useful ideas and practical information on all the current and future trends in logistics and supply chain management. Written by an author of contributors who are acknowledged experts in their fields, this fully updated book focuses on areas of particular current interest.

I thank all members of my team who have helped in the preparation of the book. My special thanks go to "Random Publications" who have published the book.

– *Nitin Johari*

Contents

1

Introduction to Logistics

WHAT IS LOGISTICS

Over time, the profession of supply chain management has evolved to meet the changing needs of the global supply chain. According to the Council of Supply Chain Management Professionals (CSCMP)—

- "Supply chain management encompasses the planning and management of all activities involved in sourcing and procurement...and all logistics management activities. Importantly, it also includes coordination and collaboration with channel partners, which can be suppliers, intermediaries, third party service providers, and customers. In essence, supply chain management integrates supply and demand management within and across companies."

The CSCMP also defines logistics management as—

- "[The] part of supply chain management that plans, implements, and controls the efficient, effective forward and reverses flow and storage of goods, services and related information between the point of origin and the point of consumption in order to meet customers' requirement... Logistics management is an integrating function, which coordinates and optimizes all logistics activities, as well as integrates logistics activities with other functions including marketing, sales manufacturing, finance, and information technology." (CSCMP 2011)

In other words, you can consider logistics activities as the operational component of supply chain management, including quantification, procurement, inventory management, transportation and fleet management, and data collection and reporting. Supply chain management includes the logistics activities plus the coordination and collaboration of staff, levels, and functions. The supply chain includes global manufacturers and supply and demand dynamics, but logistics tends to focus more on specific tasks within a particular program health system.

This handbook focuses on specific logistics activities that are undertaken within the context of an integrated supply chain model. This model promotes collaboration and seamless linkages between the activities, levels and people responsible for managing the supply chain. Note that throughout the handbook, we use the terms *logistics* and *supply chain* interchangeably.

WHY LOGISTICS MATTERS

In the past, logistics was considered a custodial activity. Storekeepers were the custodians of supplies stored in small storerooms and large warehouses. Consequently, the science (and art) of logistics, and the people who make the health logistics system work, were not considered an important part of family planning, HIV and AIDS, or vaccination programs—to name only a few. Fortunately, as time passed, more and more program managers have come to understand how important logistics is to a program's success.

The goal of a health logistics system is much larger than simply making sure a product gets where it needs to go. Ultimately, the goal of every public health logistics system is to help ensure that every customer has commodity security. Commodity security exists when every person is able to obtain and use quality essential health supplies whenever he or she needs them. A properly functioning supply chain is a critical part of ensuring commodity security—financing, policies, and commitment are also necessary.

Effective supply chains not only help ensure commodity security, they also help determine the success or failure of any public health program. Both in business and in the public sector, decisionmakers increasingly direct their attention to improving supply chains, because logistics improvements bring important, quantifiable benefits. Well-functioning supply chains benefit public health programs in important ways by—

- Increasing program impact
- Enhancing quality of care
- Improving cost effectiveness and efficiency.

LOGISTICS INCREASES PROGRAM IMPACT

If a logistics system provides a reliable supply of commodities, more people are likely to use health services. Customers feel more confident about the health program when they have a constant supply of commodities—it motivates them to seek and use services. As the availability of a mix of contraceptive methods improves, the contraceptive prevalence rate (CPR) for the public sector increases. When a choice of contraceptive methods is available in health facilities, more women use contraception. When more women use contraception, it impacts a number of key public health indicators: maternal mortality, infant mortality, and total fertility rates all decrease.

LOGISTICS ENHANCES QUALITY OF CARE

Well-supplied health programs can provide superior service, while poorly supplied programs cannot. Likewise, well-supplied health workers can use their training and expertise fully, directly improving the quality of care for clients. Customers are not the only ones who benefit from the consistent availability of commodities. An effective logistics system helps provide adequate, appropriate supplies to health providers, increasing their professional satisfaction, motivation, and morale. Motivated staff are more likely to deliver a higher quality of service.

LOGISTICS IMPROVES COST EFFICIENCY AND EFFECTIVENESS

An effective supply chain contributes to improved cost effectiveness in all parts of a program, and it can stretch limited resources. Strengthening and maintaining the logistics system is an investment that pays off in three ways.

- It reduces losses due to overstock, waste, expiry, damage, pilferage, and inefficiency;
- It protects other major program investments; and
- It maximizes the potential for cost recovery.

For anyone reading this handbook; and for everyone who works to manage, support, and improve public health logistics systems; logistics is probably important to you already. To ensure that public sector health commodity logistics systems continue to provide commodity security and to improve program impact, quality of care, and cost efficiency, we must convince policymakers and decisionmakers that contributions to strengthening logistics systems will result in increased overall program effectiveness. We must show them that for any public health program to deliver high-quality, comprehensive services; and to ensure commodity security, a robust logistics system for managing health commodities must be in place. We must demonstrate to them that logistics matters.

LOGISTICS SYSTEM

During your lifetime, you will encounter hundreds of logistics systems—in restaurants, stores, warehouses, and many other places. This handbook describes logistics systems for health programs; however, if you understand a simple example of a logistics system, you will be able to understand almost any health logistics system.

A restaurant is one example of a simple logistics system.

- The kitchen is a storage facility; the food is held there until it is delivered to the customer.
- Waiters provide the transportation; they carry the food from the kitchen to the customer.
- The tables are the service delivery points, where customers sit to order and eat the food.

For customers, a restaurant is not a logistics system; it is a place to eat. You probably never thought of a restaurant as a logistics system. Your expectations for a restaurant, however, are directly related to logistics.

What expectations do you have when you go out to a restaurant for a meal?

You may expect that the—

- Restaurant will be attractive and pleasing
- Server will provide excellent customer service
- Food you order will be available
- Food will be served promptly
- Correct order will be delivered to your table
- Food will be of acceptable quality
- Food will be of acceptable quantity
- Cost of the meal will correspond to the value.

These customer expectations define the purpose of a logistics system—it ensures that the right goods, in the right quantities, in the right condition, are delivered to the right place, at the right time, for the right cost. In logistics, these rights are called the six rights. Whether the system supplies soft drinks, vehicles, or pens; or manages contraceptives, essential drugs, or other commodities, these six rights always apply.

LOGISTICS CYCLE: ORGANIZING LOGISTICS SYSTEM ACTIVITIES

Logistics management includes a number of activities that support the six rights. Over the years, logisticians have developed a model to illustrate the relationship between the activities in a logistics system; they call it the logistics cycle.

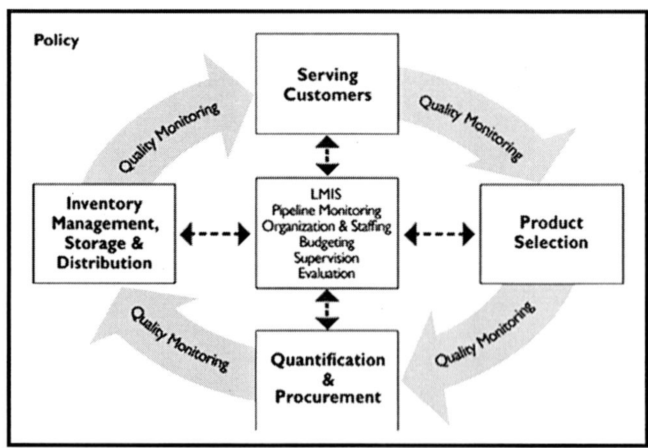

Fig. The Logistics Cycle

You will first notice that the cycle is circular, which indicates the cyclical or repetitive nature of the various elements in the cycle. Each activity—serving customers, product selection, quantification and procurement, and inventory management—depends on and is affected by the other activities. For example, product selection is based on serving customers. What would happen if, for a medical reason, we select a product that is not authorized or registered for use in a country program? We would need to rethink our decision and order a product that is authorized and registered for use. This decision would, in turn, affect our procurement and storage, two other activities in the logistics cycle. The activities in the center of the logistics cycle represent the management support functions that inform and impact the other elements around the logistics cycle.

In the next few sections, you will look briefly at all the elements shown in the logistics cycle, including the—

- Major activities in the cycle
- Heart of the logistics cycle
- Quality monitoring of the activities
- Logistics environment—policies and adaptability of the system.

MAJOR ACTIVITIES IN THE LOGISTICS CYCLE

Let's briefly review the major activities in the logistics cycle:

Serving customers

Everyone who works in logistics must remember that they select, procure, store, or distribute products to meet customer needs. Storekeepers do not store drugs just for the purpose of storing; they store products to ensure that commodity security exists for every customer to obtain and use the health commodities when they need them. In addition to serving the needs of the end customer—the customer seeking health services—each person in the process is also serving the needs of more immediate customers. Storekeepers provide customer service when they issue medicines to the health facility, and the central medical stores provide customer service when they issue commodities to the district. The logistics system ensures customer service by fulfilling the six rights. Each activity in the logistics cycle, therefore, contributes to excellent customer service and to ensuring commodity security.

product selection

In any health logistics system, health programs must select products. In a health logistics system, a national formulary and therapeutics committee, pharmaceutical board, board of physicians, or other government-appointed group may be responsible for product selection. Most countries have developed essential medicine lists patterned on the World Health Organization (WHO) Model List. Products selected for use will impact the logistics system, so the logistics requirements must be considered during the product selection.

Quantification

After products have been selected, the required quantity and cost of each product must be determined. Quantification is the process of estimating the quantity and cost of the products required for a specific health program (or service), and, to ensure an uninterrupted supply for the program, determining when the products should be procured and distributed. See the suggested reading list at the end of the handbook for sources of additional information about quantification of health commodities.

Procurement

After a supply plan has been developed as part of the quantification process, quantities of products must be procured. Health systems or programs can procure from international, regional, or local sources of supply; or they can use a procurement agent for this logistics activity. In any case, procurement should follow a set of specific procedures that ensure an open and transparent process that supports the six rights.

inventory management: storage and distribution

After an item has been procured and received by the health system or program, it must be transported to the service delivery level where the client will receive the products. During this process, the products must be stored until they are sent to the next lower level, or until the customer needs them. Almost all businesses store a quantity of stock for future customer needs.

HEART OF THE LOGISTICS SYSTEM

Information is the engine that drives the logistics cycle; without information, the logistics system would not run smoothly.

Logistics management information systems

In the beginning of the cycle, managers gather information about each activity in the system and analyze that information to make decisions and coordinate future actions. For example, information about product consumption and inventory levels must be gathered to ensure that a manager knows how much of a product to procure.

Logisticians added the word *logistics* to *management information system* (MIS) to create *logistics management information system* (LMIS). Logisticians want it clear that the collection of data for managing a logistics system is a separate activity from the collection of data for other information systems, including health management information systems (HMISs). An LMIS collects data about commodities; this information is often used for activities, such as filling routine supply orders for health facilities. An HMIS collects information on the total number of patients seen or diagnosed; data from an HMIS is not used as often as LMIS data— i.e., annually—and it is used for different purposes—i.e., for evaluating program impact. Logisticians emphasize the use of logistics data for making decisions about activities within the logistics cycle.

Other activities at the heart of the logistics cycle

Other activities help drive or support the logistics cycle; they are the heart of a well-functioning logistics system. These activities include—

organization and staffing

A logistics system can only work if well-trained, efficient staff monitor stock levels, place orders, and provide products to clients. Health programs assign the appropriate resources to staff (for example, supervision authority and technical knowledge) to complete logistics activities. In fact, some countries have established national logistics management units that analyze logistics data and provide feedback throughout the system. Organization and staffing, therefore, are important parts of the cycle. For a logistics system to work correctly, logistics staff must make the six rights a top priority.

Budget

Allocation and management of finances directly affect all parts of the logistics cycle, including the quantities of products that can be procured, the amount of storage space that may be available, the number of vehicles that can be maintained, and the number of staff working in logistics. Mobilizing resources and securing a budget line item for health commodities and logistics activities is extremely important to ensure that products are available and that the logistics system operates effectively. To determine the resources needed to scale up, supply chain managers first need to assess what the expected costs are at different levels of the logistics system. When determining supply chains costs, managers should consider the cost of storage, transportation, and management; and determine what share of these costs each group will cover (i.e., Ministry of Health, donors, nongovernmental organizations [NGOs], etc.).

Supervision

Supervising the staff who work within the logistics system keeps it running smoothly and helps to anticipate needed changes. Routine, effective supervision, coupled with on-the-job training in logistics, helps to both prevent and resolve supply problems and human resource constraints.

monitoring and evaluation

Routine monitoring and periodic evaluation of the pipeline and logistics system activities help demonstrate how well the system is performing, the areas that can be improved, as well as the system's impact on service provision.

QUALITY MONITORING

It is important to understand the role of quality monitoring in ensuring an efficient and effective logistics system. In the logistics cycle, notice how *quality monitoring* appears between each activity of the logistics cycle. *Quality monitoring refers not only to the quality of the product, but also to the quality of the work.*

Between Product Selection and Quantification & Procurement

Quality monitoring plays an important role in quantifying and procuring the right products, based on the appropriate product selection and use. Products that are quantified should be on the national essential medicines list (EML), be approved and registered for use in the country, and be included in appropriate standard treatment guidelines (STGs). Also, service providers must be trained to correctly use the products before they are procured and distributed to facilities.

Between Quantification & Procurement and Inventory Management

Procurement decisions should be based on the supply plan that is developed during quantification. To ensure product quality, procurement documents must include detailed product and packaging specifications, and the expectations for quality at the time of receipt. After procurement, program managers must check the quality of health commodities before they enter the distribution system. Products that are procured should be quickly cleared through customs, or other inspections, before being distributed to facilities.

Between Inventory Management and Serving Customers

While products are received, stored, and distributed (and when customers receive them), it is important to monitor their quality. Furthermore, the quality of the storage conditions and transportation mechanisms should be monitored. The inventory control system must be designed so that, if followed, customers will receive the products they need, at the time they need them.

Between Serving Customers and Product Selection

Even after customers receive the products, the program must continue to monitor the quality. Programs must determine if customers are satisfied with the quality of the products and whether the customers are satisfied with the service they received.

Health workers must adhere to standard treatment guidelines when serving clients; they must also conduct pharmacovigilance. Quality monitoring of both the product and the service is critical to the success of efforts to promote the appropriate use of products. Customers should correctly use the products they receive and be satisfied with them and with the service they received. The results of monitoring customer satisfaction can be used to inform decisionmakers about changes in product selection and use for the next procurement cycle. Remember, serving customers is at the top of the logistics cycle and that means getting the right goods to those customers.

POLICY AND ADAPTABILITY

In addition to the elements in the logistics cycle, two additional factors—policy and adaptability— directly relate to the logistics system.

Policy

Government regulations and procedures affect all elements of the logistics system. Many country governments have established policies on the selection of medical products (usually based on essential medicine lists), how items are procured (for example, international competitive bidding or using prequalified manufacturers); when items are distributed; where and how items are stored; and the quantities customers receive (often called *dispensing protocols*). Fiscal and budget policies are often some of the most influential policies affecting a logistics system, whether related to securing funding for product procurement; or to pay for critical infrastructure, such as storerooms and transportation. Health program managers and other personnel dedicated to logistics can influence these policies, but they may face great challenges when trying to implement or change them. These managers and personnel should stay up-to-date on current policies and complete them, as specified.

adaptability

Adaptability is a characteristic of all successful logistics systems. Logistics systems must be designed to be flexible and adapt to constantly changing circumstances, such as changes in demand for a product, or changes in funding policies for logistics activities. You cannot redesign the logistics system every time a new product is introduced, or when consumption increases. In one sense, adaptability speaks to the logistics system's ability to successfully obtain the resources that are necessary to address changes in demand. For example, as demand increases, the logistics system needs to be flexible enough to respond to the increase in the quantities of products that will move through the system. This may mean building more warehouses and purchasing more vehicles, or increasing the frequency of resupply to avoid the need for larger storage facilities. The system's ability to meet these needs—its adaptability—will impact commodity availability. As governments continue to propose ways to reform the entire health sector—such as decentralization, integration, or cost recovery—the logistics system must continue to function when reforms are implemented. To function, a logistics system must be adaptable.

KEY LOGISTICS TERMS

Many of the terms in this handbook have a specific meaning for logistics; definitions in a dictionary may not be the same as the definitions we use. The key logistics terms used throughout the handbook are defined below and in the glossary at the back of this handbook.

- Supplies, commodities, goods, materials, products, and stock. These items flow through a logistics system. The terms are used interchangeably throughout this handbook.

- Users, clients, patients, and customers. The people who receive or use supplies. The terms are used interchangeably throughout this handbook.
  - *Users* is familiar to anyone who collects information about *new* or *continuing* users, such as in family planning programs. *Users* can also refer to people who use a product that is not given to a client or patient but is used for them, such as an HIV test kit or a laboratory reagent. In those examples, the counselor or the lab technician is the *user* of the product.
  - *Clients* usually refers to someone who receives a treatment or service. For example, they could be a family planning client and receive contraceptives; or they could be a client and receive a service, such as a test for malaria or TB.
  - *Patients* is a term often associated with clinic patients receiving treatment for an illness, such as those in an antiretroviral therapy (ART) program.
  - *Customers* is a term typically used by the private sector; it helps reinforce the concept of *customer service*. In public health programs, all users, clients, and patients are considered to be *customers* in the same way a commercial business thinks of its customers: the service provider, health center, and laboratory are there to serve the customer. The concept of customer service can also be applied between levels of a logistics system—the regional or provincial warehouse is the customer of the central warehouse.
- consumption, dispensed, dispensed to user, usage data. Data on the quantity of goods given to or used by customers. The terms are used interchangeably throughout this handbook.
- service delivery point. Any facility where users receive supplies related to health services. Service delivery points (SDPs) are usually hospitals and health centers, but may also include mobile units, community-based distributors, laboratories, and health posts. These facilities are called SDPs because services are provided and products are used or dispensed at these locations.
- pipeline. The entire chain of physical storage facilities and transportation links through which supplies move from the manufacturer to the user, including port facilities, central warehouse, regional warehouses, district warehouses, all SDPs, and transport vehicles, including community-based distribution networks.
  - Like a water pipeline, the logistics system has *tanks* and *physical pipes* (the warehouses and means of transportation) that store and move *water* (the product) to the *home* (the SDP).

- Unlike a water pipeline, which is usually continuous, a health logistics pipeline requires transportation to move supplies periodically from one warehouse to another. In geographically diverse countries, supplies are moved in various ways, including small boats, buses, and even bicycles.

- lead time. The time between when new stock is ordered and when it is received and available for use. When logistics managers evaluate how well a logistics system is meeting the six rights, they measure the lead time and try to reduce it. Goods should be available to customers at *the right time*—before the customer asks for the product. Lead time can be calculated within the entire in-country system, from arrival in port to the end user, between specific levels of the system, or even the procurement lead time from when a product is ordered with the manufacturer until it arrives in port.

When you calculate lead time, it is especially important to include all the time up to when the stock is *available for use*. Stock that has been received, but not inspected, recorded, and put on the shelf, is not ready to be issued and is not available to be used. To satisfy the client's need, stock must be available for the customer when they request or need it.

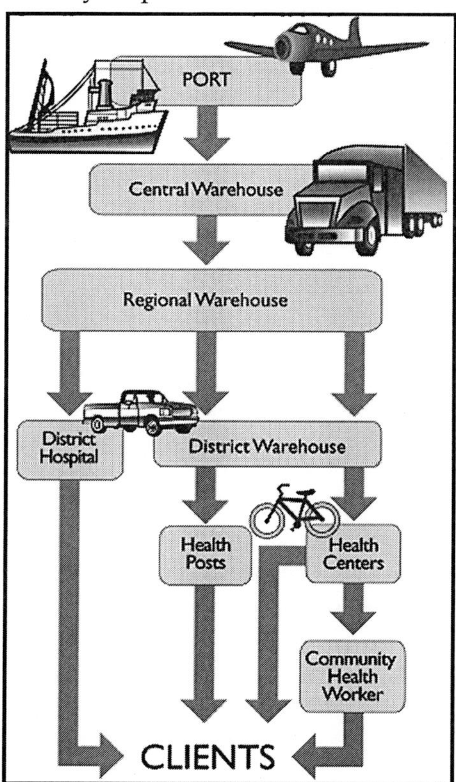

Fig. Typical Public Sector In-Country Supply Pipeline

MORE LOGISTICS TERMS

Several common logistics terms can be defined by comparing them to an opposing term—*allocation* and *requisition* resupply, *dispensed* and *issues* data, and *vertical* and *integrated* systems. The following sections compare each of these paired terms. Although we could define many more concepts, these basic comparisons are fundamental and we refer to them throughout the handbook.

ALLOCATION (PUSH) VERSUS REQUISITION (PULL)?

Placing orders is a routine activity in logistics. In most logistics systems, an order is placed for new supplies every month, or every quarter, from an SDP to a higher level. In some logistics systems, the quantity to be resupplied is calculated by the person *placing* the order. This is called a *requisition* (or *pull)* system. In other systems, the quantity to be resupplied is determined by the person who *fulfills* the order. This is called an *allocation* (or *push)* system.

- In a *requisition* system, the person who *receive*s the supplies calculates the quantities of supplies required.
- In an *allocation* system, the person who *issues* the supplies calculates the quantities of supplies required.

Returning to our restaurant example, at an all-you-can-eat buffet, customers select the types of food to put on their plate and how much to take; they decide how hungry they are and select their meals, accordingly. The server does not tell the customer what to eat—the customer decides. These restaurants use a *requisition* system. In contrast, at home, the cook usually decides what and how much to serve, based on the family's taste and the available ingredients—this is *an allocation* system.

However, if information systems work efficiently and are automated (in many parts of the private sector, for example); and different levels can access the same information, at the same time, and have the capacity to conduct calculations, then the differences between the allocation and the requisition systems fade. The main issues to consider are data visibility (i.e., what data is available where and when), human resource requirements (i.e., can existing personnel do the mathematical calculations?), and level of budget authority (i.e., does the individual health facility control its own funds so it can operate in a requisition system, or does the district control commodity funding, making an allocation system necessary?).

Both allocation and requisition approaches can be used in one system; however, it is usually inefficient to combine the two among facilities at the same level. For example, a requisition system can be used from the central level to the regional level, and an allocation system from the regional level to the SDP. But, only one system should be used within each level. Imagine the frustration and confusion at the regional warehouse

if some health facilities are requisitioning supplies while others need supplies allocated to them. For the pipeline to work, the proper quantities must be ordered and shipped in the shortest time possible. Using two systems at one level only adds to confusion and delays.

It is also important that, when a logistics system is designed, the lower level and the higher level understand who decides what quantities are to be ordered. If staff at the higher level think it is an allocation system, and staff at the lower level think it is a requisition system, lower-level staff may become confused when the quantity they receive is not the same as the quantity they ordered. If this happens often enough, lower-level staff may assume that they will never receive what they order and stop ordering.

CONSUMED VERSUS ISSUED?

Logistics systems fulfill the six rights for the customer; therefore, all decisions in logistics should be based on information about the products that the customer is given or uses. Logistics systems need to track information about the quantities of a product actually put in the hands of the customers. After a customer receives a product, we say that it is consumed; even if it is wasted or discarded, the logistics system will still need to resupply the item, regardless of its ultimate use. (Outside the field of logistics, of course, knowing how customers use or discard the supplies they receive is of great interest.)

Information about the quantity of products given to customers is called *dispensed-to-user data*, often abbreviated as *dispensed data* or *consumption data*. Because an SDP is the only place where supplies are given directly to customers, this is the only level where we can collect dispensed-to-user data. *Usage data* is another term with a meaning similar to dispensed to user, except that it is used by the consumer but is not dispensed directly to them (i.e., laboratory reagents, HIV test kits, etc.). For these products, consumption (usage) data must come from the facility or level where the products are used (the laboratory, the testing site, etc.).

The supply pipeline includes all intermediate storage facilities. The term for information on the movement of products between any two storage facilities is *issues data*. For example, when the regional level distributes supplies to the district level, the data on the quantity of product moved is issues data. Or, when a hospital pharmacy store gives supplies to other departments or wards in the hospital, or to the dispensary, this is also issues data.

Whenever possible, logistics decisions for planning should be based on consumption data. If the regional warehouse issued 50,000 condoms to the district warehouse last quarter, should it issue the same number this quarter? The answer is *not necessarily*, because condoms may be piling up in the district warehouse. The issue quantity will be more accurate if information is available on the quantity of condoms that were dispensed to users during that time period. Throughout this handbook, we emphasize the importance of using consumption data for decisionmaking. In systems that do not have consumption data, issues data can be used as a substitute. When you use issues data, however, always use issues data from the lowest level possible. For example, issues data from districts to health facilities are preferred to data from the central warehouse to districts; because district issues should better reflect customer demand. Even better, issues data from the facility store to the dispensary will be a closer estimate of actual consumption. Because the relationship between issues data and customer demand is not exact, particularly at the higher the level of the issues data, collecting the actual dispensed-to-user data should be a priority for logistics systems that do not have dispensed-to-user data available.

PRODUCT INTEGRATION

Many countries have several parallel logistics systems for selecting, procuring, and distributing different types of supplies to clients. Often health programs—family planning, maternal and child health, malaria control, TB control, or HIV and AIDS—each manage and distribute supplies for their programs. These programs are called disease-specific programs (sometimes called *vertical* programs); because, historically, they often have separate standard operating procedures and distribution channels and may be managed by separate management units at the central level.

Recently, however, many countries have moved toward product integration, i.e., combining the management of some or all logistics functions for different commodity categories (i.e., family planning, HIV, malaria, and TB) into a shared supply chain. For example, a system that manages contraceptives for the family planning program might also manage oral rehydration salts (ORS), vitamin A, and other products for the maternal and child health program.

Within a given country, some logistics functions may remain separate, where others are combined. For example, contraceptives, nevirapine for preventing mother-to-child transmission (PMTCT), and HIV test kits may be procured by separate programs, but they may also, subsequently, be stored and transported together. Procurement, in this example, is said to be separate (or vertical), where the storage and transport functions are integrated.

When you determine which logistics functions to combine, you need to consider and make trade-offs between the handling requirements of particular products (i.e., cold chain, short shelf life), and the cost of the functions, and customer service (i.e., ensuring that merging the distribution of different products will not disrupt service). You may read more about the logistics system design considerations for product integration in chapter 10; also, see the suggested reading list at the end of the book for information about how product integration can affect logistics.

SUPPLY CHAIN INTEGRATION

This handbook distinguishes between product integration (described above) and supply chain integration. By *supply chain integration,* we mean a performance-improving approach that develops seamless linkages between the various actors, levels, and functions within a given supply chain to maximize customer service. The objectives of supply chain integration are to improve efficiency and reduce redundancy, thus improving product availability and, often, reducing costs. Performance-enhancing measures can take many forms: logistics management units, joint strategic plans, information sharing mechanisms, and technical working groups. In Rwanda, for example, the Family Planning Technical Working Group (FPTWG) was formed to improve coordination and minimize duplication of effort. Through regular meetings and sharing information, the group has fostered trust among partners; which has, in turn, contributed to improvements in commodity security: forecasts and procurements are executed in a reasonable time, stockouts are minimized, and more providers are trained and facilities are upgraded throughout the country. The end result of the group's efforts is improved efficiency and better customer service. This handbook focuses on the logistics of the supply chain and how the integration of particular functions within that chain can create a higher level of service.

In the supply chain industry, other sectors and organizations have different ways of considering integration; therefore, you may see different language or definitions. In the public health arena, however, the focus is on streamlining the supply chains of disease-specific programs. Therefore, this handbook illustrates how you can create functions that work well together, how to build or strengthen the connections between those functions, and how these activities can support a reliable supply of quality products.

2

The Logistics Sector in India

The Indian economy has been growing at an average rate of more than 8% over the last four years, putting enormous demands on its productive infrastructure. Whether it is the physical infrastructure of roads, ports, water, or power, or the digital infrastructure of broadband networks and telecommunication, or the service infrastructure of logistics — all are being stretched beyond their capabilities. Interestingly, this is leading to an emergence of innovative practices that will allow businesses and public services to operate at a higher growth rate in an environment in which the support systems are concurrently being augmented. In this chapter, we describe the status of the evolving logistics sector in India and innovations therein through interesting business models, as well as the challenges that the sector will face in the years to come.

Broadly speaking, the Indian logistics sector, as elsewhere, comprises the entire inbound and outbound segments of the manufacturing and service supply chains. Of late, the logistics infrastructure has received a lot of attention both from business and industry and from policy makers. However, the role of the management of this infrastructure in effective competition has been somewhat underemphasized. Although inadequate logistics infrastructure has the effect of creating bottlenecks in the growth of an economy, the logistics management regimen has the capability to overcome infrastructure disadvantages in the short run while providing cutting-edge competitiveness in the long term.

This presents a number of challenges as well as opportunities for the Indian economy. Several models seem to be emerging based on the critical needs of the Indian economy, and these can stand as viable models for other global economies as well. Two key areas require attention in the management of logistics chains across the Indian business sectors: cost and reliable value-added services. Logistics costs have been estimated at 13–14% of Indian GDP, which is higher than that of the United States (8%), but lower than that of China (21%). The service reliability of the logistics industry in emerging markets such as India has been seen as slow and as requiring significant engagement time with the customers, thereby incurring high indirect variable costs. However, the Indian logistics story is one of islands of excellence accompanying a general improvement on almost all parameters. It is this aspect that we explore further in this chapter. In the next section, we offer a brief introduction to some of the peculiarities of the Indian logistics sector. Following this, we discuss the determinants of growth in this industry and highlight several interesting initiatives that point toward a renewal of the sector. We close with a discussion of the challenges facing the logistics sector now and in the future.

HISTORICAL DEVELOPMENT

SOME PECULIARITIES OF INDIAN SUPPLY CHAINS

The Indian logistics sector has typically been driven by the objective of reducing transportation costs that were inordinately high due to the regional concentration of manufacturing and geographically diversified distribution activities, as well as inefficiencies in infrastructure and accompanying technology. Freight movement has slowly been shifting from rail to road, with implications for the quality of transfer, the timeliness of delivery, and consequently costs — except for commodities, which move over long distances predominantly via the extensive rail network. The transportation industry is fragmented and largely unorganized.

A large number of independent players with regional or national permits carry freight, often with a small fleet of one or two single-axle trucks. This segment carries a large percentage of the national load and almost all of the regional load. It comprises owners and employees with inadequate skills, narrow perspectives, and limited ability to organize or manage their operations effectively. Low cost has been traditionally achieved by employing low-level technology, offering low wages, scrimping on equipment maintenance, and overloading trucks beyond capacity. Often, transportation cartels regulate the supply of trucks and transport costs. Price competition among a large number of service providers in the industry also has contributed to lower cost. However, the long-run average cost of transport operations across the entire supply chain may not turn out to be low.

Logistics spending is increasing, sometimes dramatically, across various industrial sectors in India. Steel, pharmaceuticals, food and agri-business, and automotives are the sectors that have been growing most rapidly in the national economy — and it is no surprise that their logistics costs have been increasing at a faster rate. The low change in order processing and administrative costs in the cement sector could possibly be due to the use of call centers by various producers for order processing and dispatch planning. The steel and pharmaceutical sectors have seen maximum changes in component costs. The distribution practice of pushing goods down the channel might be responsible for the high increase in inventory and warehousing costs in the pharmaceutical industry. Investments in new cold chains and losses might be the causes of high change in warehousing, packaging, and loss-related costs. Warehousing has typically been dominated by small players with small capacities and poor deployment of handling, stacking, and monitoring technologies. While warehousing issues have had a detrimental effect on almost all sectors, the food sector has suffered the most, due to low levels of investment in cold chains and allied machinery. Erratic power outages have also required a more manual operation, with less dependence on technology. Another factor that has affected both the location and the cost of operating a warehouse has been the "octroi tax", in response to which firms have been locating warehouses outside city limits and have delayed moving goods into the retail network as long as possible. The tax has also led firms to develop an unholy business-government nexus to avoid the tax and extraction of rents.

The use of technology to increase productivity and service — both IT and engineering equipment — is still quite limited. An inappropriate evaluation of the benefits of technology has led to the higher usage of manual labor across the logistics industry, whether in distribution activities or within plants. Many firms try to compete through the advantage of low wages, which in turn necessitate hiring low-skilled or unskilled personnel, thereby sacrificing the possibility of longrun productivity-related gains. Understanding the linkage between inventory and transport planning is the key to reduce the operational costs of distribution.

In a survey of Indian manufacturing firms, Chandra and Sastry found that 98% of the firms have a contract with trucking companies for making dispatches, while only 11% own their own fleet of trucks. While 36% of these firms use third-party logistics (3PL) service providers for making dispatches, only about 30% use 3PL service providers for procuring materials from their suppliers. In the survey, only 21% of firms report the use of some software for scheduling dispatches. Somehow, transport planning has received little attention within operations despite the fact that about 10% of the cost of sales is associated with physical distribution.

Transport planning does not appear to have received the required attention. An understanding of the overall structure of Indian supply chains will lead to a better appreciation of many of the issues raised earlier. In Chandra and Sastry's survey, about 4% of firms have fewer than five suppliers, about 85% of firms have fewer than five plants, about 14% of firms have fewer than five regional distributors, and about 9% of firms have fewer than five retailers. Similar statistics are obtained for other ranges of suppliers, plants, distributors, and retailers. It is worth noting that 63% of firms have more than 100 suppliers, while about 39% of firms have more than 100 distributors and 77% of firms have more than 100 retailers. In addition, about 17% of firms claim to have more than 500 suppliers. The corresponding figures for distributors and retailers are 22 and 54%, respectively. This is perhaps where difficulties in managing logistics in India lie: the larger the number of suppliers or distributors, the higher the cost of co-ordination.

When we look at the spatial distribution of plants and suppliers, the above statement becomes even stronger. Of the sample firms that operate more than one plant, 48% of these plants are located more than 100 km, apart, 33% of these plants are located more than 500 km apart, and 18% of these plants are located more than 1000 km apart. Similarly, on an average, only 4% of suppliers are located within 5 km of the manufacturing plant, while about 13% are located within 5–25 km of the plant, 16% are located within 25–100 km of the plant, and about 67% of suppliers have facilities that are more than 100 km away from the plants. Past governmental policies may have forced some firms to locate plants further away from each other. However, this may be coming back to haunt these firms today, as the cost of co-ordination increases and the ability to provide a quick response to customer requirements therefore decreases.

This problem is exacerbated with suppliers. Manufacturers must either develop suppliers separately for each location, or else material has to travel longer distances if the plants all have a common supplier. The logistics challenge in such an environment is immense: build the infrastructure; manage the requirements of the changing structure of various sectors' supply chains; change industrial policies to facilitate efficient production and movement of goods and services; deploy effective managerial practices and technology to enhance competitiveness through better management of logistics networks and develop new models for new sectors, in the service sectors as well as in traditional areas such as agri-business. The logistics industry in India is transforming itself very interestingly despite its peculiarities by developing innovative business models and by chipping away at structural and policy-based rigidities. In a later section, we discuss some of these innovative initiatives that are leading the renewal of the logistics industry in India.

CURRENT AND FUTURE TRENDS

THE CHANGING LOGISTICS INFRASTRUCTURE

With rising consumer demand and the resulting growth in global trade, infrastructure support in terms of rails, roads, ports, and warehouses holds the key to the success of the economy. In this section, we provide a brief overview of the status of the logistics infrastructure in India and the current initiatives, both private and public, in this area. Goods are transported predominantly by road and rail in India. Road transport is controlled by private players, whereas rail transport is handled by the central government. The second largest network in the world, India's roads contribute to 65% of the freight transport. Road is preferred over rail because of its cost effectiveness and flexibility. Rail, on the other hand, is preferred because of its containerization facility and its ease in transporting ship containers and wooden crates. The sea is another complementary mode of transport: 95% of India's foreign trade is by sea. India has 12 major ports, 6 each on the east and west coasts, and 185 minor ports. There is also evidence of an acrossthe-board increase in freight traffic for all modes, indicating increased logistics activity.

The percentage change in road, rail, air, and sea cargo traffic has increased between 2001 and 2005 from 5% to 14%, 4% to 7.5%, 6% to 20%, and 3.5% to 11%, respectively. In keeping with the increasing demand for road transportation, the National Highways Authority of India (NHAI) has been strengthening and widening national highways in multiple phases. As part of the National Highways Development Project (NHDP), work on the development of the Golden Quadrilateral and the north-south and east-west links started in 1998. This project will build 13,000 km of expressways that will connect the nation. NHAI is investing about USD650 million towards the development of an Intelligent Transportation System (ITS), which will make transport services on the highways efficient and will automate many processes, including toll collection.

Because of the growing opportunity and potential for high revenue, the Ministry of Railways has been taking measures to expand rail connectivity and recapture the market share of freight business. By focusing on improving wagon utilization, the Railways have managed to reduce the freight cost from 61 paise per net ton km (ntkm) in 2001 to 56 paise per ntkm in 2005. At present, freight trains run on the same railway tracks as passenger trains, at an average speed of about 25 kmph. With the proposed dedicated west and east freight corridors, however, the freight trains are expected to run at 100 kmph. The west and east rail corridors of 1469 km and 1232 km, respectively, will be built with investments of USD2.60 billion and USD2.40 billion and will be equipped with the latest centralized traffic control systems.

The Indian Railways has also decided to collaborate with bulk users of freight transport to build the rail network in a Public-Private Partnership (PPP) mode. The first project on this line comprises nine public and private sector companies that are building an 82 km rail line between Haridarpur and Paradip at a cost of USD120 million. Recently, several steel companies have also shown an interest in linking iron and coal mines in Orissa via a 98 km rail line. An efficient multimodal transportation system is quite essential for the diverse Indian geography and economy, as it allows players to choose the most economic mode of transport given their product and customer requirements and sourcing location. To allow for the smooth operation of trade through multiple modes, India has a separate governing body, the Director General of Shipping, which works under the Multimodal Transportation of Goods Act of 1993. Its function is to frame rules and grant licenses to operators providing door-to-door service using multiple modes. Multimodal transport in India, through rail, was a monopoly of the Container Corporation of India until 2005. However, with licenses being given to 13 new private players, rail trade should improve considerably. In order to encourage trade by small-scale industries, the Indian Railways has started a "road-railer" system in which container vehicles are capable of running both on highways hauled by trucks and on rail. In 1998–1999, the Konkan Railway pioneered the "roll-on, roll-off " (RO-RO) concept between Mumbai (Kolad) and Goa (Verna). Privately owned trucks are loaded with their goods and are then driven onto a rake of flat cars and carried to the destination. In 2005–2006, the ports handled 456.20 million tons of cargo traffic — a doubling of capacity over 2000–2001.

This is expected to increase to 700 million tons by 2011–2012. To keep pace with the growing demand, the government plans to increase port capacities to about 1 billion tons per annum over the next six years. Under the National Maritime Development Programme (NMDP), the government is encouraging public-private partnership in the building and maintenance of ports. This scheme will cover 276 port-related projects at an investment cost of USD12.40 billion. With the rising congestion levels at major ports and with high average turnaround and waiting times, the government has decided to develop minor ports in seven states to ease the traffic at the major ports. The operational performance of various ports in India is improving but the pace is slow, and delays, particularly those due to the port authority, need to be reduced further through better planning, execution, and technology. The estimated cost of the development of these minor ports is expected to be about USD350 million.

In addition to the public-private partnerships, the private sector is expected to invest USD7.67 billion over the next six years. Currently, 15 private-sector projects are operational at various major ports, and four more are under implementation. One of these aims to build the deepest port in the world, at an investment of USD1 billion. This project is being handled by a three-firm Chinese consortium with a Mumbai-based partner, Zoom Developers.

Interestingly, firms like Ambuja Cement have been using barges for the transport of clinkers from their factories to crushing and packaging plants all over the coast, thereby reducing transport costs considerably. The Sethusamudram Ship Channel Project, which is creating a deep-sea channel across the Palk Strait between India and Sri Lanka, will allow for the direct and efficient transport of big ships between the western and eastern coasts of India. Right now, these ships have to sail around Sri Lanka's coast, thereby incurring an additional 30 hours of sailing time. A flurry of activity is underway that is enhancing the infrastructure capacities in the country. It is hoped that these developments will reduce the extent of congestion at the major ports and perhaps lead to the specialization of certain ports, with their accompanying technology and managerial practices; for instance, ports in Gujarat are eminently poised to focus on chemical and textile exports. Improvements in planning, however, through the deployment of IT, advanced planning tools, and better managerial practices, remain largely ignored.

DETERMINANTS OF LOGISTICS GROWTH IN INDIA

The Indian logistics business is valued at USD14 billion and has been growing at a compound annual growth rate (CAGR) of 7% to 8%. As mentioned earlier, logistics costs represent 13% to 14% of the country's GDP. The market is fragmented, with thousands of players offering partial services in logistics; it is estimated that there are about 400 firms capable of providing some level of integrated service. The economy is expected to grow about 10% over the next 10 years, and sectors including chemicals, petrochemicals, pharmaceuticals, metals and metal processing, fast-moving consumer goods (FMCG), textile, retail, and automotives are projected to grow the fastest.

New business models are emerging as new firms, both domestic and foreign, enter the market. As a result of the ensuing competition, domestic market growth and linkages with global supply chains promise to change the face of the logistics industry beyond recognition. In this section, we examine how these are going to determine the growth of the sector. The scale of operations in manufacturing is changing, and so are the markets and sourcing geographies. Growth in manufacturing in India has happened across clusters located in different parts of the country, for example, Ludhiana, NCR, Baddi and Dehradun in the north; Rajkot, Jamnagar, Pune, and Mumbai in the west; and Coimbatore, Vishakapatnam, Bangalore, Hosur, Chennai, Puducherry, and Sriperumbudur in the south. Assembly plants at these locations are being fed with raw materials and intermediate products from all over the country and abroad.

Moreover, distribution networks with emerging hubs in Indore and Nagpur supply all of India as well as foreign countries. These networks are going to increase the nature and extent of the movement of goods and services across the country. The growth in the distribution networks has been accompanied by the expansion of domestic production capacity as well as a big multinational entry into the Indian manufacturing scene. As the volume of production grows, so will the extent of movement of goods either to the ports for export or to the rest of the country. Some of the large players to enter or expand significantly in the Indian market recently have been Reliance Retail, Big Bazaar Hypermart, Pantaloon, and RPG in retail; Nokia, LG, Samsung, Motorola, Sony, and Blue Star in consumer electronics; Bajaj, Hero Honda, Maruti-Honda, Toyota, Audi, Volkswagen, Renault, and Volvo in the automotive sector; and Holcim in cement. We expect that their operations will drive the growth of the logistics industry. The liberalizing Indian economy is experiencing the entry of large domestic and global firms into new businesses as well as the enlargement of the distribution network of many regional Indian firms. The announcement of large retail projects by Reliance and Bharti will bring new technology, add additional warehouse capacity, and require fast and reliable movement of goods across the country. Reliance is considering establishing large warehouses in Thailand to take advantage of low-cost sourcing from Southeast Asia once the Free Trade Agreement with Thailand gets finalized.

Similarly, regional food and grocery retail leaders such as Subhiksha which are present very extensively in the South Indian market are now entering the rest of the country, with more than 600 new retail stores in 2007. Their logistics strategies and needs are being very significantly transformed by this nationwide expansion. New retail chains are entering the nonmetro towns and non-state capitals. The growth of the courier industry post-liberalization has helped change the parameters of service evaluation in the industry from cost alone to cost, time, and reliability. This sector has also seen number alliances between regional and local players, especially in the small package market, creating networks of small players that are not only cost-effective but also more flexible than the large national players. This segment of the industry has taken advantage of the plentiful manpower and is gradually moving away from "angadiyas," or manual intercity couriers, to a more organized network that shares transport infrastructure. Courier firms even work together to consolidate subpackages from various small couriers into a single large courier bag to be transported by air cargo or road transport rather by several manual couriers via train. This allows small couriers to save on service and share fixed costs.

The entry of large 3PL carriers, including FedEx and DHL, and the expansion of domestic networks of Indian firms such as Gati and Shreyas Shipping is also transforming the nature of services and business practices across the sector. Another trend driving growth in this sector has been the consolidation among the logistics players. Mergers and acquisitions among Indian and multinational logistics firms are starting to increase the reach of the multinationals' 3PLs in the domestic market while consolidating the business.

Consolidation is expected to be beneficial both to the service providers and to the consumers. Initially, multinational 3PL firms provided only customs-clearance and freight-forwarding services to their international clients. With a growing logistics market, however, we should see a shift in this trend. The complexity of managing the supply chain in the pre-consolidation era is illustrated by the experience of Nokia. Logistics activity for Nokia's India hub was maintained by a large number of service providers, and co-ordination and handover were a problem at times. With its acquisition of Blue Dart, DHL is now able to provide seamless end-to-end integrated supply chain solutions. Downstream distribution channels have also seen some consolidation. Manufacturing firms, particularly in the FMCG sector, have started to reduce the number of wholesalers so as to increase the reach of — and consequently the returns to — each wholesaler. This also induces them to invest in new productivity-enhancing technology and effective managerial practices.

Technology in the logistics chain is being upgraded, bringing better visibility to customers' skimming. The introduction of more efficient transport technology and mobile communication has the potential to change the logistics practices in the industry. Increasing competition and the low levels of IT penetration also imply that the scope for change is immense and imminent. The agri-business sector's supply chain, for example, has changed significantly with increasing investment in cold-chains across the country. Through these chains, fruits and vegetables can be transported long distances and the milk grid is able to pick up liquid milk from, and deliver it to, remote areas more frequently. Here, the role of co-operatives like AMUL has been exemplary in increasing the size of the distribution network and reorganizing the supply network very efficiently, which has built up enormous social capital — a pre-requisite for growth in emerging economies.

Low levels of penetration of hand-held technologies for order processing and tracking, product tracking, and material handling accessories, as well as IT for improved decision making, can be seen as opportunities for growth. Mobile technologies also hold the potential for the rapid use of information for real-time decision making and for co-ordinating both inbound and outbound logistics. Indian customers exhibit strong value- and variety-seeking behavior; hence, the development of capabilities in the process of product and service delivery will create loyalty. For firms entering India, the biggest challenges are to co-ordinate with multiple service providers, understand the regulatory requirements, and establish capacity in the supply chain. One of the key weaknesses in the approach of many new firms is their inability to quickly understand Indian business conventions and market dynamics. Indian product and logistics markets are highly segmented, with growth happening in the low-cost and value-conscious segments.

Firms that recognize this cost-conscious environment and deploy technology that will deliver a cost-based advantage will gain in this market. Moreover, firms must be ready to participate in the building of local infrastructure in terms of warehouse capacity and technology networks. This may be seen as a strategic activity. The application of IT in the logistics industry as well as in client industries is an interesting opportunity that is waiting to be exploited. The co-ordination of the logistics markets of the SMEs with appropriate products also represents a valuable area of potential development. Government policies have been another driver of change in the logistics industry. The trend toward a higher road-cargo traffic relative to rail is going to require better logistics control and co-ordination. The Golden Quadrilateral road project and the East and West rail corridors are expected to change the reactivity of Indian firms through shorter lead times and lower maintenance costs for transport equipment. These projects also have the potential to reduce procedural delays on highways by decreasing the number of checks and related stoppages of vehicles.

The impact on perishable goods will be the most significant. Thirteen states and three union territories have already amended the state laws allowing private sector participation in the direct purchase of farm produce from farmers, which is making procurement more efficient and is bringing better technology as well as products into the rural production and distribution network. In addition, banks have developed venture capital funds for logistics players. The *Small Industries Development Bank of India* (SIDBI), for instance, has invested USD2.3 million in the Mumbai-based firm Direct Logistics. The unbundling of the logistics supply chain — including the physical pick-up, storage, and movement of goods, as well as allied services such as invoicing, order management, freight forwarding, customs clearance, and octroi tax management — will lead to new business opportunities and further value-added for the customers.

An interesting example is that of the Reliance Connect Service Centers, which have been established on Indian highways by Reliance along with petrol stations. The Connect Centers provide a place for truckers to relax; send information to parent firms on their location, completed transactions, etc.; receive material/instructions; and remit money to the parent firms. They have become a "one-stop shop" helping truckers and their companies to keep in touch. Similarly, once the *value added tax* (VAT) is introduced, it will simplify the process of goods servicing and will lead to the rationalizing of many operational decisions.

The potential effect of the emergence of a strong service industry on logistics performance is not well understood. Perhaps a new business segment will emerge that is technology-driven and will help co-ordinate activities across business channels. For example, there is a need to integrate the flow of information, goods, and services between medical physicians, diagnostics center, hospitals and nursing homes, and retail medical outlets — all of which are uncoordinated, independent entities at the moment. This could range from the digital transmission of MRI scans from a diagnostics center to a physician's computer, to blood collection and delivery from various city centers to nursing homes and blood banks or directly to dispersed operating rooms. The role of a co-ordinating agency becomes organizationally valuable in such an environment.

The need is to link physical logistics processes with communication technologies, building on the strengths of the IT and mobile communication industries.

Transforming the Auto Components Replacement Supply Chain

Changing government policies and consumer preferences have significantly affected the distribution supply chain of Indian companies, posing new challenges for various channel partners. We view this transformation process through the lens of the auto components replacement market supply chain and discuss its implications below. In a study of this process, we surveyed 21 manufacturers and 22 channel members spread equally in northern and western clusters of the auto-components industry in India. In 2004–2005, the auto-component industry produced parts worth USD6.7 billion, with 57% of the demand coming from the replacement market. Low entry barriers have led to a large number of players in the replacement market: there are about 400 firms in the organized sector and more than 5000 in the unorganized sector.

Another feature of this subsector is the long duration of ownership of vehicles in India, which leads to a significant demand for replacement parts. Anecdotal evidence indicates that customers' willingness to pay for parts ecreases with the length of car ownership. This has led to an intense segmentation of the parts market by price. Pre-1991, this industry was still in a nascent stage. It was characterized by few manufacturers and low demand. Consequently, the distribution network was flat. Availability of spare parts was a key issue, with long delivery lead-times, and manufacturers sought large order sizes. This also led to the growth of unbranded parts or parts branded by regional producers in the replacement market. Products were sold chiefly on the basis of the seller's personal relationship with the buyer; quality, brand, and price were not the selling propositions. Maruti Udyog Ltd. created a network of suppliers of quality parts for its vehicles, and Hero Honda did the same for its motorcycles.

Post-1991, the liberalization of the automotive industry led to the entry of many foreign auto players. Because of the impending automobile industry boom and high margins for distributors, the demand for spare auto parts was expected to grow. The distribution channel was modified, with the entry of two more channel members, namely, wholesalers and semi-wholesalers. The latter were smaller versions of the former and locally oriented. The period 1994–2007 saw a major transformation of the distribution structure. OEMs started to operate in the replacement market through a parallel supply chain selling parts through their service stations.

Additionally, the entry of a large number of channel members caused semi-wholesalers to move out of the supply chain: they either moved up the chain to become wholesalers or moved down to become retailers. To strengthen the co-ordination of this extended supply chain and to buffer against the differential tax structure across states, companies started to operate with carry and forwarding agents. Transportation-related activities were carried out by all the members of the supply chain. Manufacturers used 3PL services for transferring their stock to C&FA and distributor locations. But thereafter, transportation activity was solely managed by the channel members themselves. An analysis of the available IT infrastructure and its usage pattern for all the channel members in our survey indicates that there is a high variation in the usage of IT in the replacement market supply chain. Among the surveyed firms, 87% use ERP packages, most of which are customized and developed locally.

The main impediment to the use of branded packages is the high cost of purchase and implementation. These packages are used to generate sales reports, order from suppliers, account for financial transactions, and track the level of inventory at plants and C&FA. Manufacturers order their stock from suppliers mostly via email. In order to track inventory in the channel, firms also make IT investments both at C&FA and within the firm. Linking the C&FA to the company website enables firms to check stock status at the C&FA and reduce the order-processing and customer-response times. Larger firms are also providing a similar set-up for their distributors. Since the C&FA is mostly owned and managed by the firms, manufacturers are also able to check the inventory status, dispatching status, and customer records. Distributors have invested in computers primarily for keeping track of the inventory and updating accounting details. On the other hand, the rest of the channel partners generally do not even own computers. Parts are ordered primarily over the phone.

Interestingly, most distributors were found to be following a periodic review policy, while the rest of the channel members were following a continuous review policy because of their low sales volume. Post-2007, with the implementation of a uniform tax structure all states, there will be some changes in the way firms operate. The C&FA will, perhaps, become redundant, as most manufacturers will prefer to deal directly with distributors. The concept of an exclusive distributor is likely to vanish. It is also expected that with the increase in variety of components, distributors might become wholesalers and will stock multiple brands of the same product. Two parallel distribution channels are expected to be in operation — the OEM chain and the non-OEM chain.

The OEM network will primarily handle passenger-car replacement parts and the non-OEM distribution network will sell parts for light commercial vehicles, heavy commercial vehicles, 2-wheelers, and 3-wheelers, as the car customer is becoming more brand-conscious even when replacing parts. Further, we perceive that more-advanced automobiles, free trade agreements with other Asian countries, and the VAT are going to change the way the replacement market operates.

There will be a rationalization of this market in terms of the number of firms competing, thereby leading to an improvement in quality, delivery time, and availability of parts. The size of the firms is expected to increase, with an emergence of large national players. This may reduce the number of producers exclusively focusing on the local markets.

CHALLENGES AHEAD

Several challenges remain in the Indian logistics sector, and its future success will depend on the ability of the industry to overcome these hurdles. Some of these impediments are at the policy level, while others are at the firm level. At the policy level, the issues of infrastructure and the integration of the nation's logistics network remain the two most critical areas that require attention. The growth of infrastructure since 1991 has been quite extensive as well as strategic — linking the key industrial, consumption, and trans-shipment centers. However, some apparent weaknesses need to be addressed. Poor road conditions increase vehicle turnover, increasing operating cost and reducing efficiency.

Movement beyond the Golden Quadrilateral is required to bring goods from upcountry production sources to main shipment centers. The growth rate for expressways thus must increase. National highways are being upgraded, but they account for a meager 2% of the total road network. More importantly, due to the non-contiguous development of expressways, truck traffic must frequently move from the expressway onto old national highways and back. This is inconvenient and restricts the utilization of the excellent road network that is being developed. The pricing of the toll on these expressways, especially for cargo traffic, has also been a deterrent to its usage — hence, the price elasticity of this demand needs to be better understood, and appropriate price packages should be developed for heavy users. The role of transport technology is also crucial: once the cost of manufacturing multiaxle trucks comes down, this market will see higher penetration and consequently lower per-unit cost of transportation. Volvo is currently trying to develop this market, but the volume of high capacity trucks continues to be low.

The East and West bulk rail transport corridor will divert some traffic from the roads, provided that the secondary movement can be minimized and the issue of the security of the goods is adequately addressed. Similarly, river navigation in north and northeastern India may offer useful options for cargo movement in the hinterland, where road congestion is high. Freight vehicles run only 250–300 km per day in India, as compared to 800–1000 km in developed countries. Interstate checkposts, surprise checks, and unauthorized hold-ups on highways create bottlenecks. Entry taxes into cities for goods also create procedural bottlenecks. The Motor Vehicles Act and the Motor Transport Workers Act that regulate driver licensing and loading norms, and the duty hours of drivers, respectively, require modification to address the quality of services in this sector. Similarly, while the regional permits that allow a truck to ply between certain states come at a lower cost, it limits the flexibility of truckers to convert opportunities. The Indian logistics market remains fragmented on this account, and the national market does not appear as one integrated entity. Harmonization of taxes, procedures, and policies across states is required to facilitate a seamless flow of goods and services.

For instance, if there were a nationwide broadband logistics IT-network, then a trucker starting in Chennai could file all the required papers in Chennai, get all inspections done there, and move without interruptions to, say, Jammu. Each state entry point could have access to these papers, and they could flag the truck through their checkpost as it arrived with no stoppages or delays. Today, it can take anywhere from half-an-hour to several hours to get the papers and goods inspected at each checkpost. The issue of inspections could be taken care of by the use of sealed container carriers. This and similar changes in process technology are needed to increase the effectiveness and responsiveness of the transport network. In privatizing the operations of railway container traffic, new entrants are expected to face serious problems. Because of limited manufacturing capacity for producing rail cars, these firms will have to import them, at significant expense. Huge investments in storage capacities near railway stations will also add to the cost.

All these factors will increase the entry barriers for private operators. Moreover, the tariff structure and revenue sharing will still be a hindrance to the success of public-private partnership projects in infrastructure development. While the use of IT for logistics management is increasing, it is largely limited to large firms. This represents an opportunity for firms to further improve decision-making abilities across the supply chain and reduce costs further. For instance, order processing and delivery status are two areas that exhibit a certain weakness in servicing. With the growth of the IT sector in India, these are clearly areas that could gain from the IT sector's engagement. Manufacturing firms could collaborate with the extensive network of call centers to manage order processing and the actual integration of order servicing with the physical supply chain. Similarly, there is a role for the emergence of a segment in the logistics chain that manages dispatch information and performs delivery tracking across manufacturers for their customers. Only a few thousand vehicles out of a total of several million currently have a tracking system.

Truck manufacturers could integrate the tracking technology in their products, and IT servicing firms could then provide an information service that would track the movement of these vehicles, providing information to distribution firms that would allow them to track both the consignment and the truck better. Currently, the best service is that provided by Reliance Connect at their petrol pumps on the highways, where truckers can stop and call their firms to inform them of their whereabouts. Such service providers will continue to be valuable to the very small trucking companies that have proliferated in the logistics industry and which do not have the wherewithal to either install or operate their own IT systems. As the concentration in the industry increases, the need to manage a larger number of trucks, routes, warehouses, and customers will require decision-support systems that perform dynamic planning and scheduling. The IT base is indeed at a low level, and firms will need to compete on the basis of actual logistics costs instead of clever accounting practices before the sector will see increased IT penetration. As the need for visibility in the supply chain increases, better technology applications will also appear.

Another area that will see tremendous growth is the outsourcing of logistics services. While logistics outsourcing has been in existence for several decades, it has been limited to transportation and warehousing. Post-liberalization, the country has seen the outsourcing of value-added services such as freight forwarding, fleet management, import/export and customs clearance, order fulfillment, and consulting services such as distribution network planning. These are still the early years for the 3PL service providers, and a recent survey cites a lack of trust and awareness as the key hurdles to its growth. Service taxes on outsourced costs and the need to establish multiple warehousing facilities in order to avoid double taxation have also been found to undermine the 3PL business.

According to the survey, most of the 3PL service providers offer limited services. In the future, their role as co-ordinators will require that they offer a wider menu of value-added services. They also have the potential to integrate SME channels through a variety of logistics services and technology across a network of small producers. The logistics industry is evolving rapidly, and it is the interplay of infrastructure, technology, and new types of service providers that will determine whether the industry is able to help its customers reduce their logistics costs and provide effective service. Changing government policies on taxation and the regulation of service providers will also play an important role in this process.

Co-ordination across various government agencies still requires approval from multiple ministries and this is a road block for multimodal transport in India. Ports, roads, railways, and container freight operations are all currently managed by different ministries in the Indian government. At the firm level, the logistics focus will have to move toward the reduction of cycle times in order to offer greater value-added to their customers. These are just a few of the issues that must be resolved, or at least addressed, before the logistics industry can flourish and grow in India.

3

Transportation

AIR TRANSPORTATION IN INDIA

Air transportation in India is under the purview of the Department of Civil Aviation, a part of the India's Ministry of Civil Aviation and Tourism. In 1995 the Indian government owned two airlines and one helicopter service, and private companies owned six airlines. The government-owned airlines dominated India's air transportation in the mid-1990s. Air India is the international carrier; it carried more than 2.2 million passengers in FY 1992. Indian Airlines is the major domestic carrier and also runs international flights to nearby countries.

It carried 9.8 million passengers in FY 1989, when it had a load factor of more than 80 percent in its fifty-nine airplanes. Analysts, however, attributed this high load factor to a shortage of capacity rather than efficiency of operation. A major expansion was planned for the 1990s, but an airplane crash in 1990 and a pilots' strike in 1991 damaged the airline, which carried only 7.8 million passengers in FY 1992. Two other accidents in 1993, plus several hijackings, put constraints on the growth of both airlines. A third government-owned airline, Vayudoot, was also a domestic carrier in the early 1990s. It provided feeder service between smaller cities and the larger places served by Air India and Indian Airlines.

By 1994 Indian Airlines had taken over Vayudoot. Another publicly owned company, Pawan Hans, runs helicopter service, mostly to offshore locations and other areas that cannot be served by fixed-wing aircraft. In 1995 India's six private airlines accounted for more than 10 percent of domestic air traffic. Both the number of carriers and their market share are expected to rise in the mid-1990s. The four major private airlines are East West Airlines, Jagsons Airlines, Continental Aviation, and Damania Airways. In addition to the Indian-owned airlines, many foreign airlines provide international service. In 1995 forty-two airlines operated air services to, from, and through India. In the mid-1990s, India had 288 usable airports. Of these, 208 had permanent-surface runways and two had runways of more than 3,659 meters, fifty-nine had runways of between 2,400 and 3,659 meters, and ninety-two had runways between 1,200 and 2,439 meters. There are major international airports at Bombay, Delhi, Calcutta, Madras, and Thiruvananthapuram under the management of the International Airport Authority of India. International service also operates from Marmagao, Bangalore, and Hyderabad. A consortium of Indian and British companies signed a memorandum of understanding with the state government of Maharashtra in June 1995 to build a new international airport for Bombay, across the harbor from the main city and to be linked by a cross-harbor roadway. Major regional airports are located at Ahmadabad, Allahabad, Pune, Srinagar, Chandigarh, Kochi, and Nagpur.

AVIATION POLICIES IN INDIA

REGULATORY FRAMEWORK

- In the context of a multiplicity of airlines, airport operators and the possibility of oligopolistic practices, there is need for an autonomous regulatory authority which could work as a watchdog, as well as a facilitator for the sector, prescribe and enforce minimum standards for all agencies, settle disputes with regard to abuse of monopoly and ensure level playing field for all agencies. Therefore, a statutory autonomous Civil Aviation Authority will be constituted. The basic objectives of setting up of the Authority will be to ensure aviation safety, security and effective regulation of air transport in the country in the liberalised environment.
- The functions of the CAA will be as under:
  - Ensure level playing field for all agencies and
  - Ensure that there are no unfair trade practices and market dominance through encouragement of entry and fostering of competition in accordance with Competition Policy of the Government;
  - Ensure that these agencies and personnel continuously fulfil the standards;
  - Issue license to these agencies and personnel;
  - Regulate tariff;
  - Set the standards for various agencies and personnel of civil aviation sector;
  - Study and analyse the trends in international and domestic civil aviation, project likely future scenario and publish periodical reports.
  - Take appropriate preventive/corrective/punitive action against the agencies and personnel for violations of set standards;
- The agencies mentioned above include airport, airport-operators, passenger aircraft operators, cargo aircraft operators, helicopters, private aircraft operators, flying clubs, aero-sports clubs, security

agency, training institute, air-travel operators or any other agency having role in civil aviation sector.

- The personnel mentioned above include pilots, flight engineers, navigators, cabin crew, flight despatchers, aircraft maintenance engineers/ technicians, air traffic controllers and personnel engaged in the maintenance of communication, navigation, surveillance/ air traffic management systems and other ground aids.

- A comprehensive Indian Aviation Law will be framed to replace the existing Acts relating to aviation and security which will be in tune with the present day civil aviation scenario, and would also put the proposed CAA in place.
- Civil Aviation Authority will also be required to make available information regarding passenger and cargo traffic including regular analysis in an appropriate consolidated format on a commercial basis.
- Civil Aviation Authority will be required to publish Annual Report on the Air Safety and Security Environment in the country.
- Civil Aviation Authority will conduct safety and security audit including flight inspections of the concerned agencies to ensure that they are meeting the prescribed standards.

PERSONAL SECTOR PARTICIPATION

- Private sector participation will be a major thrust area in the civil aviation sector for promoting investment, improving quality and efficiency and increasing competition.
- Competitive regulatory framework with minimal controls will be created to encourage entry and operation of private airlines/ airports.
- Private sector investment in the construction/ upgradations/ operation of new as well as existing airports including cargo related infrastructure will be encouraged.
- Rationalization of various charges and price of ATF/AVGas will be undertaken to render operation of smaller aircraft viable so as to encourage major investment in feeder and regional air services by the private sector.
- Training Institutes for pilots, flight engineers, maintenance personnel, air-traffic controller, security will be encouraged in private sector.
- Private sector investment in non-aeronautical activities like shopping complex, golf course, entertainment park, aero-sports etc. near airports will be encouraged to increase revenue, improve viability of airports and to promote tourism. CAA will ensure that this is not at the cost of primary aeronautical functions, and is consistent with the security requirements.

- Government will gradually reduce its equity in PSUs in the sector.
- Government will encourage employee participation through issue of shares and ESOP.

AIRPORT ROAD AND RAIL NETWORK

- The Government will aim at ensuring adequate world class airport infrastructure capacity in accordance with demand, ensuring maximum utilization of available capacities and efficiently managing the airport infrastructure by increasing involvement of private sector.
- Greenfield airport will be permitted by the Government where
  - The existing airport is unable to meet the projected requirement of traffic or
  - A new focal point of traffic emerges with sufficient viability and
  - The new location is normally not within an aerial distance of 150 kilometers of an existing airport
- Encouragement will be given to development/ construction in private sector of small airstrips/ helipads/heliports, which are smaller and cheaper to construct. These will be particularly suitable in remote hilly or island areas, large business, city centres, factory locations and at other important nodal points. This will also facilitate increase in small aircraft operations
- Private sector participation
  - Private sector will be free to undertake
    a. Construction and operation of new airports/airstrips/ helipads/heliports including cargo complexes, express cargo terminals, cargo satellite cities and cargo handling facilities
    b. Upgradation and operation of existing airports/airstrips/ helipads/heliports in consultation with the existing operator including cargo complexes, Express cargo terminals, cargo satellite cities and cargo handling facilities
  - Foreign equity participation will be permitted up to 74 % with automatic approval and 100 % with special permission of government
  - Private sector participation will include participation of state government, urban local bodies, private companies, individuals and joint ventures on Build-Own-Operate basis or any other pattern of ownership and management depending on the circumstances.
  - Restructuring of major airports of Airports Authority of India will be undertaken through long-term lease to private investors for efficient management, improvement of standards of services/ facilities and attracting private investment
  - At privately managed airports, air traffic control and aviation

security will continue to be provided by the Airports Authority of India and customs and immigration facilities by respective Government departments.
- The equipment needed for any service would normally be provided by the agency responsible for the service and an equitable system would be established for sharing of revenue between different agencies. Keeping in view their respective investments and responsibilities.

- All airports/airstrips/helipads/heliports used for scheduled air-transport services will be licensed by Civil Aviation Authority.
- Airport/ airstrip/ heliport/ helipad operators will follow ICAO guidelines for levying airport/ airstrip/ heliport/ helipad charges based on cost recovery principle. The CAA would put in a place a regulatory mechanism to prevent abuse of monopolistic nature of such infrastructure.
- An objective and well-defined transparent mechanism for allocation of slots at airports will be ensued at all times.
- CAA will ensure fair play between different airport/ airstrip/ heliport/ helipad operators and user agencies so that no airport/ airstrip/ heliport/ helipad operator is accused of discriminating against any particular airline or any other user. Similarly, Government will ensure that no airport-operator is discriminated against with regard to allotment as point of call, if there is demand for air services from such airport.
- More international gateways shall be provided. It would be ensured that there is at least one international airport in every region of the country in order to give a boost to trade and tourism and adequate capacity in all the routes.
- Major thrust will be given for increasing the share of commercial revenue from non-aeronautical sources by giving total freedom to airport/ airstrip/ heliport/ helipad operators in the matter of raising non-aeronautical revenue
- New Ground Handling regulations with following broad particulars envisage:
  - At airports managed by AAI, new private investors have been allowed by AAI to undertake ground handling besides national carriers and self-handling by carriers which will increase competition resulting in improvement in services and reduction in costs.
  - At private airports, at least limited competition will be mandatory.
- A rationalized dynamic system for airport charges for AAI airports will be introduced for

  - Optimum utilization of airport by using peak and off-peak time charges,
  - Increasing revenue of airport operators
  - Promoting airports in far-flung regions by having varying airport charges from airport to airport depending upon the facilities available at the airport.
  - Promoting use of small aircraft
- A new Directorate of Lands shall be established in AAI and land use guidelines will be formulated for utilizing vacant land.
  - Vacant land at airports will be evaluated for construction of aviation related activities.
  - For optimal exploitation of airport land for civil aviation purposes, private-sector/ State Government participation would be welcome.
  - Land at such airports where there is no likelihood of future use for civil aviation purposes will be utilized for other commercial purposes like gold courses, tennis, etc. either by AAI itself or in joint venture.
  - Effective steps will be taken for removing encroachments from AAI land and if necessary, comprehensive rehabilitation package will be formulated.
- Cargo handling
  - Infrastructure like satellite freight cities with multi-modal transport, cargo terminals, cold storage centres, automatic storage and retrieval systems, mechanized transport of cargo, dedicated express cargo terminals with airside and city side openings, computerization and automation etc. will be set up on priority basis.
  - Private sector participation in cargo handling will be encouraged.
  - Efficient Electronic Data Interchange systems will be developed and linked amongst all stakeholders in the trade.
  - Air cargo complexes and dedicated express cargo terminals will be integral part of all major airports.
- Operation of airports would be in accordance with the provisions relating to prevention of air, water and noise pollution.
- Guidelines for naming of airports will be formulated to ensure that the airports are named after the cities they are situated in as per international norms.
- Air Traffic services
  - Air Traffic controllers will be licensed by CAA.
  - AAI will continue to provide Air Traffic Services over the Indian air Space as per standards set by CAA in accordance with ICAO norms.

- Approach and aerodrome control services may be provided by licensed ATCs engaged by the airport operators
- New satellite based CNS/ATM systems will be introduced as per ICAO's Regional Plan
- India to have a significant say in the provision of new satellite based CNS/ATM services in Asia- pacific/ SAARC regional airspace
- Fresh Air traffic Services and Controlling procedures will be evolved for helicopters and small aircraft to exploit their inherent advantages and to reduce the cost of their operations and efficient use of airspace without compromising safety. This will also give boost to Flying Clubs.
- Efforts will be made for Civil-Military co-ordination for
    a. Greater sharing of civil and military airspace for unidirectional air-corridors and straightening of air-routes to save fuel and time,
    b. Uniform air-traffic procedures,
    c. Additional slots for civilian flights at military airports,
    d. Sharing of revenues at civil enclaves

DOMESTIC PASSENGER AND CARGO AIR TRANSPORT

- ATF will be taken out from administered price mechanism for petroleum prices. The price of ATF for domestic airline will, therefore, be governed by market and customs duty. Airlines will also be permitted import of ATF.
- Capacity induction will be regulated with a view to ensuring safety, security and preventing unhealthy levels of capacity.
- Flying clubs, Aerosports like hang-gliding, ballooning, heli-skiing, para-jumping etc. will be promoted by encouraging private investment and formulating liberalized guidelines in consultation with users. This will include rationalized Avgas prices and liberalized air space control.
- Foreign equity up to 25% and Non-Resident Indian investment up to 100% will be permitted for domestic passenger transport services. However, participation from foreign airlines either directly or indirectly will not be permitted. Substantive ownership and effective control by Indians will be a pre-requisite.
- Government and CAA will ensure that there is no discrimination between different passenger and cargo air-operators.
- Helicopter operations will be given a new boost by a total change in outlook. At present, fixed wing norms with minor changes are broadly applied to rotary wing aircraft. Fresh guidelines will be formulated in consultation with user industry from the point of view of rotary wing aircraft. Fresh Air Traffic Services and controlling

procedures, which exploit the inherent advantages of helicopter without compromising safety, will be evolved. This will also reduce the cost of operations of helicopters and efficient use of airspace. Encouragement will be given to use of helicopters in the areas of heli-tourism, adventure sports, mountaineering/ trekking, point-to-point heli-services to bypass traffic congestion on the road, connecting remote areas and islands in Northeast, Andaman and Nicobar and Lakshdweep, religious places, sky crane for construction/ laying of transmission lines etc.

- It is necessary that both airline operations as well as airport infrastructure be treated as mutually dependent and complementary and given similar concessions to promote a balanced growth of the sector. Therefore, airline operations and acquisition of aircraft should be given the status of "infrastructure ".
- Permission to start scheduled passenger and cargo air transport service would be given by government on demonstration of competency, minimum capital requirement and viability of the company to provide a safe and reliable service. CAA may also fix a minimum number of aircraft for scheduled operators permit.
- Private sector participation in providing domestic passengers and cargo air transport services will be encouraged.
- Special consideration will also be given to Private operators and Corporate operators by way of rationalized Avgas prices, encouragement for construction of smaller airstrips/helipad et. in private sector.
- The government will encourage provision of safe passenger and cargo air transport services to every region of the country at economic prices.
- There will be freedom to operate non-revenue and passenger charter and cargo flights to any foreign destinations. Indian passport holders will also be allowed to travel on these flights.
- Wet leasing of foreign registered aircraft by operators will be permitted only in special circumstances like grounding of aircraft, augmentation of capacity for short term, to meet the capacity requirements for handling natural calamities, etc.

PROMOTION OF COMMON AVIATION AND PETITE AIRCRAFT OPERATION

- Single engine aircraft of seating capacity upto 10 seats can be permitted for passenger charter and cargo flights. Such operations shall be in accordance with the single engine operation guidelines and over land areas having no hilly terrain or other obstructions.
- There is a need to change the traditional concept of airport

development, ownership and operations in view of the economics of small aircraft/charters operations. Participation of state Government, urban local bodies, airline/ aircraft operators, other private investors will be encouraged in development, upgradation and management of small airports/ airstrips. These airports will be distinct from traditional airport and will be bare-bone type with no frills. Such airports need not be mandatorily manned and onus of ensuring security and safety of operations will rest on the aircraft operator in conjunction with the local administration/ bodies, etc. This will encourage the operation of small aircraft/ air taxis, as operators themselves or in collaboration with State Government/ Urban local bodies/ residents of a specific locality, factory, nearby factories, tourist operators will be able to manage such airports/ airstrip flexibly and efficiency at reduced cost. This will boost passenger transport and tourism

- There is need to open up the country and tap the latent demand for air services in many parts of the country currently not on the air map. However, the traffic profile in these areas does not permit viable operations of jet. Even smaller aircraft operations are not viable because of the high cost of operation and high break-even factor.
- Therefore, Aviation Turbine Fuel for turbo prop aircraft operations will be provided at par with price for international air services, with a cap of 4% on sales tax. Operation of smaller aircraft/ charters will be further encouraged through rationalization of airport charges, Inland Air Travel Tax and Avgas prices. For the North-East region, IATT has been fully exempted on all routes. Government will consider extending similar facilities to other category II areas.
- While Route-Dispersal Guidelines do help in providing air services in the remote and inaccessible areas, further measures are required to encourage widespread air-connectivity. Passenger and cargo air transport services to many regions will not be possible unless operation of small aircraft is made economically viable either on stand alone basis or in conjunction with major trunk routes.

WORLDWIDE AIR TRANSPORT

- Air India and Indian Airlines would be guaranteed the use of traffic rights actually being utilised by them for five years following privatisation.
- Efforts will be made by national carriers to join global alliances in their own commercial interest and in the interest of travelling passengers through code-sharing, exchange of frequent- flier programmes etc.

- Government will also establish, in the long run, an objective and well-defined mechanism for sharing of international traffic rights amongst all airlines in a transparent manner.
- Government will ensure that there will be no discrimination between different airport operators in allotting capacity to foreign carriers as per bilateral agreements if demand exists.
- Government will ensure that traffic rights are utilized to the maximum extent possible through direct operations, creation of virtual equipment by way of joint flights, code sharing arrangements etc. by the two national carriers i.e. Air India and Indian Airlines. Other domestic carriers who fulfill the minimum criteria for designation as Indian carrier to operate international passenger flights will also be permitted to meet this objective. Initially, they may be permitted to fly to neighbouring countries against unutilised rights subject to right of first refusal by national carriers. The requirement of substantial ownership and effective control of the airlines by Indians would continue to be operative.
- Liberal bilateral rights will be given for promoting international operations to less developed regions of the country as well as to ill-connected far away countries to promote trade and tourism in those regions.
- The Government will aim at ensuring adequate capacity to fully meet the requirement of international trade and tourism.
- There will be freedom to international tourist Charter operation to different custom airports.
- There will be no restriction on international cargo flights. However, they will not be allowed to carry domestic cargo on their flights within the country.
- Tourist charters from domestic airports to foreign destinations will also be permitted subject to safeguards for scheduled operations.

TOURISM AND TRADE PROMOTION

- Tourism and trade sectors are closely linked to civil aviation sector. Therefore it is important that airport infrastructure and air services are planned keeping in view the requirement and promotion of these sectors. Multi-modal approach will be used for planning to ensure better connectivity.
- A thrust for international tourism in India will be given by
  - Providing freedom to International Tourist Charters to all airports linking places of tourist interest
  - Declaring additional airports as international airports resulting in easy connectivity and better services,
  - Upgradation of airports at places of Tourist interest like Buddhist circuit, sanctuaries, beach resorts etc.

- Encouraging private sector participation in building tourist infrastructure near airports like transport services from airports to nearby cities, golf courses, amusement park, business centres, duty free shopping complexes of international class, aviation recreation activities, adventure aviation, hang-gliding, microlight aircraft, parachuting etc
- Efforts will be made to issue visa on arrival at the airport in larger number of cases.
- Improvement in passenger facilitation and sensitisation of personnel of immigration, customs, security and AAI at airport to make them more courteous and passenger friendly.

• For promotion to trade and industries, following steps will be undertaken:
  - Abolition of On-Board Courier Scheme to facilitate courier trade
  - Introduction of "Known Shipper " scheme for reducing dwell time in exports by doing away with "cooling off" requirement
  - Introduction of Electronic Data Interchange interlinking trade agencies, customs, immigration for faster efficient trade transactions
  - Private sector participation in cargo handling for increasing competition and improved services.

FUNCTIONING OF INDIAN CARRIERS

MAIN AIRLINES IN INDIA

There has been a revolution in air travel in India in the last decade. Ever since the government launched its open sky policy and allowed private players to enter the arena there has been a sea change in the airline industry in India. Air travel has become cheaper and more affordable and the number of people traveling by air has gone up drastically. Consequently, Indian Airports too have changed for the better. Airports in India have become more swanky and passenger friendly. Here is some useful information on airlines and airports in India.

SOME WELL-KNOWN DOMESTIC AIRLINES

Air Deccan

Air Deccan is India's first low-cost airline. It is a part of Deccan Aviation Private Limited, India's largest private heli-charter company. Air Deccan was established in 2003 and started operations in August that year with regular scheduled flights from Bangalore to Mangalore and Hubli. Captain G R Gopinath, is the Managing Director of Air Deccan and is one of the founders of Air Deccan. The other founder is Captain KJ Samuel. Air Deccan has grown rapidly since it first started air operations in 2003. It has revolutionized air travel in India and has brought air travel with in the reach of common man. Air Deccan was the first airline in India to link second rung cities like Hubli, Madurai and Visakhapatnam to metros like Bangalore and Chennai. The airline went public in May 2006. The proceeds from the IPO will be used to set up a training centre in Bangalore and a maintenance facility in Chennai. Presently, Air Deccan covers 57 destinations in India, which is more than any other airline in India. The Air Deccan fleet consists of 31 aircrafts. These include 13 Airbus A320-200, 5 ATR 42-320, 9 ATR 42-500, and 5 ATR 72-212A. Air Deccan has massive expansion plans. The company has acquired 30 Airbus A320s, which are to be deployed starting in 2007.

Air India

Air India is India's national Airline. Air India's history can be traced to October 15, 1932. On this day J.R.D. Tata, the father of Civil Aviation in India and founder of Air India, took off from Drigh Road Airport, Karachi, in a tiny, light single-engine de Havilland Puss Moth on his flight to Mumbai via Ahmedabad. Air India was earlier known as Tata Airlines. At the time of its commencement, Tata Airlines consisted of one Puss Moth, one Leopard Moth, one palm-thatched shed, one whole time pilot, one part-time engineer, and two apprentice-mechanics. Tata Airlines was converted into a Public Company under the name of Air India in August 1946. On March 8, 1948, Air India International Limited was formed to start Air India's international operations. On June 8, 1948, Air India started its international services with a weekly flight from Mumbai to London via Cairo and Geneva with a Lockheed Constellation aircraft. In early 1950s due to deteriorating financial condition of various airlines, the Government decided to nationalize air transport. On August 1, 1953 two autonomous corporations were created. Indian Airlines was formed with the merger of eight domestic airlines to operate domestic services, while Air India International was established to operate the overseas services. The word 'International' was dropped in 1962. With effect from March 1, 1994, the airline has been functioning as Air India Limited. Air India's worldwide network today covers 44 destinations by operating services with its own aircraft and through code-shared flights. Important destinations covered by Air India are Bangkok, Hongkong, Jakarta, Kuala Lumpur, Osaka, Singapore, Tokyo, Seoul, Dar-es-Salam, Nairobi, Frankfurt, London, Paris, Birmingham, Abu Dhabi, Al Ain, Bahrain, Dammam, Doha, Dubai, Jeddah, Muscat, Riyadh, Kuwait, Los Angeles, Chicago, Newark, New York, and Toronto. Air India's fleet consists of 38 aircrafts. These include 12 Boeing 747-400, 1 Boeing 747-400 COMBI, 2 Boeing 747-300 COMBI, 19 Airbus 310-300, and 4 Boeing 777-200.

Air Sahara

Air Sahara is one of India's leading private airlines. It is part of the multi-crore Sahara India Pariwar. Air Sahara was established on September 20, 1991 and began operations on December 3, 1993 with a fleet of two Boeing 737-200 aircrafts. It was then known as Sahara Airlines. Sahara Airlines was rebranded as Air Sahara on October 2, 2000. On March 22, 2004 Air Sahara became an international carrier with the start of flights from Chennai to Colombo.

Presently, Air Sahara connects to 24 domestic and 4 international destinations with 134 daily direct flights and offer 13900 seats per day. Domestic destinations include important cities like Delhi, Bangalore, Mumbai, Kolkata, Lucknow, Hyderabad, Pune, Chennai along with regional destinations like Ahmedabad, Gorakhpur, Allahabad, Bhubaneshwar and Ranchi. International destinations covered by Air Sahara are Colombo, Kathmandu, Singapore, and Chicago. Four more international destinations: Kuala Lumpur, Bangkok, Hongkong and London are proposed to be covered soon.

Air Sahara currently has a fleet of 27 aircrafts. These include 1 Boeing 767, 5 Boeing 737-800, 8 Boeing 737-700, 4 Boeing 737-400, 2 Boeing 737-300, and 7 CRJ -200. Air Sahara also provides chartered helicopter services from Delhi & Mumbai. Its fleet of helicopters include 3 ECUREUILS AS-355-NM2, and 1 DAUPHIN AS-365-NM2.

Indian Airlines

Indian Airlines, India's premier airline, has now been renamed as Indian. But Indian Airlines had establish itself as such a strong brand name that majority of people are still not aware that its name has been changed to Indian. Indian Airlines is fully owned by the Government of India and came into came into being with the enactment of the Air Corporations Act 1953. Indian Airlines began its operation on 1st August 1953 and was entrusted with the responsibility of providing air transportation within the country as well as to the neighbouring countries. Indian Airlines came into existence after nationalization of eight private airlines. At the time of nationalization, Indian Airlines inherited a fleet of 99 aircraft consisting of various types of aircrafts. With nationalization Indian Airlines started modernization in Indian civil aviation industry. Year 1964 heralded the beginning of the jet era in Indian Airlines when the Caravelle aircraft was inducted into the fleet. Continuous upgradation in its fleet has been going on ever since. Presently, Indian Airlines, together with its fully owned subsidiary Alliance Air, has a fleet of 70 aircraft. Another 43 new aircrafts are expected to be inducted in Indian Airlines by November 2006. Indian Airlines transport network spans from Kuwait in the west to Singapore in the east and covers 76 destinations. The Indian Airlines international network covers Kuwait, Oman, UAE, Qatar and Bahrain in West Asia; Thailand, Singapore, Malaysia and Myanmar in South East Asia and Pakistan, Afghanistan, Nepal, Bangladesh, Sri Lanka and Maldives in the South Asia sub-continent.

Jet Airways

Jet Airways is India's premier private airlines. Naresh Goyal is currently the chairman of Jet Airways. Jet Airways operates over 320 flights daily to 43 destinations in India and currently controls about 40% of India's aviation market. Jet Airways was the first private airline of India to fly to international destinations. It operates daily international flights to Colombo, Kathmandu, Singapore, Kuala Lumpur and London. Jet Airways has won a number of awards in recognition of standards of its service and has also received the ISO 9001:2000 certification for its In-flight Services. Jet Airways was established on 3 May 1991 with a fleet of 4 Boeing 737-300 aircraft, with 24 daily flights serving 12 destinations. Jet Airways presently operates 55 aircrafts and is now a public limited company. Its fleet of 55 aircrafts include 3 Airbus 340-300E, 4 Boeing 737-800, 1 Airbus 330-200, 1 Boeing 737-700, 18 Boeing 737-800, 8 ATR 72-500, 2 Boeing 737-900, 12 Boeing 737-700, and 6 Boeing 737-400. Jet Airways was recently involved in a controversy. On January 19, 2006 Jet Airways announced its decision to buy fellow airlines Air Sahara for $500 million in an all-cash deal. The deal was touted as the biggest in India's aviation history. But the deal fell midway and now the two parties are involved in a fierce court battle.

Kingfisher Airline

Kingfisher Airline is a private airline based in Bangalore, India. The airline is owned by Vijay Mallya of United Beverages Group. Kingfisher Airlines started its operations on May 9, 2005 with a fleet of 4 Airbus A320 aircrafts. The airline currently operates on domestic routes. The destinations covered by Kingfisher Airlines are Bangalore, Mumbai, Delhi, Goa, Chennai, Hyderabad, Ahmedabad, Cochin, Guwahati, Kolkata, Pune, Agartala, Dibrugarh, Mangalore and Jaipur. In a short span of time Kingfisher Airline has carved a niche for itself. The airline offers several unique services to its customers.

These include: personal valet at the airport to assist in baggage handling and boarding, exclusive lounges with private space, accompanied with refreshments and music at the airport, audio and video on-demand, with extra-wide personalised screens in the aircraft, sleeperette seats with extendable footrests, and three-course gourmet cuisine. Kingfisher Airlines currently operates with a brand new fleet of 8 Airbus A320 aircraft, 3 Airbus A319-100 aircraft and 4 ATR-72 aircraft. It was the first airline in India to operate with all new aircrafts.

Kingfisher Airlines is also the first Indian airline to order the Airbus A380. It placed orders for 5 A380s, 5 A350-800 aircrafts and 5 Airbus A330-200 aircrafts in a deal valued at over $3 billion on June 15, 2005. Delivery of the A330s is due to start in late 2007, followed by the A380s in 2010 and the A350s in 2012.

AIR CORPORATIONS BILL, 1994

BILL

To provide for the transfer and vesting of the undertakings of Indian Airlines and Air India respectively to and in the companies formed and registered as Indian Airlines Limited and Air India Limited and for matters connected therewith or incidental thereto and also to repeal the Air Corporations Act, 1953.

Be it enacted by Parliament in the Forty-fifth Year of the Republic of India as follows:-

Short Title and Commencement:

- This Act may be called the Air Corporations Act, 1994.
- It shall be deemed to have come into force on the 29th day of January, 1994.

Definitions:

In this Act, unless the context otherwise requires,-

- "Appointed day" mean such date as the Central Government may, by notification in the Official Gazette, appoint under section 3;
- "Company" means "Indian Airlines Limited" or "Air India Limited" formed and registered under the Companies Act, 1956;
- "Corporations" means "Indian Airlines" and "Air India" established under section 3 of the Air Corporations Act, 1953 and "corporation" means either of the corporations.

Undertakings of corporations to vest in companies

On such date as the Central Government may, by notification in the Official Gazette, appoint, there shall be transferred to, and vest in,—

- Indian Airlines Limited, the undertaking of Indian Airlines; and
- Air India Limited, the undertaking of Air India.

General Effect of Vesting of Undertakings in the Companies

- All contracts and working arrangements subsisting immediately before the appointed day and affecting a corporation shall, in so far as they relate to the undertaking of that corporation, cease to have effect or to be enforceable against that corporation and shall be of as full force and effect against or in favour of the company in which the undertaking has vested by virtue of this Act and enforceable as fully and effectually as if, instead of the corporation, the company had been named therein or had been a party thereto.
- Any proceeding or cause of action pending or existing immediately before the appointed day be or against a corporation in relation to its undertaking may, as from that day, be continued and enforced by or against the company in which it has vested by virtue of this

Act, as it might have been enforced by or against that corporation if this Act had not been passed, and shall cease to be enforceable by or against that corporation.

- The undertaking of a corporation which is transferred to, and which vests in, a company under section 3 shall be deemed to include all assets, rights, powers, authorities and privileges and all properties, movable and immovable, real or personal, corporeal or incorporeal, in possession or reservation, present or contingent, of whatever nature and wheresoever situate, including lands, works, workshops, aircraft, cash balances, capital reserves, reserve funds, investments, tenancies, leases and book debts and all other rights and interests arising out of such property as were immediately before the appointed day in the ownership, possession or power of that corporation in relation to its undertakings, whether within or outside India, all books of account and documents relating thereto and shall also be deemed to include all borrowings, liabilities and obligations of whatever kind then subsisting of that corporation in relation to its undertaking.

Licenses, etc., to be Deemed to have been Granted to Companies

With effect from the appointed day, all licenses, permits, quotas and exemptions granted to a corporation in connection with the affairs and business of that corporation under any law for the time being in force, shall be deemed to have been granted to the company in which the undertaking of that corporation has vested.

Tax Exemption or Benefit to Continue to have Effect:

- Where any exemption from, or any assessment with respect to, any tax has been granted or made or any benefit by way of set off or carry forward, as the case may be, of any unabsorbed depreciation or investment allowance or other allowance or loss has been extended or is available to a corporation under the income-tax Act, 1961, such exemption, assessment or benefit shall continue to have effect in relation to the company in which the undertaking of that corporation has vested.
- Where any payment made by a corporation is exempt from deduction of the tax at source under any provision of the Income-tax Act, 1961, the exemption from tax will continue to be available as if the provisions of the said Act made applicable to the corporation were operative in relation to the company in which the undertaking of that corporation has been vested.
- The transfer and vesting of the undertaking or any part thereof in terms of section 3 shall not be construed as a transfer within the meaning of the Income-tax Act, 1961 for the purposes of capital gains.

Guarantee to be Operative

Any guarantee given for or in favour of a corporation with respect to any loan or lease finance shall continue to be operative in relation to the company in which the undertaking of that corporation has vested by virtue of this Act.

Provisions in Respect of Officers and Other Employees of Corporations:

- Every officer or other employee of a corporation serving in its employment immediately before the appointed day shall, in so far as such officer or other employee is employed in connection with the undertaking which has vested in a company by virtue of this Act become, as from the appointed day an officer or other employee, as the case may be, of the company in which the undertaking has vested and shall hold his office or service therein by the same tenure, at the same remuneration, upon the same terms and conditions, with the same obligations and with the same rights and privileges as to leave, passage, insurance, superannuation scheme, provident fund, other funds, retirement, pension, gratuity and other benefits as he would have held under that corporation if its undertaking had not vested in the company and shall continue to do so as an officer or other employee, as the case may be, of the company or until the expiry of a period of six months from the appointed day if such officer of other employee opts not to be the officer or other employee of the company, within such period.
- Notwithstanding anything contained in the Industrial Disputes Act, 1947 or in any other law for the time being in force, the transfer of the services of any officer or other employee of a corporation to a company shall not entitles such offer or other employee to any compensation under this Act or under any other law for the time being in force and no such claim shall be entertained by any court, tribunal or other authority.
- Notwithstanding anything contained in this Act or in the Companies Act, 1956 or in any other law for the time being in force or in the regulations of a corporation, no Director of the Board, Chairman, Manageing Director or any other person entitled to manage the whole or a substantial part of the business and affairs of that corporation shall be entitled to any compensation against that corporation or against the company, as the case may be, for the loss of office or for the premature termination of any contract of management entered into by him with that corporation.
- Tax exemption granted to Provident Fund or Pilots Group Insurance and Superannuation Scheme would continue to be applied to the company.
- The officers and other employees who have retired before the

appointed day from the service of a corporation and are entitled to any benefits, rights or privileges shall be entitled to receive the same benefits, rights or privileges from the company in which the undertaking of that corporation has vested.

- The trusts of the Provident Fund or Pilots Group Insurance and Superannuation Scheme of the corporation and any other bodies created for the welfare of officers or employees would continue to discharge their functions in the company as was being done hitherto in the corporation.
- Where an officer or other employee of a corporation opts under sub-section not to be in the employment or service of the company in which the undertaking of that corporation has vested, such officer or other employee shall be deemed to have resigned.

Power of Central Government to Provide Instructions

The Central Government may give to a company directions as to the exercise and performance by that company of its functions, and that company shall be bound to give effect to any such directions.

Power to Remove Difficulties:

- Every order made under sub-section shall be laid before each House of Parliament.
- If any difficulty arises in giving effect to the provision of this Act, the Central Government may, by order published in the Official Gazette, not inconsistent with the provisions of this Act, remove the difficulty:
- Provided that no such order shall be made after the expiry of a period of two years from the coming into force of this Act.

Repeal of Act 27 of 1953 and Cases of Corporations:

- On the appointed day, the Air Corporations Act, 1953 shall stand repealed.
- The corporations shall, with the repeal of the Air Corporations Act, 1953, cease to exist.

Repeal and Saving:

- Notwithstanding such repeal of the Air Corporations Ordinance, 1994, anything done or any action taken under the said Ordinance shall be deemed to have been done or taken under the corresponding provisions of this Act.
- The Air Corporations Ordinance, 1994 is hereby repealed.

RAIL TRANSPORT

Rail transport is the transport of passengers and goods by means of wheeled vehicles specially designed to run along railways or railroads. Rail transport is part of the logistics chain, which facilitates the international trading and economic growth in most countries. A typical railway/railroad track consists of two parallel rails, normally made of steel, secured to cross-beams, termed sleepers or 'ties'. The sleepers maintain a constant distance between the two rails; a measurement known as the 'gauge' of the track. To maintain the alignment of the track, it is either laid on a bed of ballast or else secured to a solid concrete foundation, and the whole is referred to as Permanent way. Railway rolling stock, which is fitted with metal wheels, moves with low frictional resistance when compared to road vehicles; on the other hand locomotives and power cars normally rely solely for traction on the point of contact of the wheel with the rail whence they obtain adhesion i.e. the part of the transmitted axle load that makes the wheel "adhere" to the smooth rail. Whilst this is usually sufficient under normal dry rail conditions, adhesion can be reduced or even lost through the presence of unwanted material on the rail surface, such as grease, ice or dead leaves.

GENERAL

Rail transport is an energy-efficient and capital-intensive means of mechanized land transport and is a component of logistics. Rails, which along with various engineered components, are part of the permanent way. They provide very smooth and hard surfaces on which the wheels of the train may roll with a minimum of friction. As an example, a typical modern wagon can hold up to 125 tons of freight on two four-wheel bogies/trucks. The contact area between each wheel and the rail is tiny, a strip no more than a few millimetres wide, and hence suffers very little friction. Furthermore, the track distributes the weight of the train evenly, allowing significantly greater loads per axle/ wheel than in road transport, leading to less wear and tear on the permanent way.

This can save energy compared with other forms of transportation, such as road transport which depends on the friction between rubber and road. Trains also have a small frontal area in relation to the load they are carrying, which cuts down on forward air resistance and thus energy usage, although does not necessarily account for the effect of side winds. In all, under the right circumstances, a train needs 50-70% less energy to transport a given tonnage of freight than does road transport. Due to these various benefits, rail transport is a major form of public transport in many countries. In Asia, for example, many millions use trains as regular transport in India, China, South Korea and Japan.

It is also widespread in European countries. By comparison, intercity rail transport in the United States is relatively scarce outside the Northeast Corridor, although a number of major U.S. cities have heavily-used, local rail-based passenger transport systems or light rail or commuter rail operations. The vehicles traveling on the rails are arranged in a series of individual powered or unpowered vehicles linked together, called a train; this can include the locomotive where present. A locomotive is a powered vehicle used to haul a train of unpowered vehicles; calling a locomotive a "train" is a common popular misnomer. A string of unpowered vehicles without the locomotive is also termed a train; in the U.S.A. individual unpowered vehicles are known as cars and are divided according to the role: for a passenger-carrying vehicle the term carriage is used, whilst a freight-carrying vehicle is known as a freight car; in Britain, a freight car would be called a wagon. An individual powered passenger vehicle is known as a railcar or a power car; when one or more as these are coupled to one or more unpowered trailer cars as an inseparable unit, this is called a railcar set; several sets coupled together make up a multiple unit.

Collectively, rail vehicles of all types are known as rolling stock. As a result, rail transport is a major form of public transport in many countries. In Asia, for example, many millions use trains as regular transport in India, China, South Korea and Japan. It is also widespread in European countries. By comparison, intercity rail transport in the United States is relatively scarce outside the Northeast Corridor, although a number of major U.S. cities have heavily-used, local rail-based passenger transport systems or light rail or commuter rail operations.

HISTORY

The earliest evidence of a railway found thus far was the 6 kilometers Diolkos wagonway, which transported boats across the Corinth isthmus in Greece during the 6th century BC. Trucks pushed by slaves ran in grooves in limestone, which provided the track element, preventing the wagons from leaving the intended route. The Diolkos ran for over 1300 years, until 900 AD. The first horse-drawn wagonways also appeared in ancient Greece, with others to be found on Malta and various parts of the Roman Empire, using cut-stone tracks. Railways began re-appearing in Europe after a hiatus following the collapse of the Roman Empire from around 1550, usually operating with wooden track.

The first railways in Great Britain were constructed in the early 17th century, mainly for transporting coal from mines to canal wharfs where it could be transferred to a boat for onward shipment. Early examples of this can be found in Broseley in Shropshire, where wooden rails and flanged wheels were utilised, as on a modern railway. However, the rails were liable to wear out under the pressure, and had to be replaced. In 1768, the Coalbrookdale Iron Works laid cast iron plates on top of the wooden rails, providing a more durable load-bearing surface.

From the late 18th century, iron rails began to appear, with the British civil engineer William Jessop designing smooth iron edge rails, which were to be used in conjunction with flanged iron wheels. Jessop used this innovation on a route between Loughborough and Nanpantan, Leicestershire in 1789. In

1803, Jessop opened the Surrey Iron Railway in south London, arguably the world's first horse-drawn public railway. The first locomotive to haul a train of wagons on rails was designed by Cornish engineer Richard Trevithick, and was trialled in 1804 on a plateway at Merthyr Tydfil, South Wales. Although the locomotive successfully hauled the train, the rail design was not a success, partly because its weight broke a number of the brittle cast-iron plates. Despite this setback, another area of South Wales pioneered rail operations, when, in 1806, a horse-drawn railway was built between Swansea and Mumbles: the Swansea-Mumbles railway started carrying fare-paying passengers in 1807 – the first in the world to do so.

In 1811, John Blenkinsop designed the first successful and practical railway locomotive. He patented a system of moving coals by a rack railway worked by a steam locomotive, and a line was built connecting the Middleton Colliery to Leeds. The locomotive was built by Matthew Murray of Fenton, Murray and Wood. The Middleton Railway was the first railway to successfully use steam locomotives on a commercial basis. It was also the first railway in Great Britain to be built under the terms laid out in an Act of Parliament. Blenkinsop's engine had double-acting cylinders and, unlike the Trevithick pattern, no flywheel. Due to previous experience of broken rails, the locomotive was made very light and this brought concerns about insufficient adhesion, so instead of driving the wheels directly, the cylinders drove a cogwheel through spur gears, the cogwheel providing traction by engaging with a rack cast into the side of the rail. The Stockton and Darlington Railway opened in northern England in 1825 to be followed five years later by the Liverpool and Manchester Railway, considered to be the world's first "Inter City" line.

The rail gauge was used for the early wagonways, and had been adopted for the Stockton and Darlington Railway. The 4 ft 8½ in width became known as the international "standard gauge", used by about sixty per cent of the world's railways. The Liverpool and Manchester Railway, on the other hand, proved the viability of rail transport when, after organising the Rainhill Trials of 1829, Stephenson's Rocket successfully hauled a load of 13 tons at an average speed of 12 miles per hour. The company took the step of working its trains from its opening entirely by steam traction. Railways then soon spread throughout the United Kingdom and the world, and became the dominant means of land transport for nearly a century, until the invention of aircraft and automobiles, which prompted a gradual decline in railways. The first railroad in the United States may have been a gravity railroad in Lewiston, New York in 1764.

The 1810 Leiper Railroad in Pennsylvania was intended as the first permanent railroad, and the 1826 Granite Railway in Massachusetts was the first commercial railroad to evolve through continuous operations into a common carrier. The Baltimore and Ohio, opened in 1830, was the first to evolve into a major system. In 1867, the first elevated railroad was built in New York. In 1869, the symbolically important transcontinental railroad was completed in the United States with the driving of a golden spike at Promontory, Utah. The development of the railroad in the United States helped reduce transportation time and cost, which allowed migration towards the west. Railroads increased the accessibility of goods to consumers, thus allowing individuals and capital to flow westward.

The use of overhead wires conducting electricity, invented by Granville T. Woods in 1888, amongst several other improvements, led to the development of electrified railways, the first of which in the United States was operated at Coney Island from 1892. Richmond, Virginia had the first successful electrically-powered trolley system in the United States. Designed by electric power pioneer Frank J. Sprague, the trolley system opened its first line in January, 1888. Richmond's hills, long a transportation obstacle, were considered an ideal proving ground. The new technology soon replaced horse-powered streetcars. Diesel and electric trains and locomotives replaced steam in many countries in the decades after World War II. In the USSR the phenomenon of children's railways was developed since the 1930s. Fully operated by children, they were extracurricular educational institutions, where teenagers learnt railway professions.

A lot of them are functioning in post-Soviet states and Eastern European countries. Many countries since the 1960s have adopted high-speed railways. On April 3, 2007, the French TGV set a new train speed record. The train, with a modified engine and wheels, reached 574.8 km/h. The record attempt took place on the new LGV Est line between Paris and Strasbourg using a specially equipped TGV Duplex train. The overhead lines had also been modified for the attempt to carry 31,000 V rather than the line's normal 25,000 V. On 24 August 2005, the Qingzang railway became the highest railway line in the world, when track was laid through the Tanggula Mountain Pass at 5,072 meters above sea level in the Tanggula Mountains, Tibet.

OPERATIONS

A railway can be broken down into two major components. Basically these are the items which "move", the rolling stock, that is the locomotives, passenger carrying vehicles, freight carrying vehicles and those which are "fixed", usually referred to as its infrastructure. This category includes the permanent way and buildings.

SIGNALLING

Railway signalling is a system used to control railway traffic safely, essentially to prevent trains from colliding. Being guided by fixed rails, trains are uniquely susceptible to collision; furthermore, trains cannot stop quickly, and frequently operate at speeds that do not enable them to stop within sighting distance of the driver. Most forms of train control involve movement authority being passed from those responsible for each section of a rail network to the train crew. The set of rules and the physical equipment used to accomplish this determine what is known as the method of working, method of operation or safeworking. Not all these methods require the use of physical signals and some systems are specific to single track railways.

RIGHT OF WAY

Railway tracks are laid upon land owned or leased by the railway. Owing to the requirements for large radius turns and modest grades, rails will often be laid in circuitous routes.

Public carrier railways are typically granted limited rights of eminent domain. In many cases in the 19th century railways were given additional incentives in the form of grants of public land. Route length and grade requirements can be reduced by the use of alternating earthen cut and fill, bridges, and tunnels, all of which can greatly increase the capital expenditures required to develop a right of way, while significantly reducing operating costs and allowing higher speeds on longer radius curves. In densely urbanized areas such as Manhattan, railways are sometimes laid out in tunnels to minimize the effects on existing properties.

SAFETY AND RAILWAY DISASTERS

Trains can travel at very high speed; however, they are heavy, are unable to deviate from the track and require a great distance to stop. Although rail transport is considered one of the safest forms of travel, there are many possibilities for accidents to take place. These can vary from the minor derailment, a head-on collision with another train coming the opposite way and collision with an automobile at a level crossing/grade crossing. Level crossing collisions are relatively common in the United States where there are several thousand each year killing about 500 people - although the comparable figures in the United Kingdom are 30 and 12. The most important safety measures are railway signalling and gates at level/grade crossings. Train whistles warn others of the presence of a train, while trackside signals maintain the distances between trains.

In the United Kingdom, vandalism or negligence is thought responsible for about half of rail accidents. Railway lines are zoned or divided into blocks guarded by combinations of block signals, operating rules, and automatic-control devices so that one train, at most, may be in a block at any time. Such traffic control is done in a similar way to air traffic control. Compared with road travel, railways remain relatively safe. Annual death rates on roads are over 40,000 in the United States and about 3,000 in the United Kingdom, compared with 1,000 rail-related fatalities in the United States and under 20 in the UK.

TRACK

A typical railway/railroad track consists of two parallel steel rails, generally anchored perpendicular to beams, termed sleepers or ties, of timber, concrete, or steel to maintain a consistent distance apart, or gauge. The rails and perpendicular beams are usually then placed on a foundation made of concrete or compressed earth and gravel in a bed of ballast to prevent the track from buckling as the ground settles over time beneath and under the weight of the vehicles passing above. The vehicles travelling on the rails are arranged in a train; a series of individual powered or unpowered vehicles linked together, displaying markers. These vehicles move with much less friction than do vehicles riding on rubber tires on a paved road, and the locomotive that pulls the train tends to use energy far more efficiently as a result.

Trackage, consisting of sleepers/ties and rails, may be prefabricated or assembled in place. Rails may be composed of segments welded or bolted, and may be of a length comparable to that of a railcar or two or may be many hundreds of feet long. The surface of the ballast is sloped around curves to reduce side forces. This reduces the forces tending to displace the track, reduces the tendency to overturn at high speed, and makes for a more comfortable ride for standing cattle and standing or seated passengers in trains. This will be optimal at only one particular speed, however.

TRACK COMPONENTS

Railways are highly complex feats of engineering, with many hours of planning and forethought required for a successful outcome. The first component of a railway is the route, which is planned to provide the least resistance in terms of gradient and engineering works. As such, the trackbed is heavily engineered to provide, where possible, a level surface. As such, embankments are constructed to support the track, in order to provide a compromise in terms of the route's average elevation. With this in mind, sundry structures such as bridges and viaducts are constructed in an attempt to maintain the railway's elevation, and gradients are kept within manageable constraints.

Where such items are not always justified, such as in hilly terrain, where routes may require long detours to avoid such features, a cutting or tunnel is dug or bored through the obstacle. Once the sundry engineering works are completed, a bed of stone is laid over the compacted trackbed to ensure drainage around the ties and even distribution of pressure over a wider area, locking the track-work in place. This crushed stone is firmly tamped to prevent further settling and to lock the stones. Minor watercourses are led through pipes before the grade is raised. The base of the trackage consists of treated wood or concrete "ties", also known as "sleepers". These ensure the proper distance between the rails and anchor the rail structure to the roadbed through the use of Plates. These are attached to the top of the ties in order to provide a secure housing for the rails. After placement of the rail atop the plate, spikes are driven through holes in the plate and into the tie where they are held by friction. The top of the spike has a head that clamps the rail. Alternatively, lag bolts may be used to retain the clamps; this is preferred since screws do not tend to loosen. The spaces between and surrounding the ties are filled with additional ballast to stabilize the rail assembly against movement.

POINTS

Points or switches, technically known as turnouts, are the means of directing a train onto a diverging section of track, for example, a siding, a branch line, or a parallel running line. Laid similar to normal track, a point typically consists of a frog, check rails and two switch rails. The switch rails may be moved left or right, under the control of the signalling system, to determine which path the train will follow.

MAINTENANCE

Spikes in wooden ties can loosen over time, whilst split and rotten ties may be individually replaced with a concrete substitute. Should the rails settle owing to soil subsidence they may be lifted by specialized machinery and additional ballast tamped down to form a level elevation. Periodically, ballast must be removed and replaced with clean ballast to ensure adequate drainage, especially if wooden ties are used. Culverts and other passages for water must be kept clear lest water is impounded by the trackbed, causing landslips. Where trackbeds are placed along rivers, additional protection is usually placed to prevent erosion during times of high water, whilst Bridges are another important item requiring inspection and maintenance.

EURO RAIL

The European rail network, or Eurail as most Americans refer to it, is a complex web of rail lines serving over 30,000 European cities. North Americans are best to associate Europe's rail network with our Interstate road system. Virtually every city is serviced somehow. Over 80,000 train departures a day make traveling from city to city fast, comfortable and care free. Today, its meaning couldn't be more appropriate. Upgrades in services, trains and tracks leaves little chance of boredom en route, but it's still leisurely enough to relax and absorb the changing scenery.

From hills, farms, and snowcapped mountains to castles peaking through the forest, rail travellers need only worry whether to stop by the dining car for lunch, chat with fellow passengers, or simply enjoy the view. Of course there's always time to catch up on some needed rest. Packaged group tours offer an inexpensive option for many travellers, but they offer little free time or deviation from the itinerary. Traveling Europe on your own by rail gives you the opportunity to see what you like, when you like. You also have the opportunity to mingle with Europeans who are sharing the train ride with you, which is part of the reason to go to Europe. Trains offer romance and aura that cannot be found in any other method of transportation. Just the mention of the Orient Express conjures visions of exquisite dining, intrigue and mystery. While many of the original famous trains have been upgraded by modern high-speed international trains, the thrill is still there. Traveling Europe by train is unique, enjoyable and memorable.

AMTRAK

The National Railroad Passenger Corporation, doing business as Amtrak, is a quasi-governmental corporation that was organized on May 1, 1971, to provide intercity passenger train service in the United States. "Amtrak" is a portmanteau of the words "American" and "track". All of Amtrak's preferred stock is owned by the Federal government. The members of its board of directors are appointed by the President of the United States and are subject to confirmation by the United States Senate. Common stock was issued in 1971 to railroads that contributed capital and equipment; its current holders consider it worthless but declined a 2002 buy-out offer by Amtrak. Amtrak employs nearly 19,000 people. It operates passenger service on 21,000 miles of track primarily owned by other railroads connecting 500 destinations in 46 states. Some routes serve Canada. In fiscal year 2006, Amtrak served 24.3 million passengers, a company record. According to estimates for fiscal year 2007, Amtrak has served over the 25 million passenger mark, a 6% increase from last year.

PASSENGER RAIL SERVICE BEFORE AMTRAK

The history of Amtrak begins with the decline of privately-operated passenger rail. From the middle 19th century until approximately 1920, if a person traveled from one city to another in the United States, the trip almost certainly was by rail. By 1910, close to 100% of intercity passenger trips were made by railroad. All of those services were provided by private, for-profit organizations. Approximately 65,000 railroad passenger cars were in operation in 1929. For a long time after 1920, passenger rail's popularity plateaued and there were a series of pullbacks and tentative recoveries.

Rail passenger revenues declined dramatically between 1920 and 1934, but in the mid-1930s, railroads reignited the popular imagination with service improvements and introductions of new, diesel-powered streamliners, such as the gleaming silver Pioneer Zephyr and Flying Yankee. Even with the improvements, on a relative basis, ridership continued to erode and by 1940 railroads held a far less dominant 67% share of all passenger-miles in the United States. World War II broke the malaise. During the war, troop movements and restrictions on use of automobile fuel generated a sixfold increase in passenger traffic from the low point of the Depression. After the war, railroads rejuvenated overworked and neglected fleets with a multitude of fast and often luxurious streamliners — epitomized by the Super Chief and California Zephyr — which inspired the last major resurgence in passenger rail travel. In 1948, Santa Fe CEO Fred G. Gurley reported a "complete reversal of our passenger traffic picture", with 1947 revenues exceeding those of 1936 by 220%.Inspired by America's leadership, European and Japanese railroads also launched their own streamlined, high-speed rail services. The postwar resurgence was short-lived.

In 1946, there remained 45% fewer passenger trains than in 1929, and the pace of decline quickened despite railroad optimism. Passengers disappeared, and so did the trains. Between 1946 and 1964, the annual number of passengers declined from 770 to 298 million. The number of U.S. commuter trains declined by more than 80%, from greater than 2,500 in 1954 to fewer than 500 in 1969. Few trains generated profits; most produced losses. Broad-based passenger rail deficits appeared as early as 1948 and by the mid-1950s railroads claimed aggregate annual losses on passenger services of more than $700 million. By 1965, only 10,000 rail passenger cars were in operation, 85% fewer than in 1929. Passenger service was provided on only 75,000 miles of track, a stark decline. Passenger rail service in the United States showed the signs of underinvestment. Rail facilities suffered from decrepit equipment, cavernous and nearly empty stations in dangerous urban centres, and management that seemed intent on driving away the few remaining customers. The 1960s also saw the end of railway post office revenues, which had helped some of the remaining trains break even despite the dearth of passengers.

CAUSES OF DECLINE OF PASSENGER RAIL

The causes of the decline of passenger rail were complex. The industry was hobbled by government regulation and labour inflexibility, which undermined passenger rail just as the industry faced an explosion of competition from massively subsidized automobile and airplane transportation. All this marked the path to oblivion. Rail interests were structured to sell access to elaborate, efficient, roads at a profit; they could not compete for passengers with parallel turnpikes, air strips, and highways in the sky. The competing modes were in many ways convenient and faster. They fostered independence. But most importantly, as the costs of running a passenger railroad rose, highways in particular were cheaper, as they were built with public funds and without a profit motive. The decline was a failure of a business model as much as the failure of a technology.

GOVERNMENT REGULATION AND LABOUR ISSUES

Passenger rail's vibrancy first was interrupted by government intervention brought about by the Interstate Commerce Commission. Just after the turn of the 20th century, populist rate-setting schema and a WWI wartime nationalization of the rail industry erased ample railroad profits, reversed growth of the rail system, and contributed to massive underinvestment from approximately 1910 to 1921. Meanwhile, labour costs advanced, and with them passenger fares, which discouraged passenger traffic just as automobiles gained a foothold. Later the ICC intervened in other ways, also to the detriment of passenger rail.

In 1947, the ICC ruled that passenger trains could not exceed 79 mph without special in-cab signaling systems; the systems were derided as unnecessary and prohibitively expensive, and after issuance of the regulation, plans to develop intercity high-speed rail services were shelved. In 1958, the ICC was authorized to allow or reject modifications and eliminations of passenger routes. Many routes at that time required beneficial pruning, but the ICC delayed action by an average of eight months and when it did authorize modifications, the ICC insisted that unsuccessful routes be merged with profitable ones. Thus, fast, popular rail service was transformed into slow, unpopular service. The ICC was even more critical of corporate mergers. Many combinations, which railroads sought to compete, were delayed for years and even decades, such as the merger of the New York Central Railroad and Pennsylvania Railroad, into what eventually became Penn Central, and the Delaware, Lackawanna and Western Railroad and Erie Railroad into the Erie Lackawanna Railroad. By the time the ICC approved the mergers in the 1960s, disinvestments by the federal government, years of deteriorating equipment and station facilities and the flight of passengers to the air and car had taken their toll and the mergers were unsuccessful.

At the same time, government insisted that railroads carry a substantial tax burden. A World War II-era excise tax of 15% on passenger rail travel survived until 1962. Local governments, far from providing needed support to passenger rail, viewed rail infrastructure as a ready source for property tax revenues. In one extreme example, in 1959 the Great Northern Railroad, which owned about a third of one percent of the land in Lincoln County, Montana, was assessed more than 91% of all school taxes in the county. Railroads also were saddled with antiquated work rules and an inflexible relationship with labour unions. Work policies did not adapt to technological change. Average train speeds doubled from 1919 to 1959, but unions resisted efforts to modify their existing 100 to 150 mile work days. As a result, railroaders' work days were roughly cut in half, from 5 to 7½ hours in 1919, down to 2½ to 3¾ hours in 1959. Labour rules also perpetuated positions that had been obviated by technology. Between 1947 and 1957, passenger railroad financial efficiency dropped by 42% per mile.

SUBSIDIZED COMPETITION

While passenger rail faced internal and governmental pressures, new challenges appeared that undermined the dominance of passenger rail: highways and commercial aviation. The passenger rail industry wilted as government backed these upstarts with billions of dollars in construction. Beginning roughly in the WWI era, cars became more attainable to most Americans. Soon, government actively began to support with public funds a non-profit network of roads not subject to property taxation that rivaled and then surpassed the for-profit network that the railroads had built in previous generations with corporate capital.

The Federal Highway Act funded the Interstates, local governments built compatible networks of local roads, and all told between 1921 and 1955 governmental entities financed more than $93 billion worth of pavement, construction, and maintenance. In turn, more Americans embraced the flexibility, convenience and privacy of personal transportation by automobile over public transit alternatives. Intercity bus services also saw declines. In the 1950s, a second and more formidable threat appeared: affordable commercial aviation. Government at many levels supported aviation. Governmental entities spawned sprawling urban and suburban airports, and funded construction of massive highways to provide access to the airports.

RAIL PASSENGER SERVICE ACT

In 1967, the National Association of Railroad Passengers was formed to lobby for government funding to assure the continuation of passenger trains. Its lobbying efforts were hampered by the opposition of the Democratic Party to any sort of subsidies to the privately-owned railroads, and Republican Party opposition to the nationalization of the railroad industry. The proponents were aided by the fact that few in the federal government wanted to be held responsible for the seemingly-inevitable extinction of the passenger train, which most regarded as tantamount to political suicide. The urgency of the need to solve the passenger train problem was heightened by the bankruptcy filing of the Penn Central, the dominant railroad in the Northeastern United States, on June 21, 1970. Under the Rail Passenger Service Act of 1970, Congress created the National Railroad Passenger Corporation to subsidize and oversee the operation of intercity passenger trains. The Act provided that

- Any railroad operating intercity passenger service could contract with the NRPC, thereby joining the national system.
- Participating railroads bought into the NRPC using a formula based on their recent intercity passenger losses. The purchase price could be satisfied either by cash or rolling stock; in exchange, the railroads received NRPC common stock.
- Any participating railroad was freed of the obligation to operate intercity passenger service after May 1, 1971, except for those services chosen by the Department of Transportation as part of a "basic system" of service and paid for by NRPC using its federal funds.

- Railroads that chose not to join the NRPC system were required to continue operating their existing passenger service until 1975 and thenceforth had to pursue the customary Interstate Commerce Commission approval process for any discontinuance or alteration to the service.

For some time, there was a veto threat from President Richard M. Nixon. The veto never materialized and the act was signed into law on October 30, 1970. The original working brand name for NRPC was Railpax, but shortly before the company started operating it was changed to Amtrak.

The Nixon administration and many Washington insiders viewed the NRPC as a politically expedient way for the President and Congress to give passenger trains the one "last hurrah" demanded by the public. Cynics expected Amtrak to quietly disappear as public interest waned. Proponents also hoped that government intervention would be short-lived, but their view was that Amtrak would soon support itself. Neither view has yet proved correct. Popular support has allowed Amtrak to continue in operation longer than critics imagined while financial results have made infeasible a return to private operation.

EARLY DAYS

Amtrak began operations May 1, 1971. The corporation was molded from the passenger rail operations of 20 out of 26 major railroads in operation at the time. The railroads made contributions of rolling stock, equipment, and capital. In return, they received approval to discontinue their own passenger services, and at least some acquired common stock in Amtrak. Notably, Amtrak received no railroad track or right-of-way at its inception. Railroads that shed passenger operations were expected to host Amtrak trains on their tracks, for a fee.

There was a period of adjustment. All of Amtrak's routes were continuations of prior service, although Amtrak immediately pruned about half of the existing passenger rail network. Out of the 364 trains that were operated previously, Amtrak only continued 182. On the trains that were continued, to the extent possible, schedules were retained with only minor changes from the Official Guide of the Railways. Former names largely were continued.

Several major corridors initially became freight-only, including New York Central Railroad's Water Level Route across New York and Ohio and Grand Trunk Western Railroad's Chicago to Detroit service, although service soon returned to the Water Level Route with introduction of the Lake Shore. Reduced passenger train schedules created headaches. A 19-hour layover became necessary for eastbound travel on the James Whitcomb Riley between Chicago and Newport News. Amtrak also inherited problems dealing with station facilities, most notably stations with deferred maintenance, and redundant facilities resulting from competing companies that served the same areas. On the day it started Amtrak was given the huge responsibility of rerouting passenger trains from the then seven existing train terminals in Chicago into just one, Union Station. In New York Amtrak had to pay to maintain Penn Station and Grand Central Terminal due to lack of track connections to bring trains from upstate New York into Penn Station, a problem that was not rectified until the building of the Empire Connection in 1991. In many cases Amtrak had to abandon service into the huge old Union Stations such as ones in Cincinnati, Saint Paul, Buffalo, Detroit, Kansas City, and Saint Louis and route trains into smaller Amtrak-built facilities down the line. On the other hand, merged operations also presented efficiencies such as the combination of three West Coast trains into the Coast Starlight, running from San Diego to Seattle.

The Northeast Corridor received an Inland Route via Springfield, Massachusetts, thanks to support from New York, Connecticut and Massachusetts. The North Coast Hiawatha was implemented as a second Pacific Northwest route. The Milwaukee to St. Louis Abraham Lincoln and Prairie State routes also commenced. The first all-new Amtrak route, not counting the Coast Starlight, was the Montrealer/Washingtonian. That route was inaugurated September 29, 1972, along Boston and Maine Railroad and Canadian National Railway track that had last seen passenger service in 1966. Amtrak soon had the opportunity to acquire railway. Following the bankruptcy declaration of several northeastern railroads in the early 1970s, including the Penn Central which owned and operated the Northeast Corridor, Congress passed the Railroad Revitalization and Regulatory Reform Act of 1976. A large part of the act was directed to the creation of a Conrail, but in addition the law enabled transfer to Amtrak of the vital Northeast Corridor railway from Boston, Massachusetts to Washington, DC.

That trackage became Amtrak's crown jewel. In subsequent years, various short route segments not needed for freight operations were transferred to Amtrak. Nevertheless, in general, Amtrak remained dependent on freight railroads for access to most of its routes. Amtrak fell far short of achieving financial independence in its first decade, but it did find modest success rebuilding ridership. Outside factors discouraged competing modes of transportation, such as fuel shortages which increased costs of automobile and airline travel, and airline strikes which disrupted airline operations. Intensive investments in Amtrak's track, equipment and information resources also made Amtrak more relevant to America's transportation needs. Amtrak's ridership increased from 16.6 million in 1972 to 21 million in 1981.

POLITICAL INFLUENCES

Unlike many large businesses, subsequent to its formation Amtrak has had only one active investor: the United States government. Like most investors, the Federal government has demanded a degree of accountability. Determination of congressional funding and selection of Amtrak's leadership have been infused with political considerations. Funding levels and capital support have varied over time. Political pressures extend to Amtrak's very route structure.

As with any federally supported activity, the more states and congressional districts served, the more political support in Congress. Some members of Amtrak's board and executive leadership have had little or no experience with railroads. Conversely, Amtrak also has benefited from the interest of highly motivated and politically-oriented public servants. For example, in 1982, former U.S. Secretary of the Navy and retired Southern Railway head W. Graham Claytor, Jr., brought his naval and railroad experience to the job.

Claytor had served briefly as an acting U.S. Secretary of Transportation in the cabinet of President Jimmy Carter in 1979, and came out of retirement to lead Amtrak after the disastrous financial results during the Carter administration. He was recruited and strongly supported by John H. Riley, an attorney who was the highly skilled head of the Federal Railroad Administration under the Reagan Administration from 1983-1989. Secretary of Transportation Elizabeth Dole also tacitly supported Amtrak. Claytor seemed to enjoy a good relationship with the Congress for his 11 years in the position. Of course, politics aside, that may have also been because he was perceived to have done a good job in reducing costs and living within a smaller appropriation, albeit through extensive use of short-term debt.

MODERN HISTORY

Ridership stagnated at roughly 20 million passengers per year amid uncertain government aid from 1981 to about 2000. Ridership increased in the 2000s after implementation of capital improvements in the Northeast Corridor and rises in automobile fuel costs. Since 2002, Amtrak has had four consecutive years of record ridership. During fiscal year 2006, Amtrak reported more than 24.3 million passengers, its highest total to date. According to Amtrak, an average of more than 67,000 passengers ride on up to 300 Amtrak trains per day. In the 1990s, Claytor was succeeded at Amtrak's helm by career public servants who inherited the goal of operational self-sufficiency. First, Thomas Downs was assumed the leadership.

Downs had overseen the Union Station project, which experienced substantial delays and cost overruns. Downs inherited monumental financial goals and departed after guiding Amtrak narrowly through a cash crunch. George Warrington succeeded Downs in January, 1998. Warrington previously led Amtrak's Northeast Corridor Business Unit. Warrington's sought to meet the requirements of a legislatively-imposed glide-path to self-sufficiency, excluding railroad retirement tax act payments. Passengers became "guests" and there were expansions into express freight work, but the financial plans failed. Amtrak's inroads in express freight delivery created additional friction with competing freight operators, including the trucking industry. Warrington also had the burden of delays in implementation of the new Acela Express high-speed trainsets, which promised to be a strong source of income and favourable publicity along the Northeast Corridor between Boston and Washington DC. Under Warrington, Amtrak could not add sufficient express revenue or cut sufficient other services to break even. David L. Gunn was selected as president in April 2002.

By that time, self-sufficiency was falling out of favour as a realistic goal. Gunn had a strong reputation as a straightforward and experienced manager. He was not one to shy away from conflict with others. Years earlier, Gunn's refusal to "do politics" put him at odds with the WMATA board, which included representatives from the District of Columbia and suburban jurisdictions in Maryland and Virginia. Gunn was an accomplished public servant and railroad person and his successes before Amtrak earned him a great deal of credibility, despite a sometimes-rough relationship with politicians and labour unions. Gunn was polite but direct in response to congressional criticism. In a departure from his predecessors' promises to make Amtrak self-sufficient in the short term, the Gunn administration took the stance that no form of passenger transportation in the United States is self-sufficient as the economy is currently structured, and that Amtrak should not be judged by different standards than other transport modes. Highways, airports, and air traffic control all require large government expenditures to build and operate, coming from The Highway Trust Fund and Aviation Trust Fund paid for by user fees, highway fuel and road taxes and in the case of The General Fund by people who own cars and do not. These expenditures are indirect subsidies unlike Amtrak's which fall under the watchful scrutiny of Congress when budget allocations are made yearly.

Before a congressional hearing, Gunn answered a demand by leading Amtrak critic Arizona Senator John McCain to eliminate all operating subsidies by asking the Senator if he would also demand the same of the commuter airlines, upon whom the citizens of Arizona are dependent. McCain, usually not at a loss for words when debating Amtrak funding, did not reply. Gunn's tenure was punctuated by successes in reducing layers of management overhead in Amtrak. He eliminated almost all of the controversial express business. His policy was that continued deferred maintenance would become a safety issue, which Amtrak would not tolerate. The policies improved labour relations to some extent, even as Amtrak's ranks of unionized and salaried workers have been reduced. November 9, 2005, David Hughes, Amtrak's Chief Engineer, succeeded Gunn as interim president. Given Gunn's solid performance, many Amtrak supporters feared that Gunn's removal was Amtrak's death knell. On August 29, 2006, Alexander Kummant was named as Gunn's permanent replacement effective September 12, 2006. Kummant has expressed a commitment to see that Amtrak continues to operate a national rail network. He does not envision separating the Northeast corridor under separate ownership. He has said that shedding the system's long distance routes would amount to selling off national assets that are on par with national parks, and that Amtrak's abandonment of these routes would be irreversible. He has recommended annual congressional funding of Amtrak in the amount of $1 billion for ten years. He said that this investment is moderate, in light of Federal investment in other modes of transportation. He compared the cost of four or five highway interchanges with the costs of providing one hundred mile-per-hour high-speed rail service for several hundred miles.

PUBLIC FUNDING

Amtrak commenced operations in 1971 with $40 million in direct Federal aid, $100 million in Federally insured loans, and a somewhat larger private contribution. Officials expected that Amtrak would break even by 1974, but those expectations proved unrealistic and annual direct Federal aid reached a 17-year high in 1981 of $1.25 billion. During the Reagan administration, appropriations were halved. By 1986, Federal support fell to a decade low of $601 million, almost none of which were capital appropriations. In the late 1980s and early 1990s, Congress continued the reductionist trend even while Amtrak expenses held steady or rose.

Amtrak was forced to borrow to meet short-term operating needs, and by 1995 Amtrak was on the brink of a cash crisis and was unable to continue to service its debts. In response, in 1997 Congress authorized $5.2 billion for Amtrak over the next five years – largely to complete the Acela capital project – on the condition that Amtrak submit to the ultimatum of self-sufficiency by 2003 or liquidation. Amtrak made financial improvements during the period, but ultimately did not achieve self sufficiency. In the aftermath of the September 11, 2001, terrorist attacks, during which Amtrak kept running while airlines were grounded, the value of a national passenger rail service was briefly acknowledged in Washington. But when Congress returned to work following the attacks, the airlines received a $15 billion bailout package, and inattention toward Amtrak resumed. In 2004, a stalemate in Federal support of Amtrak forced cutbacks in services and routes as well as resumption of deferred maintenance.

In fiscal 2004 and 2005, Congress appropriated about $1.2 billion for Amtrak, $300 million more than President George W. Bush had requested. However, the company's board requested $1.8 billion through fiscal 2006, the majority of which would be used to bring infrastructure, rolling stock, and motive power back to a state of good repair. In Congressional testimony, the Department of Transportation's inspector-general confirmed that Amtrak would need at least $1.4 billion to $1.5 billion in fiscal 2006 and $2 billion in fiscal 2007 just to maintain the status quo. In 2006, Amtrak received just under $1.4 billion, with the condition that Amtrak would reduce food and sleeper service losses. Thus, dining service were simplified and now require two fewer on-board service workers. Only Auto Train and Empire Builder services continue regular made onboard meal service. State governments have partially filled the breach left by reductions in Federal aid. Several states have entered into operating partnerships with Amtrak, notably California, Pennsylvania, Illinois, Michigan, Oregon, Washington, North Carolina, Oklahoma, Wisconsin and Vermont, as well as the Canadian province of British Columbia, which provides some of the resources for the operation of the Cascades route.

CONTROVERSY

Aid to Amtrak by government was controversial from the beginning. Formation of Amtrak in 1971 was criticized as a bailout serving corporate rail interests and union railroaders, not the traveling public. Critics assert that Amtrak has proven incapable of operating as a business and does not provide valuable transportation services meriting public support, a "mobile money-burning machine." They argue that subsidies should be ended, national rail service terminated, and the Northeast Corridor turned over to private interests. "To fund a Nostalgia Limited is not in the public interest." Proponents point out that the government heavily subsidizes the Interstate Highway System and many aspects of passenger aviation. Massive government aid of those forms of travel was a primary factor in the decline of passenger service by privately owned railroads in the 1950s and 60s. Amtrak still, indirectly, through fees to host railroads, pays property taxes that highway users do not pay.

Advocates assert that Amtrak only should be expected to be as self-sufficient as those competing modes. In other words, it should not be expected to be self sufficient at all. Proponents also argue that rail passenger service merits public support because it is safer and more energy efficient than competitors, and often more convenient and comfortable. Amtrak serves many communities which have no air service or other public transportation. If rail operations received favourable treatment and capital support on par with automobile infrastructure and air transport, proponents argue that rail passenger service in America would not be so humble and would be more relevant to a greater number of transportation needs.

LABOUR ISSUES

Intractable positions staked out by labour leaders were blamed for part of the decline of passenger rail service in the early to middle 20th century, and labour union clout was widely credited with facilitating the creation of Amtrak in 1971. Many trade union jobs were saved by the bailout. In recent times, efforts at reforming passenger rail have addressed labour issues. In

1997, Congress released Amtrak from a prohibition on contracting for labour outside of the corporation, opening the door to privatization. Since that time, many of Amtrak's employees have been working without a contract. The most recent contract, signed in 1999, was mainly retroactive. New Amtrak president Kummant seems poised to follow a cooperative posture with Amtrak's trade unions. He has ruled out plans to privatize large parts of Amtrak's unionized workforce.

AMTRAK OPERATIONS AND SERVICES

Amtrak no longer is required by law to operate a national route system, although it nonetheless is encouraged to strive to do so. At the present time, Amtrak has some presence in all but two of the 48 contiguous states. Service on the Northeast Corridor between Washington, DC and Boston, Massachusetts, and between Philadelphia, Pennsylvania and Harrisburg, Pennsylvania is powered by overhead wires. Across the rest of the system, diesel locomotion is utilized. Frequency of service on routes varies widely, from three trips weekly on the Sunset Limited from Los Angeles, California to New Orleans, Louisiana, to service several times per hour weekdays on the Northeast Corridor from New York City to Washington, DC. Amtrak also operates a captive bus service, Thruway Motorcoach, that provides connections to train routes. The most popular and heavily-used routes are those on the Northeast Corridor, which include the Acela Express, and Regional.

Those routes serve Boston, Massachusetts, New York City, Philadelphia, Pennsylvania, Washington, DC, and many communities in between. Four of the six busiest stations by boardings are located on the corridor: New York; Washington; Philadelphia, and Boston. The remaining members of the top six are: Chicago and Los Angeles. Amtrak trains have both names and numbers. Train routes are named to reflect the rich and complex history of the route itself, or of the area traversed by the route. Each individual scheduled run of the route is assigned a number. As a general rule, even-numbered routes run north and east while odd-numbered routes run south and west. Some routes, such as the Pacific Surfliners, use the opposite numbering system, inherited from the previous operators of similar routes, such as the Santa Fe Railroad.

INTERMODAL CONNECTIONS

Intermodal connections between Amtrak trains and other transportation are available at many stations. With few exceptions, Amtrak rail stations that are located in downtown areas have connections to local public transit. Amtrak also code shares with Continental Airlines, providing service between Newark Liberty International Airport and Philadelphia 30th St, Wilmington, Stamford, and New Haven. In addition, Amtrak serves airport stations at Milwaukee and Baltimore. Amtrak coordinates Thruway Motorcoach service to extend many of its routes, particularly in California.

GAPS IN SERVICE

Outside the Northeast Corridor, Amtrak was a niche player. In 2003, Amtrak accounted for 0.1% of US intercity passenger miles. In fiscal year 2004, Amtrak routes served over 25 million passengers, while in calendar year 2004 commercial airlines served over 712 million passengers. Amtrak provides some rail service in 46 states. The only states that are not served by Amtrak are Hawaii, Alaska, and South Dakota. Wyoming lost rail service in the 1997 cuts, but is still served by Amtrak's Thruway Motorcoaches. Amtrak serves many states only nominally through stations along borders and/or away from major population areas.

Many major cities in the Midwest, West, and South have two or fewer trains per day, such as Atlanta, Denver, Cincinnati, Indianapolis, and Minneapolis/Saint Paul. Amtrak's reliance on freight railroads has also been a cause for its elimination of service. Passenger rail service was entirely discontinued to Phoenix, Arizona in 1997, after the Union Pacific Railroad, which owns the tracks that served Phoenix, announced it was abandoning the right of way.

Amtrak did not have the funds to maintain the trackage thus today the city is only served only by Thruway Motorcoach. In 1983 the Palmetto was truncated from Saint Petersburg to Tampa due to Amtrak not being able to take on the costs of maintaning the Seaboard Coast Line drawbridge that took the train over Tampa Bay. Damage to railroad track caused by Hurricane Katrina interrupted service on the Sunset Limited.

Originally the train departed from Orlando, Florida, but the track damage along the Gulf coast caused the train to originate at New Orleans, Louisiana. The track's owner, CSX, completed repairs by early 2006 but Amtrak service has not resumed over one year later, leaving the intermediate stations between Orlando and New Orleans without any Amtrak service. Several significant Amtrak routes have been eliminated due to lack of funding since 1971, creating other gaps. The east-west train feeding Kansas City with New York and Washington D.C. known as the National Limited was cut, leaving the only direct links between the Midwest and East through Chicago. The North Coast Hiawatha between Chicago and Seattle provided only reduced service between Chicago and the Pacific Northwest.

The last link with the vaunted Chicago - Florida services of such trains as the City of Miami, the Dixie Flagler, and the South Wind, was broken when the Floridian was discontinued in October 1979. In 1997, the Desert Wind and Pioneer were discontinued, along with service to Las Vegas, Boise, and all of Wyoming. In 2003 and 2005 Amtrak also discontinued the Kentucky Cardinal ending all service to Louisville, and the Three Rivers which provided another direct and daily New York to Chicago service through Pennsylvania. Also throughout the seventies Amtrak had also provided many secondary cities in Pennsylvania such as Reading and Bethlehem with service, yet has since discontinued it. All these gaps in service remain major concerns in the Amtrak system.

GUEST REWARDS

Amtrak operates a loyalty programme called Guest Rewards, which is similar to the frequent flyer programmes offered by many airlines. Guest Rewards members accumulate points by riding Amtrak and through other activities. Members can redeem these points for free or discounted Amtrak tickets and other awards.

FREIGHT

Amtrak Express provides small package and less-than-truckload shipping services between more than 100 cities. Amtrak Express also offers station-to-station shipment of human remains to many express cities. At smaller stations, funeral directors must load and unload the shipment onto and off the train. Amtrak hauled mail for the United States Postal Service and time-sensitive freight, but discontinued these services in October 2004. On most parts of the few lines that Amtrak owns, trackage rights agreements allow freight railroads to use its trackage.

COMMUTER SERVICES

Through various commuter services, Amtrak serves an additional 61.1 million passengers per year in conjunction with state and regional authorities in California, Washington, Maryland, Connecticut, and Virginia. Amtrak's Pacific Surfliner, Capitol Corridor, and San Joaquins are mostly funded by a state transit authority, Caltrans, and not the Federal government.

TRAINS AND TRACKS

Most tracks on which Amtrak operates are owned by freight railroads. Amtrak operates over all seven Class I railroads in the United States, as well as several short lines — the Guilford Rail System, New England Central Railroad and Vermont Railway. Other sections are owned by terminal railroads jointly controlled by freight companies or by commuter rail agencies. The arrangement has two notable impacts on Amtrak operations. The host railroad is responsible for maintenance and occasionally Amtrak has suffered service disruptions from untimely track rehabilitation. When host railroads have simply refused to maintain their tracks to Amtrak's needs, Amtrak occasionally has been compelled to pay the host to maintain the tracks. Also, Amtrak enjoys priority over the host's freight traffic only for a specified window of time. When a passenger train misses that window, host railroads may direct passenger trains to follow lumbering freight traffic, severely exacerbating even minor delays.

TRACKS OWNED BY AMTRAK

Along the Northeast Corridor and in several other areas, Amtrak owns 730 route-miles of track, including 17 tunnels consisting of 29.7 miles of track and 1,186 bridges consisting of 42.5 miles of track. Amtrak owns and operates the following lines:

Northeast Corridor

The Northeast Corridor between Washington, D.C. and Boston via Baltimore, Philadelphia, Newark and New York is largely owned by Amtrak, working cooperatively with several state and regional commuter agencies. Amtrak's portion was acquired in 1976 as a result of the Railroad Revitalization and Regulatory Reform Act.

- Boston to the Massachusetts/Rhode Island state line
- 118.3 miles, Massachusetts/Rhode Island state line to New Haven, Connecticut
- 240 miles, New Rochelle, New York to Washington, D.C.

The part of the line from New Haven to the New York/Connecticut border is owned by the state of Connecticut, while the portion from Port Chester to New Rochelle is owned by the state of New York. The Connecticut Department of Transportation and the Metropolitan Transportation Authority operate this line through Metro-North Railroad.

Philadelphia to Harrisburg Main Line

This line runs from Philadelphia to Harrisburg, Pennsylvania. As a result of a successful investment partnership with the commonwealth of Pennsylvania, signal and track improvements were completed in October 2006, and now allow all-electric service with a top speed of 110 mph to run along the corridor. 104 miles, Philadelphia to Harrisburg

Empire Corridor

- 11 miles, New York Penn Station to Spuyten Duyvil, New York
- 35.9 miles, Stuyvesant to Schenectady, New York
- 8.5 miles, Schenectady to Hoffmans, New York

New Haven-Springfield Line

- 60.5 mi, New Haven to Springfield

Other Tracks

- Chicago-Detroit Line—98 miles, Porter, Indiana to Kalamazoo, Michigan

- Chicago-Detroit Line—4 miles in Detroit, Michigan, CP Townline to CP West Detroit
- Post Road Branch—12.42 miles, Post Road Junction to Rensselaer, New York

Amtrak also owns station and yard tracks in Chicago; Hialeah; Los Angeles; New Orleans; New York City; Oakland; Orlando; Portland, Oregon; Saint Paul, Minnesota; Seattle; and Washington, D.C. Amtrak owns the Chicago Union Station Company and Penn Station Leasing. It has a 99.7% interest in the Washington Terminal Company and 99% of 30th Street Limited. Also owned by Amtrak is Passenger Railroad Insurance.

INDIAN RAILWAYS

Indian Railways, abbreviated as IR, is a Department of the Government of India, under the Ministry of Railways, and is tasked with operating the rail network in India. The Ministry is headed by a cabinet rank Railways Minister, while the Department is managed by the Railway Board. Indian Railways is not a private corporate body; however, of late IR has been trying to adopt a corporate management style. Indian Railways has a total state monopoly on India's rail transport. It is one of the largest and busiest rail networks in the world, transporting sixteen million passengers and more than one million tonnes of freight daily. IR is the world's largest commercial or utility employer, with more than 1.6 million employees, and is second to the Chinese Army in highest number of employees. The railways traverse the length and breadth of the country; the routes cover a total length of 63,140 km. As of 2002, IR owned a total of 216,717 wagons, 39,263 coaches and 7,739 locomotives and ran a total of 14,444 trains daily, including about 8,702 passenger trains. Railways were first introduced to India in 1853. By 1947, the year of India's independence, there were forty-two rail systems. In 1951 the systems were nationalized as one unit, becoming one of the largest networks in the world. Indian Railways operates both long distance and suburban rail systems.

HISTORY

A plan for a rail system in India was first put forward in 1832, but no further steps were taken for more than a decade. In 1844, the Governor-General of India Lord Hardinge allowed private entrepreneurs to set up a rail system in India. Two new railway companies were created and the East India Company was asked to assist them. Interest from investors in the UK led to the rapid creation of a rail system over the next few years. The first train in India became operational on 1851-12-22, and was used for the hauling of construction material in Roorkee. A year and a half later, on 1853-04-16, the first passenger train service was inaugurated between Bori Bunder, Bombay and Thana. Covering a distance of 34 km, it was hauled by three locomotives,

Sahib, Sindh and Sultan. This was the formal birth of railways in India. The British government encouraged new railway companies backed by private investors under a scheme that would guarantee an annual return of five percent during the initial years of operation. Once established, the company would be transferred to the government, with the original company retaining operational control.

The route mileage of this network was about 14,500 km by 1880, mostly radiating inward from the three major port cities of Bombay, Madras and Calcutta. By 1895, India had started building its own locomotives, and in 1896 sent engineers and locomotives to help build the Uganda Railway. Soon various independent kingdoms built their own rail systems and the network spread to the regions that became the modern-day states of Assam, Rajasthan and Andhra Pradesh. A Railway Board was constituted in 1901, but decision-making power was retained by the Viceroy, Lord Curzon. The Railway Board operated under aegis of the Department of Commerce and Industry and had three members: a government railway official serving as chairman, a railway manager from England and an agent of one of the company railways. For the first time in its history, the Railways began to make a tidy profit. In 1907, almost all the rail companies were taken over by the government. The following year, the first electric locomotive appeared. With the arrival of the First World War, the railways were used to meet the needs of the British outside India.

By the end of the First World War, the railways had suffered immensely and were in a poor state. The government took over the management of the Railways and removed the link between the financing of the Railways and other governmental revenues in 1920, a practice that continues to date with a separate railway budget. The Second World War severely crippled the railways as trains were diverted to the Middle East, and the railway workshops were converted into munitions workshops. At the time of independence in 1947, a large portion of the railways went to the then newly formed Pakistan. A total of forty-two separate railway systems, including thirty-two lines owned by the former Indian princely states, were amalgamated as a single unit which was christened as the Indian Railways. The existing rail networks were abandoned in favour of zones in 1951 and a total of six zones came into being in 1952. As the economy of India improved, almost all railway production units were indigenised. By 1985, steam locomotives were phased out in favour of diesel and electric locomotives. The entire railway reservation system was streamlined with computerisation in 1995.

PASSENGER SERVICES

Indian Railways operates 8,702 passenger trains and transports 15 million daily across twenty-five states and three union territories. Sikkim, Arunachal Pradesh and Meghalaya are the only states not connected. The passenger division is the most preferred form of long distance transport in most of the country. A standard passenger train consists of eighteen coaches, but some popular trains can have up to 24 coaches. Coaches are designed to accommodate anywhere from 18 to 72 passengers, but may actually accommodate many more during the holiday seasons and on busy routes. The coaches in use are vestibules, but some of these may be dummied on some trains for operational reasons. Freight trains use a large variety of wagons. Each coach has different accommodation class; the most popular being the sleeper class. Up to nine of these type coaches are usually coupled. Air conditioned coaches are also attached, and a standard train may have between three and five air-conditioned coaches. Online passenger ticketing, introduced in 2004, is expected to top 100,000 per day by 2008, while ATMs in many stations will be equipped to dispense long-distance tickets by the end of 2007.

PRODUCTION SERVICES

The Indian Railways manufactures a lot of its rolling stock and heavy engineering components. This is largely due to historical reasons. As with most developing economies, the main reason is import substitution of expensive technology related products. This was relevant when the general state of the national engineering industry was immature. Production Units, the manufacturing plants of the Indian Railways, are managed directly by the ministry. The General Managers of the PUs report to the Railway Board. The Production Units are:

- Diesel Locomotive Works, Varanasi
- Chittaranjan Locomotive Works, Chittaranjan
- Diesel-Loco Modernisation Works, Patiala
- Integral Coach Factory, Chennai
- Rail Coach Factory, Kapurthala
- Rail Wheel Factory, Bangalore
- Rail Spring Karkhana, Gwalior
- Bharat Earth Movers Limited, Bangalore

BEML is not part of railways, but they do manufacture the coaches for IR and Metro coaches for DMRC and going forward for Bangalore Metro also.

SUBURBAN RAIL

Many cities have their own dedicated suburban networks to cater to commuters. Currently, suburban networks operate in Mumbai, Chennai, Kolkata, Delhi, Hyderabad and Pune. Hyderabad, and Pune do not have dedicated suburban tracks but share the tracks with long distance trains. New Delhi, Chennai and Kolkata have their own metro networks, namely the New Delhi Metro, the Chennai MRTS- Mass Rapid Transport System, same as other local EMU suburban service as in Mumbai and Kolkata etc., but with dedicated tracks mostly laid on a flyover and the Kolkata Metro, respectively. Suburban trains that handle commuter traffic are mostly electric multiple units. They usually have nine coaches or sometimes twelve to handle rush hour traffic. One unit of an EMU train consists of one power car and two general coaches. Thus a nine coach EMU is made up of three units having one power car at each end and one at the middle.

The rakes in Mumbai run on direct current, while those elsewhere use alternating current. A standard coach is designed to accommodate 96 seated passengers, but the actual number of passengers can easily double or triple with standees during rush hour. The Kolkata metro has the administrative status of a zonal railway, though it does not come under the seventeen railway zones. The Suburban trains in Mumbai handle more rush then any other suburban network in India. The network has three lines viz, western, central and harbour. It's considered to be the lifeline on Mumbaia Central Lines start from Chhatrapati Shivaji Terminus and runs for more than 100 km till Kasara and Western Line starting from Churchgate runs again for more than 100 km till Dahanu Road. It is thus longest suburban rail in the world. So also, it is busiest suburban network in the world, in the sense that it carries more than 5 million passengers each day. On 11 July 2006 six bombs were set off on these trains, targeted at the general public.

FREIGHT

IR carries a huge variety of goods ranging from mineral ores, fertilizers and petrochemicals, agricultural produce, iron & steel, multimodal traffic and others. Ports and major urban areas have their own dedicated freight lines and yards. Many important freight stops have dedicated platforms and independent lines. Indian Railways makes 70% of its revenues and most of its profits from the freight sector, and uses these profits to cross-subsidise the loss-making passenger sector. However, competition from trucks which offer cheaper rates has seen a decrease in freight traffic in recent years. Since the 1990s, Indian Railways has switched from small consignments to larger container movement which has helped speed up its operations. Most of its freight earnings come from such rakes carrying bulk goods such as coal, cement, food grains and iron ore.

Indian Railways also transports vehicles over long distances. Trucks that carry goods to a particular location are hauled back by trains saving the trucking company on unnecessary fuel expenses. Refrigerated vans are also available in many areas. The "Green Van" is a special type used to transport fresh food and vegetables. Recently Indian Railways introduced the special 'Container Rajdhani' or CONRAJ, for high priority freight. The highest speed notched up for a freight train is 100 km/h for a 4,700 metric tonne load. Recent changes have sought to boost the earnings from freight. A privatization scheme was introduced recently to improve the performance of freight trains.

Companies are being allowed to run their own container trains. The first length of an 11,000 km freight corridor linking India's biggest cities has recently been approved. The railways has increased load limits for the system's 220,000 freight wagons by 11%, legalizing something that was already happening. Due to increase in manufacturing transport in India that was augmented by the increase in fuel cost, transportation by rail became advantageous financially. New measures such as speeding up the turnaround times have added some 24% to freight revenues.

NOTABLE TRAINS AND ACHIEVEMENTS

The Darjeeling Himalayan Railway, a narrow gauge railway that still regularly uses steam as well as diesel locomotives is classified as a World Heritage Site by UNESCO. The route started earlier at Siliguri and now at New Jalpaiguri in the plains in West Bengal and traverses tea gardens en route to Darjeeling, a hill station at an elevation of 2,134 metres. The highest station in this route is Ghum. The Nilgiri Mountain Railway, in the Nilgiri Hills in southern India, is also classified as a World Heritage Site by UNESCO. It is also the only rack railway in India. The Chatrapati Shivaji Terminus railway station in Mumbai is another World Heritage Site operated by Indian Railways.

The Palace on Wheels is a specially designed train, frequently hauled by a steam locomotive, for promoting tourism in Rajasthan. The Maharashtra government did try to introduce the Deccan Odyssey along the Konkan route, but it did not enjoy the same success as the Palace on Wheels. The Samjhauta Express is a train that runs between India and Pakistan. However, hostilities between the two nations in 2001 saw the line being closed. It was reopened when the hostilities subsided in 2004. Another train connecting Khokhrapar and Munabao is the Thar Express that restarted operations on February 18, 2006; it was closed down after the 1965 Indo-Pak war. The Kalka Shimla Railway till recently featured in the Guinness Book of World Records for offering the steepest rise in altitude in the space of 96 kilometres. The Lifeline Express is a special train popularly known as the "Hospital-on-Wheels" which provides healthcare to the rural areas. This train has a carriage that serves as an operating room, a second one which serves as a storeroom and an additional two that serve as a patient ward.

The train travels around the country, staying at a location for about two months before moving elsewhere. Among the famous locomotives, the Fairy Queen is the oldest running locomotive on the mainline in the world today, though the distinction of the oldest surviving locomotive that has recently seen service belongs to John Bull. Kharagpur railway station also has the distinction of being the world's longest railway platform at 1072 m. The Ghum station along the Darjeeling Toy Train route is the second highest railway station in the world to be reached by a steam locomotive. Indian Railways operates 7,566 locomotives; 37,840 Coaching vehicles and 222,147 freight wagons. There are a total of 6,853 stations; 300 yards; 2,300 goods-sheds; 700 repair shops and a total workforce of 1.54 million. The shortest named station is Ib and the longest is Sri Venkatanarasimharajuvaripeta. The Himsagar Express, between Kanyakumari and Jammu Tawi, has the longest run in terms of distance and time on Indian Railways network. It covers 3,745 km in about 74 hours and 55 minutes. The Trivandrum Rajdhani, between Delhi's Nizamuddin Station and Trivandrum, travels non-stop between Vadodara and Kota, covering a distance of 528 km in about 6.5 hours, and has the longest continuous run on Indian Railways today. The Bhopal Shatabdi Express is the fastest train in India today having a maximum speed of 140 km/h on the Faridabad-Agra section. The fastest speed attained by any train is 184 km/h in 2000 during test runs. This speed is much lower than fast trains in other parts of the world. The difference in these speeds could be in part attributed to the fact that the trains run on existing tracks, which were not designed for such high speeds.

ORGANISATIONAL STRUCTURE

Indian Railways is a department of the Government, being owned and controlled by the Government of India, via the Ministry of Railways rather than a private company. As of 2007, the Railway Ministry is currently headed by Laloo Prasad Yadav, the Union Minister for Railways and assisted by two junior Ministers of State for Railways, R. Velu and Naranbhai J. Rathwa. Indian Railways is administered by the Railway Board, which has six members and a chairman. Each of the sixteen zones is headed by a General Manager who reports directly to the Railway Board. The zones are further divided into divisions under the control of Divisional Railway Managers. The divisional officers of engineering, mechanical, electrical, signal & telecommunication, accounts, personnel, operating, commercial and safety branches report to the respective Divisional Manager and are in charge of operation and maintenance of assets. Further down the hierarchy tree are the Station Masters who control individual stations and the train movement through the track territory under their stations' administration. In addition to the zones, the six production units are each headed by a General Manager, who also reports directly to the Railway Board. In addition to this the Central Organisation for Railway Electrification, Metro Railway, Calcutta and construction organisation of N F Railway are also headed by a General Manager. CORE is located at Allahabad. This organisation undertakes electrification projects of Indian Railway and monitors the progress of various electrification projects all over the country. Apart from these zones and production units, a number of Public Sector Undertakings are under the administrative control of the ministry of railways. These PSU units are:

- Container Corporation Limited

- Dedicated Freight Corridor Corporation of India
- Indian Railway Finance Corporation
- Indian Railways Catering and Tourism Corporation
- IRCON International Ltd. – Construction Division
- Konkan Railway Corporation
- Mumbai Rail Vikas Corporation
- Rail Vikas Nigam Limited
- Railtel Corporation of India – Telecommunication Networks
- RITES Ltd. – Consulting Division of Indian Railways

Centre for Railway Information Systems is an autonomous society under Railway Board, which is responsible for developing the major software required by Indian Railways for its operations.

RAIL BUDGET AND FINANCES

The Railway Budget deals with the induction and improvement of existing trains and routes, the modernisation and most importantly the tariff for freight and passenger travel. The Parliament discusses the policies and allocations proposed in the budget. The budget needs to be passed by a simple majority in the Lok Sabha. The comments of the Rajya Sabha are non binding. Indian Railways are subject to the same audit control as other government revenue and expenditures. Based on the anticipated traffic and the projected tariff, the level of resources required for railway's capital and revenue expenditure is worked out.

While the revenue expenditure is met entirely by railways itself, the shortfall in the capital expenditure is met partly from borrowings and the rest from Budgetory support from the Central Government. Indian Railways pays dividend to the Central Government for the capital invested by the Central Government. As per the Separation Convention, 1924, the Railway Budget is presented to the Parliament by the Union Railway Minister, two days prior to the General Budget, usually around 26 February. Though the Railway Budget is separately presented to the Parliament, the figures relating to the receipt and expenditure of the Railways are also shown in the General Budget, since they are a part and parcel of the total receipts and expenditure of the Government of India. This document serves as a balance sheet of operations of the Railways during the previous year and lists out plans for expansion for the current year.

The formation of policy and overall control of the railways is vested in Railway Board comprising the Chairman, Financial Commissioner and other functional Members for Traffic, Engineering, Mechanical, Electrical and Staff matters. As per the 2006 budget, Indian Railways earned Rs. 54,600 crores. Freight earnings increased by 10% from Rs. 30,450 cr in the previous year. Passenger earnings, other coaching earnings and sundry other earnings increased by 7%, 19% and 56% respectively over previous year. Its year end fund balance is expected to stand at Rs. 11,280 cr. Around 20% of the passenger revenue is earned from the upper class segments of the passenger segment. The overall passenger traffic grew 7.5% in the previous year. In the first two months of India's fiscal year 2005–06, the Railways registered a 10% growth in passenger traffic, and a 12% in passenger earnings. A new concern faced by Indian Railways is competition from low cost airlines that has recently made its début in India.

In a cost cutting move, the Railways plans to minimise unwanted cessations, and scrap unpopular routes. Indian railways suffer from deteriorating finances and lack the funds for future investment. Last year, India spent $28 billion, or 3.6% of GDP, on infrastructure. The main problem plaguing the Railways is the high accident rate which stands at about three hundred a year. Although accidents such as derailment and collisions are less common in recent times, many are run over by trains, especially in crowded areas. Indian Railways have accepted the fact that given the size of operations, eliminating accidents is an unrealistic goal, and at best they can only minimize the accident rate. Human error is the primary cause blamed for mishaps. The Konkan Railway route suffers from landslides in the monsoon season, which has caused fatal accidents in the recent past. Contributing to the Railways' problems are the antiquated communication, safety and signaling equipment. One area of upgrading badly required is an automated signaling system to prevent crashes.

A number of train accidents happened due to a manual system of signals between stations. However, the changeover to a new system would require a substantial investment. It is felt that this would be required given the gradual increase in train speeds and lengths, that would make accidents more dangerous. In the latest instances of signaling control by means of interlinked stations, failure-detection circuits are provided for each track circuit and signal circuit with notification to the signal control centres in case of problems. However, this is available in a very small subset of the total Railways. Aging colonial-era bridges and century-old tracks also require regular maintenance and upgrading. In recent years Indian Railways has claimed that it has achieved a financial turnaround, with operating profits expected to improve by 83.7%.

Credit for this achievement has been claimed by current Indian Railway Minister, Mr Lalu Prasad Yadav who claims to have brought a significant improvement in operating efficiency of goods traffic after he took over as Railway Minister in May 2004. The Rajdhani Express and Shatabadi Express are the fastest and most luxurious trains of Indian Railways, though they face increasing pressure from air travel, as the trains travel only 80 km per hour and their food and service is not competitive. To modernize Indian Rail and to bring it at par with the developed world, would require a massive investment of about US$100 billion. Sixth Pay Commission has been constituted in India to review the pay structure of the Government employees and its recommendations are expected by the end of 2008 and based on its recommendations, the salaries of all Railways officers and staff are expected to be revised with retrospective effect. If previous Pay Commissions are taken as indicator then this revision will not be less than 50% upwards and it may hit Railways bottomlines severely and possibly mitigate all the good work of the Railways. Sanitation and use of modern technology in that area has been a problem.

Although Indian Rail has announced the introduction of dry toilets in the trains, so far not much headway has been made and the train toilets continue to drop the wastes on the rail tracks. Plans to upgrade stations, coaches and services are on track. Twenty-two of the largest stations are due for an overhaul when a private company is picked for the job. New LHB German coaches, manufactured in India, were scheduled to be introduced in 2007 on the daily run of the prestigious East Central Railway Patna-New Delhi Radjhani Express. These coaches will enhance the safety and riding comfort of passengers, and in time will eventually replace thousands of old model coaches throughout Indian Railways. Three new manufacturing units will be set up to produce state-of-the-art locomotives and coaches. Channel music, TV screens showing the latest films, and optional menus from five-star hotels are soon to be introduced on the Rajdhani and Shatabdi Express. Base kitchens and food services across the system are also slated for a makeover. More importantly, a whole new IT management infrastructure will be developed to better handle ticketing, freight, rolling stock, terminals, and rail traffic.

PALACE ON WHEELS

The Palace on Wheels is a special heritage tourist train, which has been modified to incorporate fourteen saloons, two restaurant cum kitchen cars, one Bar cum Lounge, a library and four service cars. The cabins of each saloon are attached with bath and shower. This train is a complete example of luxury travel and has all the facilities of a five star hotel or resort. It is a seven-day trip. The train departs from Delhi Cantt station and arrives at Jaipur, Rajasthan on second day; the third day is in Jaisalmer, the fourth in Jodhpur, fifth in Ranthambore Tiger Sanctuary and Chittaurgarh Fort and the sixth day is spent in Jaipur. On the seventh day the train goes to Agra before concluding the journey at Delhi Cantt Station on the eighth day. This train journey is a source of attraction for tourists from all over the world. The train chugs out of Delhi cantonment on a week-long run through Rajasthan every Wednesday night, with a trip also inbuilt to Agra and the Taj Mahal. Turban-wearing attendants take over from the moment you arrive at the platform, assigning you your coupes and detailing all the facilities that are on board. The train moves by night and arrives each morning at a new destination, where new experiences await you. If you are an early riser, you will see the sun rise over the horizon of the desert, a golden orb that flames in pastel colour before it ignites into brilliant orange as it mounts higher. So it has done for million years, and so it has been watched on its journey by thousands of them, residents of the desert; Suryavanshi and Chandravanshi, descended from the Sun and the Moon – incredible! It is not easy it is to believe but it is all true!

ROYAL ORIENT TRAIN

The Royal Orient train is one of the world's most exotic trains. The journey by the Royal orient train is a rare delight. It is an experience that takes you back to the times of Rajas and Maharajas. As you embark on your journey by the Royal Orient train, you get to explore two of the most fascinating and culturally rich states of India, Gujarat and Rajasthan. The journey by the Royal Orient train is a memorable experience as you get to see different facets of Indian culture. A joint venture of the Tourism Corporation of Gujarat and the Indian Railways, the Royal Orient promises you to showcase the best of Indian culture and heritage. Your experience on the Royal Orient will be unique and unforgettable; in a luxurious setting with personalized services from liveried attendants. There are thirteen coaches and saloons, named after erstwhile kingdoms of Rajputana. So get ready to experience the journey of lifetime as we promise to explore the rich cultural heritage of Rajasthan and Gujarat! The Royal Orient train is fitted with all the modern conveniences you would expect in five star hotels. Every cabin is clean, comfortable and furnished tastefully. The cabins have spacious baths attached to them, equipped with running hot and cold water. In addition to this there are multi-cuisine restaurants that offer you the dishes of your choice. The Royal Orient train also has a bar on board. And if you are a book lover and passionate about reading, there's a library on the Royal Orient train to pass off time in your favourite way.

THE DECCAN ODYSSEY

This Luxury Maharaja Train is a joint venture between Indian Railways & Maharashtra Tourism & onboard services are managed by staff of internationally renowned Taj Group of Hotels. This Royal train tries to recreate the Era of Peshwas-medieval time Feudal Lords of Western India & there are additional facilities of Presidential Suite Cabins, Spa & Massage treatments, Conference Lounge Car, Business Centre etc. The 7 Nights Deccan Odyssey Train Tour operates Annually from October to April Ex. Mumbai every Wednesday & highlight of the Luxury Train Tour are the Golden beaches of Goa & World Heritage Cave sites of Ajanta Ellora. The Air-Conditioned Luxury Train Tour offers combination of richly furnished Deluxe Cabins & Presidential Suites; & All Passenger Cabins have private attached toilets with shower cubicles & daily refurbished with 5 Star hotel quality toiletries. There are Two Dining Cars, One Bar Saloon with smoking lounge area, Conference

Area/recreation saloon with small Business Centre, Spa Saloon with mini-gym. Each passenger Saloon has four Deluxe Cabins & is serviced by a private attendant/ butler, who looks after tea/coffee service & housekeeping.

TOY TRAIN OF DARJEELING

Trains came to India in the early part of the last century — among the very first and most novel, is the famous Toy Train of Darjeeling. It is 117 years old having made its maiden trip in the September of 1881. Officially known as the Darjeeling Himalayan Railway, it is as much a pioneering work of achievement, projecting not only its engineering ingenuity but also a historic development of the 19th century British convalescent centre in the remote north eastern Himalayas. In 1870, an agent working for the Eastern Bengal Railway came up with a brilliant idea to reduce the costs of transport. His name Franklyn Prestage — the idea — the Toy Train. It took eight long years for Prestage to submit his scheme to Lt. Governor Sir Ashley Eden, who gave it immediate sanction. Named the Darjeeling Steam Tramway Co., it was changed to The Darjeeling Himalayan Railway Co. on September 15th 1881. It remained as such till it was taken over by the Indian Government on Oct. 20, 1948.

The construction had begun in 1879 and with the zeal shown by the workers, the first 20 miles from Siliguri to Tindharia station was opened in March 1880 for the Viceroy's special train only. After a further 11 miles to Kurseong were completed, it was opened to the public on August 23 of that year. Sonada was reached on February 1, 1881, the summit of Ghoom on April l4th, 1881 and finally on July 4th 1881 the baby locomotive and three coaches puffed right through to Darjeeling-a total of 50.75 miles. In 1914, the Darjeeling Himalayan Railway was further extended down south towards Kishanganj and close to the Nepalese frontier for jute traffic and in 1915. Meantime the DHR was extended from Siliguri toward Sevoke by 10 miles and further to the north 16 miles on Kalimpong road. Until 1878, the journey from Calcutta to Darjeeling took from 5 to 6 days by the East Indian Railway from Howrah to Sahebganj, then by steam ferry across the Ganges to Charcoal, then by bullock carts on the river opposite Danger Hat, after crossing again by bullock cart or 'palki' to Purnea, Kishanganj, Titalya and Siliguri whence the ascent commenced via the Punkhabari road which finally joins the present cart road at Kurseong. In 1878, Siliguri was put on the map of the railway, the journey was cut to two days and another six to seven hours to Darjeeling.

INDIARAIL PASS

Foreign tourists, who wish to experience India by train, can enjoy special facilities earmarked for them. These are explained in greater details below.

- *Special Quota:* Several important trains have a special quota for foreign tourists. This can be availed on payment of US Dollars or

Pound Sterling. Tourists without foreign currency will be allotted the special quota on production of the exchange certificates issued by any nationalized bank. At the time of reservation, the passport number and the country of origin should be mentioned.

- *Assistance Cells:* Major Reservation Centres have special Cells to help foreign tourists plan their itinerary, reserve their tickets and render any assistance required.
- *The International Tourist Bureau:* Situated on the first floor of New Delhi Railway station provides personalized service and assistance to foreign tourists and NRIs regarding reservations, itinerary planning and other inquiries. This Bureau is manned by trained staff and tourist guides, fluent in foreign languages for any assistance.
- *Indrail Pass:* This travel ticket has been created especially for foreign tourists and Indian nationals residing abroad. This ticket is available for a special time period from 1/2 day to 90 days. Indrail Passes should be used within one year of issue. Validity period starts from the date of the first train journey and ends on the midnight of the last journey.

AVAILABILITY OF INDRAIL PASSES

- In India, Indrail Passes are available for sale in Railway Offices at: Agra Cantt, Agra City, Ahmedabad, Amritsar, Aurangabad, Bangalore City, Calcutta, Chandigarh, Chennai, Gorakhpur, Hyderabad, Jaipur, Mumbai, New Delhi, Puttaparthi Town Booking Agency, Rameswaram, Secundrabad, Trivandrum Central, Vadodara, Varanasi, Vasco da Gama and Vijayawada.
- Certain recognized Travel Agents are also authorized to sell these passes in Delhi, Mumbai, Calcutta and Chennai.

BENEFITS ON INDRAIL PASS

Travel as you like. Priority on Rail Reservation from Foreign Tourist Quota. Children below 5 years travel free and those between 5 & 12 years are charged half fares. Free meals on Rajdhani Express/Shatabdi Express trains. No sleeper surcharge on Night journey. No extra charge for Travel by Superfast Trains. No reservation fee for berths and seats. Free bedrolls on 1st AC/2nd AC/3 Tier AC.

TIPS FOR BUYING INDRAIL PASS

- For Single Journey you should purchase Half Day/One Day pass as the validity of these passes are for 12 hours and 24 hours respectively from the time of you begin the journey.
- For Half Day/One Day pass in case of Rajdhani, you are eligible to use one class lower than you pay for the class. E.g. If you pay for

AC class, then you will be eligible to travel by First Class/AC-2tier, AC-3 Tier/AC Chair Car.

WATER TRANSPORT

Water transportation is the intentional movement of water over large distances. Methods of transportation fall into three categories: Aqueducts, which include pipelines, canals, and tunnels; container shipment, which includes transport by truck and tanker; and towing, where a tugboat is used to pull an iceberg or a large water bag along behind it. Due to its weight, the transportation of water is very energy intensive. Unless it has the assistance of gravity, a canal or long-distance pipeline will need pumping stations at regular intervals. In this regard, the lower friction levels of the canal make it a more economical solution than the pipeline. Water transportation is also very common along rivers and oceans.

SHIP TRANSPORT

Ship transport is primarily used for the carriage of people and non-perishable goods, generally referred to as cargo. Although the historic importance of sea travel has lost much importance due to the rise of commercial aviation, it is still very effective for short trips and pleasure cruises. Nonetheless, sea transport remains the largest carrier of freight in the world. While slower than air transport, modern sea transport is a highly effective method of moving large quantities of non-perishable goods. More than 6 billion tons of cargo were delivered by sea in 2005. In addition to cargo carriage, one can consider scientific voyages and races as forms of ship transport. Transport by water is significantly less costly than transport by air for trans-continental shipping. Ship transport is often international by nature, but it can be accomplished by barge, boat, ship or sailboat over a sea, ocean, lake, canal or river. This is frequently undertaken for purposes of commerce, recreation or military objectives. When a cargo is carried by more than one mode, the transport is termed intermodal. Ships have long been used for warfare, with applications from naval supremacy to piracy, invasions and bombardment. Aircraft carriers can be used as bases of a wide variety of military operations. Ship transport is used for a variety of unpackaged raw materials ranging from chemicals, petroleum products, and bulk cargo such as coal, iron ore, cereals, bauxite, and so forth. So called "general cargo" covers goods that are packaged to some extent in boxes, cases, pallets, barrels, and so forth. Since the 1960s containerization has revolutionized ship transport.

CRUISE SHIP

A cruise ship or a cruise liner is a passenger ship used for pleasure voyages, where the voyage itself and the ship's amenities are considered an essential part of the experience. Cruising has become a major part of the tourism industry, with millions of passengers each year as of 2006. The industry's rapid growth has seen nine or more newly built ships catering to a North American clientele added every year since 2001, as well as others servicing European clientele. Smaller markets such as the Asia-Pacific region are generally serviced by older tonnage displaced by new ships introduced into the high growth areas. Cruise ships operate on a mostly set roundabout courses, returning with their passengers to their originating port. In contrast, ocean liners do "line voyages" in open seas, are strongly built to withstand the rigors of transoceanic voyages, and typically ferry passengers from one point to another, rather than on round trips. Some liners also engage in longer trips which may not lead back to the same port for many months.

FERRY

A ferry is a form of transport, usually a boat or ship, but also other forms, carrying passengers and sometimes their vehicles. Ferries are also used to transport freight and even railroad cars. Most ferries operate on regular, frequent, return services. A foot-passenger ferry with many stops, such as in Venice, is sometimes called a water bus or water taxi. Ferries form a part of the public transport systems of many waterside cities and islands, allowing direct transit between points at a capital cost much lower than bridges or tunnels.

4

Transaction Cycle

INTRODUCTION

Earlier we used to follow account period settlement for settling all the trades in the stock market. Account period in NSE was from Wednesday to the following Tuesday. This means trades done on Wednesday, Thursday, Friday, Monday and Tuesday will be paid-in on Tuesday and paid-out on the following Wednesday. This was a time consuming process. An investor who had bought the shares will have to wait till the following Wednesday to get the delivery of shares, so he will be unable to reap the benefit of rising prices during the period. Also, the shares being in physical form created a lot of problem for the buyer as they had to be sent to the company or their R&TA (Registrar & Transfer Agent) for getting the ownership changed of the securities.

While on BSE, the cycle commenced on Monday and ended on Friday. At the end of this period, the net obligations of all the brokers were calculated and the brokers settle their respective obligations as per the rules, bye-laws and regulations of the clearing corporation.

Account period is a system that encourages liquidity in the market because people can buy and sell without having to pay immediately - almost like using a credit card. But the flip side of the system is that the longer it takes between a trade (a buy or sell) and actual settlement, the riskier the system is.

Nowadays, the scenario has totally changed. The clearing and settlement system has become very transparent and therefore, people have also started having faith in the market and its operations. The use of super computers to carry out the trades and to maintain their records has actually made the market operations crystal clear. Apart from the state of art information technology, the latest innovations include:

- Emergence of clearing corporation to assume counterparty risks; we will be discussing this later in this chapter.
- Replacement of account period settlement by rolling settlement system leading to shorter settlement cycles,

- Dematerialization of securities has been adopted in place of physical securities; we will be discussing this later in this unit.
- Electronic transfer of securities through book entry system; we will be discussing this later in this unit.
- Fine tune risk management system, etc.; we will be discussing this later in this unit.

Though many of these have not been implemented fully as they are yet to reach the masses and penetrate the whole market. One of the greatest achievements of the current system is settlement of trades within three working days, i.e. T+2 rolling settlement which has replaced account period settlement, which used to take at least a week to define the obligations. Rolling settlement has now been introduced for all securities.

Rolling settlement involves shrinking the netting period to one day. This is part of the historical progression that we have followed in India's equity market. The length of the netting period has gone from an undisciplined fortnight to a disciplined week, and with rolling period it now goes to a day.

TRANSACTION CYCLE

A transaction cycle depicts the steps followed by a client in order to execute a trade wherein a buy order matches with a sell order. The Following steps are followed incompleting a transaction cycle:

- *Step 1:* The above cycle is initiated by a client who wants to either buy or sell securities. In that case, he has to make a decision regarding the same. A decision is taken by the client after considering the liquidity conditions and requirements or reshuffles his holdings in response to changes in the market conditions or perceptions.
- *Step 2:* He then selects a broker and instructs him to place buy/sell order on an exchange.
- *Step 3:* The order is converted to a trade as soon as it finds a matching sell/buy order.
- *Step 4:* The trades are netted to determine the obligations of the trading members to deliver securities/funds as per settlement schedule.
- *Step 5:* Buyer/seller delivers funds/securities and receives securities/funds and acquires ownership of the securities.

We will be elaborating this transaction cycle in detail with the chapters in this unit. But before that we need to understand the role of the agencies that helps in the smooth functioning of the transaction cycle.

SETTLEMENT AGENCIES

The NSCCL, along with other agencies like clearing members, custodians, clearing banks and depositories settles trades executed on the exchange. The roles of each of the entities are explained below.

NATIONAL SECURITIES CLEARING CORPORATION LIMITED (NSCCL)

The NSCCL, a wholly owned subsidiary of NSE, was incorporated in August 1995. NSCCL commenced clearing operations in April 1996. It was set up for the following purposes:

- To bring and sustain confidence in clearing and settlement of securities;
- To promote and maintain, short and consistent settlement cycles;
- To provide counter-party risk guarantee, and
- To operate a tight risk containment system.

NSCCL carries out the clearing and settlement of the trades executed in the Equities and Derivatives segments and operates Subsidiary General Ledger (SGL) for settlement of trades in government securities. It performs the following tasks:

- Clears all trades;
- Determines obligations of members;
- Arranges for pay-in of funds and securities;
- Arranges for pay-out of funds and securities;
- Assumes the counter-party risk of each member and guarantees financial settlement.
- It also undertakes settlement of transactions on other stock exchanges like, the Over the Counter Exchange of India.

Through NSCCL, we have been able to up-grade the clearing and settlement procedures in the Indian Stock Market and have brought Indian financial markets in line with international markets.

CLEARING MEMBERS

Clearing members are responsible for settling the trades done on all the counters. Settling the trades involves taking the responsibility of making available the resources required on time, i.e. making available the funds and securities on the settlement day.

Settlement day would mean T+2 day. Funds are made available through the clearing banks where the clearing member has his account and securities are made available through the depository participant. In case of trades done on the capital market segment, all trading members have to be their own clearing members too, i.e. they only have to settle the trades done by them (every TM has to be his own CM). In case of trades done in 'Future and Option' market, clearing member can be a separate entity than trading member as the volume of trades done in this segment is huge. A clearing member has to get himself registered with NSCCL.

CUSTODIANS

As the name suggests, the custodians perform the task of keeping the securities in a safe manner/custody. They hold the documentary proof of securities, keeping the title of securities intact in the name of the holder. In NSCCL, custodian is only a clearing member and not a trading member. A custodian is required to settle the trades only after confirming to the NSCCL that it will be settling the trade or not. If it takes the obligation, it will have to settle the trades and if not, then the obligation is assigned back to the trading member for whom the custodian works.

CLEARING BANKS

Clearing banks act as a link between the clearing members and the NSCCL for the settlement of funds, i.e. pay-in and pay-out of funds. Every clearing member gets an account opened with a clearing bank for this purpose only. A clearing bank works on the instructions of the clearing member. A clearing member after defining the obligations in terms of funds informs the clearing bank about the obligations to be fulfilled. The clearing bank makes available the funds required on the pay-out day to meet the obligations on time.

DEPOSITORIES

A depository is an organisation created under Companies Act 1956 for the purpose of facilitating electronic transfer of securities in a dematerialized environment/form. The clients/investors do not open an account with the depository. Instead that job is performed by the agents of depositories known as depository participants.

There are 2 depositories in India, namely, NSDL & CDSL. A clearing member/Custodian opens a securities pool account (demat) with a depository participants of these depositories to make the securities available in the account on the settlement day. As per the instructions, the depository transfers the securities electronically.

PROFESSIONAL CLEARING MEMBERS (PCM'S)

Professional Clearing Members (PCMs) are special category of members who undertake to clear & settle trades done by the brokers/traders who have appointed them to do the job. They take the responsibility of clearing the trades done by their clients & in no circumstances; they perform the task of trading.

The clearing banks and the depository act as an interface between the NSCCL and the clearing members/custodians. Let us now understand the process that is followed in settlement.

SETTLEMENT PROCESS

There are basically three tasks that are performed in the process of buying and selling of securities. They are:

- Trading
- Clearing
- Settlement

Trading basically deals with putting an order and its execution. Clearing deals with determination of obligations, in terms of funds and securities. Settlement means that the trade will be completed and NSCCL acts as a counter party and takes an obligation for the same. It has created a faith in the investors that all the trades would be settled and in no case any investor will have to face any problem of insufficient funds and securities. NSCCL acts as a buyer to every seller and a seller to every buyer. This principle is called novation. In case of default by any party, the NSCCL takes action against the defaulter. The following steps are followed in the settlement of a trade:

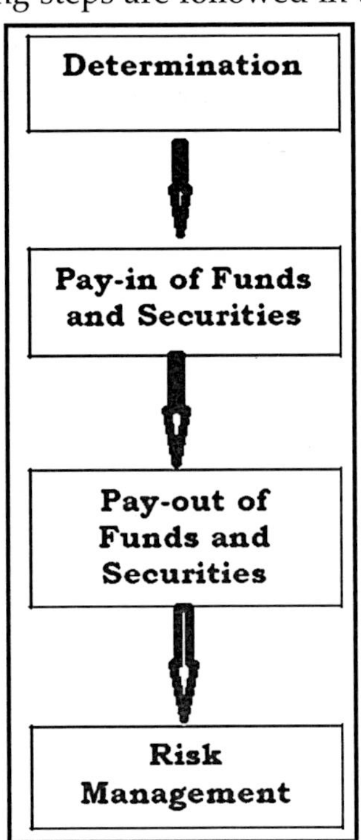

- *Step 1: Determination of obligations:* Obligations are determined by NSCCL for the traders and acts as a central counter-party (CCP) to the members. It determines the obligations of the members as what they ought to give and receive on the due date.
- *Step 2: Pay-in of funds and securities:* The members, after knowing their obligations, make available the funds and securities to NSCCL. The member's depository having obligation to pay-in the securities; get an instruction from the NSCCL to pass the required entry for the transfer of securities to them. For the members having an obligation to pay-in funds, NSCCL gives an instruction to the clearing banks for the same.
- *Step 3: Pay-out of funds and securities:* After processing the shortages of funds and securities and arranging for the movement of the same,

NSCCL sends out electronic instructions to the clearing banks/ depositories to pass the required entries for the same.

- *Step 4: Risk management:* Since there is a time lag between execution of trade and its settlement, there are chances of default. To minimize the risk of defaults, NSCCL has framed a comprehensive risk management and surveillance system. Under this, the organization keeps a check through various systems (on-line and off-line monitoring) and in case of default panelizes the respective trader for the same.

RISKS IN SETTLEMENT

A sound risk management system is integral to an efficient clearing and settlement system. NSE introduced for the first time in India, risk containment measures that were common internationally but were absent from the Indian securities markets. Counter-party risk and System risk are two kinds of risks that are intrinsic in a settlement system. Let discuss these risks further in this section.

COUNTERPARTY RISK

This basically arises even if one of the parties does not discharge their obligation fully and on time. This broadly has two components, namely replacement cost risk i.e. pre-settlement risk and principal risk, which arises during settlement.

Replacement Cost Risk

A type of risk resulting from a situation in which a party to a trade knows that the counter party will be unable to meet the obligations of the trade, and thus a new replacement trade will have to be entered into. Hence known as "replacement-cost risk", which refers to the cost associated with replacing the original trade. Of course, there is a good chance that the above task will not be done at the same price, since the market has probably moved since the trade was first done.

For example, Ram sold 100 shares of Reliance at 10:00 am @ Rs.2600 without having them, in anticipation that the price of Reliance will fall during the day and he will cover his position intraday by buying those 100 shares at a lower price. His observations went wrong and instead of Reliance price falling it raised throughout the day and at 3:00 pm the price of a Reliance share was at Rs.3000. Resulting in a loss of Rs.400 per share * 100 shares = Rs.40000.

He decides to inform his broker about his non-fulfilling of his commitment and delivering short his obligation of giving 100 shares of Reliance. The broker decides to cover this position of Ram on his own account by buying 100 Reliance to make his net obligation zero. By the time his order was executed the price of Reliance was at Rs.2900. Hence the replaced transaction was at a cost of Rs.300 per share. If Ram is unable to pay this cost, it will result as a replacement cost risk for the broker and in-turn to the system.

Principal Risk

Principal risk is the risk that arises when the buyer/seller has not received the shares/funds but has fulfilled his obligation of making payment/delivery of shares. This has been reduced by having a central counterparty such as NSCCL which becomes the buyer to every seller and the seller to every buyer.

For example, Ram bought 100 shares of Reliance on Monday @ Rs.2600 and made good his obligation by paying his broker Rs.2600*100 = Rs.2,60,000. As a result of this Ram is expecting a delivery of his 100 Reliance shares by T+2 days (Wednesday). If the counterparty (seller) to this transaction defaults in his commitment of giving delivery of these 100 shares and if the system does not assure giving back at least this money (principal) paid by the buyer, then this result's into a principal risk. As mentioned principal risk is reduced by having a central counterparty to all trades in the form of NSCCL. What NSCCL assures Ram is that he will get his 100 shares or his money Rs.2,60,000 will be returned back with some surplus (the penalty collected from the defaulting seller's broker), but instead on T+2 day (Wednesday) it will be given on T+5 day (Monday). NSCCL will make it possible by buying 100 shares for the buyer on behalf of the defaulting seller from the auction market. We will discuss the functioning of the auction market in the next chapter.

Liquidity Risk

Liquidity risk is the risk of that party which is unable to liquidate its position because of the default of another party. Suppose, the buyer has paid for the securities but has not received the delivery on time as the seller had short sold the securities. So the buyer will be able to sell his shares only when he receives the delivery after the NSCCL has bought them for the buyer on behalf of the seller from the auction market. So, here the buyer is bearing a liquidity risk because of the counterparty default.

For example, Ram bought shares on Monday, and normally he should get the shares on Wednesday but did not get them as the seller had defaulted. He will only get the shares on the following Monday when the NSCCL will buy the shares for the buyer on behalf of the seller from the auction market. Suppose, by this time, the prices went up, the buyer cannot off-load his holdings as he doesn't have the delivery of shares. He will get the delivery only on Monday and may be the prices might go down by that time.

Third Party Risk

Another variant of counterparty risk is the third party risk which arises if the parties to trade are permitted or required to use the services of a third party which fails to perform. For example, the failure of a clearing bank which helps in payment can disrupt settlement. This risk is reduced by allowing parties to have accounts with multiple banks. Similarly, the users of custodial services face risk if the concerned custodian becomes insolvent, acts negligently or commits fraud.

SYSTEM RISK

Second set of risk in settlement is system risk which comprises of operational, legal and systemic risk.

Operational Risk

Operational risk is defined as the risk of loss resulting from inadequate or failed internal processes, people and systems, or from external events. Such as, error, fraud, outages etc. Although the risks apply to any organisation in business it is of particular relevance to the financial/banking regime where regulators are responsible for establishing safeguards to protect against systemic failure of the system and in-turn the economy.

Legal Risk

Legal risk is risk from uncertainty due to legal actions or uncertainty in the applicability or interpretation of contracts, laws or regulations.

Systemic Risk

Systemic risk might arise when the default by one of the parties leads to the default of other parties too. This has a multiplying effect and can cause a failure in the system. To avoid such problems, the exchange has strict rules and regulations on margining, capital adequacy standards, settlement guarantee funds and legal backing for settlement activity. We will discuss this in the later chapters of this unit.

SUMMARY

- Clearing refers to the process of comparing trades before settlement date or the determination of the net obligations of the broker participants (for both securities and cash).
- The settlement process refers to the exchange of cash and securities on the contractual settlement date. The settlement date can be agreed upon at trade execution or can be prescribed by local trading conventions.
- Central counterparty (CCP) - A CCP acts as counterparty to every buy and sell trade, a process known as "novation". NSCCL acts as a CCP in India for all the trades done on NSE. This process concentrates counterparty risk and provides settlement guarantee.
- The agencies which participate in the process of settlement are NSCCL, clearing members, custodians, depositories and NSE.
- There are several risks that may arise in the process of settlement. They are broadly classified as counterparty risk and system risk.

5

Recording of Transfer Pricing and Taxation

INTRODUCTION

A small operation managed by a few individuals was the typical beginning of a large corporation with a hundred operating affiliates dispersed around the world. Decision making was highly centralized and lines of communication were short. As the company grew, the founding management team found it more difficult to keep matters under control. This problem was greatly exacerbated when operations within the company became physically separated. Centers of activity in different locations called for a different style of management. Funneling of all decisions from diverse locations through a small group of individuals, who no longer possess the necessary intimate awareness of the circumstances surrounding each decision, is a surefire prescription for stifling growth. Growth is the name of the game for modern corporations.

Growth entails individual operating affiliates taking appropriate action to enhance productivity, market share, and the scope of a company's product line. It has been found that operating affiliates physically separated from the parent organization can best achieve these objectives under a decentralized style of management. Responsibility now falls on the shoulders of the manager of an operating affiliate to make the necessary decisions that will lead to improved financial results, the universal measure of performance. The parent organization takes on a new role as coordinator and monitor of activities now that responsibility for operations has been transferred to the operating units. Far from playing a passive role, the parent organization focuses its attention on optimizing the performance of its semiautonomous operating affiliates. To do this, the parent organization must establish, and articulate, a set of strategic goals and allocate limited corporate resources to the various operating affiliates to best achieve these goals.

It must ensure that the short-term action plans of the operating affiliates are in accord with its long-term plans. Top management positions in the operating affiliates must be filled with individuals capable of leading their affiliates in the right direction and an incentive system must be set up to induce managers to orient their thinking to the goals of the company. Finally, the parent organization must set up a financial reporting and control system to monitor its global operations, to provide necessary information for the making of decisions and to evaluate the performance of the affiliate managers. Although operating affiliates appear to be semiautonomous units in that they are given a wide spectrum of decision-making responsibility in managing their local operations, they are not independent centers of corporate activity. They are often united in manufacturing and marketing a common product line, in the course of which they routinely buy and sell finished goods, components, or raw materials from one another. These intra company exchanges of goods, components, and raw materials require a transfer price.

The parent organization sets the transfer price after considering various factors with an eye on optimizing corporate performance as a whole. Transfer prices are often not negotiated and agreed on by the actual buyers and sellers of the goods and components being shipped between operating affiliates. Yet transfer prices directly affect the revenue and cost of goods sold, and therefore, the profitability of the operating affiliates. Because the affiliate managers are monitored by a financial reporting and control system that scrutinizes their financial results, one can expect that affiliate managers have an entirely different perspective on transfer pricing than the executives of the parent organization. Transfer pricing can easily embroil executives of the parent organization and the managers of operating affiliates in endless disputes. Some firms have even established an administrative panel for reviewing transfer prices to resolve sharp differences of opinion between those responsible for managing operating affiliates and those responsible for setting transfer prices.

TRANSFER PRICES AND TAXES

A global company with operations in many nations must deal with a new dimension of complexity in establishing transfer prices, which is not present when a company operates solely within the confines of a single nation. A company whose operations are within a single nation pays the same taxes on profits regardless of the transfer pricing policy. The consolidation process, whether for financial or tax accounting purposes, eliminates intra company transactions to arrive at either a book profit or a before-tax profit. When a company transacts business through affiliate companies in different nations, however, transfer pricing provides a mechanism for shifting taxable profits between tax jurisdictions.

Tax authorities in various nations are concerned with the notion that transfer pricing, often set by parent organizations outside their jurisdiction, is based on minimizing taxes paid in their jurisdictions. There certainly is an element of truth in this contention, but there are other considerations in administering transfer prices than minimizing taxes. The setting of transfer prices provides a way of moving funds internationally for a variety of purposes, of circumventing currency exchange controls that threaten to choke the operations of a company, of minimizing the deleterious impact of other artificial barriers to trade such as duties and tariffs, and of reducing currency risk exposure. A transfer pricing policy attempts to satisfy a multiple set of objectives. Some of these objectives call for high transfer prices, whereas others require low transfer prices. A company must select what it considers to be an optimal transfer price, which is a compromise price for best achieving divergent objectives. This optimal transfer price may not be the one that minimizes taxes on profits. The selected transfer price may not be satisfactory both to the local tax authority and to the manager of an affiliate if it reduces the reported profitability of the affiliate. However, setting the transfer price is critical to optimizing the financial performance of the corporation as a whole, given the conditions that prevail at a point in time.

MINIMIZING TAXES

Tax authorities of most countries have guidelines or controls that are expected to be complied with in setting transfer prices. Management is not free to arbitrarily select transfer prices without having to substantiate their transfer price decisions. Nevertheless, there is still an element of choice where a selected transfer price may reduce the tax burden of a company. Suppose that a company consists of a parent organization and two operating affiliates—one in nation A, where the tax rate on profits is 30 percent, and one in nation B, where the tax rate on profits is 40 percent. The tax is applied to each affiliate's gross margin for illustrative purposes. The affiliate in nation A makes a product that is entirely sold through the affiliate in nation B. Two cases are considered—a low and a high transfer price.

Case I-Low Transfer Price

	Nation A Tax 30%	Nation B Tax 40%	Consolidated
Sales	$2000	$3200	$3200
Cost of Goods Sold	1500	2000	1500
Gross Margin	500	1200	1700
Tax	150	480	630
Net Income	$350	$720	$1070

Everything made in a factory in nation A is sold through a marketing organization in nation B. Therefore, total sales in nation A, calculated on the basis of an administered transfer price, is also the cost of goods sold in nation B. Sales in nation B of $3,200 is the net consolidated sales for the company, because all goods produced in nation A are sold in nation B. The actual cost of manufacturing the goods in nation A is $1,500. Because nation B does not add value to the goods, the consolidated cost of goods sold for the company is also $1,500. The consolidated tax is the sum of the $150 and the $480 paid to the tax authorities of nations A and B, respectively. The consolidated net income is $1,070, the sum of the net incomes of the two affiliates. Suppose that the transfer price is increased from $2,000 to $2,500 for goods shipped between the two affiliates. Consolidated sales, cost of goods sold, and gross margin are unaffected by the change in the transfer price, because it is netted out in the consolidation process. Taxes paid in each nation are no longer the same because of the change in the transfer price. In case II, the increase in the transfer price shifts the profit to Nation A, which has the lower tax rate. The affiliate in nation A earns more taxable income and pays more in taxes than in case I.

The affiliate in nation B earns less taxable income and pays less in taxes in case II than in case I. The net effect, as seen by comparing case II with case I, is that the company as a whole is paying less in taxes, which increases its consolidated net income. It is true that had the two nations the same tax rate, the total taxes paid by the company, and the consolidated net income, would not be affected by changes in the transfer price. Even so, transfer prices determine what portion of total taxes are to be paid to the tax authority in nation A and to the tax authority in Nation B. Although the parent organization may be relatively insensitive concerning to whom it pays taxes, needless to say, the tax authorities are very much concerned as to which is collecting taxes. The problem is compounded, from the point of view of a tax authority, because the transfer price is probably set by a parent organization not under its jurisdiction.

The importance of transfer pricing to both managers and tax authorities can be appreciated when it is realized that between 40 percent and 60 percent of international trade involves goods moving between affiliates of the same company. Corporate decisions on transfer prices do have a meaningful impact on what a tax jurisdiction collects. There are nations, islands, and localities where tax authorities exhibit little interest in transfer prices. Ireland, Puerto Rico, and other nations or areas designated as free trade zones or having special tax privileges may not tax corporate profits, or have a very low tax rate.

These nations or locales are interested in companies building plants on their soil for the social benefits that accrue from employment of individuals who might otherwise be unemployed. Companies operating in such nations or locales can substantially decrease their overall tax rate. The effective reduction in tax rates depends on the transfer prices of imported components and semi finished goods and the transfer prices of exported finished goods. Granting tax concessions is one way for a nation to attract companies. At this time, eastern European nations offer tax incentives but do not have a prescribed accounting methodology to calculate profits, which makes it impossible to quantify the tax benefit. More than one company has set up an operation in eastern Europe to later discover that the government had a much different version in mind of the nature of the tax benefits than the investors anticipated. Such shortsightedness by government officials has a deleterious impact on attracting other companies. Many nations are discovering that viewing business solely as a way to fill the public coffers may not be in their long-term best interests. Within the United States, states with high corporate tax rates have experienced companies moving to states with low corporate tax rates.

The higher they raise their corporate tax rates, the less they collect in taxes. As once companies moved from one state to another, now they move from one nation to another. In selecting a potential site, a businessman considers many factors, of which taxes are but one. Some of these are social and political stability; a system of commercial law to resolve disputes; a set of acceptable accounting practices (both to assess tax liabilities and evaluate tax incentives); a labour force with the requisite skills and will to work; and an infrastructure of transportation, communication, and utility and social (education, medical care) services. There are more locations that offer good potential sites for factories than before.

Managers no longer feel that their factories must be anchored to one nation and have learned to manage far-flung operations. Nations must now compete for factories. Tax authorities in developed nations are beginning to realise that they may end up collecting less tax revenue in their eagerness to collect more tax revenue by raising tax rates. The United States was forced to repeal a luxury tax on pleasure boats because pleasure boat construction virtually ceased with the passage of the new tax. New Jersey was forced to repeal a sales tax on trucks when truck selling companies moved their operations to nearby Pennsylvania. In both cases, tax revenues fell when tax rates were raised, and the tax authorities were forced to rescind tax increases. In a global economy, companies are mobile and will relocate to avoid especially burdensome taxes.

INTERNATIONAL FUNDING

Businesses operating in hard currency nations have the advantage of being able to transfer and convert currencies as necessary. Many nations, however, have currencies that lack convertibility, the so-called soft currencies. Transfer pricing provides a means of moving funds from one country to another, when direct currency convertibility is not possible. If a nation has an affiliate that completes the manufacturing process and sells its output within that nation, funds can be moved out of that nation by increasing the transfer price for goods imported by the affiliate. The same objective can be accomplished by increasing the charges for services rendered by the parent organization to the affiliate, such as selling and administrative (S&A) fees, research and development (R&D) expenses, financial charges on transferred assets, and royalties for rights to patents and dividends. Sometimes currency exchange controls focus on the amount of dividends that can be paid by an affiliate to its parent. A quasi-dividend can be paid by raising the transfer price of goods moving into the nation or by increasing corporate fees, financial charges, and royalty payments. Some nations with severe restrictions on dividend outflows will permit increases in transfer prices and service fees.

These quasi-dividend payments are allowed because the local government recognizes that few companies can afford the luxury of investing in a nation that prohibits the company from earning a return on its investment. However, actions such as these that drain funds out of a soft currency nation eventually result in some sort of currency exchange restriction. This often results in affiliate profits accumulating in a currency that may not be particularly desirable. Sometimes currency exchange restrictions can be bypassed by the affiliate making an investment, or lending funds, to an affiliate in another nation.

CONTROLLING REPORTED PROFITS

Shifts in transfer prices, corporate administrative fees, and other parent company charges to an affiliate are means of managing the affiliate's reported profitability. It may be in the interest of a parent organization to lower the reported profitability of an affiliate for reasons other than tax minimization. These include deflecting union demands for higher wages, reducing political pressure to nationalize or expropriate a profitable affiliate, and dissuading potential competitors from entering the market. Lowering profitability is also a way to counter price controls that limit profitability. If a government has set price controls based on the cost of production plus a limited markup for profits, increases in the transfer price of goods sent to the affiliate lowers the profit margin of goods sold in that nation. This may permit goods to be sold at government decreed profit margins with the company as a whole still able to earn its normal profits. A few nations have tax rates that are linked to profitability.

The greater the profitability, the higher the tax rate. The logic behind this taxation policy is that there is a level of profits on investment that seems "excessive" to the government. Such excessive profitability should be punished by the government, and there is no greater punishment than taking away the excess profits through a higher tax rate. By increasing the transfer price of goods being imported into the nation, the degree of profitability is decreased, lowering the tax rate and, presumably, restoring respectability in the eyes of the government. Alternatively, it may be in the interests of the parent organization to enhance the profitability of an affiliate. This may be done by lowering the transfer price of imported goods. One reason for enhancing the profitability of an affiliate is to provide sufficient financial resources to the affiliate for it to withstand price cutting by competitive companies. Improving an affiliate's profitability, even at the cost of paying more in taxes, may allow the affiliate to borrow needed funds for operation from local banks and other financial institutions, to improve its credit rating to qualify for lower interest loans and to fund capital outlays from its own resources.

CIRCUMVENTING EXCHANGE CONTROLS

Governments with soft currencies often limit the amount of their currency that companies operating in their nations can exchange for other currencies. Their motivation is to discourage the selling of the domestic soft currency and the buying of a hard currency, which would exert downward pressure on the value of the local currency. In other words, exchange controls are set up to keep a soft currency from becoming softer. From the point of view of a parent organization, restricting hard currency outflows inhibits an affiliate's ability to pay for imported components or other items necessary for its operations. Transfer prices for the needed components can be kept artificially low to expand the volume of goods that are being imported into a soft currency nation.

This sustains an affiliate's manufacturing operation without exceeding government decreed restrictions on converting soft currency to hard currency. But there is an adverse consequence because such a course of action results in a parent corporation accumulating even larger amounts of soft currency. These holdings of soft currency are constantly losing purchasing power through inflation. The soft currency cannot be converted to a more desirable currency because of currency exchange restrictions and the soft currency, which has little value within the nation, has no value outside the nation. One of the knottiest problems associated with an operating affiliate in a soft currency nation is funding of hard currency imports necessary for its operation and obtaining a hard currency return on a hard currency investment. Some companies will not set up an operation in a soft currency nation unless there is a prearranged means to earn hard currency to pay for hard currency imports and to provide a hard currency return on a hard currency investment. Pepsi Cola struck a barter deal for producing its soft drink in the former Soviet Union.

Its soft ruble revenue, net of soft ruble expenses, is exchanged for Russian built tankers, which are then sold for hard currencies. Oil companies will not set up operations in the Commonwealth of Independent States, and other soft currency nations, unless they receive a share of the output, which is shipped out of the nation and sold for hard currency. The easiest way for a company to earn hard currency in a soft currency nation would be to export a portion of its output to hard currency nations. However, most soft currency nations do not permit the hard currency revenue to remain with the company. The hard currency revenue is exchanged for an equivalent amount of soft currency, which is then credited to the exporter's bank account. In essence, the national government receives the hard currency revenue from exports and pays soft currency to the exporter. Sometimes international banks are at fault for imposing this condition on a nation as a means to guarantee repayment of international debt. Regardless of whether the nation or the international banks impose this condition, it is self-defeating because the economic development of a developing nation is held back by the inability of companies to earn sufficient hard currency to justify their investments.

MINIMIZING DUTIES AND TARIFFS

Duties and tariffs imposed on goods imported into a nation can be reduced by lowering the transfer price. This is the exact opposite of reducing taxes on profits by increasing the transfer price. Because the tariff rate is usually less than the tax rate on profits, lowering transfer prices to reduce import tariffs often results in a higher tax on profits. In some nations, however, tariffs on certain imported goods and commodities are not set by a corporate-determined transfer price but by an internationally posted price. This can be done only for generic goods (steel) or commodities (oil), where there is an active market with published and verifiable prices. Sometimes tax authorities will reference costs not to a "transfer price" cost but to an internationally agreed standard.

One example of this is tanker rates in the oil business. An oil company can manage the profitability, and therefore, the tax liability, of a refinery by the transfer price associated with international tanker transportation for moving oil to and from a refinery. The tax authorities of many nations and the oil companies have agreed to a panel of experts determining a fair and representative tanker rate that is used for the computation of taxes independent of the transfer price, or internal cost, that oil companies charge for shipping oil among their affiliates. This eliminates arguments between tax authorities and oil companies concerning the appropriate shipping charge. Determining the optimal transfer-pricing policy is further complicated when a nation in which an affiliate operates has an export subsidy programme or provides a tax credit on the value of exports. It may be advantageous to lower transfer prices to an affiliate whose output is exported to third parties or other affiliates in other nations to take advantage of these tax incentives.

The optimal transfer price depends on the nature of the export subsidy or tax credit, the volume of the affiliate's output that is exported from the nation, the relationship between taxes on profits and the generation of tax credits and on the capacity of the affiliate to utilize the tax credit or export subsidy. The nature of the taxes paid in a nation in the form of income taxes, duties and tariffs on imported goods, and export subsidies or tax credits on exported goods influence the setting of transfer prices. There is no hard and fast rule on whether a high or a low transfer-pricing policy is best for a company. The particular circumstances of a company's operations in a nation and the nature of taxes and subsidies determine the best transfer-pricing policy. A transferpricing system integrated into a financial reporting and control system should be capable of analyzing "what" if scenarios to evaluate the effect of different transfer-pricing policies.

REDUCING CURRENCY EXCHANGE RISK

Changes in currency exchange rates result in transaction and translation gains and losses. More importantly, they affect the competitive position of an affiliate. If an affiliate manufactures and markets its goods in a nation, and imports components from another nation, a revaluation of the currency where the finished goods are being sold relative to the currency of its purchased components reduces manufacturing costs. This makes the affiliate more competitive and profitable. A devaluation, on the other hand, increases the cost of imported components, making the affiliate less competitive and less profitable. Reality is much more complex than this simple example because affiliates may export and import components and finished goods to and from a variety of nations.

Changes in exchange rates benefit some affiliates and hurt others, and it may not be obvious because of the nature of buying and selling of goods and services. It is possible that a change in currency exchange rates that is adverse to a particular affiliate may be beneficial to the company as a whole because of the nature of the net exposure of the company to the affected currencies. Adjustments to transfer prices may affect currency holdings before an anticipated change in exchange rates takes place and may be able to restore a company's competitive position after the change has taken place. Therefore, a financial reporting and control system should have the capacity to assess changes to both transfer prices and currency exchange rates to enable the parent organization to respond both to anticipated changes in currency exchange rates and to subsequent shifts in its competitive position.

TRANSFER PRICING AND JOINT VENTURES

A joint venture partner, a local partner owning a portion of an affiliate, and a minority shareholder are going to be as interested in transfer pricing as the local tax authority. Less often, a partnership is structured on the basis of a claim, or royalty, on revenue. More often, it is a claim on profits. If one party to a venture or partnership can influence revenue, costs, and profitability through transfer pricing, then the other party or partner, or a minority shareholder, will be deservedly concerned. One way to manage transfer pricing with regard to having partners or minority shareholders is to formalize the setting of transfer prices in some verifiable manner such as a set markup above costs, another is to reference transfer prices to an observable market transaction. Either way minimizes the opportunity for one party to a partnership or joint venture to manipulate transfer prices to its advantage. If the partners, participants, and minority shareholders feel that their interests are vulnerable by virtue of the other party to a business venture controlling transfer prices, then they may not contribute to the venture that which was expected of them. Avoiding these problems can be more easily said than done. Some years ago, Ford Motor Company purchased the minority shares of its partially owned subsidiaries because the company felt that it could not administer transfer pricing in a way that was fair to all concerned. Some managements have made the strategic decision not to enter into joint ventures, or have local partners or minority shareholdings in corporate affiliates, where they can manage the profitability of the venture through transfer prices. Sometimes, the solution for a problem is to avoid the problem.

TRANSFER PRICING AND MANAGERIAL PERFORMANCE EVALUATION

It may be in the interest of the corporation as a whole to transfer in components that are more highly priced than those an affiliate can purchase from other sources. It may be in the interest of the corporation as a whole to transfer goods made in one affiliate to another affiliate for less than what the affiliate can sell them for to third parties. Although the corporation may gain by such a set of transfer prices for goods moving among affiliates, it does not serve the interests of the affiliate managers if they are subsequently judged on profitability. This dichotomy of purpose in establishing a transfer-pricing policy for the good of the whole company, yet holding managers of affiliates accountable for profits that are contaminated, so to speak, by transfer prices has not been successfully addressed when transfer prices are different from market prices. In fact, this is one potent argument in favour of companies having transfer pricing policies based on the market price for comparable goods. If transfer prices are set at the price for goods exchanged between unrelated parties, then there is no dichotomy of purpose in setting transfer prices and measuring performance.

Managers of affiliates can be judged in an unbiased fashion on the profitability of their operations because they are buying and selling at market prices—the same prices that would prevail if they were independent companies. The disadvantage of letting the market set transfer prices is that the parent corporation can no longer utilize transfer pricing as a means to pursue the overall optimization of the financial performance of the corporation. One possible approach to the dysfunctional aspects of setting transfer prices at other than market prices and measuring management performance of affiliates is to isolate and separately state the amount of inter company "profit" or "loss" that each affiliate is experiencing in its transactions with other affiliates. This approach provides the parent organization with information on whether an affiliate is suffering from unwarranted decreased profitability or enjoying unwarranted increased profitability because of transfer pricing.

SETTING TRANSFER PRICES BY COST OF PRODUCTION

There are two general approaches for setting transfer prices: the cost of production and market prices associated with third party, or unrelated, transactions. The cost-of-production approach bases the price of goods to be transferred between affiliates on the variable cost of production, an allowance for fixed costs that are general in nature and are apportioned over the entire product line, and an allowance for fixed costs that can be apportioned among the individual products. This latter category usually includes research and development costs and selling and administrative costs. The remaining components may include financial fees and royalties associated with tangible and intangible assets to be apportioned to individual products and the selection of an appropriate profit margin.

The variable cost of production includes labour, material, and other direct costs that are consumed in the production of an item. If the policy of the company is to hire and fire (lay off) factory workers as production rises and falls, then labour is a variable cost. If a company is reluctant to let go of their workers when sales decline, then factory labour should be considered part of fixed costs. Factory labour costs are usually part variable and part fixed. Other variable costs can be the unit financing and utility costs associated with machinery and processes used in the manufacture of a particular product and unit shipping costs. These costs can also be treated as fixed costs depending on how the company's cost accounting system is set up. Fixed costs are all costs not included in variable costs. Fixed costs are the financing or depreciation costs of the factory; the overhead costs of marketing, accounting, and supervision; the cost of inventories, warehouses, insurance, utilities, communication, property taxes, and other non-variable cost items. Fixed costs may not be entirely fixed in that there is some variation as production levels change.

For instance, bonuses, which would be considered part of the fixed costs of having an executive suite, rise and fall with profits, which are related to production levels. The number of staff personnel in marketing, accounting, engineering, and other overhead functions can vary with the production level. Some elements of fixed costs are allocated in the transfer price setting mechanism in a way that fairly apportions the fixed cost burden among the various products. Other elements of fixed costs can be apportioned more on the basis of the benefit derived by an individual product. One of these is research and development, where the allocation can be made over a product line in proportion to the degree of R&D expenditures associated with the development of an individual product.

Although there is general agreement that this is a fair way to apportion R&D expenses of successful undertakings, there is lack of agreement on how to apportion R&D expenses for failed projects. Some maintain that the allocation of expenses associated with failed R&D projects should be apportioned to all products on the basis that every product should bear the risk of failed R&D efforts. Others object on the grounds that had the R&D effort succeeded, a particular product might not have benefited. Therefore, it makes no sense for the transfer price to contain the cost of a failed R&D effort, which, had it succeeded, would not be part of the transfer price of the product. The question as to the proper treatment of failed R&D projects is not an internal accounting matter. Tax authorities are interested in who takes the write off of a failed R&D project. In the United States, the Internal Revenue Service (IRS) is concerned whether a transfer price contains a provision for failed R&D expenditures.

If a transfer price contains only that portion of R&D expenditures that were successful with regard to a particular product, then failed R&D projects of a U.S. corporation are being written off solely against U.S. income. A portion of the tax loss write-off is passed on to the tax authority of another nation by including an element of failed R&D expenditures in the transfer price. Another fixed cost element that can be separated and apportioned in a different manner than general fixed costs are services provided to an individual product. These may be coordination and control expenses associated with a product; costs for enhancing the efficiency of operations for manufacturing the product or expanding the scope of its market; and the costs of recruiting and training of management and operations personnel associated with manufacturing, marketing, and repairing or servicing the product. The allocation of these service costs to individual products provides another element in deriving their transfer prices.

The derivation of the transfer price also includes elements for tangibles and intangibles associated with a product. Tangibles are the plant, equipment, and other physical assets dedicated to the manufacture of the product. Part of the transfer price provides a financial return for tangibles based on their value. Intangibles represent the technical knowledge and expertise and applicable patents that can be allocated to a particular product. The transfer price also contains an element that provides a company with a return on intangibles. Intangible costs within a transfer price cannot be capriciously determined by management because intangible costs affect taxable profits. For this reason, the IRS has established guidelines for determining the intangible cost element in a transfer price.

An intangible cost element must be present if there are intangible costs associated with the manufacture or marketing of a product and must be so identified. Intangible costs can be proportioned in relation to the income attributable to the intangibles by units of production, sales, net or gross profits, or other reasonable methods. The fee for intangible property incorporated in a transfer price must be similar to what would have been arranged with an independent third party. The last part of the cost approach in setting transfer prices is determining the proper profit margin on the goods made by one affiliate and shipped to another. This may be the average profit margin for the company as a whole or a profit margin associated with a specific product line. Regardless, the stipulated profit margin must be reconciled in some manner with the profitability of the company or a product line to satisfy the tax authorities. The need for reconciliation of the profit and the various cost elements of the transfer price with the tax authorities sometimes results in the tax group within the finance department of a company being responsible for administering transfer prices. However, this choice may hinder general management from using transfer prices as a means to achieve corporate objectives.

The chief advantage of the cost of production approach for setting transfer prices is that the costs are available and are subject to quantification. For this reason, the production cost approach has been more common in the past than the market price approach. The chief disadvantage is that there is no real incentive for an affiliate to improve its manufacturing process, to enhance its efficiency, or to take steps to lower costs. Mistakes, errors, inefficiencies in manning or machinery, management inattention to detail, worker carelessness, and excessive remuneration of white and blue collar workers alike may all be incorporated in the determination of costs and passed on to the affiliates in the transfer price. Another disadvantage is that both the tax authority and the affiliates may object to the nature of the apportionment of R&D, S&A, tangibles, and intangibles among the various products and the assigned profit margin.

SETTING TRANSFER PRICES BY MARKET PRICES

The disadvantages associated with the cost-of-production method of setting transfer prices can be mostly avoided by referencing transfer prices to third party transactions for identical, or nearly identical, products. If an affiliate can obtain the item being purchased from a third party for a certain price, then that price can be the basis for setting the transfer price. The proponents of market-oriented transfer prices maintain that letting the market set the transfer price is inherently more fair than a production-cost-based system because one affiliate is not supporting the inefficiencies of another. If an affiliate receives only the global competitive price for its products, then there is an incentive for it to take whatever actions are needed to correct the inefficiencies in its operations that are resulting in higher costs.

In a truly decentralized operation, managers are expected to make their decisions on an independent basis, and unrelated companies are permitted to compete for the business of an affiliate, along with other affiliates. The parent organization does not set transfer prices and has little or no influence over the decisions made by the managers of the affiliates. No favour or special consideration is shown to fellow affiliates in the competitive process of selecting suppliers for components and goods. The hope, of course, is that everyone is kept on his or her competitive toes to produce salable goods at the lowest possible cost. This managerial philosophy, where each affiliate is treated as an independent company, is sometimes referred to as the small business unit (SBU) management philosophy. The disadvantage is that, although each affiliate is focused on optimizing its operations, the end result may be suboptimal performance of the corporation as a whole. Suppose that affiliate X produces all of a component (part X) for a number of widget manufacturing affiliates. Total demand for part X is 2 million per year. Affiliate X has $10 million in fixed annual costs, which include a profit margin on the investment in manufacturing facilities plus a return on the R&D investment for the development of part X. The variable costs for manufacturing part X is $5. The transfer price based on the fixed and variable costs of affiliate X supplying all other affiliates with part X is $10.

VOLUME OF SALES: 2,000,000

Fixed Costs	$10,000,000
Variable Costs at $5 per Unit	10,000,000
Total Costs	$20,000,000
Transfer Price Based on Cost of Making 2,000,000	$10.00

Affiliate A is free to cut its best deal and obtains a quote of $9.50 from another company. Affiliate A does what is best for maximizing its profits and purchases 200,000 part X's from a third party for $9.50 rather than pay $10 to affiliate X. Affiliate X has lost a contract for 200,000 part X's and now operates on a basis of a sales volume of 1,800,000 per year.

VOLUME OF SALES: 1,800,000

Fixed Costs	$10,000,000
Variable Costs at $5 per Unit	9,000,000
Total Costs	$19,000,000
Transfer Price Based on Cost of Making 1,800,000	$10.56

The remaining affiliates must pay a higher price because there is less sales volume to cover the fixed costs of affiliate X. The increase in transfer price to cover the fixed and variable costs is essentially equivalent to treating fixed costs as a component of variable costs, which it is not. Nevertheless, affiliate X must cover all its costs. When affiliate X announces the increase in price, affiliate B concludes a deal with a third party at $9.75 causing another loss of 200,000 for affiliate X.

VOLUME OF SALES: 1,600.000

Fixed Costs	$10,000,000
Variable Costs at $5 per Unit	8,000,000
Total Costs	$18,000,000
Transfer Price Based on cost of Making 1,600,000	$11.25

Now it's time for affiliate C to say goodbye to affiliate X, as it maximizes its profit by reducing the cost of part X by paying $10.50 to another outside source. This is higher than the $10 price that applied when all the affiliates received part X from affiliate X. It is clear from the continuation of this exercise that, as each affiliate maximizes its profits by cutting costs, the corporation as a whole is being sub optimized. Even if the various affiliates do not pay more than an average price of $10 per unit for part X in purchasing all part X's from outside sources, the global company is stuck with an affiliate with no sales and a fixed annual cost of $10 million that represents, in large measure, financing costs on plant and equipment. It is highly likely that the fixed costs in affiliate X contain an allowance for R&D expenses and product development that have to be recouped in the operation of a company, but do not have to be recouped by another company if it is essentially manufacturing a copy of part X.

Copying is fairly common in global commerce because patent protection is limited to the nation issuing the patent. Global companies often obtain patents in a number of nations, but this may not be possible for all nations. A company may manufacture a copy of a product in one of these nations. Although it is true that affiliate X is free to pursue patent infringement action against sales in a particular nation where it has patent protection, the time involved in enforcement proceedings and the legal expenses may make such protection prohibitively expensive. Furthermore, there is no internationally recognized legal structure to handle patent infringements. In addition to R&D expenses, the fixed costs of affiliate X may also contain a service element for the benefit of the affiliates purchasing its output that may not be provided by third parties. By each affiliate "doing its own thing," the R&D and service costs cannot be covered.

One principal problem associated with using market reference points for transfer pricing is that the affiliates may be shipping components and parts that are not readily available from other firms. Most components and parts are specifically designed for a company's product line and are not available from third parties unless contracted for by an affiliate. Market prices for similarly designed components that cannot be actually used in the company's product line may not be relevant. Moreover, the quality inherent in third-party quotes for similar parts may not be up to the standards imposed on products made within a global corporate family.

There is no easy answer as to which approach for determining transfer prices should be followed. Both have their adherents and detractors. Either approach restricts transfer prices to something related to third-party, or market, transactions or to the cost of manufacture. Surveys have shown that nations seem to exhibit cultural preferences as to which approach to follow and as to what motivates companies in setting transfer prices. Companies in some countries favour costbased transfer prices, whereas companies in other nations favour market-based transfer prices. U.S. based corporations have historically preferred setting transfer prices by the cost approach because the necessary data is available, whereas the necessary data for setting transfer prices on the basis of market transactions may not be available. Oftentimes, market quotes for uniquely designed parts and components may have to be derived rather than observed because there are no market transactions for the precise item. Should General Motors set its transfer price on carburetors being shipped to Europe based on its cost of production or on what Toyota charges its U.S. transplants? The two carburetors are not the same and do not have the same cost of production.

Furthermore, there may not be a data base available for prices for carburetors sold between related and unrelated parties from which to derive a market price. Preferences change with time. Surveys done in the 1970s indicated that the preponderance of U.S. companies were motivated by tax minimization in setting transfer prices. More recent surveys indicate that companies are more interested in setting transfer prices on the basis of measuring the performance of affiliate managers and of providing reliable and unbiased information for the making of decisions. This change in attitude in U.S. companies may be the result of the United States becoming a relative tax haven compared to other nations. Its corporate tax rate of 34 percent, plus state taxes, is less than in many other industrialized nations, where tax rates range between 40 percent and 55 percent. A U.S. company's total tax bill may, in fact, be reduced by allocating more profits to the United States.

Regardless of changes in attitudes as to what is important in setting transfer prices, the essential point is that there is no unanimity on which approach to use and on what motivates companies in setting transfer prices. Up to this point, an important assumption has been that the parent company has real control over transfer prices to manage corporate cash flows and the profits reported by affiliates and to overcome artificial barriers to trade in the form of custom duties, currency exchange, and price controls. Some recent surveys suggest that competitive forces and market conditions within a nation seem to be more important in setting transfer prices than decisions made by a parent organization. If transfer prices are being set by exogenous commercial forces, then the presumption that a parent organization is able to achieve optimal financial performance of a global family of affiliates through the careful orchestration of transfer pricing is being challenged.

TAX CONSIDERATIONS

Taxation and transfer pricing are intimately entwined, because transfer pricing of goods, parts, and components moving in and out of a nation has a direct impact on taxes on profits and on the amount of duties and tariffs paid to the tax authority. The discussion on transfer pricing based on the cost-of-production approach shows an intimate involvement with the tax authority in the methodology for calculating various elements of the transfer price. There is little uniformity on taxation among nations. Taxes range from taxation of a corporation's activities to the "water's edge" or on its global earnings, the so-called "unitary tax." The state of California invented the unitary tax in the 1930s when movie companies in California began moving out of the state to avoid state taxes.

A unitary tax was applied against the global earnings of a company and the tax was determined by the proportion of a company's sales, property, and payroll within the state to its global sales, property, and payroll. The resulting tax had no relation to the degree of profitability of a company's operation in California. A company could operate at a loss in California and still pay a tax based on its global profits. Needless to say, both foreign governments and multinational companies have vigorously fought the unitary tax. A number of court decisions confirmed or restricted unitary taxation over the years.

Ultimately, opposition to the unitary tax succeeded. In November 1991, Alaska was the last state to abandon having a company's state tax liability based on the global earnings of the company. The unitary tax still exists in a truncated form, where earnings are restricted to the "water's edge." The state tax is calculated on the portion of a company's activities within a state as compared to its activities within the United States. Although most other countries limit their assessment on what is to be taxed to the operations of a company within their jurisdiction, there is no universal agreement as to what constitutes revenue and expenses in the calculation of taxable income and no uniformity on tax rates. Every nation decides what is subject to taxation and the applicable tax rates.

The complexity of tax regulations, in general, and the diversity of tax laws among nations are such that it is necessary for an affiliate to retain the technical expertise necessary to understand and comply with local tax regulations. The parent organization must retain the technical knowledge for its own tax jurisdiction and have sufficient knowledge of tax matters elsewhere to coordinate tax planning among the various affiliates. The vigour with which tax payments are enforced varies among nations. Some countries with seemingly high tax rates permit an underground economy to flourish without much in the way of enforcing tax payments. The other side of the coin is the willingness of companies to adhere to tax laws. In some nations, a businessman who scrupulously follows the tax laws and pays what is owed to the tax authority will find himself at a competitive disadvantage.

NATURE OF TAXES

Taxes can be direct or indirect. The United States relies more on direct taxation, which is applied to each taxable entity. A U.S. corporation is taxed at 34 percent on its profits. If a corporation pays a dividend to its shareholders, then the next taxable entity, the individual, pays a tax, which may be 28 percent or more. This is double taxation. Some nations, such as Germany, have two corporate tax rates on profits—one for retained profits and the other for distributed profits in the form of dividends.

A lesser tax rate applies to profits that are distributed to shareholders to reduce the degree of double taxation. Europe relies more on indirect taxes—particularly, the value added tax (VAT). The VAT is basically a tax applied to each stage of the production process and is not directly associated with the degree of profitability. Indeed, only a small portion of a VAT is associated with profits. Suppose that a company's manufacturing operations has the following financial results.

Wages, rents, interest, profit	$400,000
Outside purchases of goods and services for which VAT has already been paid	600,000
Total sales	$1,000,000

The additive method is to apply the VAT rate, say 10 percent, to all costs associated with the production of goods, including profit and excluding purchases of goods and services from third parties for which the VAT has already been paid. In this case, $400,000 of a company's activities falls into this category resulting in a VAT of $40,000. A simpler method of calculation is to take the gross sales of the company ($1,000,000), subtract all purchases of goods and services for which VAT has already been paid ($600,000), and apply the VAT rate to the balance ($400,000). Either method yields the same result.

The VAT is essentially equivalent to a national sales tax, because every company associated with the production and marketing of goods and providing services pays a tax on whatever value it adds to the goods or services. The value added tax, like a sales tax, is a tax on consumption, whereas U.S. taxes are on income and profits. Value added tax rates vary widely from country to country and according to the nature of the business. Certain European countries have low VAT rates (5 percent) for business transactions associated with food and high VAT rates (40 percent) for luxury products. Others attempt to have one rate that applies to most forms of commerce. Because the VAT is not paid on items that have already been exposed to a value added tax, and with the European economy becoming more integrated, there is a powerful incentive for the European Community to harmonize VAT rates and coordinate the handling of VAT payments for products or components shipped between members of the European Community.

The amounts of value added by a company are frequently disclosed in European financial statements. In the excerpt from the British company, the company had gross revenues of 3,213 million pounds in 1987 of which 919.1 million pounds represents added value by the company. Of the total of 919.1

million pounds of added value, 496.8 million pounds was paid to the company's employees, 157.1 million pounds was paid in taxes to government tax authorities, and the remainder was paid to the internal and external providers of capital.

U.S. TAXATION OF GLOBAL COMPANIES

Nations have different ways of taxing global companies domiciled within their jurisdiction. If a parent corporation is domiciled in the United States, it does not pay taxes in the United States on profits earned by incorporated affiliates in other nations, unless the nation is considered a tax haven. This, in the United States, is known as Subpart F income, which will be discussed later under rein voicing centers. Unlike an incorporated affiliate, a branch of a U.S. company located in a foreign nation is taxed directly on its earnings regardless of whether the earnings are remitted to the home office or not. The taxes paid on remitted and unremitted earnings are not the same, in that unremitted earnings have to be translated to U.S. dollars before a tax liability can be assessed, and therefore, are influenced by changes in currency exchange rates.

Taxes can also be calculated on the basis of the increase in the net worth of the branch, which can also be affected by changes in currency exchange rates. Sometimes a U.S. company will first open a branch operation in another country to permit startup losses to flow back to the parent organization. When the branch becomes profitable, it may be reorganized as a wholly owned subsidiary, reducing the company's overall tax liability. U.S. based companies usually operate in the global market through operating affiliates whose stock is owned by the parent corporation. The parent corporation pays U.S. taxes only on the profits generated from dividends, royalties, and other service payments and fees paid by a non-U.S. domiciled affiliate to the parent organization.

Taxes paid on profits by affiliates in their nations of domicile can be treated either as a tax credit or a tax deduction by the parent organization in the calculation of its U.S. taxes. To the degree that a tax paid on profits to a foreign government is treated as a tax credit, the net effect of a company paying taxes on its profits in a foreign country is that these taxes are essentially paid for by the U.S. government foregoing an equivalent amount of U.S. source based tax revenue.

Obviously, taxes paid to foreign governments must pass certain criteria set forth by the Internal Revenue Service to be considered for a tax credit. Foreign tax credits apply to taxes paid on foreign source profits calculated in a conventional way as U.S. source profits. Tax credits are also available for foreign government withholding taxes on dividends, interest payments, and royalties paid by a foreign-based affiliate to a U.S. parent company. There is a maximum permissible limit on tax credits linked to the ratio of foreign source income to total worldwide income multiplied by the tax liability of U.S. operations. This effectively limits the foreign tax credit to the U.S., not the foreign, tax rate. A company doing business in a nation with a higher tax rate on profits than in the United States does not receive a tax credit equal to the taxes paid to the foreign government. The tax credit is based on the U.S. tax rate. With U.S. tax rates being lower than in most other industrialized nations, U.S. based global companies are not being fully compensated by tax credits on foreign income taxes. This may provide an incentive to shift taxable income back to the United States through changes in transfer prices. The U.S. tax authorities permit a credit for taxes paid on profits to other nations under the notion of tax equity and tax neutrality.

The principle of tax equity implies that a U.S. taxpaying entity with an operation in another nation should not pay more in taxes than having the operation domiciled in the United States. Were the equity principle absolutely true, a U.S. taxpaying entity would be indifferent, or neutral, to whether the operation was located in another nation or in the United States. Some maintain that the U.S. tax code does not adhere to the tax neutrality principle because a company doing business in New York City does not obtain a tax credit on its federal taxes for taxes paid to the state and city of New York on profits made in their jurisdiction. A company with an affiliate in another nation not only receives a tax credit, which neutralizes its foreign and U.S. income taxes, but does not have to pay U.S. taxes on its foreign source earnings until those earnings are remitted to the parent in the form of a dividend, a royalty payment, or an equivalent thereof. As long as foreign source profits remain in the coffers of the affiliate, no taxes are due to the U.S. government, even though, under special circumstances, the affiliate may lend these funds to the parent company. Deferral of dividend payments is essentially an interest-free loan made by the U.S. government to the foreign affiliate of a U.S. parent company on the amount of U.S. taxes due if, and when, these funds are repatriated to the U.S. parent. The principles of equity and neutrality built into the U.S. tax code were designed to provide an incentive for U.S. firms to invest overseas as part of the national policy of rebuilding war-torn nations. U.S. companies would be better off confining their activities within the United States, and would not invest in foreign affiliates, if the profits of these foreign affiliates were exposed to double taxation.

Qualified foreign taxes, which cannot be utilized as tax credits, may be used as a tax deduction. A tax deduction is not as valuable as a tax credit. Tax deductions apply when there are not sufficient U.S. taxes to be shielded by tax credits, or where the overall limitation on tax credits has been exceeded. Tax deductions can be carried back or carried forward, whichever is more useful.

REIN VOICING CENTERS

Some companies have set up rein voicing centers to manage all intra company trading of products. A rein voicing centre is at a single location, buying the output of the manufacturing affiliates and selling it to the marketing affiliates. Each affiliate receives or pays in its own currency, thus concentrating all intra company transaction currency exposure at the rein voicing centre. The centre possesses the necessary data to assess the net currency exposure of intra company transactions and can enter into appropriate currency hedges. The centre may also receive better quotes from currency exchange dealers because all intra company currency exchange transactions are done at one location.

The rein voicing centre can mark up the price of all products flowing through the centre to cover its administrative expenses. If there is little or no profitability associated with the operations of a rein voicing centre, it does not matter where the rein voicing centre is located from a tax viewpoint. However, it is possible to increase the markup to the point where corporate profit can be diverted from the nations where the goods are manufactured and marketed to the nation where the rein voicing centre is located. Now the location of the rein voicing centre is critical from a tax viewpoint. In the 1960s, the U.S. government became concerned with the accumulation of profits in rein voicing centers located in tax havens. Tax havens were characterized as nations imposing no, or a very low, tax on profits, having a high degree of bank secrecy, and little or no currency controls.

These nations consider financial activities of importance to their economy, provide modern communication facilities, and promote themselves as offshore financial centers. Bahamas, Bermuda, Cayman Islands, Liberia, Panama, and Vanuatu have been identified as tax havens. It is possible to "run" a rein voicing centre through these nations without a physical presence of personnel or products. Profits can be easily diverted to tax havens by increasing the markup on selling prices, thus reducing tax liabilities to the nations where the products are manufactured and marketed. If the criterion for determining a tax haven is satisfied, then the income earned by a rein voicing centre, or any corporate entity in the declared tax haven, is deemed Subpart F income. This income flows directly to the U.S. parent corporation and is taxed as though the income was earned in the United States.

TAXATION IMPACT ON TRANSFER PRICING

Companies operating in the United States are guided by Section 482 of the Internal Revenue Code when setting transfer prices. Specifically, the IRS, through the Secretary of the Treasury, has the right to "distribute, apportion, or allocate gross income, deductions, credits, or allowances... between or among... businesses, if he determines that such distribution, apportionment, or allocation is necessary in order to prevent evasion of taxes. The IRS has been granted wide latitude to do whatever it wants if the IRS deems that dealings between a U.S. parent and its affiliates do not meet its standards.

For instance, the IRS can reallocate income and deductions if loans have been made between a parent corporation and an affiliate at an unrealistic interest rate. Unrealistic interest rates are those that would not occur for similar transactions between unrelated third parties. This also applies to charging for services and use of property, and transfers of tangible and intangible property including lease payments and royalties. A reference to IRS guidelines has already been made in discussing R&D and intangible costs in setting transfer prices by the production cost approach.

Basing transfer pricing on published data rather than corporate derived prices is another example of the close working relationship, voluntary or not, between tax authorities and managers responsible for transfer prices. In general, the IRS standard for determining transfer pricing, and other dealings between a parent and its affiliates, is whether it is an "arm's-length" transaction—one that would occur between a company and a third party having no affiliation other than the commercial transaction under consideration. This is independent of whether the transfer price is based on the cost of production or on market prices. If the transfer price between affiliates is seemingly out of line with a price that would have been charged to an unrelated party, then the IRS has the right to reallocate income or deductions according to what it feels to be the appropriate transfer price. The IRS specifies various methods for establishing an appropriate transfer price. The preferred one is the comparable uncontrolled price method where prices are the same for goods sold to affiliate and to nonaffiliated companies. The price for goods sold to an unrelated third party establishes the transfer price for goods transferred to an affiliate.

This method does not work when goods are not sold to third parties, but are totally transferred between affiliates. Under these circumstances, the second method for setting the transfer price is the resale price method. This is the price for which the company would sell the item to an unspecified third party. The third party would add the same comparable value as the affiliate and sell the completed product with an appropriate markup. By netting the market price of the appropriate markup and the value added to the product by an affiliate, one can "back into" an appropriate transfer price from the point of view of the tax authority. The third method is the "cost plus" method, where the IRS permits three different ways of allocating costs (full absorption, direct cost, and incremental cost).

All these methods leave some margin of discretion as to what is the appropriate transfer price. If all these fail, as they frequently do for high-technology products, customized components, or subassemblies, then so-called fourth methods are permitted, such as determining transfer pricing on the basis of a predetermined profit for the foreign firm's operations and, through a netting process of accounting for applicable costs, establishing an appropriate transfer price. Regardless of the methodology, the burden of proof in supporting a transfer price is with the taxpayer, not the IRS. To confuse matters more, there have been occasions when the tax courts have rejected the notion of arm's-length transfer pricing in settling tax disputes between corporations and the IRS.

OTHER NATIONS' POLICIES CONCERNING TRANSFER PRICING

The tax authority in Canada views transfer pricing of goods similar to the way the United States does. Transfer pricing for services differs in that it is based on a pro rata sharing of actual incurred costs between the parent corporation and its affiliate, and not necessarily at an arm's-length price. Tax authorities in Japan follow a system comparable to that of the United States. German tax code provisions permit the reallocation of domestic source income if revenue or income has been shifted to another nation through a transaction that is different from those that would have been entered into by unrelated parties. In other words, transfer pricing should be arm's-length, although the code is not specific in defining arm's-length pricing.

The United Kingdom is similar to Germany in not specifically defining arm's-length pricing. The Inland Revenue may adjust taxable income based on fairness and arm's-length criteria. Disputes between corporations and Inland Revenue agents are frequently settled by negotiation, resulting in some sort of compromise between the two parties. This is unlike in Germany, where the adjustments made by the tax authorities are considered final, and unlike in the United States, where adjustments are litigated in tax courts. Tax authorities in many nations are currently taking a much closer look at transfer pricing practices. Recently, the U.K. Inland Revenue recast the accounts of one non-British company operating in the United Kingdom and assessed back taxes of nearly 2 billion pounds.

In the United States, there is growing political pressure for the IRS to take more vigorous action against foreign-owned companies operating through U.S. based affiliates. This pressure stems from the realization that the aggregate expenses for foreign-owned businesses operating in the United States exceed aggregate revenues. This means that, in the aggregate, foreign-owned subsidiaries are claiming to operate at a loss, although individual foreign-owned subsidiaries may be paying taxes on profits. Some foreign-owned affiliates operating in the United States have a twenty-year string of consecutive losses.

This is not considered a realistic appraisal of performance because there are few profit-motivated foreign-based parent companies that would support twenty years of successive losses were they real. Poor or nonexistent profits for foreign-based affiliates operating in the United States are blamed on transfer pricing. Transfer price manipulation is felt to have resulted in tax underpayments of between $12 and $50 billion. Legislation was passed in 1989 to require foreign-owned businesses in the United States to keep records, in

English, of transactions with foreign related parties. Much of this legislation has to do with substantiating transfer pricing on either a cost or arm's length transaction with an unrelated third party. A growing risk associated with manipulating transfer prices for the purpose of tax minimization. The risk is that the tax authorities will recast the company's statements with their own version of the proper transfer price, thus exposing a company to the risk of double taxation. Most nations have entered into tax treaties with various other nations with regard to taxing of affiliates of parent organizations domiciled in the treaty nations.

These treaties determine withholding taxes on dividends, interest, and royalties; relief from double taxation; and the types of taxes and organizations covered by the treaty. Overall exposure to taxation can be reduced by judicious structuring of the legal corporate entities of a parent company and its affiliates in accordance with the provisions of these treaties. Some of these treaties contain formal agreements for the mutual examination of the tax returns of affiliates of a parent company. The tax returns of affiliates and parent organizations are exchanged and examined by the tax authorities to determine correct tax liabilities, detect tax avoidance maneuvers, scrutinize transfer pricing practices, and exchange information useful to the tax authorities. These treaties also provide a forum for one tax authority to complain about the actions taken by another, when these actions are deemed detrimental to its interests. Recent developments in international cooperation of tax authorities include the establishment of a formal agreement on transfer prices.

The mutual agreement of various nations to reference a published source for tanker rates in determining oil company tax liabilities is an example of this. Australia and the United States are attempting to grant "advance determinations" of the proper transfer price for Australian companies' dealings with their U.S. affiliates. A recent survey has shown that about half of IRS tax examinations of multinational companies involve transfer prices. If a mutually agreeable methodology could be arranged between a company and the IRS, many of these tax examinations could be eliminated. The IRS is attempting to develop a procedure whereby a company and the IRS would mutually agree to a transfer-pricing agreement covering the distribution of finished goods, sales of raw materials and components, general and administrative expenses, and managerial and technical services. If the taxpayer develops an acceptable transfer-pricing methodology, then the taxpayer and the IRS would enter into an advance-pricing agreement.

The IRS would limit its examinations to an audit to ensure that the taxpayer has complied with the agreement. However, the taxpayer is obliged to submit pricing data of independent transactions, or an adequate substitute, to show that the transfer price possesses the necessary attributes of an arm's-length transaction. The taxpayer is also responsible to show that the agreed transfer-pricing methodology is generating acceptable transfer prices from an arm's-length perspective. The preference of tax authorities in many nations for arm's-length transfer pricing may act as an inducement to switch from the cost-of-production to the market price approach in setting transfer prices because, presumably, they are one and the same. The financial and taxation departments of multinational, or global, companies must deal daily with what are considered to be the most pressing issues in international accounting today. Those involved with transfer pricing must measure the consequences of their transfer-pricing decisions both on corporate profits and on current and potential tax liabilities. Potential tax liabilities, stemming from tax authorities rejecting management's transfer price decisions, and substituting their own, are enormous. This must weigh heavily on the shoulders of those responsible for setting transfer prices.

6

Supply Chain Management

Supply chain management (SCM) is the management of the flow of goods. It includes the movement and storage of raw materials, work-in-process inventory, and finished goods from point of origin to point of consumption. Interconnected or interlinked networks, channels and node businesses are involved in the provision of products and services required by end customers in a supply chain. Supply chain management has been defined as the "design, planning, execution, control, and monitoring of supply chain activities with the objective of creating net value, building a competitive infrastructure, leveraging worldwide logistics, synchronizing supply with demand and measuring performance globally."

SCM draws heavily from the areas of operations management, logistics, procurement, and information technology, and strives for an integrated approach.

ORIGIN OF THE TERM AND DEFINITIONS

The term "supply chain management" entered the public domain when Keith Oliver, a consultant at Booz Allen Hamilton (now Booz & Company), used it in an interview for the Financial Times in 1982. The term was slow to take hold. It gained currency in the mid-1990s, when a flurry of articles and books came out on the subject. In the late 1990s it rose to prominence as a management buzzword, and operations managers began to use it in their titles with increasing regularity.

Commonly accepted definitions of supply chain management include:

- The management of upstream and downstream value-added flows of materials, final goods, and related information among suppliers, company, resellers, and final consumers
- The systematic, strategic coordination of traditional business functions and tactics across all business functions within a particular company and across businesses within the supply chain, for the purposes of improving the long-term performance of the individual companies and the supply chain as a whole
- A customer-focused definition is given by Hines: "Supply chain

strategies require a total systems view of the links in the chain that work together efficiently to create customer satisfaction at the end point of delivery to the consumer. As a consequence, costs must be lowered throughout the chain by driving out unnecessary expenses, movements, and handling. The main focus is turned to efficiency and added value, or the end-user's perception of value. Efficiency must be increased, and bottlenecks removed. The measurement of performance focuses on total system efficiency and the equitable monetary reward distribution to those within the supply chain. The supply chain system must be responsive to customer requirements."

- The integration of key business processes across the supply chain for the purpose of creating value for customers and stakeholders
- According to the Council of Supply Chain Management Professionals (CSCMP), supply chain management encompasses the planning and management of all activities involved in sourcing, procurement, conversion, and logistics management. It also includes coordination and collaboration with channel partners, which may be suppliers, intermediaries, third-party service providers, or customers. Supply chain management integrates supply and demand management within and across companies. More recently, the loosely coupled, self-organizing network of businesses that cooperate to provide product and service offerings has been called the *Extended Enterprise*.

A supply chain, as opposed to supply chain management, is a set of organizations directly linked by one or more upstream and downstream flows of products, services, finances, or information from a source to a customer. Supply chain management is the management of such a chain.

Supply chain management software includes tools or modules used to execute supply chain transactions, manage supplier relationships, and control associated business processes.

Supply chain event management (SCEM) considers all possible events and factors that can disrupt a supply chain. With SCEM, possible scenarios can be created and solutions devised.

In many cases the supply chain includes the collection of goods after consumer use for recycling. Including third-party logistics or other gathering agencies as part of the RM re-patriation process is a way of illustrating the new endgame strategy.

PROBLEMS ADDRESSED

Supply chain management addresses the following problems:

- Distribution network configuration: the number, location, and network missions of suppliers, production facilities, distribution centers, warehouses, cross-docks, and customers.
- Distribution strategy: questions of operating control (e.g., centralized,

decentralized, or shared); delivery scheme (e.g., direct shipment, pool point shipping, cross docking, direct store delivery, or closed loop shipping); mode of transportation (e.g., motor carrier, including truckload, less than truckload (LTL), parcel, railroad, intermodal transport, including trailer on flatcar (TOFC) and container on flatcar (COFC), ocean freight, airfreight); replenishment strategy (e.g., pull, push, or hybrid); and transportation control (e.g., owner operated, private carrier, common carrier, contract carrier, or third-party logistics (3PL)).

- Trade-offs in logistical activities: The above activities must be coordinated in order to achieve the lowest total logistics cost. Trade-offs may increase the total cost if only one of the activities is optimized. For example, full truckload (FTL) rates are more economical on a cost-per-pallet basis than are LTL shipments. If, however, a full truckload of a product is ordered to reduce transportation costs, there will be an increase in inventory holding costs, which may increase total logistics costs. The planning of logistical activities therefore takes a systems approach. These trade-offs are key to developing the most efficient and effective logistics and SCM strategy.
- Information: The integration of processes through the supply chain in order to share valuable information, including demand signals, forecasts, inventory, transportation, and potential collaboration.
- Inventory management: Management of the quantity and location of inventory, including raw materials, work in process (WIP), and finished goods.
- Cash flow: Arranging the payment terms and methodologies for exchanging funds across entities within the supply chain.

Supply chain execution means managing and coordinating the movement of materials, information and funds across the supply chain. The flow is bi-directional. SCM applications provide real-time analytical systems that manage the flow of products and information throughout the supply chain network.

FUNCTIONS

Supply chain management is a cross-functional approach that includes managing the movement of raw materials into an organization, certain aspects of the internal processing of materials into finished goods, and the movement of finished goods out of the organization and toward the end consumer. As organizations strive to focus on core competencies and becoming more flexible, they reduce their ownership of raw materials sources and distribution channels. These functions are increasingly being outsourced to other firms that can perform the activities better or more cost effectively. The effect is to increase the number of organizations involved in satisfying customer demand, while reducing managerial control of daily logistics operations. Less control and more supply chain partners led to the creation of the concept of supply chain management. The purpose of supply chain management is to improve trust and collaboration among supply chain partners, thus improving inventory visibility and the velocity of inventory movement.

IMPORTANCE

Organizations increasingly find that they must rely on effective supply chains, or networks, to compete in the global market and networked economy. In Peter Drucker's (1998) new management paradigms, this concept of business relationships extends beyond traditional enterprise boundaries and seeks to organize entire business processes throughout a value chain of multiple companies.

In recent decades, globalization, outsourcing, and information technology have enabled many organizations, such as Dell and Hewlett Packard, to successfully operate collaborative supply networks in which each specialized business partner focuses on only a few key strategic activities. This inter-organisational supply network can be acknowledged as a new form of organisation. However, with the complicated interactions among the players, the network structure fits neither "market" nor "hierarchy" categories. It is not clear what kind of performance impacts different supply network structures could have on firms, and little is known about the coordination conditions and trade-offs that may exist among the players. From a systems perspective, a complex network structure can be decomposed into individual component firms. Traditionally, companies in a supply network concentrate on the inputs and outputs of the processes, with little concern for the internal management working of other individual players. Therefore, the choice of an internal management control structure is known to impact local firm performance.

In the 21st century, changes in the business environment have contributed to the development of supply chain networks. First, as an outcome of globalization and the proliferation of multinational companies, joint ventures, strategic alliances, and business partnerships, significant success factors were identified, complementing the earlier "just-in-time", lean manufacturing, and agile manufacturing practices. Second, technological changes, particularly the dramatic fall in communication costs (a significant component of transaction costs), have led to changes in coordination among the members of the supply chain network.

Many researchers have recognized supply network structures as a new organisational form, using terms such as "Keiretsu", "Extended Enterprise", "Virtual Corporation", "Global Production Network", and "Next Generation Manufacturing System". In general, such a structure can be defined as "a group of semi-independent organisations, each with their capabilities, which collaborate in ever-changing constellations to serve one or more markets in order to achieve some business goal specific to that collaboration".

The security management system for supply chains is described in ISO/ IEC 28000 and ISO/IEC 28001 and related standards published jointly by the ISO and the IEC.Supply Chain Management draws heavily from the areas of operations management, logistics, procurement, and information technology, and strives for an integrated approach.

HISTORICAL DEVELOPMENTS

Six major movements can be observed in the evolution of supply chain management studies: creation, integration, and globalization, specialization phases one and two, and SCM 2.0.

CREATION ERA

The term "supply chain management" was first coined by Keith Oliver in 1982. However, the concept of a supply chain in management was of great importance long before, in the early 20th century, especially with the creation of the assembly line. The characteristics of this era of supply chain management include the need for large-scale changes, re-engineering, downsizing driven by cost reduction programs, and widespread attention to Japanese management practices.

INTEGRATION ERA

This era of supply chain management studies was highlighted with the development of electronic data interchange (EDI) systems in the 1960s, and developed through the 1990s by the introduction of enterprise resource planning (ERP) systems. This era has continued to develop into the 21st century with the expansion of Internet-based collaborative systems. This era of supply chain evolution is characterized by both increasing value added and cost reductions through integration.

A supply chain can be classified as a stage 1, 2 or 3 network. In a stage 1–type supply chain, systems such as production, storage, distribution, and material control are not linked and are independent of each other. In a stage 2 supply chain, these are integrated under one plan and is ERP enabled. A stage 3 supply chain is one that achieves vertical integration with upstream suppliers and downstream customers. An example of this kind of supply chain is Tesco.

GLOBALIZATION ERA

The third movement of supply chain management development, the globalization era, can be characterized by the attention given to global systems of supplier relationships and the expansion of supply chains over national boundaries and into other continents. Although the use of global sources in organizations' supply chains can be traced back several decades (e.g., in the oil industry), it was not until the late 1980s that a considerable number of organizations started to integrate global sources into their core business. This era is characterized by the globalization of supply chain management in organizations with the goal of increasing their competitive advantage, adding value, and reducing costs through global sourcing.

SPECIALIZATION ERA (PHASE I): OUTSOURCED MANUFACTURING AND DISTRIBUTION

In the 1990s, companies began to focus on "core competencies" and specialization. They abandoned vertical integration, sold off non-core operations, and outsourced those functions to other companies. This changed management requirements, by extending the supply chain beyond the company walls and distributing management across specialized supply chain partnerships.

This transition also refocused the fundamental perspectives of each organization. Original equipment manufacturers (OEMs) became brand owners that required visibility deep into their supply base. They had to control the entire supply chain from above, instead of from within. Contract manufacturers had to manage bills of material with different part-numbering schemes from multiple OEMs and support customer requests for work-in-process visibility and vendor-managed inventory (VMI).

The specialization model creates manufacturing and distribution networks composed of several individual supply chains specific to producers, suppliers, and customers that work together to design, manufacture, distribute, market, sell, and service a product. This set of partners may change according to a given market, region, or channel, resulting in a proliferation of trading partner environments, each with its own unique characteristics and demands.

SPECIALIZATION ERA (PHASE II): SUPPLY CHAIN MANAGEMENT AS A SERVICE

Specialization within the supply chain began in the 1980s with the inception of transportation brokerages, warehouse management, and non-asset-based carriers, and has matured beyond transportation and logistics into aspects of supply planning, collaboration, execution, and performance management.

Market forces sometimes demand rapid changes from suppliers, logistics providers, locations, or customers in their role as components of supply chain networks. This variability has significant effects on supply chain infrastructure, from the foundation layers of establishing and managing electronic communication between trading partners, to more complex requirements such as the configuration of processes and work flows that are essential to the management of the network itself. Supply chain specialization enables companies to improve their overall competencies in the same way that outsourced manufacturing and distribution has done; it allows them to focus on their core competencies and assemble networks of specific, best-in-class partners to contribute to the overall value chain itself, thereby increasing overall performance and efficiency. The ability to quickly obtain and deploy this domain-specific supply chain expertise without developing and maintaining an entirely unique and complex competency in house is a leading reason why supply chain specialization is gaining popularity.

Outsourced technology hosting for supply chain solutions debuted in the late 1990s and has taken root primarily in transportation and collaboration categories. This has progressed from the application service provider (ASP) model from roughly 1998 through 2003, to the on-demand model from approximately 2003 through 2006, to the software as a service (SaaS) model currently in focus today.

SUPPLY CHAIN MANAGEMENT 2.0 (SCM 2.0)

Building on globalization and specialization, the term "SCM 2.0" has been coined to describe both changes within supply chains themselves as well as the evolution of processes, methods, and tools to manage them in this new "era". The growing popularity of collaborative platforms is highlighted by the rise of TradeCard's supply chain collaboration platform, which connects multiple buyers and suppliers with financial institutions, enabling them to conduct automated supply-chain finance transactions.

Web 2.0 is a trend in the use of the World Wide Web that is meant to increase creativity, information sharing, and collaboration among users. At its core, the common attribute of Web 2.0 is to help navigate the vast information available on the Web in order to find what is being bought. It is the notion of a usable pathway. SCM 2.0 replicates this notion in supply chain operations.

It is the pathway to SCM results, a combination of processes, methodologies, tools, and delivery options to guide companies to their results quickly as the complexity and speed of the supply chain increase due to global competition; rapid price fluctuations; surging oil prices; short product life cycles; expanded specialization; near-, far-, and off-shoring; and talent scarcity.

SCM 2.0 leverages solutions designed to rapidly deliver results with the agility to quickly manage future change for continuous flexibility, value, and success. This is delivered through competency networks composed of best-of-breed supply chain expertise to understand which elements, both operationally and organizationally, deliver results, as well as through intimate understanding of how to manage these elements to achieve the desired results. The solutions are delivered in a variety of options, such as no-touch via business process outsourcing, mid-touch via managed services and software as a service (SaaS), or high-touch in the traditional software deployment model.

BUSINESS PROCESS INTEGRATION

Successful SCM requires a change from managing individual functions to integrating activities into key supply chain processes. In an example scenario, a purchasing department places orders as its requirements become known. The marketing department, responding to customer demand, communicates with several distributors and retailers as it attempts to determine ways to satisfy this demand. Information shared between supply chain partners can only be fully leveraged through process integration.

Supply chain business process integration involves collaborative work between buyers and suppliers, joint product development, common systems, and shared information. According to Lambert and Cooper (2000), operating an integrated supply chain requires a continuous information flow. However, in many companies, management has concluded that optimizing product flows cannot be accomplished without implementing a process approach. The key supply chain processes stated by Lambert are:

- Customer relationship management
- Customer service management
- Demand management style
- Order fulfillment
- Manufacturing flow management
- Supplier relationship management
- Product development and commercialization
- Returns management

Much has been written about demand management. Best-in-class companies have similar characteristics, which include the following:

- Internal and external collaboration
- Initiatives to reduce lead time
- Tighter feedback from customer and market demand
- Customer-level forecasting

One could suggest other critical supply business processes that combine these processes stated by Lambert, such as:

- Customer service management process: Customer relationship management concerns the relationship between an organization and its customers. Customer service is the source of customer information. It also provides the customer with real-time information on scheduling and product availability through interfaces with the company's production and distribution operations. Successful organizations use the following steps to build customer relationships:
  - Determine mutually satisfying goals for organization and customers

- Establish and maintain customer rapport
- Induce positive feelings in the organization and the customers

- Procurement process: Strategic plans are drawn up with suppliers to support the manufacturing flow management process and the development of new products. In firms whose operations extend globally, sourcing may be managed on a global basis. The desired outcome is a relationship where both parties benefit and a reduction in the time required for the product's design and development. The purchasing function may also develop rapid communication systems, such as electronic data interchange (EDI) and Internet linkage, to convey possible requirements more rapidly. Activities related to obtaining products and materials from outside suppliers involve resource planning, supply sourcing, negotiation, order placement, inbound transportation, storage, handling, and quality assurance, many of which include the responsibility to coordinate with suppliers on matters of scheduling, supply continuity, hedging, and research into new sources or programs.
- Product development and commercialization: Here, customers and suppliers must be integrated into the product development process in order to reduce the time to market. As product life cycles shorten, the appropriate products must be developed and successfully launched with ever-shorter time schedules in order for firms to remain competitive. According to Lambert and Cooper, managers of the product development and commercialization process must:
  - Coordinate with customer relationship management to identify customer-articulated needs;
  - Select materials and suppliers in conjunction with procurement; and
  - Develop production technology in manufacturing flow to manufacture and integrate into the best supply chain flow for the given combination of product and markets.
- Manufacturing flow management process: The manufacturing process produces and supplies products to the distribution channels based on past forecasts. Manufacturing processes must be flexible in order to respond to market changes and must accommodate mass customization. Orders are processes operating on a just-in-time (JIT) basis in minimum lot sizes. Changes in the manufacturing flow process lead to shorter cycle times, meaning improved responsiveness and efficiency in meeting customer demand. This process manages activities related to planning, scheduling, and supporting manufacturing operations, such as work-in-process storage, handling, transportation, and time phasing of components, inventory at manufacturing sites, and maximum flexibility in the

coordination of geographical and final assemblies postponement of physical distribution operations.

- Physical distribution: This concerns the movement of a finished product or service to customers. In physical distribution, the customer is the final destination of a marketing channel, and the availability of the product or service is a vital part of each channel participant's marketing effort. It is also through the physical distribution process that the time and space of customer service become an integral part of marketing. Thus it links a marketing channel with its customers (i.e., it links manufacturers, wholesalers, and retailers).
- Outsourcing/partnerships: This includes not just the outsourcing of the procurement of materials and components, but also the outsourcing of services that traditionally have been provided in house. The logic of this trend is that the company will increasingly focus on those activities in the value chain in which it has a distinctive advantage and outsource everything else. This movement has been particularly evident in logistics, where the provision of transport, warehousing, and inventory control is increasingly subcontracted to specialists or logistics partners. Also, managing and controlling this network of partners and suppliers requires a blend of central and local involvement: strategic decisions are taken centrally, while the monitoring and control of supplier performance and day-to-day liaison with logistics partners are best managed locally.
- Performance measurement: Experts found a strong relationship from the largest arcs of supplier and customer integration to market share and profitability. Taking advantage of supplier capabilities and emphasizing a long-term supply chain perspective in customer relationships can both be correlated with a firm's performance. As logistics competency becomes a critical factor in creating and maintaining competitive advantage, measuring logistics performance becomes increasingly important, because the difference between profitable and unprofitable operations becomes narrower. A.T. Kearney Consultants (1985) noted that firms engaging in comprehensive performance measurement realized improvements in overall productivity. According to experts, internal measures are generally collected and analyzed by the firm, including cost, customer service, productivity, asset measurement, and quality. External performance is measured through customer perception measures and "best practice" benchmarking.
- Warehousing management: To reduce a company's cost and expenses, warehousing management is carrying the valuable role

against operations. In the case of perfect storage and office with all convenient facilities in company level, reducing manpower cost, dispatching authority with on time delivery, loading & unloading facilities with proper area, area for service station, stock management system etc.

THEORIES

Currently there is a gap in the literature on supply chain management studies: there is no theoretical support for explaining the existence or the boundaries of supply chain management. A few authors, such as Halldorsson et al., Ketchen and Hult, and Lavassani et al., have tried to provide theoretical foundations for different areas related to supply chain by employing organizational theories. These theories include:

- Resource-based view (RBV)
- Transaction cost analysis (TCA)
- Knowledge-based view (KBV)
- Strategic choice theory (SCT)
- Agency theory (AT)
- Channel coordination
- Institutional theory (InT)
- Systems theory (ST)
- Network perspective (NP)
- Materials logistics management (MLM)
- Just-in-time (JIT)
- Material requirements planning (MRP)
- Theory of constraints (TOC)
- Total quality management (TQM)
- Agile manufacturing
- Time-based competition (TBC)
- Quick response manufacturing (QRM)
- Customer relationship management (CRM)
- Requirements chain management (RCM)
- Available-to-promise (ATP)

However, the unit of analysis of most of these theories is not the supply chain but rather another system, such as the firm or the supplier-buyer relationship. Among the few exceptions is the relational view, which outlines a theory for considering dyads and networks of firms as a key unit of analysis for explaining superior individual firm performance.

RESOURCE-BASED VIEW

The resource-based view (RBV) as a basis for the competitive advantage of a firm lies primarily in the application of a bundle of valuable tangible or intangible resources at the firm's disposal. To transform a short-run competitive advantage into a sustained competitive advantage requires that these resources are heterogeneous in nature and not perfectly mobile. Effectively, this translates into valuable resources that are neither perfectly imitable nor substitutable without great effort. If these conditions hold, the bundle of resources can sustain the firm's above average returns. The VRIO and VRIN model also constitutes a part of RBV. There is strong evidence that supports the RBV.

Key Points

The key points of the theory are:

1. Identify the firm's potential key resources.
2. Evaluate whether these resources fulfill the following criteria:
   - *Valuable* – A resource must enable a firm to employ a value-creating strategy, by either outperforming its competitors or reduce its own weaknesses. Relevant in this perspective is that the transaction costs associated with the investment in the resource cannot be higher than the discounted future rents that flow out of the value-creating strategy.
   - *Rare* – To be of value, a resource must be rare by definition. In a perfectly competitive strategic factor market for a resource, the price of the resource will be a reflection of the expected discounted future above-average returns.
   - *In-imitable* – If a valuable resource is controlled by only one firm it could be a source of a competitive advantage. This advantage could be sustainable if competitors are not able to duplicate this strategic asset perfectly. The term isolating mechanism was introduced by Rumelt to explain why firms might not be able to imitate a resource to the degree that they are able to compete with the firm having the valuable resource. An important underlying factor of inimitability is causal ambiguity, which occurs if the source from which a firm's competitive advantage stems is unknown. If the resource in question is knowledge-based or socially complex, causal ambiguity is more likely to occur as these types of resources are more likely to be idiosyncratic to the firm in which it resides. Conner and Prahalad go so far as to say knowledge-based resources are *"...the essence of the resource-based perspective"*.
   - *Non-substitutable* – Even if a resource is rare, potentially value-creating and imperfectly imitable, an equally important aspect is lack of substitutability. If competitors are able to counter the firm's value-creating strategy with a substitute, prices are driven down to the point that the price equals the discounted future rents, resulting in zero economic profits.

3. Care for and protect resources that possess these evaluations, because doing so can improve organizational performance.

The VRIN characteristics mentioned are individually necessary, but not sufficient conditions for a sustained competitive advantage. Within the framework of the resource-based view, the chain is as strong as its weakest link and therefore requires the resource to display each of the four characteristics to be a possible source of a sustainable competitive advantage.

Definitions

A subsequent distinction, made by Amit & Schoemaker is that the encompassing construct previously called "resources" can be divided into resources and capabilities. In this respect, resources are tradable and non-specific to the firm, while capabilities are firm-specific and are used to engage the resources within the firm, such as implicit processes to transfer knowledge within the firm. This distinction has been widely adopted throughout the resource-based view literature.

What constitutes a "capability"?

Makadok emphasizes the distinction between capabilities and resources by defining capabilities as "a special type of resource, specifically an organizationally embedded non-transferable firm-specific resource whose purpose is to improve the productivity of the other resources possessed by the firm". "[R]esources are stocks of available factors that are owned or controlled by the organization, and capabilities are an organization's capacity to deploy resources". Essentially, it is the bundling of the resources that builds capabilities.

What constitutes "competitive advantage"?

A competitive advantage can be attained if the current strategy is value-creating, and not currently being implemented by present or possible future competitors. Although a competitive advantage has the ability to become sustained, this is not necessarily the case. A competing firm can enter the market with a resource that has the ability to invalidate the prior firm's competitive advantage, which results in reduced rents. Sustainability in the context of a sustainable competitive advantage is independent with regard to the time frame. Rather, a competitive advantage is sustainable when the efforts by competitors to render the competitive advantage redundant have ceased. When the imitative actions have come to an end without disrupting the firm's competitive advantage, the firm's strategy can be called sustainable. This is in contrast to views of others that a competitive advantage is sustained when it provides above-average returns in the long run.

History of the resource-based view

Some aspects of theories are thought of long before they are formally adopted and brought together into the strict framework of an academic theory. The same could be said with regard to the resource-based view.

While this influential body of research within the field of Strategic Management was named by Birger Wernerfelt in his article A Resource-Based View of the Firm, the origins of the resource-based view can be traced back to earlier research. Retrospectively, elements can be found in works by Coase, Selznick (1957), Penrose (1959), Stigler (1961), Chandler (1962, 1977), and Williamson (1975), where emphasis is put on the importance of resources and its implications for firm performance. This paradigm shift from the narrow neoclassical focus to a broader rationale, and the coming closer of different academic fields (industrial organization economics and organizational economics being most prominent) was a particular important contribution.

Two publications closely following Wernerfelt's initial article came from Barney (1986a, 1986b). Even though Wernerfelt was not referenced directly, the statements made by Barney about strategic factor markets and the role of expectations can clearly be seen within the resource-based framework as later developed by Barney (1991). Other concepts that were later integrated into the resource-based framework have been articulated by Lippman and Rumelt (uncertain imitability, 1982), Rumelt (isolating mechanisms, 1984) and Dierickx and Cool (inimitability and its causes, 1989). Barney's framework proved a solid foundation upon which others might build, and its theoretical underpinnings were strengthened by Conner (1991), Mahoney and Pandian (1992), Conner and Prahalad (1996) and Makadok (2001), who positioned the resource-based view with regard to various other research fields. More practical approaches were provided for by Amit and Shoemaker (1993), while later criticism came from among others from Priem and Butler and Hoopes, Madsen and Walker.

The resource based view has been a common interest for management researchers and numerous writings could be found for same. A resource-based view of a firm explains its ability to deliver sustainable competitive advantage when resources are managed such that their outcomes can not be imitated by competitors, which ultimately creates a competitive barrier. RBV explains that a firm's sustainable competitive advantage is reached by virtue of unique resources being rare, valuable, inimitable, non-tradable, and non-substitutable, as well as firm-specific.

These authors write about the fact that a firm may reach a sustainable competitive advantage through unique resources which it holds, and these resources cannot be easily bought, transferred, or copied, and simultaneously, they add value to a firm while being rare. It also highlights the fact that not all resources of a firm may contribute to a firm's sustainable competitive advantage. Varying performance between firms is a result of heterogeneity of assets and RBV is focused on the factors that cause these differences to prevail.

Fundamental similarity in these writings is that unique value-creating resources will generate a sustainable competitive advantage to the extent that no competitor has the ability to use the same type of resources, either through acquisition or imitation. Major concern in RBV is focused on the ability of the firm to maintain a combination of resources that cannot be possessed or built up in a similar manner by competitors. Further such writings provide us with the base to understand that the sustainability strength of competitive advantage depends on the ability of competitors to use identical or similar resources that make the same implications on a firm's performance. This ability of a firm to avoid imitation of their resources should be analyzed in depth to understand the sustainability strength of a competitive advantage.

Barriers to imitation of resources

Resources are the inputs or the factors available to a company which helps to perform its operations or carry out its activities. Also, these authors state that resources, if considered as isolated factors, do not result in productivity; hence, coordination of resources is important. The ways a firm can create a barrier to imitation are known as "isolating mechanisms", and are reflected in the aspects of corporate culture, managerial capabilities, information asymmetries and property rights. Further, they mention that except for legislative restrictions created through property rights, the other three aspects are direct or indirect results of managerial practices.

King mentions inter-firm causal ambiguity may results in sustainable competitive advantage for some firms. Causal ambiguity is the continuum that describes the degree to which decision makers understand the relationship between organizational inputs and outputs. Their argument is that inability of competitors to understand what causes the superior performance of another (inter-firm causal ambiguity), helps to reach a sustainable competitive advantage for the one who is presently performing at a superior level. Holley and Greenley state that social context of certain resource conditions act as an element to create isolating mechanisms and quote Wernerfelt (1986) that tacitness (accumulated skill-based resources acquired through learning by doing) complexity (large number of inter-related resources being used) and specificity (dedication of certain resources to specific activities) and ultimately, these three characteristics will result in a competitive barrier.

Referring back to the definitions stated previously regarding the competitive advantage that mentions superior performance is correlated to resources of the firm and consolidating writings of King stated above, we may derive the fact that inter-firm causal ambiguity regarding resources will generate a competitive advantage at a sustainable level. Further, it explains that the depth of understanding of competitors—regarding which resources underlie the superior performance—will determine the sustainability strength of a competitive advantage. Should a firm be unable to overcome the inter-firm causal ambiguity, this does not necessarily result in imitating resources. As to Johnson and Mahoney, even after recognizing competitors' valuable resources, a firm may not imitate due to the social context of these resources or availability of more pursuing alternatives. Certain resources, like company reputation, are path-dependent and are accumulated over time, and a competitor may not be able to perfectly imitate such resources.

They argue on the basis that certain resources, even if imitated, may not bring the same impact, since the maximum impact of the same is achieved over longer periods of time. Hence, such imitation will not be successful. In consideration of the reputation of fact as a resource and whether a late entrant may exploit any opportunity for a competitive advantage, Kim and Park mention three reasons why new entrants may be outperformed by earlier entrants. First, early entrants have a technological know-how which helps them to perform at a superior level. Secondly, early entrants have developed capabilities with time that enhance their strength to out-perform late entrants. Thirdly, switching costs incurred to customers, if they decide to migrate, will help early entrants to dominate the market, evading the late entrants' opportunity to capture market share. Customer awareness and loyalty is another rational benefit early entrants enjoy.

However, first mover advantage is active in evolutionary technological transitions, which are technological innovations based on previous developments. The same authors further argue that revolutionary technological changes (changes that significantly disturb the existing technology) will eliminate the advantage of early entrants. Such writings elaborate that though early entrants enjoy certain resources by virtue of the forgone time periods in the markets, rapidly changing technological environments may make those resources obsolete and curtail the firm's dominance. Late entrants may comply with the technological innovativeness and increased pressure of competition, seeking a competitive advantage by making the existing competencies and resources of early entrants invalid or outdated. In other words, innovative technological implications will significantly change the landscape of the industry and the market, making early movers' advantage minimal. However, in a market where technology does not play a dynamic role, early mover advantage may prevail.

Analyzing the above-developed framework for the Resource-Based View, it reflects a unique feature, namely, that sustainable competitive advantage is achieved in an environment where competition does not exist. According to the characteristics of the Resource-based view, rival firms may not perform at a level that could be identified as considerable competition for the incumbents of the market, since they do not possess the required resources to perform at a level that creates a threat and competition. Through barriers to imitation, incumbents ensure that rival firms do not reach a level at which they may perform in a similar manner to the former. In other words, the sustainability of the winning edge is determined by the strength of not letting other firms compete at the same level. The moment competition becomes active, competitive advantage becomes ineffective, since two or more firms begin to perform at a superior level, evading the possibility of single-firm dominance; hence, no firm will enjoy a competitive advantage. Ma agrees stating that, by definition, the sustainable competitive advantage discussed in the Resource based view is anti-competitive. Further such sustainable competitive advantage could exist in the world of no competitive imitation.

Based on the empirical writings stated above, RBV provides the understanding that certain unique existing resources will result in superior performance and ultimately build a competitive advantage. Sustainability of such an advantage will be determined by the ability of competitors to imitate such resources.

However, the existing resources of a firm may not be adequate to facilitate the future market requirement, due to volatility of the contemporary markets. There is a vital need to modify and develop resources in order to encounter the future market competition.

An organization should exploit existing business opportunities using the present resources while generating and developing a new set of resources to sustain its competitiveness in the future market environments; hence, an organization should be engaged in resource management and resource development. Their writings explain that in order to sustain the competitive advantage, it is crucial to develop resources that will strengthen the firm's ability to continue the superior performance.

Any industry or market reflects high uncertainty and, in order to survive and stay ahead of competition, new resources become highly necessary. Morgan agrees, stating that the need to update resources is a major management task since all business environments reflect highly unpredictable market and environmental conditions. The existing winning edge needed to be developed since various market dynamics may make existing value-creating resources obsolete.

Criticism

Priem and Butler raised four key points of criticism:

- The RBV is tautological, or self-verifying. Barney has defined a competitive advantage as a value-creating strategy that is based on resources that are, among other characteristics, valuable. This reasoning is circular and therefore operationally invalid.
- Different resource configurations can generate the same value for firms and thus would not be competitive advantage
- The role of product markets is underdeveloped in the argument
- The theory has limited prescriptive implications

However, Barney provided counter-arguments to these points of criticism.

Further criticisms are:

- It is perhaps difficult (if not impossible) to find a resource which satisfies all of the Barney's VRIN criteria.
- There is the assumption that a firm can be profitable in a highly competitive market as long as it can exploit advantageous resources, but this may not necessarily be the case. It ignores external factors concerning the industry as a whole; a firm should also consider Porter's Industry Structure Analysis (Porter's Five Forces).
- Long-term implications that flow from its premises: A prominent source of sustainable competitive advantages is causal ambiguity. While this is undeniably true, this leaves an awkward possibility: the firm is not able to manage a resource it does not know exists, even if a changing environment requires this. Through such an external change, the initial sustainable competitive advantage could be nullified or even transformed into a weakness.
- Premise of efficient markets: Much research hinges on the premise that markets in general or factor markets are efficient, and that firms are capable of precisely pricing in the exact future value of any value-creating strategy that could flow from the resource. Dierickx and Cool argue that purchasable assets cannot be sources of sustained competitive advantage, just because they can be purchased. Either the price of the resource will increase to the point that it equals the future above-average return, or other competitors will purchase the resource as well and use it in a value-increasing strategy that diminishes rents to zero.
- The concept of rarity is obsolete: Although prominently present in Wernerfelt's original articulation of the resource-based view (1984) and Barney's subsequent framework (1991), the concept that resources need to be rare to be able to function as a possible source of a sustained competitive advantage is unnecessary. Because of the implications of the other concepts any resource that follows from the previous characteristics is inherently rare.
- Sustainable: The lack of an exact definition of sustainability makes its premise difficult to test empirically. Barney's statement that the competitive advantage is sustained if current and future rivals have ceased their imitative efforts is versatile from the point of view of developing a theoretical framework, but is a disadvantage from a more practical point of view, as there is no explicit end-goal.

The relational view is an extension of the resource-based view for considering networks and dyads of firms as the unit of analysis to explain relational rents, i.e., superior individual firm performance generated within that network/dyad.

CHANNEL COORDINATION

Channel coordination (or supply chain coordination) aims at improving supply chain performance by aligning the plans and the objectives of individual enterprises. It usually focuses on inventory management and ordering decisions in distributed inter-company settings. Channel coordination models may involve multi-echelon inventory theory, multiple decision makers, asymmetric information, as well as recent paradigms of manufacturing, such as mass customization, short product life-cycles, outsourcing and delayed differentiation. The theoretical foundations of the coordination are based chiefly on the contract theory. The problem of channel coordination was first modeled and analyzed by Anantasubramania Kumar in 1992.

The decentralized decision making in supply chains leads to a dilemma situation which results in a suboptimal overall performance called double marginalization. Recently, partners in permanent supply chains tend to extend the coordination of their decisions in order to improve the performance for all of the participants. Some practical realizations of this approach are Collaborative Planning, Forecasting, and Replenishment (CPFR), Vendor Managed Inventory (VMI) and Quick Response (QR).

The theory of channel coordination aims at supporting the performance optimization by developing arrangements for aligning the different objectives of the partners. These are called coordination mechanisms or schemes, which control the flows of information, materials (or service) and financial assets along the chains. In general, a contracting scheme should consist of the following components:

- Local planning methods which consider the constraints and objectives of the individual partners,
- An infrastructure and protocol for information sharing, and
- An incentive scheme for aligning the individual interests of the partners.

The appropriate planning methods are necessary for optimizing the behavior of the production. The second component should support the information visibility and transparency both within and among the partners and facilitates the realization of real-time enterprises. Finally, the third component should guarantee that the partners act upon to the common goals of the supply chain.

The general method for studying coordination consists of two steps. At first, one assumes a central decision maker with complete information who solves the problem. The result is a first-best solution which provides bound on the obtainable system-wide performance objective. In the second step one regards the decentralized problem and designs such a contract protocol that approaches or even achieves the performance of the first-best.

A contract is said to coordinate the channel, if thereby the partners' optimal local decisions lead to optimal system-wide performance. Channel coordination is achievable in several simple models, but it is more difficult (or even impossible) in more realistic cases and in the practice. Therefore the aim is often only the achievement of mutual benefit compared to the uncoordinated situation. Another widely studied alternative direction for channel coordination is the application of some negotiation protocols. Such approaches apply iterative solution methods, where the partners exchange proposals and counter-proposals until an agreement is reached. For this reason, this approach is commonly referred to as collaborative planning. The negotiation protocols can be characterized according to the following criteria:

- The initial proposal is most frequently generated by the buyer company which is called upstream planning. By contrast, when the initiator is the supplier, it is referred to as downstream planning. In several cases there already exists an initial plan (e.g., using rolling schedules or frame plans). There are also some protocols where the initial plan is generated randomly.
- In order to guarantee finite runtime, the maximal number of rounds should be determined. In addition, the protocol should also specify the number of plans offered in each round. When the number of rounds or plans is high, the practical application necessitates fast local planner systems in order to quickly evaluate the proposals and generate counter-proposals.
- Generally, the negotiation protocols cannot provide optimality, and they require some special conditions to assure convergence.
- The counter-proposals usually define side-payments (compensations) between the companies in order to inspire the partner deviating from its previously proposed plan.

An also commonly used instrument for aligning plans of different decision makers is the application of some auction mechanisms. However, "auctions are most applicable in pure market interactions at the boundaries of a supply chain but not within a supply chain3, therefore they are usually not considered as channel coordination approaches.

Characteristics of coordination schemes

There are several classifications of channel coordination contracts, but they are not complete, and the considered classes are not disjoint. Instead of a complete classification, a set of aspects are enumerated below which generalizes the existing taxonomies by allowing classification along multiple viewpoints.

Problem characteristics

Horizon

Most of the related models consider either one-period horizon or two-period horizon with forecast update. In the latter, the production can be based on the preliminary forecast with normal production mode or on the updated forecast with emergency production, which means shorter lead-time, but higher cost. Besides, the horizon can consist of multiple periods and it can be even infinite. The practically most widespread approach is the rolling horizon planning, i.e., updating and extending an existing plan in each period.

Number of products

Almost all contract-based models regard only one product. Some models study the special cases of substitute or complementary products. However, considering more products in the general case is necessary if technological or financial constraints—like capacity or budget limits—exist.

Demand characteristic

On one hand, the demand can be stochastic (uncertain) or deterministic. On the other hand, it can be considered static (constant over time) or dynamic (e.g., having seasonality).

Risk treatment

In most of the models the players are regarded to be risk neutral. This means that they intend to maximize their expected profit (or minimize their expected costs). However, some studies regard risk averse players who want to find an acceptable trade-off considering both the expected value and the variance of the profit.

Shortage treatment

The models differ in their attitude towards stockouts. Most authors consider either backlogs, when the demand must be fulfilled later at the expense of providing lower price or lost sales which also includes some theoretical costs (e.g., loss of goodwill, loss of profit, etc.). Some models include a service level constraint, which limits the occurrence or quantity of expected stockouts. Even the 100% service level can be achieved with additional or emergency production (e.g., overtime, outsourcing) for higher costs.

Parameters and variables

This viewpoint shows the largest variations in the different models. The main decision variables are quantity-related (production quantity, order quantity, number of options, etc.), but sometimes prices are also decision variables. The parameters can be either constant or stochastic. The most common parameters are related to costs: fixed (ordering or setup) cost, production cost and inventory holding cost. These are optional; many models disregard fixed or inventory holding costs. There exist numerous other parameters: prices for the different contracts, salvage value, shortage penalty, lead-time, etc.

Basic model and solution technique

Most of the one-period models apply the newsvendor model. On two-period horizon, this is extended with the possibility of two production modes. On a multiple period horizon the base-stock, or in case of deterministic demand the EOQ models are the most widespread. In such cases the optimal solution can be determined with simple algebraic operations. These simple models usually completely disregard technological constraints; however, in real industrial cases resource capacity, inventory or budget constraints may be relevant. This necessitates more complex models, such as LP, MIP, stochastic program, and thus more powerful mathematical programming techniques may be required.

As for the optimization criteria, the most usual objectives are the profit maximization or cost minimization, but other alternatives are also conceivable, e.g., throughput time minimization. Considering multiple criteria is not yet prevalent in the coordination literature.

Decentralization characteristics

Number and role of the players

The most often studied dilemmas involve the two players and call them customer and supplier (or buyer-seller). There are also extensions of this simple model: the multiple customers with correlated demand and the multiple suppliers with different production parameters. Multi-echelon extensions are also conceivable, however, sparse in the literature. When the coordination is within a supply chain (typically a customer-supplier relation), it is called vertical, otherwise horizontal. An example for the latter is when different suppliers of the same customer coordinate their transportation. Sometimes the roles of the participants are also important. The most frequently considered companies are manufacturers, retailers, distributors or logistic companies.

Relation of the players

One of the most important characteristics of the coordination is the power relations of the players. The power is influenced by several factors, such as possessed process know-how, number of competitors, ratio in the value creation, access to the market and financial resources.

The players can behave in a cooperative or opportunistic way. In the former case, they share a common goal and act like a team, while in the latter situation each player is interested only in its own goals. These two behaviors are usually present in a mixed form, since the opportunistic claims for profitability and growth are sustainable usually only with a certain cooperative attitude. The relation can be temporary or permanent. In the temporary case usually one- or two-period models are applied, or even an auction mechanism. However, the coordination is even more important in permanent relations, where the planning is usually done in a rolling horizon manner. When coordinating a permanent supply relation, one has to consider the learning effect, i.e., players intend to learn each other's private information and behavior.

Goal of the coordination

The simplest possible coordination is aimed only at aligning the (material) flows within the supply chain in order to gain executable plans and avoid shortages. In a more advanced form of coordination, the partners intend to improve supply chain performance by approaching or even achieving the optimal plan according to some criteria. Generally, a coordinated plan may incur losses for some of the players compared to the uncoordinated situation, which necessitates some kind of side-payment in order to provide a win-win situation. In addition, even some sort of fairness may be required, but it is not only hard to guarantee, but even to define.

Most of the coordination approaches requires that the goal should be achieved in an equilibrium in order to exclude the possibility that an opportunistic player deviates from the coordinated plan.

Information structure

Some papers study the symmetric information case, when all of the players know exactly the same parameters. This approach is very convenient for cost and profit sharing, since all players know the incurring system cost. The asymmetric case, when there is an information gap between the players is more realistic, but poses new challenges. The asymmetry typically concerns either the cost parameters, the capacities or the quantities like the demand forecast. The demand and the forecast are often considered to be qualitative, limited to only two possible values: high and low. In case of stochastic demand, the uncertainty of the forecasts can also be private information.

Decision structure

The decision making roles of the players depend on the specified decision variables. However, there is a more-or-less general classification in this aspect: forced and voluntary compliance. Under forced compliance the supplier is responsible for satisfying all orders of the customer, therefore it does not have the opportunity to decide about the production quantity. Under voluntary compliance, the supplier decides about the production quantity and it cannot be forced to fill an order. This latter is more complex analytically, but more realistic as well. Even so, several papers assume that the supplier decides about the price and then the customer decides the order quantity.

Game theoretic model

From the viewpoint of game theory the models can take cooperative or non-cooperative approaches. The cooperative approach studies, how the players form coalitions therefore these models are usually applied on the strategic level of network design. Other typical form of cooperative games involves some bargaining framework—e.g., the Nash bargaining model—for agreeing upon the parameters of the applied contracts. On the other hand, on the operational level, the non-cooperative approach is used. Usually the sequential Stackelberg game model is considered, where one of the players, the leader moves first and then the follower reacts. Both cases—the supplier or the customer as the Stackelberg leader—are widely studied in the literature. In case of information asymmetry, a similar sequential model is used and it is called principal–agent setting. The study of the long-term supply relationship can also be modeled as a repeated game. To sum up, a collaboration generally consists of a cooperative, followed by a non-cooperative game. However, most researches concentrate only on one of the phases.

Involvement of a mediator

Some coordination mechanisms require the existence of an independent, trusted third party. If such a mediator exists, the powerful theory of the market mechanism design can be applied for channel coordination. Although at first glance the involvement of a third party seems to be unrealistic, in the area of planning such mediators already exist as application service providers.

Contract types

There are many variants of the contracts, some widespread forms are briefly described below. Besides, there exist several combinations and customized approaches, too.

Two-part tariff

In this case the customer pays not only for the purchased goods, but in addition a fixed amount called franchise fee per order. This is intended to compensate the supplier for his fixed setup cost.

Sales rebate

This contract specifies two prices and a quantity threshold. If the order size is below the threshold, the customer pays the higher price, and if it is above, she pays a lower price for the units above the threshold.

Quantity discount

Under quantity discount contract, the customer pays a wholesale price depending on the order quantity. This resembles to the sales rebate contract, but there is no threshold defined. The mechanism for specifying the contract can be complex. The contract has been applied in many situations, for example, in an international supply chain with fluctuating exchange rates.

Capacity options

While advance capacity purchase is popular in the supply chain practice, there are situations where a manufacturer prefers to delay its capacity purchase to have better information about the uncertain demand.

Buyback/return

With these types of contracts the supplier offers that it will buy back the remaining obsolete inventory at a discounted price. This supports the sharing of inventory risk between the partners. A variation of this contract is the backup agreement, where the customer gives a preliminary forecast and then makes an order less or equal to the forecasted quantity. If the order is less, it must also pay a proportional penalty for the remaining obsolete inventory. Buyback agreements are widespread in the newspaper, book, CD and fashion industries.

Quantity flexibility

In this case the customer gives a preliminary forecast and then it can give fixed order in an interval around the forecast. Such contracts are widespread in several markets, e.g., among the suppliers of the European automotive industry.

Revenue sharing

With revenue sharing the customer pays not only for the purchased goods, but also shares a given percentage of her revenue with the supplier. This contract is successfully used in video cassette rental and movie exhibition fields. It can be proved, that the optimal revenue sharing and buyback contracts are equivalent, i.e., they generate the same profits for the partners.

Options

The option contracts are originated from the product and stock exchange. With an option contract, the customer can give fixed orders in advance, as well as buy rights to purchase more (call option) or return (put option) products later. The options can be bought at a predefined option price and executed at the execution price. This approach is a generalization of some previous contract types.

VMI contract

This contract can be used when the buyer does not order, only communicates the forecasts and consumes from the inventory filled by the supplier. The VMI contract specifies that not only the consumed goods should be paid, but also the forecast imprecision, i.e., the difference between the estimated and realized demand. In this way, the buyer is inspired to increase the forecast quality, and the risk of market uncertainty is shared between the partners.

JUST IN TIME

Just in time (JIT) is a production strategy that strives to improve a business return on investment by reducing in-process inventory and associated carrying costs. To meet JIT objectives, the process relies on signals or Kanban between different points, which are involved in the process, which tell production when to make the next part. Kanban are usually 'tickets' but can be simple visual signals, such as the presence or absence of a part on a shelf. Implemented correctly, JIT focuses on continuous improvement and can improve a manufacturing organization's return on investment, quality, and efficiency. To achieve continuous improvement key areas of focus could be flow, employee involvement and quality.

JIT relies on other elements in the inventory chain as well. For instance, its effective application cannot be independent of other key components of a lean manufacturing system or it can "end up with the opposite of the desired result." In recent years manufacturers have continued to try to hone forecasting methods such as applying a trailing 13-week average as a better predictor for JIT planning; however, some research demonstrates that basing JIT on the presumption of stability is inherently flawed.

Philosophy

The philosophy of JIT is simple: the storage of unused inventory is a waste of resources. JIT inventory systems expose hidden cost of keeping inventory, and are therefore not a simple solution for a company to adopt it. The company must follow an array of new methods to manage the consequences of the change. The ideas in this way of working come from many different disciplines including statistics, industrial engineering, production management, and behavioral science. The JIT inventory philosophy defines how inventory is viewed and how it relates to management.

Inventory is seen as incurring costs, or waste, instead of adding and storing value, contrary to traditional accounting. This does not mean to say JIT is implemented without an awareness that removing inventory exposes pre-existing manufacturing issues. This way of working encourages businesses to eliminate inventory that does not compensate for manufacturing process issues, and to constantly improve those processes to require less inventory. Secondly, allowing any stock habituates management to stock keeping. Management may be tempted to keep stock to hide production problems. These problems include backups at work centers, machine reliability, process variability, lack of flexibility of employees and equipment, and inadequate capacity.

In short, the Just-in-Time inventory system focus is having "the right material, at the right time, at the right place, and in the exact amount", without the safety net of inventory. The JIT system has broad implications for implementers.

Transaction cost approach

JIT helps in keeping inventory to minimum in a firm. However, a firm may simply be outsourcing their input inventory to suppliers, even if those suppliers don't use Just-in-Time. Newman (1994) investigated this effect and found that suppliers in Japan charged JIT customers, on average, a 5% price premium.

Environmental concerns

During the birth of JIT, multiple daily deliveries were often made by bicycle. Increased scale has required a move to vans and trucks (lorries). Cusumano (1994) highlighted the potential and actual problems this causes with regard to gridlock and burning of fossil fuels. This violates three JIT waste guidelines:

1. Time—wasted in traffic jams
2. Inventory—specifically pipeline (in transport) inventory
3. Scrap—fuel burned while not physically moving

Price volatility

JIT implicitly assumes a level of input price stability that obviates the need to buy parts in advance of price rises. Where input prices are expected to rise, storing inventory may be desirable. However, decision of storing higher inventory, which will mean higher inventory cost need to be weighed with increased cost due to volatility in prices.

Quality volatility

JIT implicitly assumes that input parts quality remains constant over time. If not, firms may hoard high-quality inputs. As with price volatility, a solution is to work with selected suppliers to help them improve their processes to reduce variation and costs. Longer term price agreements can then be negotiated and agreed-on quality standards made the responsibility of the supplier. Fixing up of standards for volatility of quality according to the quality circle

Demand stability

Karmarker (1989) highlights the importance of relatively stable demand, which helps ensure efficient capital utilization rates. Karmarker cost production.

Supply stability

In the U.S., the 1992 railway strikes caused General Motors to idle a 75,000-worker plant because they had no supply.

Effects

A surprising effect of JIT was that car factory response time fell to about a day. This improved customer satisfaction by providing vehicles within a day or two of the minimum economic shipping delay. Also, the factory began building many vehicles to order, eliminating the risk they would not be sold. This improved the company's return on equity.

Since assemblers no longer had a choice of which part to use, every part had to fit perfectly. This caused a quality assurance crisis, which led to a dramatic improvement in product quality. Eventually, Toyota redesigned every part of its vehicles to widen tolerances, while simultaneously implementing careful statistical controls for quality control. Toyota had to test and train parts suppliers to assure quality and delivery. In some cases, the company eliminated multiple suppliers.

When a process or parts quality problem surfaced on the production line, the entire production line had to be slowed or even stopped. No inventory meant a line could not operate from in-process inventory while a production problem was fixed. Many people in Toyota predicted that the initiative would be abandoned for this reason. In the first week, line stops occurred almost hourly. But by the end of the first month, the rate had fallen to a few line stops per day. After six months, line stops had so little economic effect that Toyota installed an overhead pull-line, similar to a bus bell-pull, that let any worker on the line order a line stop for a process or quality problem. Even with this, line stops fell to a few per week.

The result was a factory that has been studied worldwide. It has been widely emulated, but not always with the expected results, as many firms fail to adopt the full system.

The just-in-time philosophy was also applied to other segments of the supply chain in several types of industries. In the commercial sector, it meant eliminating one or all of the warehouses in the link between a factory and a retail establishment. Examples in sales, marketing, and customer service involve applying information systems and mobile hardware to deliver customer information as needed, and reducing waste by video conferencing to cut travel time.

Benefits

Main benefits of JIT include:

- *Reduced setup time.* Cutting setup time allows the company to reduce or eliminate inventory for "changeover" time. The tool used here is SMED (single-minute exchange of dies).
- *The flow of goods from warehouse to shelves improves.* Small or individual piece lot sizes reduce lot delay inventories, which simplifies inventory flow and its management.
- *Employees with multiple skills are used more efficiently.* Having employees trained to work on different parts of the process allows companies to move workers where they are needed.

- *Production scheduling and work hour consistency synchronized with demand.* If there is no demand for a product at the time, it is not made. This saves the company money, either by not having to pay workers overtime or by having them focus on other work or participate in training.
- *Increased emphasis on supplier relationships.* A company without inventory does not want a supply system problem that creates a part shortage. This makes supplier relationships extremely important.
- *Supplies come in at regular intervals throughout the production day.* Supply is synchronized with production demand and the optimal amount of inventory is on hand at any time. When parts move directly from the truck to the point of assembly, the need for storage facilities is reduced.
- *Minimizes storage space needed.*
- *Smaller chance of inventory breaking/expiring.*

Problems

Within a JIT system

Just-in-time operation leaves suppliers and downstream consumers open to supply shocks and large supply or demand changes. For internal reasons, Ohno saw this as a feature rather than a bug. He used an analogy of lowering the water level in a river to expose the rocks to explain how removing inventory showed where production flow was interrupted. Once barriers were exposed, they could be removed. Since one of the main barriers was rework, lowering inventory forced each shop to improve its own quality or cause a holdup downstream. A key tool to manage this weakness is production levelling to remove these variations. Just-in-time is a means to improving performance of the system, not an end.

Very low stock levels means shipments of the same part can come in several times per day. This means Toyota is especially susceptible to flow interruption. For that reason, Toyota uses two suppliers for most assemblies. As noted in Liker (2003), there was an exception to this rule that put the entire company at risk because of the 1997 Aisin fire. However, since Toyota also makes a point of maintaining high quality relations with its entire supplier network, several other suppliers immediately took up production of the Aisin-built parts by using existing capability and documentation.

Within a raw material stream

As noted by Liker (2003) and Womack and Jones (2003), it ultimately would be desirable to introduce synchronised flow and link JIT through the entire supply stream. However, none followed this in detail all the way back through the processes to the raw materials. With present technology, for example, an ear of corn cannot be grown and delivered to order. The same is true of most raw materials, which must be discovered and/or grown through natural processes that require time and must account for natural variability in weather and discovery. The part of this currently viewed as impossible is the *synchronised* part of flow and the *linked* part of JIT. It is for the reasons stated raw materials companies decouple their supply chain from their clients' demand by carrying large 'finished goods' stocks. Both flow and JIT can be implemented in isolated process islands within the raw materials stream. The challenge becomes to achieve that isolation by some means other than carrying huge stocks, as most do today.

Because of this, almost all value chains are split into a part made-to-forecast and a part that could, by using JIT, become make-to-order. Historically, the make-to-order part has often been within the retailer portion of the value chain. Toyota took Piggly Wiggly's supermarket replenishment system and drove it at least halfway through their automobile factories. Their challenge today is to drive it all the way back to their goods-inwards dock. Of course, the mining of iron and making of steel is still not connected to an order for a particular car. Recognising JIT could be driven back up the supply chain has reaped Toyota huge benefits and a dominant position in the auto industry. Note that the advent of the mini mill steelmaking facility is starting to challenge how far back JIT can be implemented, as the electric arc furnaces at the heart of many mini-mills can be started and stopped quickly, and steel grades changed rapidly.

Oil

It has been frequently charged that the oil industry has been influenced by JIT.

The argument is presented as follows:

- The number of refineries in the United States has fallen from 279 in 1975 to 205 in 1990 and further to 149 in 2004. As a result, the industry is susceptible to supply shocks, which cause spikes in prices and subsequently reduction in domestic manufacturing output. The effects of hurricanes Katrina and Rita are given as an example: in 2005, Katrina caused the shutdown of 9 refineries in Louisiana and 6 more in Mississippi, and a large number of oil production and transfer facilities, resulting in the loss of 20% of the US domestic refinery output. Rita subsequently shut down refineries in Texas, further reducing output. The GDP figures for the third and fourth quarters showed a slowdown from 3.5% to 1.2% growth. Similar arguments were made in earlier crises.

Beside the obvious point that prices went up because of the reduction in supply and not for anything to do with the practice of JIT, JIT students and even oil and gas industry analysts question whether JIT as it has been developed by Ohno, Goldratt, and others is used by the petroleum industry. Companies routinely shut down facilities for reasons other than the application of JIT. One of those reasons may be economic rationalization: when the benefits of operating no longer outweigh the costs, including opportunity costs, the plant may be economically inefficient. JIT has never subscribed to such considerations directly; following Waddel and Bodek (2005), this ROI-based thinking conforms more to Brown-style accounting and Sloan management. Further, and more significantly, JIT calls for a reduction in inventory capacity, not production capacity. From 1975 to 1990 to 2005, the annual average stocks of gasoline have fallen by only 8.5% from 228,331 to 222,903 bbls to 208,986 (Energy Information Administration data). Stocks fluctuate seasonally by as much as 20,000 bbls. During the 2005 hurricane season, stocks never fell below 194,000,000 bbl (30,800,000 m), while the low for the period 1990 to 2006 was 187,017,000 bbl (29,733,300 m) in 1997. This shows that while industry storage capacity has decreased in the last 30 years, it hasn't been drastically reduced as JIT practitioners would prefer.

Finally, as shown in a pair of articles in the "Oil & Gas Journal", JIT does not seem to have been a goal of the industry. In Waguespack and Cantor (1996), the authors point out that JIT would require a significant change in the supplier/refiner relationship, but the changes in inventories in the oil industry exhibit none of those tendencies. Specifically, the relationships remain cost-driven among many competing suppliers rather than quality-based among a select few long-term relationships. They find that a large part of the shift came about because of the availability of short-haul crudes from Latin America. In the follow-up editorial, the Oil & Gas Journal claimed that "casually adopting popular business terminology that doesn't apply" had provided a "rhetorical bogey" to industry critics. Confessing that they had been as guilty as other media sources, they confirmed that "It also happens not to be accurate."

Business models following similar approach

Vendor-managed inventory

Vendor-managed inventory (VMI) employs the same principles as those of JIT inventory, however, the responsibilities of managing inventory is placed with the vendor in a vendor/customer relationship. Whether it's a manufacturer managing inventory for a distributor, or a distributor managing inventory for their customers, the management role goes to the vendor. An advantage of this business model is that the vendor may have industry experience and expertise that lets them better anticipate demand and inventory needs. The inventory planning and controlling is facilitated by applications that allow vendors access to their customer's inventory data. Another advantage to the customer is that inventory cost usually remains on the vendor's books until used by the customer, even if parts or materials are on the customer's site.

Customer-managed inventory

With customer-managed inventory (CMI), the customer, as opposed to the vendor in a VMI model, has responsibility for all inventory decisions. This is similar to JIT inventory concepts. With a clear picture of their inventory and that of their supplier's, the customer can anticipate fluctuations in demand and make inventory replenishment decisions accordingly.

MATERIAL REQUIREMENTS PLANNING

Material requirements planning (MRP) is a production planning and inventory control system used to manage manufacturing processes. Most MRP systems are software-based, while it is possible to conduct MRP by hand as well.

An MRP system is intended to simultaneously meet three objectives:

- Ensure materials are available for production and products are available for delivery to customers.
- Maintain the lowest possible material and product levels in store
- Plan manufacturing activities, delivery schedules and purchasing activities.

Prior to MRP, and before computers dominated industry, reorder-point/reorder-quantity (ROP/ROQ) type methods like EOQ (Economic Order Quantity) had been used in manufacturing and inventory management. In 1964, as a response to the TOYOTA Manufacturing Program, Joseph Orlicky developed Material Requirements Planning (MRP). The first company to use MRP was Black & Decker in 1964, with Dick Alban as project leader. In 1983 Oliver Wight developed MRP into manufacturing resource planning (MRP II). Orlicky's book is entitled *The New Way of Life in Production and Inventory Management* (1975). By 1975, MRP was implemented in 150 companies. This number had grown to about 8,000 by 1981. In the 1980s, Joe Orlicky's MRP evolved into Oliver Wight's manufacturing resource planning (MRP II) which brings master scheduling, rough-cut capacity planning, capacity requirements planning, S&OP in 1983 and other concepts to classical MRP. By 1989, about one third of the software industry was MRP II software sold to American industry ($1.2 billion worth of software).

The scope of MRP in manufacturing

The basic functions of an MRP system include: inventory control, bill of material processing, and elementary scheduling. MRP helps organizations to maintain low inventory levels. It is used to plan manufacturing, purchasing and delivering activities.

"Manufacturing organizations, whatever their products, face the same daily practical problem - that customers want products to be available in a shorter time than it takes to make them. This means that some level of planning is required." Companies need to control the types and quantities of materials they purchase, plan which products are to be produced and in what quantities and ensure that they are able to meet current and future customer demand, all at the lowest possible cost. Making a bad decision in any of these areas will make the company lose money. A few examples are given below:

- If a company purchases insufficient quantities of an item used in manufacturing (or the wrong item) it may be unable to meet contract obligations to supply products on time.
- If a company purchases excessive quantities of an item, money is wasted - the excess quantity ties up cash while it remains as stock and may never even be used at all.
- Beginning production of an order at the wrong time can cause customer deadlines to be missed.

MRP is a tool to deal with these problems. It provides answers for several questions:

- *What* items are required?
- *How many* are required?
- *When* are they required?

MRP can be applied both to items that are purchased from outside suppliers and to sub-assemblies, produced internally, that are components of more complex items.

The data that must be considered include:

- The *end item* (or items) being created. This is sometimes called Independent Demand, or Level "0" on BOM (Bill of materials).
- How much is required at a time.
- When the quantities are required to meet demand.
- Shelf life of stored materials.
- Inventory status records. Records of *net* materials *available* for use already in stock (on hand) and materials on order from suppliers.
- Bills of materials. Details of the materials, components and sub-assemblies required to make each product.
- Planning Data. This includes all the restraints and directions to produce the end items. This includes such items as: Routing, Labor and Machine Standards, Quality and Testing Standards, Pull/Work Cell and Push commands, Lot sizing techniques (i.e. Fixed Lot Size, Lot-For-Lot, Economic Order Quantity), Scrap Percentages, and other inputs.

Outputs

There are two outputs and a variety of messages/reports:

- Output 1 is the "Recommended Production Schedule" which lays out a detailed schedule of the required minimum start and completion dates, with quantities, for each step of the Routing and Bill Of Material required to satisfy the demand from the Master Production Schedule (MPS).

- Output 2 is the "Recommended Purchasing Schedule". This lays out both the dates that the purchased items should be received into the facility AND the dates that the Purchase orders, or Blanket Order Release should occur to match the production schedules.

Messages and Reports:

- Purchase orders. An order to a supplier to provide materials.
- Reschedule notices. These *recommend* cancelling, increasing, delaying or speeding up existing orders.

Problems with MRP systems

First problem with MRP systems - the integrity of the data. If there are any errors in the inventory data, the bill of materials (commonly referred to as 'BOM') data, or the master production schedule, then the output data will also be incorrect ("GIGO": Garbage In, Garbage Out). Data integrity is also affected by inaccurate cycle count adjustments, mistakes in receiving input and shipping output, scrap not reported, waste, damage, box count errors, supplier container count errors,production reporting errors, and system issues. Many of these type of errors can be minimized by implementing pull systems and using bar code scanning. Most vendors in this type of system recommend at least 99% data integrity for the system to give useful results.

Second problem - systems is the requirement that the user specify how long it will take for a factory to make a product from its component parts (assuming they are all available). Additionally, the system design also assumes that this "lead time" in manufacturing will be the same each time the item is made, without regard to quantity being made, or other items being made simultaneously in the factory.

A manufacturer may have factories in different cities or even countries. It is not good for an MRP system to say that we do not need to order some material, because we have plenty thousands of miles away. The overall ERP system needs to be able to organize inventory and needs by individual factory, and inter-communicate the needs in order to enable each factory to redistribute components, so as to serve the overall enterprise.

This means that other systems in the enterprise need to work properly, both before implementing an MRP system and in the future. For example, systems like variety reduction and engineering, which makes sure that product comes out right first time (without defects), must be in place.

Production may be in progress for some part, whose design gets changed, with customer orders in the system for both the old design, and the new one, concurrently. The overall ERP system needs to have a system of coding parts such that the MRP will correctly calculate needs and tracking for both versions. Parts must be booked into and out of stores more regularly than the MRP calculations take place. Note, these other systems can well be manual systems, but must interface to the MRP. For example, a 'walk around' stock intake done just prior to the MRP calculations can be a practical solution for a small inventory (especially if it is an "open store").

The other major drawback of MRP is that takes no account of capacity in its calculations. This means it will give results that are impossible to implement due to manpower or machine or supplier capacity constraints. However this is largely dealt with by MRP II. Generally, MRP II refers to a system with integrated financials. An MRP II system can include finite/ infinite capacity planning. But, to be considered a true MRP II system must also include financials.

In the MRP II (or MRP2) concept, fluctuations in forecast data are taken into account by including simulation of the master production schedule, thus creating a long-term control. A more general feature of MRP2 is its extension to purchasing, to marketing and to finance (integration of all the functions of the company), ERP has been the next step.

Solutions to data integrity issues

Bill of material - The best practice is to physically verify the bill of material either at the production site or by un-assembling the product. Cycle count - The best practice is to determine why a cycle count that increases or decreases inventory has occurred. Find the root cause and correct the problem from occurring again. Scrap reporting - This can be the most difficult area to maintain with any integrity. Start with isolating the scrap by providing scrap bins at the production site and then record the scrap from the bins on a daily basis. One benefit of reviewing the scrap on site is that preventive action can be taken by the engineering group.

Receiving errors - Manual systems of recording what has been received are error prone. The best practice is to implement the system of receiving by ASN from the supplier. The supplier sends an ASN (Advanced Shipping Notification). When the components are received into the facility, the ASN is processed and then company labels are created for each line item. The labels are affixed to each container and then scanned into the MRP system. Extra labels reveal a shortage from the shipment and too few labels reveal an over shipment. Some companies pay for ASN by reducing the time in processing accounts payable.

Shipping Errors - The container labels are printed from the shipper. The labels are affixed to the containers in a staging area or when they are loaded on the transport. Production reporting - The best practice is to use bar code scanning to enter production into inventory. A product that is rejected should be moved to an MRB (material review board) location. Containers that require sorting need to be received in reverse. Replenishment - The best replenishment practice is replacement using bar code scanning, or via pull system. Depending upon the complexity of the product, planners can actually order materials using scanning with a min-max system.

Next Generation MRP

Demand Driven MRP

In 2011, the third edition of "Orlicky's Planning" introduced a new type of MRP called Demand Driven MRP(DDMRP). The new edition of the book was written, not by Orlicky himself (he died in 1986) but by the people who are currently marketing DDMRP. Demand Driven MRP is a multi-echelon formal planning and execution technique with five distinct components:

1. Strategic Inventory Positioning - The first question of effective inventory management is not, "how much inventory should we have?" Nor is it, "when should we make or buy something?" The most fundamental question to ask in today's manufacturing environments is, "given our system and environment, where should we place inventory to have the best protection?" Inventory is like a break wall to protect boats in a marina from the roughness of incoming waves. Out on the open ocean the break walls have to be 50-100 feet tall, but in a small lake the break walls are only a couple feet tall. In a glassy smooth pond no break wall is necessary.
2. Buffer Profiles and Level - Once the strategically replenished positions are determined, the actual levels of those buffers have to be initially set. Based on several factors, different materials and parts behave differently (but many also behave nearly the same). DDMRP calls for the grouping of parts and materials chosen for strategic replenishment and that behave similarly into "buffer profiles." Buffer profiles take into account important factors including lead time (relative to the environment), variability (demand or supply), whether the part is made or bought or distributed and whether there are significant order multiples involved. These buffer profiles are made up of "zones" that produce a unique buffer picture for each part as their respective individual part traits are applied to the group traits.
3. Dynamic Adjustments - Over the course of time, group and individual traits can and will change as new suppliers and materials are used, new markets are opened and/or old markets deteriorate and manufacturing capacities and methods change. Dynamic buffer levels allow the company to adapt buffers to group and individual part trait changes over time through the use of several types of adjustments. Thus, as more or less variability is encountered or as a

company's strategy changes these buffers adapt and change to fit the environment.

4. Demand Driven Planning - takes advantage of the sheer computational power of today's hardware and software. It also takes advantage of the new demand driven or pull-based approaches. When these two elements are combined then there is the best of both worlds; relevant approaches and tools for the way the world works today AND a system of routine that promotes better and quicker decisions and actions at the planning and execution level.
5. Highly Visible and Collaborative Execution - Simply launching Purchase Orders (POs), Manufacturing Orders (MOs) and Transfer Orders (TOs) from any planning system does not end the materials and order management challenge. These POs, MOs and TOs have to be effectively managed to synchronize with the changes that often occur within the "execution horizon." The execution horizon is the time from which a PO, MO or TO is opened until the time it is closed in the system of record. DDMRP defines a modern, integrated and greatly needed system of execution for all part categories in order to speed the proliferation of relevant information and priorities throughout an organization and supply chain.

These five components work together to greatly dampen, if not eliminate, the nervousness of traditional MRP systems and the bullwhip effect in complex and challenging environments. In utilizing these approaches, planners will no longer have to try to respond to every single message for every single part that is off by even one day. This approach provides real information about those parts that are truly at risk of negatively impacting the planned availability of inventory. DDMRP sorts the significant few items that require attention from the many parts that are being managed. Under the DDMRP approach, fewer planners can make better decisions more quickly. That means companies will be better able to leverage their working and human capital as well as the huge investments they have made in information technology.

DDMRP is most useful when applied to a CTO (Configure to Order) environment. It is inherently less suitable for MTS (Make to Stock), MTO (Make to Order) and ETO (Engineer to Order) environments. DDMRP can best be seen as a method of implementing regular MRP in specific circumstances, rather than as a new philosophy in its own right.

THEORY OF CONSTRAINTS

The theory of constraints (TOC) is a management paradigm that views any manageable system as being limited in achieving more of its goals by a very small number of constraints. There is always at least one constraint, and TOC uses a focusing process to identify the constraint and restructure the rest of the organization around it.

TOC adopts the common idiom "a chain is no stronger than its weakest link". This means that processes, organizations, etc., are vulnerable because the weakest person or part can always damage or break them or at least adversely affect the outcome. The theory of constraints (TOC) is an overall management philosophy introduced by Eliyahu M. Goldratt in his 1984 book titled *The Goal,* that is geared to help organizations continually achieve their goals. Goldratt adopted the concept with his book *Critical Chain,* published 1997. The concept was extended to TOC with respectively titled publication in 1999.

An earlier propagator of the concept was Wolfgang Mewes in Germany with publications on *power-oriented management theory* and following with his *Energo-Kybernetic System,* later renamed *Engpasskonzentrierte Strategie* as a more advanced *theory of bottlenecks*. The publications of Wolfgang Mewes are marketed through the FAZ Verlag, publishing house of the German newspaper *Frankfurter Allgemeine Zeitung*. However, the paradigm *Theory of constraints* was first used by Goldratt.

Key assumption

The underlying premise of theory of constraints is that organizations can be measured and controlled by variations on three measures: throughput, operational expense, and inventory. Throughput is the rate at which the system generates money through sales. Inventory is all the money that the system has invested in purchasing things which it intends to sell. Operational expense is all the money the system spends in order to turn inventory into throughput.

Before the goal itself can be reached, necessary conditions must first be met. These typically include safety, quality, legal obligations, etc. For most businesses, the goal itself is to make money. However, for many organizations and non-profit businesses, making money is a necessary condition for pursuing the goal. Whether it is the goal or a necessary condition, understanding how to make sound financial decisions based on throughput, inventory, and operating expense is a critical requirement.

The five focusing steps

Theory of constraints is based on the premise that the rate of goal achievement by a goal-oriented system (i.e., the system's throughput) is limited by at least one constraint. The argument by reductio ad absurdum is as follows: If there was nothing preventing a system from achieving higher throughput (i.e., more goal units in a unit of time), its throughput would be infinite — which is impossible in a real-life system. Only by increasing flow through the constraint can overall throughput be increased. Assuming the goal of a system has been articulated and its measurements defined, the steps are:

- Identify the system's constraint(s) (that which prevents the organization from obtaining more of the goal in a unit of time)

- Decide how to exploit the system's constraint(s) (how to get the most out of the constraint)
- Subordinate everything else to the above decision
- Elevate the system's constraint(s) (make other major changes needed to increase the constraint's capacity)
- Warning! If in the previous steps a constraint has been broken, go back to step 1, but do not allow inertia to cause a system's constraint.

The goal of a commercial organization is: "Make more money now and in the future", and its measurements are given by throughput accounting as: throughput, inventory, and operating expenses. The five focusing steps aim to ensure ongoing improvement efforts are centered on the organization's constraint(s). In the TOC literature, this is referred to as the *process of ongoing improvement* (POOGI). These focusing steps are the key steps to developing the specific applications mentioned below.

Constraints

A constraint is anything that prevents the system from achieving its goal. There are many ways that constraints can show up, but a core principle within TOC is that there are not tens or hundreds of constraints. There is at least one but at most only a few in any given system. Constraints can be internal or external to the system.

An internal constraint is in evidence when the market demands more from the system than it can deliver. If this is the case, then the focus of the organization should be on discovering that constraint and following the five focusing steps to open it up (and potentially remove it). An external constraint exists when the system can produce more than the market will bear. If this is the case, then the organization should focus on mechanisms to create more demand for its products or services.

Types of (internal) constraints

- *Equipment:* The way equipment is currently used limits the ability of the system to produce more salable goods/services.
- *People:* Lack of skilled people limits the system. Mental models held by people can cause behaviour that becomes a constraint.
- *Policy:* A written or unwritten policy prevents the system from making more.

The concept of the constraint in Theory of Constraints is analogous to but differs from the constraint that shows up in mathematical optimization. In TOC, the constraint is used as a focusing mechanism for management of the system. In optimization, the constraint is written into the mathematical expressions to limit the scope of the solution (X can be no greater than 5).

Please note: organizations have many problems with equipment, people, policies, etc. (A breakdown is just that – a breakdown – and is not a constraint in the true sense of the TOC concept) The constraint is the thing that is preventing the organization from getting more throughput (typically, revenue through sales) even when nothing goes wrong.

Breaking a constraint

If a constraint's throughput capacity is elevated to the point where it is no longer the system's limiting factor, this is said to "break" the constraint. The limiting factor is now some other part of the system, or may be external to the system (an external constraint). This is not to be confused with a breakdown.

Buffers

Buffers are used throughout the theory of constraints. They often result as part of the exploit and subordinate steps of the five focusing steps. Buffers are placed before the governing constraint, thus ensuring that the constraint is never starved. Buffers are also placed behind the constraint to prevent downstream failure from blocking the constraint's output. Buffers used in this way protect the constraint from variations in the rest of the system and should allow for normal variation of processing time and the occasional upset (Murphy) before and behind the constraint.

Buffers can be a bank of physical objects before a work center, waiting to be processed by that work center. Buffers ultimately buy you time, as in the time before work reaches the constraint and are often verbalized as time buffers. There should always be enough (but not excessive) work in the time queue before the constraint and adequate offloading space behind the constraint.

Buffers are *not* the small queue of work that sits before every work center in a Kanban system although it is similar if you regard the assembly line as the governing constraint. A prerequisite in the theory is that with one constraint in the system, all other parts of the system must have sufficient capacity to keep up with the work at the constraint and to catch up if time was lost. In a balanced line, as espoused by Kanban, when one work center goes down for a period longer than the buffer allows, then the entire system must wait until that work center is restored. In a TOC system, the only situation where work is in danger is if the constraint is unable to process (either due to malfunction, sickness or a "hole" in the buffer – if something goes wrong that the time buffer can not protect).

Buffer management, therefore, represents a crucial attribute of the theory of constraints. There are many ways to apply buffers, but the most often used is a visual system of designating the buffer in three colours: green (okay), yellow (caution) and red (action required). Creating this kind of visibility enables the system as a whole to align and thus subordinate to the need of the constraint in a holistic manner. This can also be done daily in a central operations room that is accessible to everybody.

Plant types

There are four primary types of plants in the TOC lexicon. Draw the flow of material from the bottom of a page to the top, and you get the four types. They specify the general flow of materials through a system, and they provide some hints about where to look for typical problems. The four types can be combined in many ways in larger facilities.

- I-plant: Material flows in a sequence, such as in an assembly line. The primary work is done in a straight sequence of events (one-to-one). The constraint is the slowest operation.
- A-plant: The general flow of material is many-to-one, such as in a plant where many sub-assemblies converge for a final assembly. The primary problem in A-plants is in synchronizing the converging lines so that each supplies the final assembly point at the right time.
- V-plant: The general flow of material is one-to-many, such as a plant that takes one raw material and can make many final products. Classic examples are meat rendering plants or a steel manufacturer. The primary problem in V-plants is "robbing" where one operation (A) immediately after a diverging point "steals" materials meant for the other operation (B). Once the material has been processed by A, it cannot come back and be run through B without significant rework.
- T-plant: The general flow is that of an I-plant (or has multiple lines), which then splits into many assemblies (many-to-many). Most manufactured parts are used in multiple assemblies and nearly all assemblies use multiple parts. Customized devices, such as computers, are good examples. T-plants suffer from both synchronization problems of A-plants (parts aren't all available for an assembly) and the robbing problems of V-plants (one assembly steals parts that could have been used in another).

For non-material systems, one can draw the flow of work or the flow of processes and arrive at similar basic structures. A project, for example is an A-shaped sequence of work, culminating in a delivered project.

Applications

The focusing steps, this process of ongoing improvement, have been applied to manufacturing, project management, supply chain/distribution generated specific solutions. Other tools (mainly the "thinking process") also led to TOC applications in the fields of marketing and sales, and finance. The solution as applied to each of these areas are listed below.

Operations

Within manufacturing operations and operations management, the solution seeks to pull materials through the system, rather than push them into the system. The primary methodology use is drum-buffer-rope (DBR) and a variation called simplified drum-buffer-rope (S-DBR). Drum-buffer-rope is a manufacturing execution methodology, named for its three components. The *drum* is the physical constraint of the plant: the work center or machine or operation that limits the ability of the entire system to produce more. The rest of the plant follows the beat of the drum. They make sure the drum has work and that anything the drum has processed does not get wasted. The *buffer* protects the drum, so that it always has work flowing to it. Buffers in DBR have time as their unit of measure, rather than quantity of material. This makes the priority system operate strictly based on the time an order is expected to be at the drum. Traditional DBR usually calls for buffers at several points in the system: the constraint, synchronization points and at shipping. S-DBR has a buffer at shipping and manages the flow of work across the drum through a load planning mechanism.

The *rope* is the work release mechanism for the plant. Orders are released to the shop floor at one "buffer time" before they are due. In other words, if the buffer is 5 days, the order is released 5 days before it is due at the constraint. Putting work into the system earlier than this buffer time is likely to generate too-high work-in-process and slow down the entire system.

Supply chain/ logistics

In general, the solution for supply chains is to create flow of inventory so as to ensure greater availability and to eliminate surpluses. The TOC distribution solution is effective when used to address a single link in the supply chain and more so across the entire system, even if that system comprises many different companies. The purpose of the TOC distribution solution is to establish a decisive competitive edge based on extraordinary availability by dramatically reducing the damages caused when the flow of goods is interrupted by shortages and surpluses. This approach uses several new rules to protect availability with less inventory than is conventionally required. Before explaining these new rules, the term Replenishment Time must be defined. Replenishment Time (RT) is the sum of the delay, after the first consumption following a delivery, before an order is placed plus the delay after the order is placed until the ordered goods arrive at the ordering location.

- Inventory is held at an aggregation point(s) as close as possible to the source. This approach ensures smoothed demand at the aggregation point, requiring proportionally less inventory. The distribution centers holding the aggregated stock are able to ship goods downstream to the next link in the supply chain much more quickly than a make-to-order manufacturer can. #:Following this rule may result in a make-to-order manufacturer converting to make-to-stock. The inventory added at the aggregation point is significantly less than the inventory reduction downstream.

- In all stocking locations, initial inventory buffers are set which effectively create an upper limit of the inventory at that location. The buffer size is equal to the maximum expected consumption within the average RT, plus additional stock to protect in case a delivery is late. In other words, there is no advantage in holding more inventory in a location than the amount that might be consumed before more could be ordered and received. Typically, the sum of the on hand value of such buffers are 25–75% less than currently observed average inventory levels.
- Once buffers have been established, no replenishment orders are placed as long as the quantity inbound (already ordered but not yet received) plus the quantity on hand are equal to or greater than the buffer size. Following this rule causes surplus inventory to be bled off as it is consumed.
- For any reason, when on hand plus inbound inventory is less than the buffer, orders are placed as soon as practical to increase the inbound inventory so that the relationship On Hand + Inbound = Buffer is maintained.
- To ensure buffers remain correctly sized even with changes in the rates of demand and replenishment, a simple recursive algorithm called Buffer Management is used. When the on hand inventory level is in the upper third of the buffer for a full RT, the buffer is reduced by one third (and don't forget rule 3). Alternatively, when the on hand inventory is in the bottom one third of the buffer for too long, the buffer is increased by one third (and don't forget rule 4). The definition of "too long" may be changed depending on required service levels, however, a general rule of thumb is 20% of the RT. Moving buffers up more readily than down is supported by the usually greater damage caused by shortages as compared to the damage caused by surpluses.

Once inventory is managed as described above, continuous efforts should be undertaken to reduce RT, late deliveries, supplier minimum order quantities (both per SKU and per order) and customer order batching. Any improvements in these areas will automatically improve both availability and inventory turns, thanks to the adaptive nature of Buffer Management.

A stocking location that manages inventory according to the TOC should help a non-TOC customer (downstream link in a supply chain, whether internal or external) manage their inventory according to the TOC process. This type of help can take the form of a vendor managed inventory (VMI). The TOC distribution link simply extends its buffer sizing and management techniques to its customers' inventories. Doing so has the effect of smoothing the demand from the customer and reducing order sizes per SKU. VMI results in better availability and inventory turns for both supplier and customer. More than that, the benefits to the non-TOC customers are sufficient to meet the purpose of capitalizing on the decisive competitive edge by giving the customer a powerful reason to be more loyal and give more business to the upstream link. When the end consumers buy more the whole supply chain sells more. One caveat should be considered. Initially and only temporarily, the supply chain or a specific link may sell less as the surplus inventory in the system is sold. However, the immediate sales lift due to improved availability is a countervailing factor. The current levels of surpluses and shortages make each case different.

Finance and accounting

The solution for finance and accounting is to apply holistic thinking to the finance application. This has been termed throughput accounting. Throughput accounting suggests that one examine the impact of investments and operational changes in terms of the impact on the throughput of the business. It is an alternative to cost accounting.

The primary measures for a TOC view of finance and accounting are: throughput, operating expense and investment. Throughput is calculated from sales minus "totally variable cost", where totally variable cost is usually calculated as the cost of raw materials that go into creating the item sold.

Project management

Critical Chain Project Management (CCPM) are utilized in this area. CCPM is based on the idea that all projects look like A-plants: all activities converge to a final deliverable. As such, to protect the project, there must be internal buffers to protect synchronization points and a final project buffer to protect the overall project.

Marketing and sales

While originally focused on manufacturing and logistics, TOC has expanded lately into sales management and marketing. Its role is explicitly acknowledged in the field of sales process engineering. For effective sales management one can apply Drum Buffer Rope to the sales process similar to the way it is applied to operations. This technique is appropriate when your constraint is in the sales process itself or you just want an effective sales management technique and includes the topics of funnel management and conversion rates.

The TOC thinking processes

The thinking processes are a set of tools to help managers walk through the steps of initiating and implementing a project. When used in a logical flow, the Thinking Processes help walk through a buy-in process:

1. Gain agreement on the problem

2. Gain agreement on the direction for a solution
3. Gain agreement that the solution solves the problem
4. Agree to overcome any potential negative ramifications
5. Agree to overcome any obstacles to implementation

TOC practitioners sometimes refer to these in the negative as working through *layers of resistance* to a change. Recently, the *current reality tree* (CRT) and *future reality tree* (FRT) have been applied to an argumentative academic paper.

Development and practice

TOC was initiated by Goldratt, who until his recent death was still the main driving force behind the development and practice of TOC. There is a network of individuals and small companies loosely coupled as practitioners around the world. TOC is sometimes referred to as "constraint management". TOC is a large body of knowledge with a strong guiding philosophy of growth.

Criticism

Criticisms that have been leveled against TOC include:

Claimed suboptimality of drum-buffer-rope

While TOC has been compared favorably to linear programming techniques, D. Trietsch from University of Auckland argues that DBR methodology is inferior to competing methodologies. Linhares, from the Getulio Vargas Foundation, has shown that the TOC approach to establishing an optimal product mix is unlikely to yield optimum results, as it would imply that P=NP.

Unacknowledged debt

Duncan (as cited by Steyn) says that TOC borrows heavily from systems dynamics developed by Forrester in the 1950s and from statistical process control which dates back to World War II. And Noreen Smith and Mackey, in their independent report on TOC, point out that several key concepts in TOC "have been topics in management accounting textbooks for decades."

People claim Goldratt's books fail to acknowledge that TOC borrows from more than 40 years of previous management science research and practice, particularly from PERT/CPM and JIT. A rebuttal to these criticisms is offered in Goldratt's "What is the *Theory of Constraints* and How Should it be Implemented?", and in his audio program, "Beyond The Goal". In these, Goldratt discusses the history of disciplinary sciences, compares the strengths and weaknesses of the various disciplines, and acknowledges the sources of information and inspiration for the thinking processes and critical chain methodologies. Articles published in the now-defunct Journal of *Theory of Constraints* referenced foundational materials. Goldratt published an article and gave talks with the title "Standing on the Shoulders of Giants" in which he gives credit for many of the core ideas of Theory of Constraints. Goldratt has sought many times to show the correlation between various improvement methods. However, many Goldratt adherents often denigrate other methodologies as inferior to TOC.

TOTAL QUALITY MANAGEMENT

Total quality management (TQM) is the organization-wide effort to install and make permanent a climate in which it continuously improves its ability to deliver high-quality products and services to customers. While there is no widely agreed-upon approach, TQM efforts typically draw heavily on the previously-developed tools and techniques of quality control. As a business phenomenon, TQM enjoyed widespread attention during the late 1980s and early 1990s before being overshadowed by ISO 9000, Lean manufacturing, and Six Sigma.

History

In the late 1970s and early 1980s, the developed countries of North America and Western Europe suffered economically in the face of stiff competition from Japan's ability to produce high-quality goods at competitive cost. For the first time since the start of the Industrial Revolution, the United Kingdom became a net importer of finished goods. The United States undertook its own soul-searching, expressed most pointedly in the television broadcast of *If Japan Can... Why Can't We?* Firms began reexamining the techniques of quality control invented over the past 50 years and how those techniques had been so successfully employed by the Japanese. It was in the midst of this economic turmoil that TQM took root.

The exact origin of the term "total quality management" is uncertain. It is almost certainly inspired by Armand V. Feigenbaum's multi-edition book *Total Quality Control* (OCLC 299383303) and Kaoru Ishikawa's *What Is Total Quality Control? The Japanese Way* (OCLC 11467749). It may have been first coined in the United Kingdom by the Department of Trade and Industry during its 1983 "National Quality Campaign". Or it may have been first coined in the United States by the Naval Air Systems Command to describe its quality-improvement efforts in 1985.

Features

There is no widespread agreement as to what TQM is and what actions it requires of organizations, however a review of the original United States Navy effort gives a rough understanding of what is involved in TQM.

The key concepts in the TQM effort undertaken by the Navy in the 1980s include:

- "Quality is defined by customers' requirements."

- "Top management has direct responsibility for quality improvement."
- "Increased quality comes from systematic analysis and improvement of work processes."
- "Quality improvement is a continuous effort and conducted throughout the organization."

The Navy used the following tools and techniques:

- The PDCA cycle to drive issues to resolution
- *Ad hoc* cross-functional teams (similar to quality circles) responsible for addressing immediate process issues
- Standing cross-functional teams responsible for the improvement of processes over the long term
- Active management participation through steering committees
- Use of the Seven Basic Tools of Quality to analyze quality-related issues

Notable definitions

While there is no generally-accepted definition of TQM, several notable organizations have attempted to define it. These include:

- United States Department of Defense (1988): "Total Quality Management (TQM) in the Department of Defense is a strategy for continuously improving performance at every level, and in all areas of responsibility. It combines fundamental management techniques, existing improvement efforts, and specialized technical tools under a disciplined structure focused on continuously improving all processes. Improved performance is directed at satisfying such broad goals as cost, quality, schedule, and mission need and suitability. Increasing user satisfaction is the overriding objective. The TQM effort builds on the pioneering work of *Dr. W. E. Deming, Dr. J. H. Juran,* and others, and benefits from both private and public sector experience with continuous process improvement."
- British Standards Institution standard BS 7850-1:1992: "A management philosophy and company practices that aim to harness the human and material resources of an organization in the most effective way to achieve the objectives of the organization."
- International Organization for Standardization standard ISO 8402:1994: "A management approach of an organisation centred on quality, based on the participation of all its members and aiming at long term success through customer satisfaction and benefits to all members of the organisation and society."
- The American Society for Quality: "A term first used to describe a management approach to quality improvement. Since then, TQM has taken on many meanings. Simply put, it is a management

approach to long-term success through customer satisfaction. TQM is based on all members of an organization participating in improving processes, products, services and the culture in which they work. The methods for implementing this approach are found in the teachings of such quality leaders as *Philip B. Crosby, W. Edwards Deming, Armand V. Feigenbaum, Kaoru Ishikawa* and *Joseph M. Juran*."

- The Chartered Quality Institute: TQM is a philosophy for managing an organisation in a way which enables it to meet stakeholder needs and expectations efficiently and effectively, without compromising ethical values."

Malcolm Baldrige National Quality Award criteria

In the United States, the Baldridge Award, created by Public Law 100-107, annually recognizes American businesses, educational institutions, and healthcase organizations that run high-quality operations. Organizations are judged on criteria from seven categories:

1. Leadership
2. Strategic planning
3. Customer focus
4. Measurement, analysis, and knowledge management
5. Workforce focus
6. Operations focus
7. Results

Example criteria are:

- *How do you obtain information on your customers' satisfaction relative to their satisfaction with your competitors?*
- *How do you select, collect, align, and integrate data and information for tracking daily operations?*
- *How do you manage your workforce, its needs, and your needs to ensure continuity, prevent workforce reductions, and minimize the impact of workforce reductions, if they do become necessary?*

Joseph M. Juran believed the Baldrige Award judging criteria to be the most widely accepted description of what TQM entails.

Standards

During the 1990s, standards bodies in Belgium, France, Germany, Turkey, and the United Kingdom attempted to standardize TQM. While many of these standards have since been explicitly withdrawn, they all are effectively superseded by ISO 9000:

- *Total Quality Management: Guide to Management Principles*, London, England: British Standards Institution, 1992, ISBN 9780580211560, OCLC 655881602, BS 7850

- Electronic Components Committee (1994), *Guide to Total Quality Management (TQM) for CECC-Approved Organizations*, Brussels, Belgium: European Committee for Electrotechnical Standardization, CECC 00 806 Issue 1
- *System zur Zukunftssicherung: Total Quality Management (TQM)*, Düsseldorf, Germany: Verein Deutscher Ingenieure, 1996, OCLC 632959402, VDI 5500
- *Total Quality and Marketing/Management Tools*, Paris, France: AFNOR, 1998, FD X50-680
- *Total Quality Management: Guide to Management Principles*, Turkish Standards Institution (TSE), 2006, TS 13133

Legacy

Interest in TQM as an academic subject peaked around 1993. The Federal Quality Institute was shuttered in September 1995 as part of the Clinton administration's efforts to streamline government. The European Centre for Total Quality Management closed in August 2009, a casualty of the Great Recession. TQM as a vaguely-defined quality management approach was largely supplanted by the ISO 9000 collection of standards and their formal certification processes in the 1990s. Business interest in quality improvement under the TQM name also faded as Jack Welch's success attracted attention to Six Sigma and Toyota's success attracted attention to Lean manufacturing, though the three share many of the same tools, techniques, and significant portions of the same philosophy.

CUSTOMER RELATIONSHIP MANAGEMENT

Customer relationship management (CRM) is a model for managing a company's interactions with current and future customers. It involves using technology to organize, automate, and synchronize sales, marketing, customer service, and technical support.

Types/variations

Marketing

CRM systems for marketing track and measure campaigns over multiple channels, such as email, search, social media, telephone and direct mail. These systems track clicks, responses, leads and deals.

Customer service and support

CRM systems can be used to create, assign and manage requests made by customers, such as call center software which helps direct customers to agents. CRM software can also be used to identify and reward loyal customers over a period of time.

Appointments

CRM systems can automatically suggest suitable appointment times to customers via e-mail or the web. These can then be synchronized with the representative or agent's calendar.

Small business

For small businesses a CRM system may simply consist of a contact manager system which integrates emails, documents, jobs, faxes, and scheduling for individual accounts. CRM systems available for specific markets (legal, finance) frequently focus on event management and relationship tracking as opposed to financial return on investment (ROI).

Social media

CRM often makes use of social media to build up customer relationships. Some CRM systems integrate social media sites like Twitter, LinkedIn and Facebook to track and communicate with customers sharing their opinions and experiences with a company, products and services. Enterprise Feedback Management software platforms such as Confirmit, Medallia, and Satmetrix combine internal survey data with trends identified through social media to allow businesses to make more accurate decisions on which products to supply.

Non-profit and membership-based

Systems for non-profit and membership-based organizations help track constituents, fund-raising, demographics, membership levels, membership directories, volunteering and communication with individuals.

Adoption issues

In 2003, a Gartner report estimated that more than $2 billion had been spent on software that was not being used. According to *KEN Insights,* less than 40 percent of 1,275 participating companies had end-user adoption rates above 90 percent. Many corporations only use CRM systems on a partial or fragmented basis. In a 2007 survey from the UK, four-fifths of senior executives reported that their biggest challenge is getting their staff to use the systems they had installed. 43 percent of respondents said they use less than half the functionality of their existing system.. Recently, it is found in a study that market research regarding consumers preference may increase the adoption of CRM among the developing countries' consumers.

Trends

Many CRM vendors offer subscription-based web tools (cloud computing) and software as a service (SaaS). Some CRM systems are equipped with mobile capabilities, making information accessible to remote sales staff. Salesforce.com was the first company to provide enterprise applications through a web browser, and has maintained its leadership position. Traditional providers have recently moved into the cloud-based market via acquisitions of smaller providers: Oracle purchased RightNow in October 2011 and SAP acquired SuccessFactors in December 2011.

The era of the "social customer" refers to the use of social media (Twitter, Facebook, LinkedIn, Google Plus, Pinterest, Instagram, Yelp, customer reviews in Amazon, etc.) by customers. CR philosophy and strategy has shifted to encompass social networks and user communities.

Sales forces also play an important role in CRM, as maximizing sales effectiveness and increasing sales productivity is a driving force behind the adoption of CRM. Empowering sales managers was listed as one of the top 5 CRM trends in 2013. Another related development is vendor relationship management (VRM), which provide tools and services that allow customers to manage their individual relationship with vendors. VRM development has grown out of efforts by ProjectVRM at Harvard's Berkman Center for Internet & Society and Identity Commons' Internet Identity Workshops, as well as by a growing number of startups and established companies. VRM was the subject of a cover story in the May 2010 issue of *CRM* Magazine.

In 2001, Doug Laney developed the concept and coined the term 'Extended Relationship Management' (XRM). Laney defines XRM as extending CRM disciplines to secondary allies such as the government, press and industry consortia. CRM futurist Dennison DeGregor describes a shift from 'push CRM' toward a 'customer transparency' (CT) model, due to the increased proliferation of channels, devices, and social media.

AVAILABLE-TO-PROMISE

Available-to-promise (ATP) is a business function that provides a response to customer order enquiries, based on resource availability. It generates available quantities of the requested product, and delivery due dates. Therefore, ATP supports order promising and fulfillment, aiming to manage demand and match it to production plans. Available-to-promise functions are IT-enabled and usually integrated in enterprise management software packages. However, ATP execution may need to be adjusted for the way a certain company operates.

Classification

A fundamental distinction between ATP functions is based on the push-pull strategy. Push-based ATP is based on forecasts regarding future demand - based on anticipation of demand, ATP quantities and availability dates are computed. A prominent example is the traditional determination of ATP based on the Master Production Schedule. The push-based approach is fundamentally limited by dependence on forecasts, which may prove inaccurate. Gross ATP represents the total available supply, Net ATP represents the supply remaining to support new demands, after existing demands have been accounted for. Pull-based models, on the other hand, dynamically allocate resources in response to actual customer orders. This means that pull-based ATP is able to balance forecast-driven resource replenishment with order-triggered resource utilization, but because resources are allocated with each coming order, the process will yield myopic results.

ATP Execution

ATP functions can be executed in real time, driven by each individual order, or in batch mode – meaning that at a certain time interval, the system checks availability for orders piled up in that period of time. The process is triggered by the need to check resource availability before making a commitment to deliver an order. For example, ATP calculation using SAP software depends on the level of "stock, planned receipts (production orders, purchase orders, planned orders and so on), and planned requirements (sales orders, deliveries, reservations, etc.)"

SUPPLY CHAIN CENTROIDS

In the study of supply chain management, the concept of centroids has become an important economic consideration. A centroid is a location that has a high proportion of a country's population and a high proportion of its manufacturing, generally within 500 mi (805 km). In the US, two major supply chain centroids have been defined, one near Dayton, Ohio, and a second near Riverside, California. The centroid near Dayton is particularly important because it is closest to the population center of the US and Canada. Dayton is within 500 miles of 60% of the US population and manufacturing capacity, as well as 60% of Canada's population. The region includes the interchange between I-70 and I-75, one of the busiest in the nation, with 154,000 vehicles passing through per day, 30–35% of which are trucks hauling goods. In addition, the I-75 corridor is home to the busiest north-south rail route east of the Mississippi River.

TAX EFFICIENT SUPPLY CHAIN MANAGEMENT

Tax efficient supply chain management is a business model that considers the effect of tax in the design and implementation of supply chain management. As the consequence of globalization, cross-national businesses pay different tax rates in different countries. Due to these differences, they may legally optimize their supply chain and increase profits based on tax efficiency.

SUSTAINABILITY AND SOCIAL RESPONSIBILITY IN SUPPLY CHAINS

Supply chain sustainability is a business issue affecting an organization's supply chain or logistics network, and is frequently quantified by comparison with SECH ratings, which uses a triple bottom line incorporating economic, social, and environmental aspects. SECH ratings are defined as social, ethical, cultural, and health' footprints. Consumers have become more aware of the environmental impact of their purchases and companies' SECH ratings and, along with non-governmental organizations (NGOs), are setting the agenda for transitions to organically grown foods, anti-sweatshop labor codes, and locally produced goods that support independent and small businesses. Because supply chains may account for over 75% of a company's carbon footprint, many organizations are exploring ways to reduce this and thus improve their SECH rating.

For example, in July 2009, Wal-Mart announced its intentions to create a global sustainability index that would rate products according to the environmental and social impacts of their manufacturing and distribution. The index is intended to create environmental accountability in Wal-Mart's supply chain and to provide motivation and infrastructure for other retail companies to do the same.

More recently, the US Dodd–Frank Wall Street Reform and Consumer Protection Act, signed into law by President Obama in July 2010, contained a supply chain sustainability provision in the form of the Conflict Minerals law. This law requires SEC-regulated companies to conduct third party audits of their supply chains in order to determine whether any tin, tantalum, tungsten, or gold (together referred to as *conflict minerals*) is mined or sourced from the Democratic Republic of the Congo, and create a report (available to the general public and SEC) detailing the due diligence efforts taken and the results of the audit. The chain of suppliers and vendors to these reporting companies will be expected to provide appropriate supporting information.

Incidents like the 2013 Savar building collapse with more than 1,100 victims have led to widespread discussions about corporate social responsibility across global supply chains. Wieland and Handfield (2013) suggest that companies need to audit products and suppliers and that supplier auditing needs to go beyond direct relationships with first-tier suppliers. They also demonstrate that visibility needs to be improved if supply cannot be directly controlled and that smart and electronic technologies play a key role to improve visibility. Finally, they highlight that collaboration with local partners, across the industry and with universities is crucial to successfully managing social responsibility in supply chains.

COMPONENTS

MANAGEMENT COMPONENTS

SCM components are the third element of the four-square circulation framework. The level of integration and management of a business process link is a function of the number and level of components added to the link. Consequently, adding more management components or increasing the level of each component can increase the level of integration of the business process link. Literature on business process re-engineering buyer-supplier relationships, and SCM suggests various possible components that should receive managerial attention when managing supply relationships. Lambert and Cooper identified the following components:

- Planning and control
- Work structure
- Organization structure
- Product flow facility structure
- Information flow facility structure
- Management methods
- Power and leadership structure
- Risk and reward structure
- Culture and attitude

However, a more careful examination of the existing literature leads to a more comprehensive understanding of what should be the key critical supply chain components, or "branches" of the previously identified supply chain business processes—that is, what kind of relationship the components may have that are related to suppliers and customers. Bowersox and Closs (1996) state that the emphasis on cooperation represents the synergism leading to the highest level of joint achievement. A primary-level channel participant is a business that is willing to participate in responsibility for inventory ownership or assume other financial risks, thus including primary level components. A secondary-level participant (specialized) is a business that participates in channel relationships by performing essential services for primary participants, including secondary level components, which support primary participants. Third-level channel participants and components that support primary-level channel participants and are the fundamental branches of secondary-level components may also be included. Consequently, Lambert and Cooper's framework of supply chain components does not lead to any conclusion about what are the primary- or secondary-level (specialized) supply chain components—that is, which supply chain components should be viewed as primary or secondary, how these components should be structured in order to achieve a more comprehensive supply chain structure, and how to examine the supply chain as an integrative one.

REVERSE SUPPLY CHAIN

Reverse logistics is the process of managing the return of goods. It is also referred to as "aftermarket customer services". Any time money is taken from a company's warranty reserve or service logistics budget, one can speak of a reverse logistics operation.

SYSTEMS AND VALUE

Supply chain systems configure value for those that organize the networks. Value is the additional revenue over and above the costs of building the network. Co-creating value and sharing the benefits appropriately to encourage effective participation is a key challenge for any supply system. Tony Hines defines value as follows: "Ultimately it is the customer who pays the price for service delivered that confirms value and not the producer who simply adds cost until that point".

GLOBAL APPLICATIONS

Global supply chains pose challenges regarding both quantity and value. Supply and value chain trends include:

- Globalization
- Increased cross-border sourcing
- Collaboration for parts of value chain with low-cost providers
- Shared service centers for logistical and administrative functions
- Increasingly global operations, which require increasingly global coordination and planning to achieve global optimums
- Complex problems involve also midsized companies to an increasing degree

These trends have many benefits for manufacturers because they make possible larger lot sizes, lower taxes, and better environments (e.g., culture, infrastructure, special tax zones, or sophisticated OEM) for their products. There are many additional challenges when the scope of supply chains is global. This is because with a supply chain of a larger scope, the lead time is much longer, and because there are more issues involved, such as multiple currencies, policies, and laws. The consequent problems include different currencies and valuations in different countries, different tax laws, different trading protocols, and lack of transparency of cost and profit.

CERTIFICATION

There are several certification programs for SCM staff development, including the Association for Operations Management (APICS), the International Supply Chain Education Alliance (ISCEA), and the Institute of Supply Chain Management (IOSCM). The APICS certification is called the Certified Supply Chain Professional (CSCP); the ISCEA certification is called the Certified Supply Chain Manager (CSCM). Additionally, the Institute for Supply Management is developing a certification called the Certified Professional in Supply Management (CPSM), focused on procurement and sourcing, also called supply management. The Purchasing Management Association of Canada is the main Canadian certifying body; its designations have global recipricocity. The main designation is the Supply Chain Management Professional (SCMP), with several others progressing toward it.

7

Inventory

The word inventory doesn't have the same meaning in the USA and in the UK:

- In American English and in a business accounting context, the word inventory is commonly used to describe the goods and materials that a business holds for the ultimate purpose of resale (or repair). In American English, the word stock is commonly used to describe the capital invested in a business, while in British English, the sentence stock shared is used in the same context.
- In the rest of the English speaking world stock is more commonly used, although the word inventory is recognised as a synonym. In British English, the word inventory is more commonly thought of as a list compiled for some formal purpose, such as the details of an estate going to probate, or the contents of a house let furnished.

In both British and American English, stock is the collective noun for one hundred shares as shares were usually traded in stocks on Stock Exchanges. For this reason the word stock is used by both American and British English in the term Stock Exchange. Inventory management is a science primarily about specifying the shape and percentage of stocked goods. It is required at different locations within a facility or within many locations of a supply network to precede the regular and planned course of production and stock of materials. The scope of inventory management concerns the fine lines between replenishment lead time, carrying costs of inventory, asset management, inventory forecasting, inventory valuation, inventory visibility, future inventory price forecasting, physical inventory, available physical space for inventory, quality management, replenishment, returns and defective goods, and demand forecasting. Balancing these competing requirements leads to optimal inventory levels, which is an on-going process as the business needs shift and react to the wider environment.

Inventory management involves a retailer seeking to acquire and maintain a proper merchandise assortment while ordering, shipping, handling, and related costs are kept in check. It also involves systems and processes that identify inventory requirements, set targets, provide replenishment techniques, report actual and projected inventory status and handle all functions related to the tracking and management of material. This would include the monitoring of material moved into and out of stockroom locations and the reconciling of the inventory balances. It also may include ABC analysis, lot tracking, cycle counting support, etc. Management of the inventories, with the primary objective of determining/controlling stock levels within the physical distribution system, functions to balance the need for product availability against the need for minimizing stock holding and handling costs.

DEFINITION

Inventory management is primarily about specifying the size and placement of stocked goods. Inventory management is required at different locations within a facility or within multiple locations of a supply network to protect the regular and planned course of production against the random disturbance of running out of materials or goods.

The scope of inventory management also concerns the fine lines between replenishment lead time, carrying costs of inventory, asset management, inventory forecasting, inventory valuation, inventory visibility, future inventory price forecasting, physical inventory, available physical space for inventory, quality management, replenishment, returns and defective goods and demand forecasting and also by replenishment Or can be defined as the left out stock of any item used in an organization.

BUSINESS INVENTORY

REASONS FOR KEEPING STOCK

There are four basic reasons for keeping an inventory

1. Time - The time lags present in the supply chain, from supplier to user at every stage, requires that you maintain certain amounts of inventory to use in this lead time. However, in practice, inventory is to be maintained for consumption during 'variations in lead time'. Lead time itself can be addressed by ordering that many days in advance.
2. Uncertainty - Inventories are maintained as buffers to meet uncertainties in demand, supply and movements of goods.
3. Economies of scale - Ideal condition of "one unit at a time at a place where a user needs it, when he needs it" principle tends to incur lots of costs in terms of logistics. So bulk buying, movement and storing brings in economies of scale, thus inventory.
4. Appreciation in Value - In some situations, some stock gains the required value when it is kept for some time to allow it reach the desired standard for consumption, or for production. For example; beer in the brewing industry

All these stock reasons can apply to any owner or product

SPECIAL TERMS USED IN DEALING WITH INVENTORY

- *Stock Keeping Unit* (SKU) is a unique combination of all the components that are assembled into the purchasable item. Therefore, any change in the packaging or product is a new SKU. This level of detailed specification assists in managing inventory.
- *Stockout* means running out of the inventory of an SKU.
- "New old stock" (sometimes abbreviated NOS) is a term used in business to refer to merchandise being offered for sale that was manufactured long ago but that has never been used. Such merchandise may not be produced anymore, and the new old stock may represent the only market source of a particular item at the present time.

TYPOLOGY

1. Buffer/safety stock
2. Reorder level
3. Cycle stock (Used in batch processes, it is the available inventory, excluding buffer stock)
4. De-coupling (Buffer stock held between the machines in a single process which serves as a buffer for the next one allowing smooth flow of work instead of waiting the previous or next machine in the same process)
5. Anticipation stock (Building up extra stock for periods of increased demand - e.g. ice cream for summer)
6. Pipeline stock (Goods still in transit or in the process of distribution - have left the factory but not arrived at the customer yet)

INVENTORY EXAMPLES

While accountants often discuss inventory in terms of goods for sale, organizations - manufacturers, service-providers and not-for-profits - also have inventories (fixtures, furniture, supplies, etc.) that they do not intend to sell. Manufacturers', distributors', and wholesalers' inventory tends to cluster in warehouses. Retailers' inventory may exist in a warehouse or in a shop or store accessible to customers. Inventories not intended for sale to customers or to clients may be held in any premises an organization uses. Stock ties up cash and, if uncontrolled, it will be impossible to know the actual level of stocks and therefore impossible to control them. While the reasons for holding stock were covered earlier, most manufacturing organizations usually divide their "goods for sale" inventory into:

- Raw materials - materials and components scheduled for use in making a product.
- Work in process, WIP - materials and components that have begun their transformation to finished goods.

- Finished goods - goods ready for sale to customers.
- Goods for resale - returned goods that are salable.
- Stocks in Transit.
- Consignment Stocks.

PRINCIPLE OF INVENTORY PROPORTIONALITY

PURPOSE

Inventory proportionality is the goal of demand-driven inventory management. The primary optimal outcome is to have the same number of days' (or hours', etc.) worth of inventory on hand across all products so that the time of runout of all products would be simultaneous. In such a case, there is no "excess inventory," that is, inventory that would be left over of another product when the first product runs out. Excess inventory is sub-optimal because the money spent to obtain it could have been utilized better elsewhere, i.e. to the product that just ran out.

The secondary goal of inventory proportionality is inventory minimization. By integrating accurate demand forecasting with inventory management, rather than to past averages, a much more accurate and optimal outcome. Integrating demand forecasting into inventory management in this way also allows for the prediction of the "can fit" point when inventory storage is limited on a per-product basis.

APPLICATIONS

The technique of inventory proportionality is most appropriate for inventories that remain unseen by the consumer, as opposed to "keep full" systems where a retail consumer would like to see full shelves of the product they are buying so as not to think they are buying something old, unwanted or stale; and differentiated from the "trigger point" systems where product is reordered when it hits a certain level; inventory proportionality is used effectively by just-in-time manufacturing processes and retail applications where the product is hidden from view.

One early example of inventory proportionality used in a retail application in the United States was for motor fuel. Motor fuel (e.g. gasoline) is generally stored in underground storage tanks. The motorists do not know whether they are buying gasoline off the top or bottom of the tank, nor need they care. Additionally, these storage tanks have a maximum capacity and cannot be overfilled. Finally, the product is expensive. Inventory proportionality is used to balance the inventories of the different grades of motor fuel, each stored in dedicated tanks, in proportion to the sales of each grade. Excess inventory is not seen or valued by the consumer, so it is simply cash sunk (literally) into the ground. Inventory proportionality minimizes the amount of excess inventory carried in underground storage tanks. This application for motor fuel was first developed and implemented by Petrolsoft Corporation in 1990 for Chevron Products Company. Most major oil companies use such systems today.

ROOTS

The use of inventory proportionality in the United States is thought to have been inspired by Japanese just-in-time parts inventory management made famous by Toyota Motors in the 1980s.

HIGH-LEVEL INVENTORY MANAGEMENT

It seems that around 1880 there was a change in manufacturing practice from companies with relatively homogeneous lines of products to horizontally integrated companies with unprecedented diversity in processes and products. Those companies (especially in metalworking) attempted to achieve success through economies of scope - the gains of jointly producing two or more products in one facility. The managers now needed information on the effect of product-mix decisions on overall profits and therefore needed accurate product-cost information. A variety of attempts to achieve this were unsuccessful due to the huge overhead of the information processing of the time. However, the burgeoning need for financial reporting after 1900 created unavoidable pressure for financial accounting of stock and the management need to cost manage products became overshadowed. In particular, it was the need for audited accounts that sealed the fate of managerial cost accounting. The dominance of financial reporting accounting over management accounting remains to this day with few exceptions, and the financial reporting definitions of 'cost' have distorted effective management 'cost' accounting since that time. This is particularly true of inventory.

Hence, high-level financial inventory has these two basic formulas, which relate to the accounting period:

1. Cost of Beginning Inventory at the start of the period + inventory purchases within the period + cost of production within the period = cost of goods available
2. Cost of goods available " cost of ending inventory at the end of the period = cost of goods sold

The benefit of these formulas is that the first absorbs all overheads of production and raw material costs into a value of inventory for reporting. The second formula then creates the new start point for the next period and gives a figure to be subtracted from the sales price to determine some form of sales-margin figure.

Manufacturing management is more interested in *inventory turnover ratio* or *average days to sell inventory* since it tells them something about relative inventory levels.

- Inventory turnover ratio (also known as inventory turns) = cost of goods sold/ Average Inventory = Cost of Goods Sold/ ((Beginning Inventory + Ending Inventory)/ 2) and its inverse

- Average Days to Sell Inventory = Number of Days a Year/ Inventory Turnover Ratio = 365 days a year/ Inventory Turnover Ratio

This ratio estimates how many times the inventory turns over a year. This number tells how much cash/goods are tied up waiting for the process and is a critical measure of process reliability and effectiveness. So a factory with two inventory turns has six months stock on hand, which is generally not a good figure (depending upon the industry), whereas a factory that moves from six turns to twelve turns has probably improved effectiveness by 100%. This improvement will have some negative results in the financial reporting, since the 'value' now stored in the factory as inventory is reduced.

While these accounting measures of inventory are very useful because of their simplicity, they are also fraught with the danger of their own assumptions. There are, in fact, so many things that can vary hidden under this appearance of simplicity that a variety of 'adjusting' assumptions may be used. These include:

- Specific Identification
- Weighted Average Cost
- Moving-Average Cost
- FIFO and LIFO.

Inventory Turn is a financial accounting tool for evaluating inventory and it is not necessarily a management tool. Inventory management should be forward looking. The methodology applied is based on historical cost of goods sold. The ratio may not be able to reflect the usability of future production demand, as well as customer demand.

Business models, including Just in Time (JIT) Inventory, Vendor Managed Inventory (VMI) and Customer Managed Inventory (CMI), attempt to minimize on-hand inventory and increase inventory turns. VMI and CMI have gained considerable attention due to the success of third-party vendors who offer added expertise and knowledge that organizations may not possess.

ACCOUNTING FOR INVENTORY

Each country has its own rules about accounting for inventory that fit with their financial-reporting rules.

For example, organizations in the U.S. define inventory to suit their needs within US Generally Accepted Accounting Practices (GAAP), the rules defined by the Financial Accounting Standards Board (FASB) (and others) and enforced by the U.S. Securities and Exchange Commission (SEC) and other federal and state agencies. Other countries often have similar arrangements but with their own accounting standards and national agencies instead.

It is intentional that financial accounting uses standards that allow the public to compare firms' performance, cost accounting functions internally to an organization and potentially with much greater flexibility. A discussion of inventory from standard and Theory of Constraints-based (throughput) cost accounting perspective follows some examples and a discussion of inventory from a financial accounting perspective.

The internal costing/valuation of inventory can be complex. Whereas in the past most enterprises ran simple, one-process factories, such enterprises are quite probably in the minority in the 21st century. Where 'one process' factories exist, there is a market for the goods created, which establishes an independent market value for the good. Today, with multistage-process companies, there is much inventory that would once have been finished goods which is now held as 'work in process' (WIP). This needs to be valued in the accounts, but the valuation is a management decision since there is no market for the partially finished product. This somewhat arbitrary 'valuation' of WIP combined with the allocation of overheads to it has led to some unintended and undesirable results.

FINANCIAL ACCOUNTING

An organization's inventory can appear a mixed blessing, since it counts as an asset on the balance sheet, but it also ties up money that could serve for other purposes and requires additional expense for its protection. Inventory may also cause significant tax expenses, depending on particular countries' laws regarding depreciation of inventory, as in Thor Power Tool Company v. Commissioner. Inventory appears as a current asset on an organization's balance sheet because the organization can, in principle, turn it into cash by selling it. Some organizations hold larger inventories than their operations require in order to inflate their apparent asset value and their perceived profitability. In addition to the money tied up by acquiring inventory, inventory also brings associated costs for warehouse space, for utilities, and for insurance to cover staff to handle and protect it from fire and other disasters, obsolescence, shrinkage (theft and errors), and others. Such holding costs can mount up: between a third and a half of its acquisition value per year.

Businesses that stock too little inventory cannot take advantage of large orders from customers if they cannot deliver. The conflicting objectives of cost control and customer service often pit an organization's financial and operating managers against its sales and marketing departments. Salespeople, in particular, often receive sales-commission payments, so unavailable goods may reduce their potential personal income. This conflict can be minimised by reducing production time to being near or less than customers' expected delivery time. This effort, known as "Lean production" will significantly reduce working capital tied up in inventory and reduce manufacturing costs.

ROLE OF INVENTORY ACCOUNTING

By helping the organization to make better decisions, the accountants can help the public sector to change in a very positive way that delivers increased value for the taxpayer's investment. It can also help to incentivise progress and to ensure that reforms are sustainable and effective in the long term, by ensuring that success is appropriately recognized in both the formal and informal reward systems of the organization.

To say that they have a key role to play is an understatement. Finance is connected to most, if not all, of the key business processes within the organization. It should be steering the stewardship and accountability systems that ensure that the organization is conducting its business in an appropriate, ethical manner. It is critical that these foundations are firmly laid. So often they are the litmus test by which public confidence in the institution is either won or lost.

Finance should also be providing the information, analysis and advice to enable the organizations' service managers to operate effectively. This goes beyond the traditional preoccupation with budgets – how much have we spent so far, how much do we have left to spend? It is about helping the organization to better understand its own performance. That means making the connections and understanding the relationships between given inputs – the resources brought to bear – and the outputs and outcomes that they achieve. It is also about understanding and actively managing risks within the organization and its activities.

FIFO VS. LIFO ACCOUNTING

When a merchant buys goods from inventory, the value of the inventory account is reduced by the cost of goods sold (COGS). This is simple where the CoG has not varied across those held in stock; but where it has, then an agreed method must be derived to evaluate it. For commodity items that one cannot track individually, accountants must choose a method that fits the nature of the sale. Two popular methods that normally exist are: FIFO and LIFO accounting (first in - first out, last in - first out). FIFO regards the first unit that arrived in inventory as the first one sold. LIFO considers the last unit arriving in inventory as the first one sold. Which method an accountant selects can have a significant effect on net income and book value and, in turn, on taxation. Using LIFO accounting for inventory, a company generally reports lower net income and lower book value, due to the effects of inflation. This generally results in lower taxation. Due to LIFO's potential to skew inventory value, UK GAAP and IAS have effectively banned LIFO inventory accounting.

STANDARD COST ACCOUNTING

Standard cost accounting uses ratios called efficiencies that compare the labour and materials actually used to produce a good with those that the same goods would have required under "standard" conditions. As long as actual and standard conditions are similar, few problems arise. Unfortunately, standard cost accounting methods developed about 100 years ago, when labor comprised the most important cost in manufactured goods. Standard methods continue to emphasize labor efficiency even though that resource now constitutes a (very) small part of cost in most cases.

Standard cost accounting can hurt managers, workers, and firms in several ways. For example, a policy decision to increase inventory can harm a manufacturing manager's performance evaluation. Increasing inventory requires increased production, which means that processes must operate at higher rates. When (not if) something goes wrong, the process takes longer and uses more than the standard labor time. The manager appears responsible for the excess, even though s/he has no control over the production requirement or the problem. In adverse economic times, firms use the same efficiencies to downsize, rightsize, or otherwise reduce their labor force. Workers laid off under those circumstances have even less control over excess inventory and cost efficiencies than their managers. Many financial and cost accountants have agreed for many years on the desirability of replacing standard cost accounting. They have not, however, found a successor.

THEORY OF CONSTRAINTS COST ACCOUNTING

Eliyahu M. Goldratt developed the Theory of Constraints in part to address the cost-accounting problems in what he calls the "cost world." He offers a substitute, called throughput accounting, that uses throughput (money for goods sold to customers) in place of output (goods produced that may sell or may boost inventory) and considers labor as a fixed rather than as a variable cost. He defines inventory simply as everything the organization owns that it plans to sell, including buildings, machinery, and many other things in addition to the categories listed here. Throughput accounting recognizes only one class of variable costs: the truly variable costs, like materials and components, which vary directly with the quantity produced

Finished goods inventories remain balance-sheet assets, but labor-efficiency ratios no longer evaluate managers and workers. Instead of an incentive to reduce labor cost, throughput accounting focuses attention on the relationships between throughput (revenue or income) on one hand and controllable operating expenses and changes in inventory on the other.

NATIONAL ACCOUNTS

Inventories also play an important role in national accounts and the analysis of the business cycle. Some short-term macroeconomic fluctuations are attributed to the inventory cycle.

DISTRESSED INVENTORY

Also known as distressed or expired stock, distressed inventory is inventory whose potential to be sold at a normal cost has passed or will soon pass. In certain industries it could also mean that the stock is or will soon be impossible to sell. Examples of distressed inventory include products that have reached their expiry date, or have reached a date in advance of expiry at which the planned market will no longer purchase them (e.g. 3 months left to expiry), clothing that is defective or out of fashion, music that is no longer popular and old newspapers or magazines. It also includes computer or consumer-electronic equipment that is obsolete or discontinued and whose manufacturer is unable to support it. One current example of distressed inventory is the VHS format. In 2001, Cisco wrote off inventory worth US $2.25 billion due to duplicate orders. This is one of the biggest inventory write-offs in business history.

STOCK ROTATION

Stock Rotation is the practice of changing the way inventory is displayed on a regular basis. This is most commonly used in hospitably and retail - particularity where food products are sold. For example, in the case of supermarkets that a customer frequents on a regular basis, the customer may know exactly where they want and where it is. This results in many customers going straight to the product they seek and do not look at other items on sale. To discourage this practice, stores will rotate the location of stock to encourage customers to look through the entire store. This is in hopes the customer will pick up items they would not normally see.

INVENTORY CREDIT

Inventory credit refers to the use of stock, or inventory, as collateral to raise finance. Where banks may be reluctant to accept traditional collateral, for example in developing countries where land title may be lacking, inventory credit is a potentially important way of overcoming financing constraints. This is not a new concept; archaeological evidence suggests that it was practiced in Ancient Rome. Obtaining finance against stocks of a wide range of products held in a bonded warehouse is common in much of the world. It is, for example, used with Parmesan cheese in Italy. Inventory credit on the basis of stored agricultural produce is widely used in Latin American countries and in some Asian countries. A precondition for such credit is that banks must be confident that the stored product will be available if they need to call on the collateral; this implies the existence of a reliable network of certified warehouses. Banks also face problems in valuing the inventory. The possibility of sudden falls in commodity prices means that they are usually reluctant to lend more than about 60% of the value of the inventory at the time of the loan.

8

Productivity and Supply

PRODUCTION AND SUPPLY

In investigating the foundations of supply and demand, we will look at demand and supply as separate headings. It doesn't matter much, logically, which we take first. Historically, the first stages of the economists' Reasonable Dialog were focused more on supply. In investigating the foundations of supply, we are investigating the economics of production and that was the central topic for the classical economists.

Adam Smith, we recall, had been very optimistic about the future economic development of the industrializing countries. With increased division of labour leading to higher wages and growing demand, he felt, production could continue to grow. However, Thomas Malthus criticized Smith's optimism. Malthus spoke for the pessimistic view and, of course, Malthus is best known for his claim that increasing population would lead to poverty. In supporting this idea, Malthus began to study the limits on production. It was this study that has made his work important particularly for Neoclassical economics.

Limits on production stem from limited resources with a given technology. With a given technology, limited quantities of inputs will yield only limited quantities of outputs. The relationship between the quantities of inputs and the maximum quantities of outputs produced is called the "production function."

The "production function." is a relationship between quantities of input and quantities of output that tells us, for each quantity of input, the greatest output that can be produced with those inputs. Malthus didn't work out the details, but he clearly had this idea in mind as he originated the key concept of Diminishing Returns.

DIMINISHING RETURNS

As we recall, Malthus is best known for his pessimistic idea that population growth would force incomes down to the subsistence level. What we are interested in here is not his conclusion, but the reasoning that took him there. Malthus argued that l and is a fixed input, but the growth of population makes labour a variable input. Malthus proposed a general law of economics, the Law of Diminishing Returns: when a fixed input is combined in production with a variable input, using a given technology, increases in the quantity of the variable input will eventually depress the productivity of the variable input. (Malthus argued that decreasing productivity of labour would depress incomes).

Was Malthus right? The answer is, of course, yes and no.

There is plenty of evidence, both observational and statistical, that the Law of Diminishing Returns is valid. For example, agricultural economists have carried out experimental tests of the theory. They have selected plots of l and of identical size and fertility and used different quantities of fertilizer on the different plots of l and. In this example, l and was the fixed input and fertilizer the variable input. They found that, as the quantity of fertilizer increased, the productivity of fertilizer declines. This is only one of many bits of evidence that the Law of Diminishing Returns is true in general.

On the other h and, in the two hundred years since Malthus wrote, on the whole, population has increased but labour productivity and incomes have not declined. On the whole, they have risen. What seems to have happened is that technology has improved. Malthus recognized that if technology improved (in agriculture, at least), that might postpone what he saw as the inevitable poverty as a consequence of rising population. Some economists and other people, believe that the Malthusian prediction will eventually come true. Perhaps: what is clear is that in two hundred years it has not. But that doesn't mean the Law of Diminishing Returns is wrong! A "law" such as this can be true in general but cannot be applied when its assumptions (such as an unchanging technology) aren't true. The "Law" isn't wrong—just inapplicable to that case.There are many valid and useful applications of the Law of Diminishing Returns in economics. In this chapter we will look at two.

- We will use Diminishing Returns and related concepts to get a better idea of the meaning of the phrase "efficient allocation of resources" and some guidelines for efficiency in that sense.
- We will explore how a business firm should direct its production in order to get maximum profits and that will give us a basis for a better underst anding of the economics of supply.

First, though, we will need to look at production and diminishing returns in general in a little more detail.

PRODUCTION FUNCTION

Production is the transformation of inputs into outputs. Inputs are the factors of production—l and, labour and capital—plus raw materials and business services. The transformation of inputs into outputs is determined by the technology in use. Limited quantities of inputs will yield only limited quantities of outputs. The relationship between the quantities of inputs and the maximum quantities of outputs produced is called the "production function. "But how do these outputs change when the input quantities vary? Let's take a look at an example of a production function.In general, we would allow for varying amounts of l and, labour and capital. However, in this example, labour will be the only input, for the sake of simplicity.

A PRODUCTION FUNCTION EXAMPLE

The production function thus contains the limitations that technology places on the firm. The mathematical forms of the production function and the utility function are identical. In one case, inputs of goods and services combine to produce utility; in the other, inputs of resources combine to produce goods or services. As one moves to the right, one reaches higher levels of production. If one can visualize this as a three-dimensional graph, one can see that the production surface rises increasingly high above the surface of the page; the isoquants indicate a hill.

Marginal Productivity

Productivity, by definition, is a ratio of output to labour input. In most statistical discussions of productivity, we refer to the average productivity of labour:

$$AP = \frac{\text{Output}}{\text{Labor Input}}$$

Average labour productivity is an important concept, especially in macroeconomics. In microeconomics, however, we will focus more on the marginal productivity. We can think of the marginal productivity of labour as the additional output as a result of adding one unit of labour, with all other inputs held steady and ceteris paribus.

In algebraic terms, an equally correct definition is:

$$MP = \frac{\Delta\text{Output}}{\Delta\text{Labor}}$$

Let's have a numerical example to illustrate the application of the theory. Suppose that:

- When 300 labour-days per week are employed the firm produces 2505 units of output per week.
- When 400 labour-days per week are employed the firm produces 3120 units of output per week.
- It follows that the change in labour input, ýÿLabor, is 100.
- It also follows that the change in output, ýÿOutput, is 615.
- Applying the formula above, we approximate the marginal productivity of labour by the quotient 615/100 = 6.15.
- We can interpret this result as follows: over the range of 300 to 400 man-days of labour per week, each additional worker adds approximately 6.15 units to output.

Of course, if we had more information, we could get a closer approximation. For example, if we had the outputs for 310, 320... 390 man-days of labour, we could see how MP varies within the range 300-400. But we can be sure that the values will be in the neighborhood of 6.15.

Now let's think a little further about the Law of Diminishing Returns.

THE LAW OF DIMINISHING MARGINAL PRODUCTIVITY

In his discussions of the Law of Diminishing Returns, Malthus did not distinguish between average and marginal productivity. However, in modern economics, we think of diminishing returns primarily in terms of marginal, not average, productivity.

Law of Diminishing Returns (Modern Statement): When the technology of production and some of the inputs are held constant and the quantity of a variable input increases continually, the marginal productivity of the variable input will eventually decline. The inputs that are held steady are called the "fixed inputs." In these pages we are treating l and and capital as fixed inputs. The inputs that are allowed to vary are called the "variable inputs." In these pages we are treating labour as the variable input. Another way to express the law of diminishing returns, is that, as the variable input increases, the output also increases, but at a decreasing rate. The marginal productivity of labour is the rate of increase in output as the labour input increases. To say that output increases at a decreasing rate when the variable input increases is another way to say that the marginal productivity declines.

Marginal Productivity

Let's extend the numerical example in the page before last and see how marginal productivity varies over a wide range of labour inputs. Here is a hypothetical example of production with the inputs of l and and labour held steady and varying quantities of labour and the output and average and marginal productivities.

Labour	Output	Average Productivity	Marginal Productivity
0	0	0	0
100	945	9.45	9.45
200	1780	8.90	8.35
300	2505	8.35	7.25
400	3120	7.80	6.15
500	3625	7.25	5.05
600	4020	6.70	3.95
700	4305	6.15	2.85
800	4480	5.60	1.75
900	4545	5.05	0.65
1000	4500	4.50	-0.45

OUTPUT DIAGRAM

Here is a picture of the relationship between the variable input and the output in the numerical example in the previous table. Notice how the slope gets flatter: as the variable input increases, output increases at a decreasing rate. This is a visualization of the Law of Diminishing Marginal Productivity.

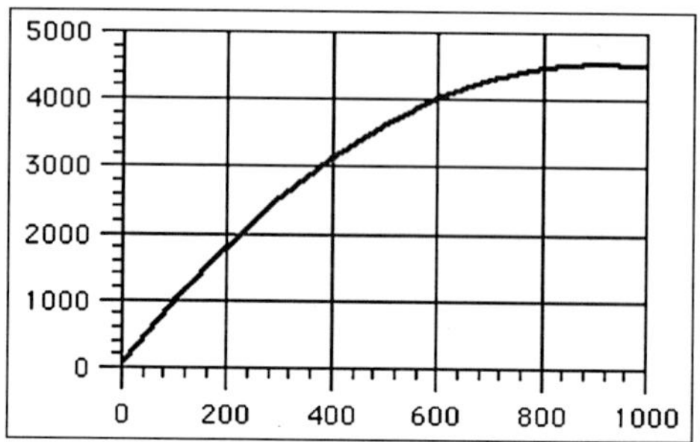

Fig. Production with Diminishing Returns

Average and Marginal Productivity Diagram

We have put some stress on the difference between average and marginal productivity. Both are important, but for a model of short-run profit-maximizing supply, marginal productivity is the more important. and the two are quite different.

Here are the average and marginal productivities for the same numerical example in the page before last. Notice how both average and marginal productivity decrease as the labour input increases. But the marginal productivity declines faster than the average productivity, pulling the average productivity down after it. The downward slope of the marginal productivity line expresses the Law of Diminishing Returns and the downward slope of the average productivity is also a result of the law.

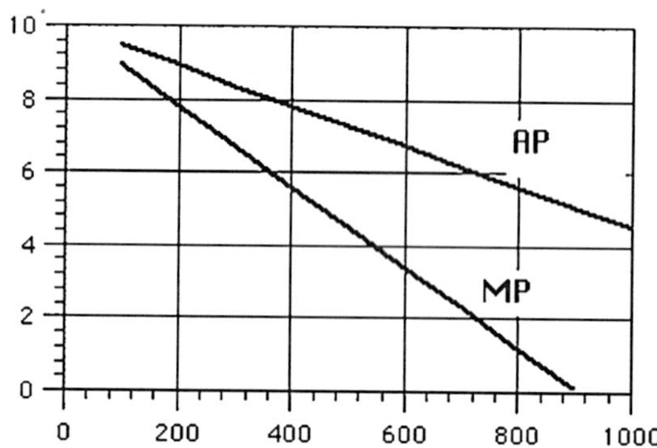

Fig. Average and Marginal Productivity

The relationship between average and marginal productivity in the diagram is important in itself and we will see similar relationships in future chapters. So let's look at it a little more closely. Average and marginal productivity will not always have the same slope. In general,

- Whenever average productivity is greater than marginal productivity, average productivity will slope downward.
- Whenever average productivity is less than marginal productivity, average productivity will slope upward.

The diagram does not show any values where average productivity is less, but a more complicated example might and then we would see the second part of the relationship visualized. To underst and the relationship, think of it this way: as we add labour input, one unit after another, we add a bit more to output at each step.

When the addition is greater than the average, it pulls the average up toward it. When the addition is less than the average, it pulls the average down toward it.

EFFICIENT ALLOCATION OF RESOURCES

Diminishing returns plays an important part in the efficient allocation of resources. For efficiency, of course, we want to give more resources to the use in which they are more productive.

But, as we give more resources to a particular use, we will observe diminishing returns—that use will become less productive. That may sound frustrating, but in fact it leads to a very important principle we can apply to the problem of efficient allocation of resources.

ALLOCATION OF LABOUR BETWEEN TWO FIELDS

Here are the Production Functions for the two Fields.

Labor Input and Output on Two Fields			
North Field		**South Field**	
labor	output	labor	output
0	0	0	0
100	9500	100	12107
200	18000	200	23429
300	25500	300	33964
400	32000	400	43714
500	37500	500	52679
600	42000	600	60857
700	45500	700	68250
800	48000	800	74858
900	49500	900	80679
1000	50000	1000	85715

The concept of marginal productivity is central to economists' underst anding of efficient allocation of resources. For an illustrative example, consider a farmer who has two fields to plant. He can grow a crop of corn (let's say) on each of them, but has a limited amount of labour to allocate between them. Let us say that the farmer can spend 1000 hours of labour, total, on the two fields. If he spends one more hour of labour on the north field, that means he has one hour less to spend on the south field.

Production Functions for the Two Fields

We can visualize the production functions for the two fields. The production function for the relatively fertile south field with a vertically dashed purple curve and the less fertile north field with a solid green curve. As we see, the south field can always produce more, with the same amount of labour, as the north field can.

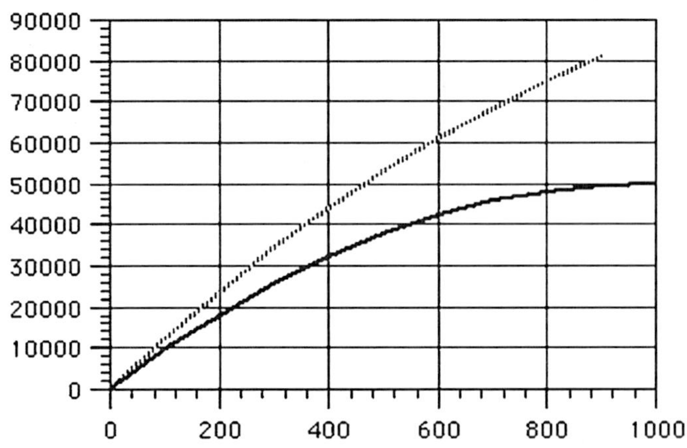

Fig. Production Functions for Two Fields

THE PROBLEM OF ALLOCATION

The farmer's "allocation problem" is: How much labour to commit to the north field and how much to the south field? One "common sense" approach might be to ab andon the infertile north field and allocate the whole 1000 hours of labour to the south field. But a little arithmetic shows that this won't work.

Here is a table that shows the correlated quantities of labour on the two fields and the total output of corn from both fields taken together.

We see that the farmer gets his largest output by allocating most, but not all, of his labour to the south field. Because of the principle of diminishing returns, however, he shouldn't put all his resources into the one field, but divide the labour resource (unevenly!) between the two. But how much should go to the north plot and how much to the south plot?

Table. Allocation of Labour and Total Output on Two Fields

Labor on North Field	Labor on South Field	Total output in bushels of corn
0	1000	85000
100	900	89600
200	800	92400
300	700	93400
400	600	92600
500	500	90000
600	400	85600
700	300	79400
800	200	71400
900	100	61600
1000	0	50000

Visualizing The Problem of Allocation

We can visualize the efficient allocation of resources with a graph like this one. The labour used on the infertile north field is measured on the horizontal axis and the total output from both fields in shown on the vertical axis. (We are assuming, of course, that all labour not used on the North field is used on the South field). The dark green curve shows how total output changes as we shift labour from the north field to the south field. Thus, the top of the curve is the interesting spot—that's where we get the most output. In this example, that's the efficient allocation of resources between the two fields. It's easy to see that we should put some labour to work on the north field—but not too much. The vertical orange line shows that the maximum output—the top of the dark green curve—comes when about 300 labour days are allocated to the north field and the rest, 700 labour days, to the south field. and that's exactly right.

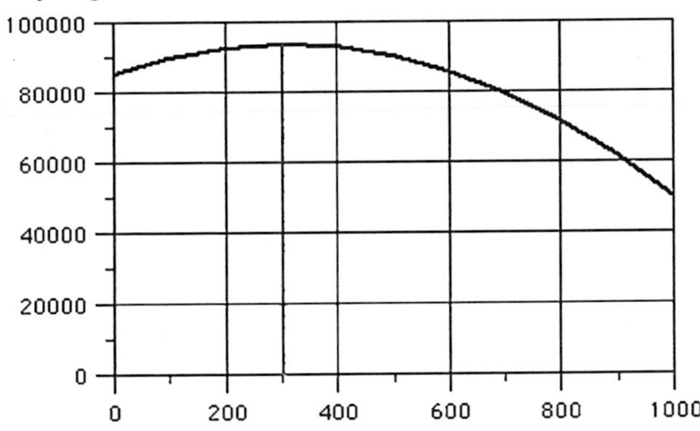

Fig. Maximum Production

It's pretty easy to see where the maximum is in this simple example. But in a more realistic example, in which there could be many more than just two dimensions, it's harder to visualize. We need a rule that we can apply in more complex, realistic examples, a rule that will tell us if we have or don't have an efficient allocation of resources.

That's where the economist's "marginal approach" comes in. The objective is to get to the top of the hill. You could call "the marginal approach" the "bug's-eye view." Think of yourself as a bug climbing up that production hill in the picture. How will you know when you are at the top?

If you were a bug, you couldn't see much. Perhaps you couldn't see to the top of the hill. But you would be able to tell if you were going up, or down, or neither. So you would just keep going as long as you were going up and stop when you were neither going up nor down. That's the way a bug gets to the top of a hill. If you were a farmer with two fields, it's a little more complicated, but the same principles apply: take it step by step. However much you may be producing, ask yourself "What would happen if I were to take one worker away from the North Field and put her to work on the South Field? How much less will the North Field produce? The answer to that question is the marginal productivity of labour on the North Field. How much more will the South Field produce? The answer to that question is the marginal productivity of labour on the South Field. So the move of labour from the North Field will increase production if the marginal productivity on the North Field is less than the marginal productivity on the South Field. Like the bug, you want to keep moving in that direction as long as production keeps getting greater, that is, as long as the marginal productivity on the North Field is less than the marginal productivity on the South Field. and you stop when further movement won't get you any higher on the hill, that is, when the marginal productivities are equal on the two fields.

Here it is:

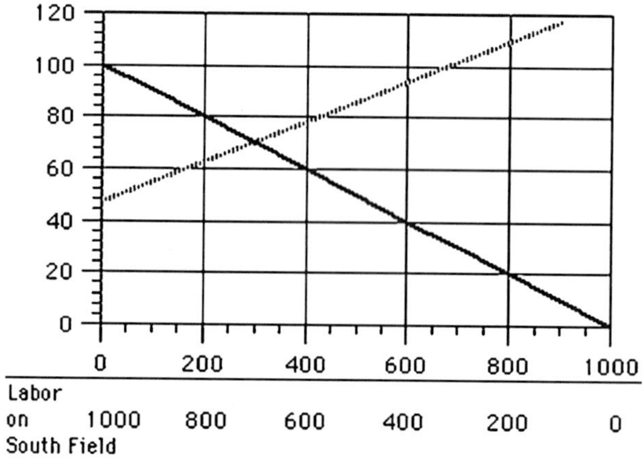

Fig. Marginal Productivity and Efficient Allocation

So now, let's visualize the marginal productivities for these two fields. But this time we will do it a slightly different way. We will measure the labour used on the infertile north field from left to right on the horizontal axis. Then, what's left is what's available for the north field, so we will measure the labour used on the south field from left to right—from 1000 hours down to zero. The marginal product on the north field is shown with the green line and the marginal product on the south field with the vertical-dashed purple line. (Remember, the marginal productivity on the south field decreases as the labour input on the south field gets bigger, so the marginal productivity on that field increases as labour used on the field gets smaller, as it does here)

MARGINAL PRODUCTIVITY

Figure shows the most efficient allocation of resources in this case. It is to allocate 300 hours of labour to the north field and 700 hours to the south field, as shown by the vertical red-orange line. For maximum output, labour is allocated so that the marginal productivity of labour on the north field is equal to the marginal productivity of labour on the south field.

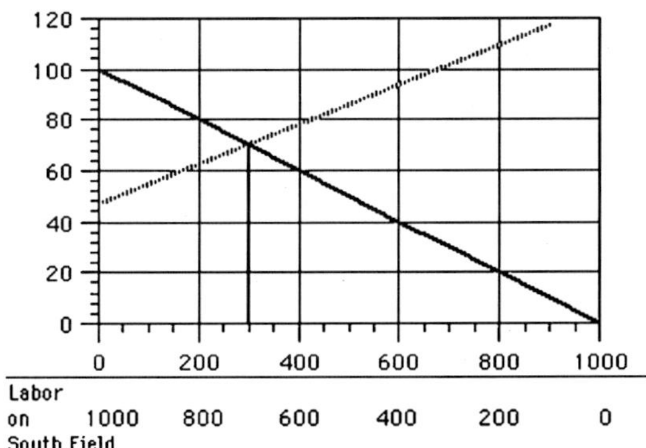

Fig. Efficient Allocation

To see why this works, think it through in reverse: what happens if the allocation of labour is not 300 to the north field and 700 to the south field? For example, suppose 200 hours are allocated to the south field and 800 to the north field. This puts us to the left of the orange line—and we read off the diagram that the marginal productivity of labour on the north field is 80 bushels of corn, while the marginal productivity on the south field is about 62.

Remembering the definition of marginal productivity, that means: if the farmer spends one additional hour on the north field, he will gain 80 bushels, while spending one less on the south field will cost him 62 bushels, leaving a net gain of 18 bushels. What has happened is that spending 800 hours of labour on the south field has pushed the "diminishing returns" on that field so far that it is less productive at the margin than the north field. and that will be true anywhere to the left of the orange line, since, in that range, the marginal productivity on the north field is always greater than the marginal productivity on the south field. Now let's see what happens if the allocation is to the right of the most efficient one—for example, suppose the farmer were to allocate 600 hours to the north field and 400 to the south field. Looking at the diagram, we see that the marginal productivity on the north field is 40 while the marginal productivity on the south field is 90.

Thus, moving an hour of labour from the north field to the south field will yield a gain of 90-40=fifty bushels of corn. and the farmer will continue to gain as he moves toward the efficient allocation from the right, because, in that range, the marginal product on the south field is always bigger than the marginal product on the north field. We have seen that the farmer can gain by reallocating his labour from either side toward the efficient output. Once he has 300 hours of labour on the north field and 700 on the south, the farmer cannot increase his output any further. That is why we think of it as the "efficient" allocation of resources. The efficient allocation of labour between the two fields. Try typing in a number between zero and one thous and in the "Labour on North Field" blank and see if you can't find the maximum total production by trial and error and notice how the marginal productivities are closer together when total production is higher.

MARGINAL PRODUCTIVITY AND THE EQUIMARGINAL PRINCIPLE

This is a quite general principle, which we may state as follows.

Rule: When the same product or service is being produced in two or more units of production, in order to get the maximum total output, resources should be allocated among the units of production in such a way that the marginal productivity of each resource is the same in each unit of production. This example may also be a little clearer example of what we mean by "efficient allocation of resources."

In the example, we have a tiny economy, consisting of one farmer and two plots of l and. When the marginal productivities on the two plots are equal, this tiny economy has an "efficient allocation of resources." Of course, real economies are more complex, but the principles governing the efficient allocation of resources are the same. This rule has a name: it is the Equimarginal Principle. The idea is to make two things equal "at the margin"—in this case, to make the marginal productivity of labour equal on the two fields.

As we will see, it has many applications in economics. In more complicated cases, we will have to generalize the rule carefully. In this example, for instance, we are allocating resources between two fields that produce the same output. When the different areas of production are producing different kinds of goods and services, it will be more complicated. But a version of the Equimarginal Principle will still apply.

THEORY OF THE FIRM

In developing the supply and demand approach to economics, economists first worked out the basis of the demand curve. By treating the demand for a product or service as a rational decision by a (primarily) self-interested individual or family, economists were able to underst and the relation of the demand for one product or service to the dem ands for other products and services and to many other forms of economic activity. It was natural to apply the same approach to supply. As a first step, we need to think about the decision-makers in supplying goods and services and what a "rational decision" to supply goods and services would mean. In economics, this is often called the "Theory of the Firm."

In the remainder of this chapter we will apply the concepts of marginal productivity and diminishing returns to the theory of the firm. First we will talk a bit about business firms and their role in a market economy, then we will return to the marginal productivity approach.

About Firms

A firm is a unit that does business on it's own account. (Firm is from the Italian, "firma, " a signature and the idea is that a firm can commit itself to a contract). Thus, the firm is the decision-maker in supplying goods and services. There are three main kinds of firms in modern market economies:

Proprietorships

A proprietorship (or proprietary business) is a business owned by an individual, the "proprietor." Many "Mom and Pop stores"—and other "Mom and Pop" businesses—are proprietorships. Some proprietorships are too small even to employ one person full time. Craftsmen, such as plumbers and painters, may have "day jobs" and work as self-employed proprietors part time after hours. Computer programmers and others may also do that. At the other extreme, some proprietary businesses employ many hundreds of workers in a wide range of specializations. In a proprietorship, the proprietor is almost always the decision-maker for the business.

Partnerships

A partnership is a business jointly owned by two or more persons. In most partnerships, each partner is legal liable for debts and agreements made by any partner. Of course, this requires a great deal of trust and thus partners generally know one another well enough to have that sort of trust. Family partnerships are very common for that very reason. (There are now a few "limited partnerships" in which some partners are protected from legal liability for the agreements made by others, beyond some limits). In many cases, one partner is designated as the managing partner and is the main decision-maker for the business.

Corporations

A corporation has two characteristics that distinguish it from most proprietorships and partnerships:

- Limited liability
- Anonymous ownership

Limited liability means that the owner of shares in a corporation cannot lose more than a certain amount if the company fails. Usually the amount is the money paid to buy the shares. Anonymous ownership means that the owner of the shares can sell them without getting the permission of anyone other than the buyer. By contrast, in most partnerships, no one partner can sell out without getting the agreement of the other partners. In such a case the continuing partners will, of course, want to know about the new partner—he will not be an "anonymous owner." In a typical corporation, the shareholders formally elect a board of directors, who in turn select the officers of the company. One of these officers, often called the "president, " will be the principle decision-maker for the firm, but he will be expected to make decisions in the interest of the shareholders.

While there are millions of proprietorships, typically very small, the biggest businesses are corporate and corporations are particularly important because of their size.

OBJECTIVES

As we recall, Malthus did not have firms in mind when he formulated the Law of Diminishing Returns. But this law has applications Malthus did not envision and we will see how to apply the law to a business firm. In the Reasonable Dialog of economics in the nineteenth century, the development of these ideas was a bit indirect. In about the eighteen-seventies, economists were rethinking the theory of consumer demand. They applied a version of "diminishing returns" and the Equimarginal Principle to determine how a consumer would divide up her spending among different consumer goods. That worked pretty well and so some other economists, especially the American economist John Bates Clark, tried using the same approach in the theory of the firm. These innovations were the beginning of Neoclassical Economics.

Following the Neoclassical approach, we will interpret "rational decisions to supply goods and services" to mean decisions that maximize—something! What does a supplier maximize? The operations of the firm will, of course, depend on its objectives. One objective that all three kinds of firms share is profits and it seems that profits are the primary objective in most cases. We will follow the neoclassical tradition by assuming that firms aim at maximizing their profits.

There are two reasons for this assumption. First, despite the growing importance of nonprofit organizations and the frequent calls for corporate social responsibility, profits still seem to be the most important single objective of producers in our market economy. Thus it is the right place to start. Second, a good deal of the controversy in the reasonable dialog of economics has centered on the implications of profit motivation. Is it true, as Adam Smith held, that the "invisible h and" leads profit-seeking businessmen to promote the general good? To assess that question, we need to underst and the implications of profit maximization.

PROFIT

Profit is defined as revenue minus cost, that is, as the price of output times the quantity sold (revenue) minus the cost of producing that quantity of output. However, we need to be a little careful in interpreting that. Remember, economists underst and cost as opportunity cost—the value of the opportunity given up. Thus, when we say that businesses maximize profit, it is important to include all costs—whether they are expressed in money terms or not.

For example, a cab-driver—the self-employed proprietor of an independent cab service—says: "I'm making a 'profit, ' but I can't take home enough to support my family, so I'm going to have to close down and get a job." The proprietor is ignoring the opportunity cost of her own labour. When those opportunity costs are taken into account, we will find that he is not really making a profit after all.

Let's say that the cab-driver makes $500 a week driving his cab, after all expenses (gasoline, maintenance, etc.) have been taken out. Suppose he can get wages (including tips!) of $800 driving for someone else, with hours no longer and about the same conditions otherwise. Then $800 is the opportunity cost of his labour and after we deduct the opportunity cost from his $500 net as an independent cabbie, he is actually losing $300 per week.

This is one of the most important reasons for using the opportunity cost concept: it helps us to underst and the circumstances that will lead people to get into and out of business. Because accountants traditionally considered only money costs, the net of money revenue minus money cost is called "accounting profit." (Actually, modern accountants are well aware of opportunity cost and use the concept for special purposes).

The economist's concept is sometimes called "economic profit." If there will be some doubt as to which concept of profit we mean, we will sometimes use the terms "economic profit" or "accounting profit" to make it clear which is intended.

THE JOHN BATES CLARK MODEL

Like any other unit, a firm is limited by the technology available. Thus, it can increase its outputs only by increasing its inputs. As usual, this will be expressed by a production function. The output the firm can produce will depend on the l and, labour and capital the firm puts to work. In formulating the Neoclassical theory of the firm, John Bates Clark took over the classical categories of l and, labour and capital and simplified them in two ways. First, he assumed that all labour is homogenous—one labour hour is a perfect substitute for any other labour hour. Second, he ignored the distinction between l and and capital, grouping together both kinds of nonhuman inputs under the general term "capital." and he assumed that this broadened "capital" is homogenous.

Of course, the simplifying assumptions aren't true—John Bates' Clark's conception of the firm is highly simplified, like a map at a very large scale.

In more advanced economics, we can get rid of the simplifying assumptions and deal with a much more realistic "map" of the business firm. But for most of this book, we'll take that on faith and stick to the simplified version Clark gave us. That will make it simpler and the principles we will discover are sound and applicable to the real world in all its complexity. In the John Bates Clark model, there are some important differences between labour and capital and they relate to the long and short run.

SHORT AND LONG RUN

A key distinction here is between the short and long run.

Some inputs can be varied flexibly in a relatively short period of time. We conventionally think of labour and raw materials as "variable inputs" in this sense. Other inputs require a commitment over a longer period of time. Capital goods are thought of as "fixed inputs" in this sense.

A capital good represents a relatively large expenditure at a particular time, with the expectation that the investment will be repaid—and any profit paid—by producing goods and services for sale over the useful life of the capital good. In this sense, a capital investment is a long-term commitment. So capital is thought of as being variable only in the long run, but fixed in the short run.

Thus, we distinguish between the short run and the long run as follows:

In the perspective of the short run, the number and equipment of firms operating in each industry is fixed. In the perspective of the long run, all inputs are variable and firms can come into existence or cease to exist, so the number of firms is also variable.

MORE SIMPLIFYING ASSUMPTIONS

The John Bates Clark model of the firm is already pretty simple. We are thinking of a business that just uses two inputs, homogenous labour and homogenous capital and produces a single homogenous kind of output.

The output could be a product or service, but in any case it is measured in physical (not money) units such as bushels of wheat, tons of steel or minutes of local telephone calls. In the short run, in addition, the capital input is treated as a given "fixed input." Also, we can identify the price of labour with the wage in the John Bates Clark model. (In a modern business firm, we have to include benefits as well as take-home wages. The technical term for the total, wages and benefits, is "employee compensation.") We will add two more simplifying assumptions. The new simplifying assumptions are:

- The price of output is a given constant.
- The wage (the price of labour per labour hour) is a given constant.

Putting them all together—just two kinds of input and one kind of output, one kind of output fixed in the short run and given output price and wage—it seems to be a lot of simplifying assumptions and it is.

They are the assumptions that fit best into many applications and the starting point for still others. Once we have simplified our conception of the firm to this extent, what is left for the director of the firm to decide.

THE FIRM'S DECISION

In the short run, then, there are only two things that are not given in the John Bates Clark model of the firm. They are the output produced and the labour (variable) input. and that is not actually two decisions, but just one, since labour input and output are linked by the "production function." Either

- The output is decided and the labour input will have to be just enough to produce that outputor
- The labour input is decided and the output is whatever that quantity of labour can produce.

Thus, the firm's objective is to choose the labour input and corresponding output that will maximize profit. Let's continue with the numerical example in the first part of the chapter.

Suppose a firm is producing with the production function shown there, in the short run. Suppose also that the price of the output is $100 and the wage per labour-week is $500.

Then let's see how much labour the firm would use and how much output it would produce, in order to maximize profits. The relationship between labour input and profits will look something like this:

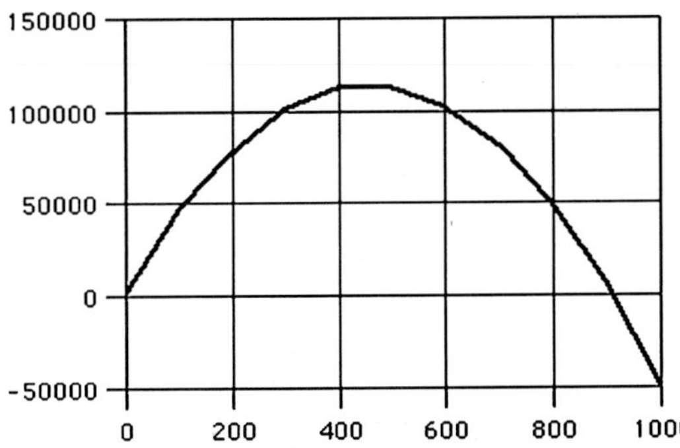

Fig. Labour Input and Profits in the Numerical Example

In the figure, the green curve shows the profits rising and then falling and the labour input increases. Of course, the eventual fall-off of profits is a result of "diminishing returns, " and the problem the firm faces is to balance "diminishing returns" against the demand for the product.

The objective is to get to the top of the profit hill. We can see that this means hiring something in the range of four to five hundred workers for the week. But just how many? The way to approach this problem is to take a bug's-eye view. Think of yourself as a bug climbing up that profit hill. How will you know when you are at the top?

THE MARGINAL APPROACH

The bug's-eye view is the marginal approach. However much labour is being employed at any given time, the really relevant question is, supposing one more unit of labour is hired, will profits be increased or decreased? If one unit of labour is eliminated, will profits increase or decrease? In other words, what does one additional labour unit add to profits? What would elimination of one labour unit subtract from profits? We can break that question down. Profit is the difference of revenue minus cost. Ask, "What does one additional labour unit add to cost? What does one additional labour unit add to revenue? The first question is relatively easy. What one additional labour unit will add to cost is the wage paid to recruit the one additional unit.

The second question is a little trickier. It's easier to answer a related question: "What does one additional labour unit add to production?" By definition, that's the marginal product—the marginal product of labour is defined as the additional output as a result of increasing the labour input by one unit. But we need a measurement that is comparable with revenues and profits, that is, a measurement in money terms. Since the price is given, the measurement we need is the Value of the Marginal Product:

Value of the Marginal Product

The Value of the Marginal Product is the product of the marginal product times the price of output. It is abbreviated VMP. To review, we have made some progress toward answering the original question. Adding one more unit to the labour input, we have

Increase in revenue = Value of marginal product

Increase in cost = Wage

So the answer to "What will one additional labour unit add to profits?" is "the difference of the Value of the Marginal Product Minus the wage." Conversely, the answer to "What will the elimination of one labour unit add to profits?" is "the wage minus the Value of Marginal Product of Labour." and in either case the "addition to profits" may be a negative number: either building up the work force or cutting it down can drag down profits rather than increasing them.

So, again taking the bug's-eye view, we ask "Is the Value of the Marginal Product greater than the wage, or less?" If greater, we increase the labour input, knowing that by doing so we increase profits by the difference, VMP-wage. If less, we cut the labour input, knowing that by doing so we increase profits by the difference, wage-VMP. and we continue doing this until the answer is "Neither." Then we know there is no further scope to increase profits by changing the labour input—we have arrived at maximum profits. Let's see how that works. Let's go back to the numerical example from earlier in the chapter and assume that the price of output is $100 per unit and the wage is $500. The value of the marginal product, $100*MP and the wage for that example.

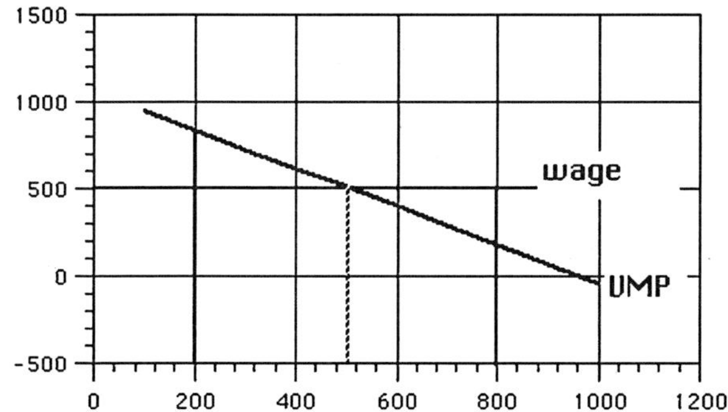

Now suppose that the firm begins by using just 200 units of labour, as shown by the orange line. The manager asks herself, "If I were to increase the labour input to 201, that would increase both costs and revenues.

By how much? Let's see: the VMP is 850, so the additional worker will add $850 to revenues. Since the wage is $500, the additional worker will add just $500 to cost, for a net gain of $350. It's a good idea to "upsize" and add one more worker.

On the other h and, suppose that the firm is using 800 units of labour, as shown by the other orange line. The manager asks herself, "If I were to cut the labour input to 799, that would cut both costs and revenues. By how much? Let's see: the VMP is 200, so the additional worker will add just $200 to revenues. Since the wage is $500, the additional worker will add just $500 to cost, for a net loss of $300. It's time to "downsize" and cut the labour force. In each case, there is an unrealized potential and the amount of unrealized potential is the difference between the VMP and the wage. The firm's profit potential will not be 100% realized until the VMP is equal to the wage. That's the "equimarginal principle" again.

THE EQUIMARGINAL PRINCIPLE

By taking the marginal approach—the bug's-eye view—we have discovered the diagnostic rule for maximum profits. The way to maximize profits then is to hire enough labour so that,

$$VMP=wage$$

where p is the price of output and VMP = p*MP the marginal productivity of labour in money terms. This is another instance of the Equimarginal Principle. The rule tells us that profits are not maximized until we have adjusted the labour input so that the marginal product in labour, in dollar terms, is equal to the wage. Since the wage is the amount that the additional (marginal) unit of labour adds to cost, we could think of the wage as the "marginal cost" of labour and express the rule as "value of marginal product of labour equal to marginal cost." But we will give a more compete and careful definition of marginal cost (of output).

Labor	Marginal Productivity	p*MP	Wage	Accounting Profit
0			500	0
	9.45	945		
100			500	44500
	8.35	835		
200			500	78000
	7.25	725		
300			500	100500
	6.15	615		
400			500	112000
	5.05	505		
500			500	112500
	3.95	395		
600			500	102000
	2.85	285		
700			500	80500
	1.75	175		
800			500	48000
	0.65	65		
900			500	4500
	-0.45	-55		
1000			500	-50000

Profit Maximization

The maximization of profits in the example. Remember, the wage is $500 per labour week. The theory tells us that profits will be biggest when the value of the marginal product is exactly equal to the wage, that is, $500. Try adjusting the number of labour weeks input and see how profits increase as the value of the marginal product gets closer to $500. *Profit Maximization*: In our numerical example, suppose that the price of output is $100 per unit and the wage is $500 per worker per period. Then the p*MP, wage and profits will be something like this.

VISUALIZING PROFIT MAXIMIZATION

What we see in the table is that the transition from 400 to 500 units of labour gives p*MP=505, very nearly VMP=wage. and that is the highest profit. So the profit-maximizing labour force is about 500 units. We can get a more exact answer by looking at a picture or tinkering with the programme example a bit. Here is a picture of the profit-maximizing hiring in this example:

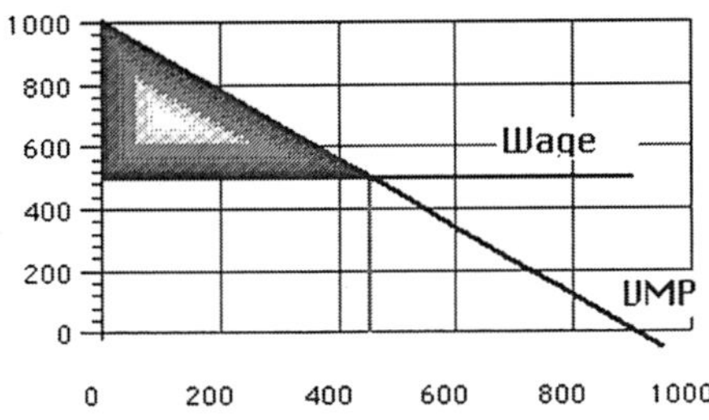

Fig. Maximizing Profit

The picture suggests that the exact amount is a bit less than 500 units of labour. If you tinker with the programme example enough, you will see that the exact profit maximizing labour input is 454.54545454545... units of labour—a repeating decimal fraction.

Notice the shaded area between the VMP curve and the price (wage) line. n the picture, the area of the shaded triangle is the total amount of payments for profits, interest and rent—in other words, everything the firm pays out for factors of production other than labour. The rectangular area below the wage line and left of the labour=454 line is shows the wage bill. Thus, the John Bates Clark model provides us with a visualization of the division of income between labour and property. We'll make use of this fact in exploring the economics of income distribution in the last Part of this chapter.

PROFIT MAXIMIZATION

We can use the diagram also to underst and why VMP=wage is the diagnostic that tells us the profit is at a maximum. Suppose the labour input is less than 500—for example, suppose labour input is 200. Than an additional labour-day of labour will add about 7.8 units to output and about $780 to the firm's sales revenue, but only $500 to the firm's costs, adding roughly $220 to profits. So it is profitable to increase the labour input from 200, or, by the same reasoning, from any labour input less than $500.

This difference between the VMP and the wage is the increase or decrease in profits from adding or subtracting one unit of labour. It is sometimes called the marginal profit and (as we observed in studying consumers' marginal benefits) the absolute value of the marginal profits is a measure of unrealized potential profits. That's why the businessman wants to adjust the labour input so that VMP-wage=0.

Let's try one more example. Suppose the labour input is 800 labour-days per week. If the firm "downsizes" to 799 labour-days, it reduces its output by just about 1.2 units and its sales revenue by about $120, but it reduces its labour cost by $500, increasing profits by about $380. Thus a movement toward the VMP=wage again increases profits by realizing some unrealized potential profit. The formula VMP=wage is a diagnostic for maximum profits because it tells us that there is no further potential to increase the profits by adjusting the labour input—marginal profit is zero. The marginal productivity rule is the key to maximization of profits in the short run. But now let's take a look at the long run perspective.

Increasing Returns to Scale and the Long Run

In microeconomics, we think of diminishing returns as a short run thing. In the long run, all inputs can be increased or decreased in proportion. Reductions in the marginal productivity of labour, due to increasing the labour input, can be offset by increasing the tools and equipment the workers have to work with. How will that come out, on net? The answer is—"it all depends!" In the long run we define three possible cases:

Decreasing Returns to Scale

If an increase in all inputs in the same proportion k leads to an increase of output of a proportion less than k, we have decreasing returns to scale. Example: If we increase the inputs to a dairy farm (cows, l and, barns, feed, labour, everything) by 50% and milk output increases by only 40%, we have decreasing returns to scale in dairy farming. This is also known as "diseconomies of scale, " since production is less cheap when the scale is larger.

Constant Returns to Scale

If an increase in all inputs in the same proportion k leads to an increase of output in the same proportion k, we have constant returns to scale. Example: If we increase the number of machinists and machine tools each by 50% and the number of st andard pieces produced increases also by 50%, then we have constant returns in machinery production.

Increasing Returns to Scale

If an increase in all inputs in the same proportion k leads to an increase of output of a proportion greater than k, we have increasing returns to scale. Example: If we increase the inputs to a software engineering firm by 50% output and increases by 60%, we have increasing returns to scale in software engineering. (This might occur because in the larger work force, some programmers can concentrate more on particular kinds of programming and get better at them). This is also known as "economies of scale, " since production is cheaper when the scale is larger. In introductory economics, we usually discuss these long run tendencies in the context of cost analysis, rather than marginal productivity analysis. However, increasing returns to scale, in particular, creates some complications for the application of marginal productivity thinking. Thus, I think there may be something to gain by exploring how increasing returns to scale goes together with marginal productivity. To keep it as simple as possible, we will look at a numerical example of a two-person labour market and a fictitious product that is produced with increasing returns to scale. Economists often like to talk about the production of "widgets, " so our fictitious industry is the widget-tying industry.

EXAMPLE OF PRODUCTION WITH INCREASING RETURNS TO SCALE

- Since this is a long run analysis, there is no fixed input. Indeed, for simplicity, there is only one input. Labour is the only input and is variable.
- Our small economy is populated by three people: Bob and John, workers and Gordon, an entrepreneur (that is, a person who will organize a business if and only if it is profitable to do so).
  - Bob, working alone, can produce output worth 2000 per week.
  - Bob's opportunity cost is 2100 per week. (That means Bob can earn 2100 in producing some other good or service).
  - John, working alone, can produce 2000 per week.
  - John's opportunity cost is 2800 per week.
- If Bob and John work together, thanks to division of labour, they can produce 5500 per week. Suppose, for example, that Gordon sets up a Widget-Tying business and hires Bob and, later, John to do the work. This is an example of "increasing returns to scale" since input increases by 100% when the second worker is hired and output increases by 175% as a result.

Why would output increase more than in proportion to inputs? First, simply having four h ands may increase productivity as the two men can simultaneously do different parts of the job. Second, each may concentrate on some part of the work, getting better at it with more practice, but leaving the other part to the other worker who also gains practice and skill in that part. (These were the kinds of advantages Adam Smith particularly stressed). Finally, each may concentrate on the tasks for which he has a greater inborn talent. Notice that the two-person widget-tying operation uses resources with an opportunity cost of 2800+2100=4900 and produces output worth 5500, for a net increase in production of 600. Evidently, it is a good thing that such a team be organized.

MARGINAL PRODUCTIVITY AND INCREASING RETURNS TO SCALE

Now, what is the marginal productivity of labour with two persons employed? With one worker, output was 2000; with two, 5500, for a difference of 3500. If either Bob or John quits, reducing the firm to 1 worker, the firm loses 3500—so 3500 is the marginal productivity of both Bob and John. That is, 3500 is the marginal productivity of labour, between 1 and 2 units of labour, not the marginal product of some specific worker who happens last. Here is the marginal productivity of labour in the form of a table. Remember, the law of diminishing marginal productivity does not apply in this long run perspective, since there is no fixed input.

Labour	Output	MP
0	0	
1	2000	2000
2	5500	3500

But see what this means. If both Bob and John are paid their marginal productivity, the wage bill is 2*3500=7000. But the product of the firm is only 5500, so Gordon ends up losing 1500. Clearly, it will not be possible to pay the marginal productivity wage. Suppose both are paid a wage less than marginal productivity. Will they continue to work for Gordon if they are paid less than marginal productivity? Yes, up to a point. Here is the supply curve of labour derived from their opportunity costs:

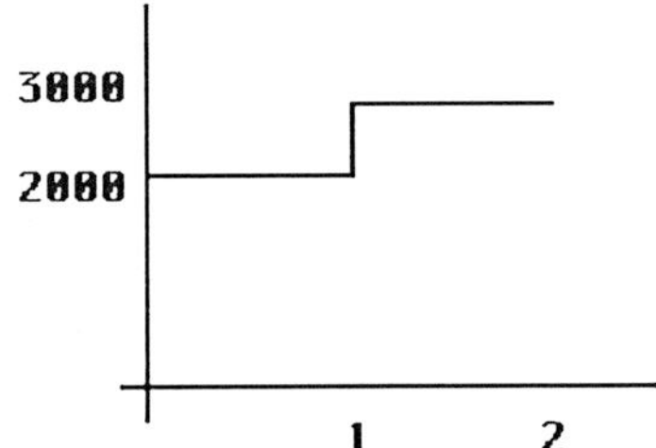

The Supply of Labour from Bob and John

How much does Gordon have to pay? Suppose Gordon starts cutting the wage. When the wage drops below 2800, John will resign and then the firm produces only 2000, not enough to pay Bob his 2100 opportunity cost, so Bob resigns too. Evidently 2800 is the least wage Gordon can pay and keep his work force. However, at a wage of 2800 per worker, Gordon's wage bill is 5600 and with an output of 5500, he is still losing 100. Not as much as before, but a loss is a loss and Gordon will choose not to set up a widget-tying enterprise.

THE DARK SIDE OF THE FORCE

Increasing returns to scale are a powerful force for increasing productivity, but the problem of organizing them efficiently is "the dark side of the force." We have seen that an enterprise that yields a net gain of 600 to society cannot be organized, in this example, without producing a loss. The market system cannot take advantage of the potentiality for gain through division of labour and increasing returns to scale in this case. This possibility was discovered by an early 20th Century British economist named Arthur Charles Pigou, but despite 80 years of discussion, this analysis is not at all widely understood, even among professional economists. Pigou thought it might be a good idea for the government to subsidize enterprises with increasing returns to scale. In this case a subsidy of 150 would make the widget-tying enterprise profitable and produce a gain of 600 in national product.

There may be another solution. Since the widget-tying enterprise adds 600 to national output but loses at least 100, we might ask, what happens to the difference of 700? The answer is that Bob gets it. Bob is paid at least 2800 but his opportunity cost is only 2100, accounting for the difference of 700. Suppose that Bob and John were not paid the same wage, but, instead, each was paid his opportunity cost plus 100. The wage bill would then be 2200+3000=5200 and Gordon would finish with a profit of 300.

Thus, wage discrimination may make it possible for the widget-tying enterprise to exist when it cannot exist so long as each worker is paid the same wage for the same work.

The conclusions are surprising and underst andably, controversial—yet the numbers support them, both in this and more complicated and abstract examples.

- Some people believe it is just that each person be paid according to her or his contribution and interpret "marginal productivity" as the person's contribution. However, this may impossible when there are increasing returns to scale, as there may not be enough output to pay everyone on that basis.
- Compromising, some would say that each person ought to be paid in proportion to her or his contribution, so that people are paid equally for the same work. That, too, may be impossible.
- Discrimination or subsidy may be necessary to allow some socially useful activities to exist.
- There may be no simple system of payment (such as supply and demand or equal pay for equal work) that will allow a socially useful enterprise with increasing returns to scale to exist.

REFLECTIONS

I think this is the reason we have organizations. If there were no increasing returns to scale, there would be little reason for any business to employ more than one person. We would instead have an economy consisting of self-employed individuals, like a yeoman agricultural system. Instead we see an economic system consisting in part of large, complicated organizations with internal arrangements and payments systems that have little to do with contributions or marginal productivity and may be discriminatory. From an abstract point of view, they may waste resources by not paying at the marginal productivity; but the benefits of increasing returns to scale are so great that, even falling far short of potential efficiency, they can still be very productive.

This is sometimes lost sight of by the organizations themselves. People naturally avoid complexity and organizations sometimes try to set up simple, market-like internal payment and fund transfer systems, hoping that this will increase efficiency. But, as we have seen, this can fail badly in the context of increasing returns to scale (and that is the context of any large productive organization).

We have recently been through such an experience at Drexel. A few years ago we went over to "revenue centered budgeting." The idea was to let the colleges retain a high proportion of the revenues they produce, through tuition, grants, contracts and so on. This would (it was felt) give the deans and college faculties more "incentive" to set up popular new programs and initiatives.

However, it wasn't possible to let the colleges keep 100%, since some money is needed to run shared services like the computer centre, student-life activities and the library, not to mention the salaries of high administrators (and we wouldn't think of mentioning that). But it couldn't be made to work. If the proportion kept by the colleges was high enough to make it profitable for them to set up new programs and initiatives, there was not enough for the purposes of the central administration; while if the proportion taken by the central administration was enough to do its job, then the colleges were losing money on their new programs and initiatives—no incentive!

So Drexel has moved away from "revenue centered budgeting" in practice, although there is still some work being done to try to work out a "revenue centered budgeting" system that will work. Here's a prediction based on the theory of increasing returns to scale: a revenue-centered budgeting system probably can be made to work, but it will be just as complex and frustrating than the centralized budgeting traditionally has been. That complexity and frustration (and large organizations) are the price we pay for the benefits of increasing returns to scale.

9

Physical Distribution: Transportation

Functions of exchange are necessarily the principal and most essential marketing functions. To give effect to the exchange functions, products must normally be supplied. Following the creation of form utility, this is done through the performance of two other marketing functions, namely, transportation and storage, which are usually designated as functions of physical distribution. In the case of tangible commodities flowing from our agricultural, mining, and manufacturing industries, the essentiality of physical distri-bution is selfevident.

Not so popularly appreciated is the extent to which the marketing of various kinds of services is also dependent upon physical distribution. The construction industry, the public utilities and communications industry, and many kinds of business and personal services could not exist in the absence of a physical flow of commodities which are required for the creation and availability of the services at times and places when and where needed. The importance of physical distribution activities, the alternative and complementary means of performing them, and their relationship to the entire marketing procedure. This is followed by a discussion of the transportation aspect of physical distribution.

WHAT IS EXPECTED OF PHYSICAL DISTRIBUTION

To a very great degree our marketing system is built upon and presupposes an economical and effective system of physical distribution. The four major types of demands that society places upon the physical distribution functions are:

- That they be adequate to meet all normal requirements of trade;
- That they provide for speedy movement, thus aiding in minimizing the time elapsing between form utility production and business use or consumption;
- That distribution services be available in number and variety to insure the efficiency of their performance;
- That the cost of providing physical distribution be reasonable and in accordance with the true worth of services rendered.

ECONOMIC BASIS FOR PHYSICAL DISTRIBUTION

The total cost of physical distribution cannot be readily ascertained. A large part of the task is handled by the public transportation and warehousing industries but much of it is accomplished within manufacturing, wholesaling, and retailing firms where physical distribution expenses are often mingled with those of other functions. Furthermore, farmers and even ultimate consumers are involved in the performance of physical distribution functions. Thus, data for the transportation and warehousing industries fall far short of measuring the total economic significance of physical distribution. The cost varies greatly among different types of products. For some which are of very high value in relation to bulk or weight (e.g., fine watches and jewelry) physical distribution costs comprise only a negligible proportion of final value. On the other hand, for commodities characterized by economic bulkiness (e.g., coal, lumber, potatoes), most of the value at place of final use or consumption consists of physical distribution expenses. The economic basis for the costs of physical distribution activities and their contribution to the productive process can be best understood by considering separately some of the specific reasons for transportation and for storage, respectively.

Reasons for Transportation

While transportation is a function necessarily performed in the marketing of all goods, it is especially costly and of unusual strategic significance in the marketing of those products which are relatively heavy or bulky, require some special form of transportation service, or must be moved considerable distances. The cost of transportation is ordinarily, however, more than offset by two distinct types of economies in the production of form utility. One is *occupational and technical division of labour,* the advantages of which can exist only under large-scale operation. With but few exceptions, industries that sell exclusively in the communities of their location cannot be operated on the most efficient scale. Transportation opens a far wider and larger market and thereby encourages large-scale industrial activity.

Second, transportation makes possible the advantages of a *geographical division of labour,* since certain communities or areas are especially well adapted for growing or making certain types of commodities. Their advantage may be due to climatic conditions, to the presence of inexpensive or adequate supplies of efficient labour, or to the proximity of necessary raw materials or semi manufactured goods.

As a result of such geographical division of labour, some communities or areas become highly specialized. They could not exist as such in the absence of modern transportation methods which take the commodities that continuously pour out in a wide stream from their farms, mines, or factories to the rest of the world and in turn bring in the necessary raw materials, supplies, and equipment.

Reasons for Storage

The most pervasive reason for storage is to meet *normal requirements of trade.* It is certainly not coincidental that most retail establishments are known as stores, and that this term, differentially prefixed, is also sometimes used to describe the facilities of wholesaling organizations as, for example, wholesale store, although it is more common to refer to a wholesale establishment as a wholesale house or *warehouse.* Considerations of etymology suggest the deep-rooted but often overlooked basic character of mercantile organizations as storehouses of merchandise. Even under modern conditions where the flow of goods from form-utility production to consumption has been greatly accelerated by improved communication and transportation facilities, normal trade inventories involve staggering quantities.

Aggregate inventory levels at the retail level ordinarily are the equivalent of about 2 months of sales of retail establishments, and inventories of wholesale establishments amount to about 1.5 months of their sales. Inventories of manufacturing establishments, consisting of materials, work in process, and finished goods, are normally the equivalent of more than 2 months of sales volume of such establishments.

While the necessity of meeting ordinary demands of trade accounts for a substantial proportion of all storage activity, a variety of specific circumstances increases the need for storage services and makes necessary the carrying of inventories substantially in excess of short-term business requirements. A second major reason for storage is the *seasonal production of goods that are consumed continuously,* as is the case of most agricultural commodities and many manufactured items which are processed from them (e.g., frozen or canned fruits and vegetables).

Third, storage is necessary for goods which are *produced regularly but which are purchased or used seasonally.* In order to manufacture economically with a reasonably uniform utilization of personnel and capital facilities, many factories that make seasonal goods, such as woolen blankets or holiday novelties, are operated almost continuously. Fourth, storage is often essential *in connection with transportation arrangements.* For example, bulk commodities such as iron ore and coal are stored in vast quantities at ports on the Great Lakes throughout much of the year, awaiting movement during the open navigation season.

A fifth requirement is for *conditioning purposes,* as illustrated by the curing of tobacco and meats, the ripening of bananas, the aging of distilled spirits, and the seasoning of lumber. Sixth, *speculative buying* by business firms in anticipation of favorable price changes often accounts for abnormal quantities of goods held in storage. An important reason for much storage activity is *public policy.* Particularly in connection with federal agricultural price support programs, vast storage facilities for basic commodities, such as wheat, cotton, and butter, have been provided solely for the purpose of removing farm surpluses from current markets. Stockpiling for defence purposes is an additional reason for the storage of certain commodities.

Physical Distribution as Economic Production

While transportation and storage are separate functions, each of major economic significance and characterized both by a high degree of occupational and institutional specialization, the values created by their performance are similar in nature and often intermingled. It is the function of transportation to convey commodities from places where their utility is relatively low to places where it is higher. Because of the location of natural resources, variations in climatic conditions, concentrations of skilled or unskilled labour, large-scale manufacturing, and a high degree of specialization, many commodities are raised or manufactured largely or exclusively in certain places or regions. As a rule, commodities are of greater value (have greater capacity of satisfying human wants and desires) when at or near points of consumption than when they are at distant points of agricultural production or manufacture. Thus the principal economic basis for transportation is enhancing the value of products by the creation of *place utility.*

The function of storage is the creation of *time utility* which is accomplished by preserving or keeping goods from the time they are grown, mined, or manufactured until they are needed or used for consumption, thereby offsetting the effects of seasonal alterations of supply and demand and adjusting the difference of time between form-utility production and consumption. Under such circumstances storage acts like a reservoir, receiving the surplus flow of goods when form-utility production exceeds demand and releasing it when scarcity is impending. It is further accomplished when goods are stored in distribution or wholesale warehouses and in retail stores in order that they may flow freely through the channels of trade, in obedience to requirements, with a sufficient reserve to ensure continuity of such a flow.

Incidental to the performance of the transportation function, goods must be stored, often for considerable periods, in railroad cars, on trucks, or in the holds of ships while en route to market. As a rule, the *time* involved in the transpor-tation process has a negative value or disutility, and every effort is ordinarily made to reduce it to a minimum. Occasionally, however, this time may be used to ripen or otherwise to condition the products transported, thereby adding to them time utility and thus further enhancing their value. Time utility may also be created when shippers and consignees utilize transportation facilities for storage purposes. To minimize the use of transportation facilities as a means for storage, a limited amount of time is ordinarily allowed for removing goods shipped in carlots after the car is delivered to the consignee, and a *demurrage* fee is charged for every day the goods remain stored in the car after the period of grace. Similarly, a limited time is allowed for the removal of smaller shipments from freight warehouses after arrival at destination. In any event, time utility is often created in connection with the movement of goods from place to place where the primary aim is the creation of place utility.

Physical Distribution Management

While transportation and storage have long been recognized as major marketing functions, a discerning awareness of their close interrelationship and their effect upon other marketing functions is a relatively recent development in the field of business management. This is explained in part by the nature of the challenge facing business leaders at different times. At an early stage of our modern industrial development, and continuing to the 1920's, the great challenge was to meet the demand of expanding markets through technology.

Emphasis was largely upon engineering innova-tion in the field of manufacturing. During and since the 1920's, with manufacturing capacity generally outstripping effective market demand, business leaders became more interested in the selling function. Emphasis tended to shift to advertising, sales promotion, and personal selling, with a view to creating markets for the output of industry. The field of physical distribution was regarded more or less as a necessary evil-a more or less fixed and uncontrollable factor. Manufacturing plant locations were more or less taken for granted, the need for storage was recognized, and it was accepted that transportation was essential to get goods from places of form utility production to successive markets. In many instances, it was believed that there was but one reasonable method of moving goods, and this was commonly rail freight.

Lack of appreciation for physical distribution as a total system is also explained by the compartmentized responsibility for specific functions in business firms. For example, a traffic manager may have the job of doing everything possible to minimize transportation costs. A warehousing manager may be judged on his ability to keep storage and handling costs low. A recommendation on the part of the traffic manager, oriented to the goal of lower transportation costs, might easily lead to an increase in the amount of necessary storage activity on the part of his employer or the firm's customers in the channel of distribution.

This interrelationship is often not appreciated when managers of departments concerned with particular functions are evaluated solely on the basis of functional performance, without investigation about the ramifications of decisions in and upon other areas of business activity. Under modern conceptions of customer-oriented marketing management, marketing has come to be viewed by management more as a total process rather than as a series of specific activities, just as academicians in this field of knowledge have done for many years. The interrelationships between marketing functions and the coordination of them with respect to the goal of meeting the needs of a market at a profit have become paramount considerations in the management of progressive firms. Specifically, in regard to physical distribution activities, this has involved an awareness of them as variable factors in the total marketing effort and in an increased emphasis upon them as an important aspect of marketing strategy. This develop-ment is attributed mainly to the following factors:

- Realization that the location of manufacturing plants and physical facilities for distribution are variable factors, at least in the long run, and that decisions in regard to such locations have an important bearing upon the ability to serve markets efficiently
- Realization that there are certain "high costs" of low-cost transportation, such as slowness, increased investment in inventories, and more damage to goods in transit; conversely, that there are certain "low costs" of high-cost transportation including flexibility, speed, lower capital requirements for inventory, reduced needs for physical facilities for storage
- The development of an increased variety of special transportation services, thus enlarging the reasonable alternative means of movement for many products; and increased competition among types of carriers and storage organizations, which are actively engaged in cooperating with manufacturing compa-nies and marketing organizations in improving physical distribution
- Developments in modern methods of automatic data processing, and the growing use of methods of quantitative analysis which, in some situations, can provide "least cost" solutions to highly complex problems involving a wide variety, of movement, handling, storage, and packaging alternatives
- Increased freight rates which, along with other types of competitive pressures, have made business firms more conscious of the need for effecting improve-ments in the total costs incurred for physical distri-bution.

As a consequence of these developments, physical distribution management emerged during the 1950's as a new and promising area of business management. Among business organizations where it has developed as a specialized activity, it is concerned with the spatial arrangement of manufacturing plants and warehousing activities, the manner in which such facilities are connected by transportation, and the satisfaction of the physical distribution requirements of the firm's customers, at minimum total costs. In some organizations, particularly large manufacturing companies, management of physical distribution often includes at least partial responsibility for a number of closely related activities, such as finished-goods inventory control, warehouse operation, order processing, finished-goods materials handling, and design of special packing, storing, or handling materials or equipment.

TRANSPORTATION

The complexities of physical distribution are examined by giving separate attention to various special features of and institutional arrangements for transportation and storage. Excluded from this discussion are matters which are largely technical or operational in nature. Emphasis is focused upon considerations which relate to alternative means of accomplishing part of the marketing task within the business enterprise, and which are also of social and economic interest because they have a bearing upon the way in which the wants of consumers are satisfied and upon the efficiency with which the marketing system operates.

In a broad sense, transportation involves all kinds of movements of persons and goods from one place to another. This includes *internal* movements within business establishments, as handled by elevators, electric stairways, and other kinds of gravity and power conveyances; it includes strictly *local* movements of people and commodities within a market area; and it includes movements *between markets.* The treatment is limited to *intermarket* or intercity movements of commodities. Internal and local market movements, while of great interest and importance, are not examined here because the former are internal management problems and the latter are largely services of marketing institutions, handled to a great extent by their own equipment, and have been given appropriate attention in the sections of this book dealing with retailing and wholesaling.

Basic Types of Freight Service

The kind and quality of service demanded of our transportation system vary with the class of freight to be moved from place to place. Even though there are numerous types of goods with multifarious physical characteristics, practically all goods may be grouped into one of two broad classes with respect to transportation service requirements. One of these consists of basic commodities that are ordinarily shipped in very large volume and require only *bulk freight service.* Illustrative of such commodities are the relatively nonperishable products of agriculture such as grains and livestock, lumber and other forest products, coal and iron ore, and some semi manufactured goods that require no special protection or service in transit.

The primary requirement of a carrier of bulk freight is ability to move tremendous physical quantities at a very low cost. Speed, special services, and conveniences are secondary considerations. Bulk freight carriers ordinarily do not compete directly with carriers of the second major class of commodities designated as *merchandise freight.* Ordinarily merchandise freight moves in smaller physical volume than bulk freight although the actual physical quantities, such as in the case of California or Florida oranges, may involve a number of full rail cars in a single shipment. The principal requirements of merchandise freight are speed of service, regular and dependable schedules, special merchandise protection, safety, and effective handling services. Cost of movement, while important, is often a secondary consideration.

Legal Forms of Transportation

There are several legal forms of transportation, each of which has a distinct role in the movement of goods. *Common carriers* are franchised by a government regulatory body. They must accept shipments from any party, maintain regular service over established routes, and move freight at published rates. As a general rule, they must obtain permission from regulatory agencies to discontinue service or to change their rates. Because of the complex pattern of regulation of common carriers, they have limited flexibility in meeting specialized transportation problems. This situation creates the opportunity for service by the other legal forms of transportation.

Contract carriers are transportation companies that provide movement service to one or various shippers. Since they are regulated much less than are common carriers and do not maintain regular schedules, their rate schedules are more easily adapted to specific situations. From the standpoint of the shipper, contract carriers may be contrasted with common carriers because of the opportunity for close relationships, resulting in more personalized service. As compared with private carriers, they provide the shipper with transportation costs which are wholly variable through the avoidance of fixed investment in transportation equipment, and eliminate certain operational problems such as maintenance, repair, and relationships with an additional labour union.

The term *private carrier* is limited to transportation service provided by the owners of goods, as illustrated by railroads operated by some steel companies, fleets of tankers operated by certain oil companies, and motor truck fleets operated by some chain grocery organizations to distribute goods from warehouses to retail stores. Private transportation for intermarket movements is economical only under conditions where relatively full utilization of transportation equipment is possible or when a highly specialized service is essential.

Trends in Modes of Transport

Goods may be transported by railroads, motor trucks, water, pipeline, or through the air. For many products, the movement from origin to market or from one market to another involves a combination of different methods. In some instances, one method of transportation is an alternative to another whereas, in some cases, there is only one practical way to accomplish movement. Trends in the relative importance of each of these modes of transportation, as measured by ton-miles of domestic intercity freight traffic. Some of the major factors affecting the relative position of each method are indicated below.

Railroads

Railroads at one time had a virtual monopoly on long distance, intercity freight movements. In 1930 they accounted for threefourths of the total ton-miles of domestic intercity freight but their *relative* position since that time has steadily diminished, owing to the increased competitive significance of oil pipelines and motor trucks. By 1960 the railroads' share of intercity freight movement was only 44 per cent.

Railroads are principally common carriers and are chiefly important as long distance haulers of bulk freight. More than 99 per cent of the tonnage shipped by rail consists of carload shipments and more than 70 per cent consists of products of mines, agriculture, and forests. In order to accommodate mass bulk movements, railroads have developed special types of equipment for coal, stone, grain, petroleum products, cement and other homogeneous products shipped in bulk. Elaborate facilities have also been provided at various points for loading and unloading such commodities. Specialized freight-carrying equipment has proved more economical for most bulk shipments, even though this often involves moving empty cars in one direction.

In the movement of merchandise freight, railroads are chiefly important in connection with long haul, large quantity shipments. Most of the merchandise freight moving by rail originates with freight forwarding companies, a special type of transportation agency discussed in a following section.

To encourage shipments of merchandise freight in economical quantities, a wide differential has been established between *c.l. (carload)* and *l.c.l. (less than carload)* freight rates. While there are some exceptions, carload rates are generally only about one-half or less of l.c.l. rates. These lower rates are justified in large part because the railroad is usually relieved of loading and assembling activities at the origin and of unloading and distribution services at terminals. An additional factor is that checking, billing and collection costs are relatively much less on full carloads than on smaller shipments. Carload shipments involve minimum weights for each commodity or class of commodity. The bulkiness or density of the commodity determines the minimum weight. For example, some items of crated furniture involve carload minimums of 16,000 pounds whereas the minimum for some iron and steel products is 40,000 pounds.

Waterways

Inland waterways, consisting of rivers, canals, and the Great Lakes, account for about 17 per cent of domestic ton-miles of intercity freight. On major rivers, such as the Mississippi and Ohio, Dieselpropelled towboats push a number of special barges which may carry as much freight as several long freight trains. The principal commodities transported on rivers are coal, coke, sand, gravel, petroleum products, semimanufactured iron and steel, grain, and cement. Most of these can be stored cheaply and therefore seasonal river transportation is satisfactory. On the Great Lakes, ore, grain, coal, and stone are carried by very large specialized cargo vessels made possible by the channel depths of the lakes and the huge locks that have been built.

Water transportation is actually much more important than indicated above because there is a large amount of *intercoastal* and *coastwise* oceanborne commerce between United States ports which is not included in the data. Large fleets of coal-carrying vessels, petroleum tankers, grain ships, and other types of ocean-going vessels operate between ports on the Atlantic, the Gulf of Mexico, and port cities in the Great Lakes Region which are accessible via the St. Lawrence Seaway.

Pipelines

By their very nature, pipelines are limited to bulk movement of liquid and gaseous products. This mode of transportation grew in importance, accounting for about 5 per cent of domestic ton-miles of intercity freight in 1930 and about 17 per cent in 1960. Although most pipelines are legally common carriers, the inflexibility of existing pipeline routes has confined the use of specific lines largely to the transportation of products of their owners who are, with some notable exceptions, major oil or gas companies. Via pipelines it is possible to transport petroleum products between major shipping points more economically than by rail, but they cannot match the economy of ocean-going tankers. For this reason, a large proportion of petroleum products consumed along the eastern seaboard is moved by a combination of pipelines and tanker service, the former connecting producing fields with ports of the Gulf of Mexico from which tankers carry the products to Atlantic ports.

Private pipelines are of considerable significance in interplant transfers of liquid materials, especially in areas such as Baton Rouge, Louisiana, where there are large concentra-tions of plants in the petro-chemical industry. In such insta-nces, the pipeline is an economical means of transporting a continuous or readily controllable flow of liquid product from one plant to another where it may undergo further processing or is otherwise used in the manufacturing process.

Truck Carriers

Freight movement by motor carrier has grown from about 4 per cent of total ton miles of intercity freight in 1930 to more than 22 per cent in 1960. About two-thirds of motor truck freight tonmiles is handled by private carriers. The foregoing figures understate the true significance of the motor truck do not include local wholesale and retail deliveries of commodities, almost all of which are accomplished by trucks.

The regular motor truck and the tractor-trailer combina-tion are natural merchandise freight carriers that enjoy advantages of flexibility and, over short distances, speed combined with low cost of movement. Not being limited by fixed routes as determined by roadbeds of railroads or natural waterways, the truck is free, to go almost anywhere, and it makes possible loading of shipments at points of origin, transporting them in a through movement without transfer, and unloading at the actual ultimate destination. Lower costs of movement for merchandise freight are experienced over short distances than by rail or by ship because the latter types require a combination of equipment involving motor trucks for pickup and delivery.

Like the railroads, motor truck common carriers have established substantial differentials in rates for *l.t.l. (less than truckload)* and *t.l. (truckload)* freight. For most commodities t.l. rates are 30 to 50 per cent less than the l.t.l. rates. In general, motor freight rates are lower than rail rates for the same commodities—especially for l.t.l. freight moving over relatively Short distances. T.l. rates tend to be slightly higher than rail c.l. rates over long distances, but since trucks are loaded at point of shipment and unloaded at destination, there is a cost advantage even in some long haul shipments when rail sidings are not available both at the location of the shipper and at the warehouse or plant of the receiver.

Air Carriers

Air freight is much more costly than surface shipment of any kind; and its use, at the current stage of development, is limited to merchandise that can stand very high transportation costs because of the urgency of delivery, high value, or great risks from perishability. In spite of substantial year-to-year advances in the total tonnage of air freight shipments, this type of service accounts for only a very small fraction of 1 per cent of total intercity freight movement. The service has, however, set new standards in speed for *long distance* freight shipments which have had a marked effect on the marketing operations of many concerns. A shipper in any major traffic city can be assured of delivery in almost any other major city the morning after the day on which the shipment is made. This may result in other advantages which partly offset the increased cost of transportation and which require a careful analysis of an entire marketing programme rather than a mere comparison of transportation costs alone. Such other advantages may include a wider area of operation, smaller inventories, reduced spoilage, elimination for the need of local warehousing in distant areas, lower packaging costs, and added sales value for products shipped by air.

Special Transportation Agencies

In addition to the actual carriers which operate the various foregoing types of transportation facilities, there are certain special agencies that perform a middleman service. In general they do not operate intercity transportation equipment themselves, but consolidate shipments in one locality, arrange for its intermarket movement by a basic method of transportation, and provide for local delivery at destination. Such agencies are especially important to originators of shipments smaller than those commonly accepted by carriers or that can be shipped economically and in cases where some specialized service is necessary.

Freight Forwarders

The function of the freight forwarder is that of consolidating l.c.l. shipments from several manufacturers, distributors, or other shippers into carload lots. By assembling a number of relatively small shipments into car lots, the forwarder obtains a carload rate from the railroad. This permits him to quote the shipper a rate which is no higher than, and usually not as high as, the regular l.c.l. rate for the merchandise. The spread between c.l. and l.c.l. rates is the forwarder's source of operating revenue. From the amount collected from shippers, he must pay the railroad the c.l. rate and the residue is used to cover the cost of soliciting business, picking up shipments for delivery, filling cars, delivering shipments to consignees, handling and settling claims, billing shippers, and to yield a net profit on the enterprise.

Use of a freight forwarder is explained mainly by the greater speed of handling l.c.l. shipments than would otherwise obtain, simply because he consolidates into one full, through car a variety of individual shipments that might otherwise travel over several railroads, with possible delays in transit due to loading and unloading at transfer points. Freight forwarders specialize in the handling of high-class merchandise freight that moves in l.c.l. quantities, but have minimum charges based on shipments of 120 pounds, thus discouraging small parcel shipments. They operate principally between major cities, and thus are able to fill cars quickly without delay in origin or in transit. They provide the shipper with the services of a traffic department, selecting the best routes and the most economical shipping techniques, and assuming the general responsibilities of a common carrier. About 60 per cent of the total tonnage of rail l.c.l. shipments is handled by freight forwarders.

When shipments involve distances of about 400 to 800 miles, forwarders often consolidate into truckloads, to be carried by regular truck lines, rather than rail carloads. Freight forwarders are not ordinarily used on shipments of less than 300 or 400 miles because of the greater efficiency with which local or regional motor truck carriers operate over such shorter distances. Although there are over 100 freight forwarding companies in the United States, three large companies enjoy most of the business. Each of these has a large number of receiving stations which are located in the strategic freight originating cities. Specialized freight forwarding companies also operate in the field of air and water transportation, providing a similar merchandise handling service.

Express

The Railway Express Agency offers a premium type of freight service ordinarily used for small shipments of valuable or highly perishable merchandise. Shipments move on schedule and at passenger train speed and can be sent to any city or village in the country which has a railway station. This is a distinct advantage over the fast freight lines operated by railroads or served by freight forwarders that are limited to connections between principal cities. The same is true of air shipments and, to some degree, even of motor trucks, since trucks operating on regular fast schedules do not attempt to service all small communities on their routes. Railway express includes both pickup and delivery service. An important advantage is the ability to insure packages for almost any amount, which accounts for the widespread use of the service in the distribution of merchandise of high unit value. Although more costly, express service is generally faster, more dependable, and involves more careful handling of merchandise than parcel post. The Railway Express Agency also makes available "air express" service, providing expedited movement, including local pickup and delivery, of small shipments by air carriers.

Parcel Post

The parcel post system, established in 1913, has had a marked effect on marketing. Large mail order companies have been important beneficiaries. Railway express was formerly the only alternative to freight charges based on a minimum shipment of 100 pounds. Many mail order shipments weighed only a few pounds and even railway express service did not provide delivery direct to customers in rural areas. By regulation, parcel post is limited to small shipments. Maximum size of parcel is 72 inches in length and girth, and maximum weight is either 40 or 20 pounds, depending upon the distance involved in the shipment. Parcel post is used when the greater speed, special handling, or insurance features of express service are not of great importance. The cost is generally lower than on shipment by rail express, although this advantage is offset to some extent by the fact that parcels are not collected directly from shippers.

Special Transportation Features

A number of special features of transportation have been developed to facilitate economical and efficient marketing and to encourage more widespread consumption of certain commodities, particularly by making possible physical distribution over more extensive geographic areas. Most such features apply to rail freight, inasmuch as it is the dominant mode of transport for long haul, large volume movement. Some of the major types of special transportation features and their relationship to marketing conditions or opportunities are indicated in the following paragraphs.

Terms of Sale and Transportation

Exact knowledge of many sales contracts is dependent upon a clear understanding of terms of sale which relate to transportation responsibility and cost. There are numerous such terms, some of which are peculiar to particular industries or particularized circumstances, but some are of such general importance that they merit explanation. One is *f.o.b.,* which means that the seller is to place the commodity "free on board" the car, or at ship side (f.a.s.), at the point of shipment. Thus the buyer is to pay the freight and other charges, and is to assume all risks of damage in transit which are not caused by the seller or which are not covered by the liability of the carrier. Unless otherwise specified, f.o.b. sales are understood to mean sales at the shipping point at an agreed price to apply as of the date of sale, usually with inspection privileges at destination. F.o.b. destination, f.o.b. Chicago, and similar terms require that the seller assume all transportation costs and risks, for he has the responsibility for the delivery of the commodity to the point designated or implied in these terms. These are known as delivered sales.

Large quantities of certain raw materials are sold on a to arrive basis. Terminal market grain dealers often send bid cards to assembly market elevators, offering to buy certain grades at specified prices, providing shipment is made within a certain number of days, usually ranging from 10 to 30. Limitations are placed on the amount that will be purchased and on the time available for acceptance, which is often the day following receipt of bids by assembly market elevators. "To arrive" means that the seller pays the freight charges and that shipment will be made for arrival at the specified destination within the indicated time limit.

Class and Commodity Rates

One of the most complex aspects of transportation is the rate structure of common carriers, particularly railroads. Two basic kinds of rates are in general use: class rates and commodity rates. In order to simplify the problem of publishing rates for thousands of individual products moving between thousands of points of origin and destination, railroads group commodities of similar bulk, weight, value, perishability, or other pertinent characteristics into classes, each of which has its own rate per 100 pounds. Thus, numerous commodities with approximately the same costs of handling and movement take the same class rate for any specified distance. *Class rates* are most important for shipments of manufactured goods and are employed by motor truck common carriers and freight forwarders in a manner similar to that used by railroads. Rates for any given class of freight vary with distance, but not directly so. They are relatively lower for long than for short hauls because terminal handling costs remain about the same for both. In order to make allowances for regional differences in the cost of and demand for transportation, various rate territories have been defined, known as the Eastern or Official, the Southern, the Western Trunk Line, the Southwestern, and the Mountain-Pacific. In each of these territories a different structure of class rates exists. Classification of specific commodities and determination of freight rate structure are the responsibility of committees representing railroads operating in each territory. Changes in product classifications and rates can be made, however, only after public formal hearings and approval of the Interstate Commerce Commission.

Commodity rates are published rates that pertain to specific products being shipped between named points of origin and destination. Commodity rates have been developed for most heavy and bulky articles which move in large volume. They apply to practically all commodities shipped in bulk and also to many kinds of merchandise freight which ordinarily move in carload lots over long distances. Generally they are lower than the class rates that would apply to the product in the absence of commodity rates. Such rates are designed to permit maximum movement of basic commodities with consideration being given to their peculiar characteristics, production and consumption conditions, and the economic need for transporting them to distant regions. Like class rates, commodity rates are subject to approval of the Interstate Commerce Commission.

Blanket Rates

Commodity rates which increase with the length of the movement often result in prohibitive transportation costs for long distance shipments of heavy or bulky products. When such commodities involve large potential freight movements, blanket or "postage-stamp" rate systems are sometimes developed in order to encourage greater distribution and consumption of the commodity in question. An important example is the case of California citrus fruit, the rate on which is the same to all points east of an arbitrary line drawn roughly north and south from Denver, Colorado. In the absence of such a rate, the freight charge would result in a price for the commodity which would be prohibitive to most consumers in eastern cities, and the movement of the commodity to such cities would be accordingly discouraged, all in favor of competitive products from Florida.

On the other hand, it is not believed that prices for the commodity would be appreciably lower in western and middle western states where consumers absorb a transportation charge somewhat higher than the actual cost of shipping to cities in these regions. Many other fresh or processed agricultural commodities, in various areas of origination, take a blanket rate to certain large destination regions, particularly when the commodities in question must compete with those originating in different areas with more favorable transpor-tation cost situations.

The grouping of a number of destinations in a large area has often contributed to decentralization of industry and wholesale trade. For example, all New England cities have been grouped for the purpose of blanket rates on a number of commodities originating at points west of Pennsylvania. The resulting equalization of raw material costs over the blanket rate area has favored the growth of industries in scattered smaller towns.

Diversion in Transit

The special privilege known as diversion in transit can be best explained by illustration. It is frequently necessary to ship apples from the northwestern states to eastern markets before they have been sold. Such cars are said to be *rolled unsold*. It is hoped that they will be sold before they arrive at a major diversion point such as Minneapolis or Chicago. Hence they are consigned to the shipper himself at one of these points, and if sold while the car is still rolling, they will then be reconsigned to the purchaser at his receiving point. If a sale is not effected, the car of apples can be reconsigned to some other eastern or southern point such as Cleveland or Louisville, depending upon developing market conditions.

If they are still unsold when they reach one of these points, the car can be again reconsigned to some other market. This can be repeated just as long as the shipments move in a forward direction. When the car is sold in markets which are in a direct line of haul from the point of origin, this is known as an *in-transit sale*. This is in contrast with a *tramp car* sale which is made to a purchaser in a market which is out of the line of haul from the originating point. For example, an eastbound car could not be reconsigned from Chicago to Des Moines, Iowa, which involves back hauling, without paying the carrier the additional rate in force for shipment between these two points.

When goods are shipped under the diversion-in-transit privilege, price and terms of sale are fixed by telegraphic offers and acceptance. If satisfactory bids are not forthcoming, the goods are diverted to the most favorable market, judging from the latest market information that is available.

All in-transit or tramp-car sales relate back to the time of issuance of the bill of lading by the carrier. Usually the buyer pays the freight on such transactions, but he assumes only the lowest authorized freight charges applicable between the point of origin and the destination stipulated in the sales agreement.

The diversion-in-transit privilege is especially valuable for shippers of products which take a blanket or postage-stamp freight rate. It is highly important also for shippers of products which cannot be stored and when the market in the city to which they were first consigned is temporarily unfavorable. The price of perishables often varies greatly in different cities on the same day, and it may be very much worth while to change the original idea as to the market in which a car of produce could be best sold and divert the car to a better market.

Through or Processing Rates. To facilitate movement of materials from distant originating points to factory locations, processing plants, or storage facilities, which are between the originating points and consuming markets, railroads have developed another special privilege, that of through rates applying to commodities which are processed or stored while in transit. Where this privilege exists, a commodity may be shipped from an originating point

- To an intermediate point
- Where the commodity is subjected to some manufacturing or commercial processing, and then reshipped to a final destination
- At a through rate which is less than the combination of the local rates from A to B and from B to C.

Through or processing rates tend to equalize the marketing advantages of competing industrial locations. For example, grain may be shipped from a grain market to an important flour milling centre where it is ground into flour and then reshipped to large consuming markets at the through rate applicable from the point of origin to the final destination of the finished product.

In such a case, the local rate on grain is usually paid on the shipment from the point of origin to the milling location; and when the flour is shipped to the consuming market, it moves at the *transit balance* which is the difference between the rate on grain from the point of origin to the final destination and the amount which was actually paid on the shipment of grain from origin to milling point. Other illustrative applications include unloading of railroad ties in transit for treatment at creosoting plants; unloading of cattle shipped from grazing areas, for purposes of fattening in feed lots at intermediate points, before reshipment to meat packing centers; and the shipping of household appliances from eastern manufacturing plants to western storage facilities where they are unloaded and later reshipped to specific market centers served from the storage facilities in question. By taking advantage of the privilege of stopping products for processing, grading, or storage, the shipper saves substantial amounts, as compared with the combination of the two separate rates which would otherwise apply. This makes it possible for shippers to serve wider market areas, encourages more effective competition among a larger number of suppliers in different regions, and contributes to a wider range of consumer choice.

Trends in Coordinated Transportation

One of the greatest obstacles to the economical and rapid physical distribution of goods has been the fact that most transportation companies are specialized in just one mode of transportation and serve a limited geographic area. At the same time, many articles of commerce must necessarily utilize two or more modes of transportation and, when distances are long, are often handled by more than one carrier involved in the same mode of transportation.

This has made it necessary to interrupt the flow of many commodities a number of times for the rehandling of goods as they are shifted from one mode of transportation to another, or from one carrier to another, or from carriers to storage facilities. Certain relatively modern developments in transportation have contributed to a substantial reduction in such delays and rehandling costs, through coordinated through movements.

Piggy Back

Loss of considerable merchandise freight revenue to motor truck carriers in the years following World War II led a number of railroads to inaugurate *piggy-back* service, which involves a form of coordination between local motor and long distance rail service. The term piggy back arises out of the practice of hauling loaded truck trailers on specially designed rail flatcars. Such trailers can be loaded at point of shipment, hauled to rail shipping facilities, placed on flatcars without any merchandise handling, moved over the rails to the destination city, hauled from rail sidings to the point of ultimate delivery, again without the need for merchandise handling at the rail facilities. Special equipment has been developed to increase the speed of loading and to reduce the weight of flatcars and truck trailers. Over long distances, piggy-back service is considerably faster than movement over the highways, since it is not affected by traffic or road conditions and does not involve the requirement of meal or rest stops for drivers.

10

Chain Stores and Voluntary Chains

Despite abundant literature on the subject, no clear-cut and universally acceptable definitions of the terms chain, chain store, or chain system have been developed. Common usage seems to relate the term chain to retail store operations and tends to neglect the existence of many chains of public utilities, banks, hotels, motion picture theatres, finance company offices, and other types which are an integral part of marketing.

Most of the best known so-called *retail* chains also operate chains of warehouses for the performance of the wholesaling functions and many also are extensively engaged in manufacturing activities. It is important, therefore, that one get an overview of the structure of chain store organizations, including the various levels on which they operate, before delving into an analysis of their competitive position and performance on the plane of retailing.

Another matter of great importance is the manner in which various independent merchants have achieved certain advantages of chain operation by voluntarily integrating their interests and activities with those of other firms, both on the retail level and on other levels of the distribution channel as well.

DEFINITION

Several criteria are useful in differentiating chain store organizations from other types which tend to resemble them in some respects. These include

- Number of establishments,
- Type of merchandise handled,
- Plane or level of operation,
- Ownership of the units,
- Management control. On the basis of these factors, *a chain or chain store system or organization may be said to consist of two or more centrally owned units, handling, on the same plane of distribution, substantially similar lines of merchandise.* This definition is in line with that used by the Federal Trade Commission in various of its studies of chain stores and it is also in accord with Census of Business classification procedures. While avoiding use of the term chain, the Census

considers a store as a member of a *multiunit* organization "if it is one of two or more stores in the same general kind of business operated by the same firm." Thus, for example, a firm is classified as a *multiunit* if it operates two or more food stores, or if it operates two or more apparel stores; but a firm operating one drugstore, a hardware store, and a furniture store would not be so classified, and all the individual stores in this case would be regarded as *single units.*

Emphasis is placed on central ownership rather than management control, and to that extent at least, chains are to be distinguished from the so-called cooperative or voluntary chains in which the retailer members preserve individual ownership. The regular chain has full control over its retail units, assumes full financial responsibility for such units, bears all loss when a unit is closed and retains all profit made by each store. In a voluntary chain, on the other hand, cooperation with the central organization is contractual; the individual store assumes full financial responsibility for its acts; all profit earned by the store is retained by its owner; when a store is forced to close its doors it is considered commercially and legally a failure and the total loss is borne by the owner and his creditors.

CLASSES OF CHAINS

Two important ways of classifying regular chains are according to the extent of area served and according to the degree to which the organization has integrated retailing with other kinds of business activities.

Geographic Basis

In terms of radius of operation, chains are generally classified as local, sectional, and national. Substantially all of the stores in *local chains* are located in or near the same metropolitan area. In almost all major cities, there are to be found local multiunit organizations in the food and drug fields. Such organizations are also rather common among department stores, clothing stores, furniture and appliance establishments, gasoline service stations, and liquor stores.

Chains are classified as *sectional* if their stores are located in some one major part of the country, such as New England, the Pacific Coast states, or any other recognized broad geographic division. Many of these are very large and are as well known to consumers within their area of operation as are the still larger national organizations.

Integration

Another useful classification is that based upon the degree of vertical integration. One group consists of retail chains *without wholesale distribution or manufacturing facilities,* thereby confining their activities to retailing. They procure merchandise through wholesalers or purchase directly from manufacturers, without special facilities for performing wholesaling functions within the company. In this group belong many local chains of only a limited number of units, also a substantial number of large organizations in the shoe, millinery, and apparel fields.

A second group consists of chains with *warehouses or wholesale distribution centers.* This is typical in all convenience goods lines where regular wholesalers are of importance in serving independent merchants. As such chains grow in size and circumvent the wholesaler, they find it necessary to provide somewhat comparable physical facilities in which wholesaling activities are performed for the organization. In fact, there is no stronger evidence of the indispensable nature of the functions of the wholesaler than the existence of chain store wholesale warehouses.

The third type consists of chains that have integrated still farther by *the performance of manufacturing activities.* This group overlaps with the second in that its members ordinarily also operate wholesale distribution centers in addition to manufacturing establishments. Outright or partial ownership of subsidiary manufacturing companies, or strong control over the activities of supplying manufacturers by furnishing specifications and taking all or a substantial part of their output is common among the mail order companies that also operate large numbers of retail stores. In the grocery trade, 63 major chains reported that they were engaged in some forms of manufacturing in 1958, and this group operated 340 manufacturing establishments, primarily to supply private brand merchandise to company stores. Sometimes integration has proceeded *forward* from manufacturing toward retailing, rather than *backward* from retailing toward manufacturing. Illustrative is the practice of certain major oil-producing companies whose principal business is done through bulk tank stations but which also operate some gasoline service stations.

Several large shoe manufacturers have acquired chains of stores and operate them as controlled outlets. A well-known example is Genesco (formerly General Shoe Corp.). While long known as a leading shoe manufacturer, this company also diversified by acquiring firms manufacturing apparel and apparel accessory items. It operates a number of separately identified shoe chains (e.g., Jarman, Holiday, I. Miller) and apparel stores (e.g., Whitehouse & Hardy, Roger Kent). It is thus apparent that to regard chains as purely retailing institutions is erroneous. Almost all of the medium-sized and larger organizations possess most of the characteristics of both retailing and wholesaling enterprises, and many are manufacturing as well as merchandising concerns.

Origin and Development of Retail Chains

The modern chain store is of comparatively recent origin. The chain idea of distribution, however, has many forerunners and prototypes. As early as 200 B.C., a certain Chinese businessman owned a chain of a great many units. A poster found in Pompeii, destroyed in A.D. 79, advertised for lease a certain property consisting of 900 retail shops. The Mitsui system of apothecary shops in Japan dates from 1643, and the company has been one of the wealthiest and most powerful businesses in that country. In the Americas, the Hudson's Bay Company operated a chain of trading posts prior to 1750. But in the United States the development of the modern chain was not started until the Great Atlantic & Pacific Tea Company was founded in 1858, although the second store was not opened until a year later.

The second of existing chains is Park & Tilford, which began business in 1840 but did not open a second store until 1860. The Jones Brothers Tea Company came into being in 1872, and the F. W. Woolworth Company proved the validity of the chain principle in the variety business about 1880. While a number of chains were established during the latter half of the nineteenth century, their real growth occurred during the present century. It is estimated that in 1900 there were but 700 chains with 4,500 stores. Each succeeding year showed an increase in the number of chains and in chain stores. At first the number of chain systems increased faster than store units, but the reverse was true during the latter half of the period, indicating a possible absorption of smaller chains by larger ones and a more rapid expansion within large chain systems.

Growth in chain store volume of sales was spectacular. As late as 1919 the estimated volume of chains was less than 5 per cent of total retail sales, but by 1929 this proportion had increased sixfold to about 30 percent. The almost phenomenal development of chain organizations during the 1920's is explained by economic and social factors. The time was ripe to apply mass methods on a more widespread basis in retail distribution where efficiency had not generally kept pace with mass production techniques in industry. The number of people living in cities was about twice that at the beginning of the century, with a large amount of the city growth coming during the 1920's. City locations are particularly desirable from the standpoint of chain store organizations, for the cost of advertising, supervision, and distribution from wholesale warehouses is low when units are highly concentrated.

The development of the automobile and the improvement of roads made it possible for rural residents to shop in cities more frequently. Between 1914 and 1920 retail prices almost doubled, with the result that most consumers became extremely price conscious. Because certain operating economies were effected, in part by a transfer of marketing functions to consumers, and because chains were able to purchase merchandise on very favorable terms in a prevailing buyers' market, they were usually able to undersell independents. It is doubtful if there was any period in our previous history when price appeals were any more in harmony with the interests of consumers.

Later Development and Current Status

The number of retail store units and sales volume importance of chains in recent decades is indicated by the following data for source and notes regarding comparability of the data):

Census of Business

Year Sales	Number of Stores in Multiunit Firms	% of Total Retail
1929	216,524	29.6%
1939	201,040	30.6
1948	162,655	29.6
1954	167,027	30.1
1958	182,735	33.7

From the standpoint of number of stores, chains had reached an apparent saturation point by 1929, followed by a decline until after 1948 when the downward trend was reversed. The volume of business transacted is, however, a much more important criterion of relative significance. During the 1930's and 1940's, chain store sales were stable at about 30 per cent of retail trade. During the latter 1950's, however, chains forged ahead, increasing their share to 33.7 per cent. Most of this increase was accounted for by chains of 11 or more stores. The decline in the number of chain stores in the period 1929-48 is explained by several factors.

One relates to a trend toward complete food stores, as opposed to earlier greater relative importance of special-ized stores such as meat markets and produce stores (once known as "green grocers"). In the 1920's, grocers tended to add meats and fruits and vegetables to their stock and thus became combination grocery stores. This trend was greatly accelerated after 1929. A second reason has been the need for grocery chains to meet the competition of supermarkets which developed in the early 1930's, by operating fewer but larger units. Third, during the 1930's many oil refineries adopted a policy of turning over the operation of company-owned stations to independent merchants. Fourth, all of these trends and policies were stimulated by special taxes levied by some states on the stores operated by chain organizations, thus encouraging the closing of small and marginal units. In some fields, however, the number of chain stores actually increased during this period. As experience proved their worth, the number of such stores was increased in the retailing of shoes, apparel, and other kinds of business.

Variations in Chain Sales Volume

Summary data for the United States as a whole do not tell the whole story of the importance of chain store sales. There are important variations by size of company, potential of the market area, and line of business.

Small Versus Large Chains

Multiunit firms that operate only a few stores are usually local organizations. Their interests, competitive situation, and methods of operation are often closer to those of independent merchants than they are to major chain store systems. As companies operating two to ten stores accounted for slightly more than one-half of all chain store units and about one-third of chain store sales volume in 1958. This is a lower proportion of total chain store sales than achieved by this group in 1948. Among the explanations for this decline are the acquisition of some small chains by larger organizations, expansion of some small chains resulting in reclassification, and greater sales volume expansion by chains of larger size.

Chains of 11 or more stores tend to operate establishments of greater sales volume size. They account for about two-thirds of chain store sales but operate slightly less than one-half of the chain store units. Especially significant are chains with more than 100 stores. This group, with about 27 per cent of chain store units, does about 42 per cent of chain store sales.

Kind of Business

In some lines of business, chains dominate the trade, in others their position is not greatly different than their average share of market for total retail trade, and in still others they are of negligible importance. Chains account for more than 80 per cent of sales in the department and variety store classifications, for more than 50 per cent of the sales of grocery and food stores, and for more than 40 per cent of sales of women's ready-to-wear and tire, battery, and automotive accessory stores. By way of contrast, they do less than 20 per cent of the volume in the hardware trade, gasoline service stations, eating and drinking places, and less than 10 per cent of the business of automobile dealers.

The lines of business which are dominated to the greatest extent by chains tend also to be lines in which large chains have a much greater share of the market than do smaller companies (two to ten stores). On the other hand, small chains tend to be of as great or greater importance than large chains in lines where the per cent of sales done by all chains is low.

Between 1948 and 1958 large chains (11 or more stores) made strong advances in share of total sales in the following lines of trade: department stores, grocery stores, and women's ready-to-wear stores. These lines of trade have been affected both by acquisition of smaller companies by large organizations and by substantial expansion of chain store units in new shopping centers.

Urban Concentration

During the early periods of development, chains tended to concentrate in large urban areas and in the most heavily populated sections of the country.

While some chains are to be found in cities of any significant size, marked concentration in the largest population centers continues to be the rule. Heavy concentration in large cities is explained in part because certain prominent chains, especially in shopping goods lines, operate only in such cities; also, in convenience lines, the number of different chains competing with each other tends to be much larger than in smaller markets.

The smaller the size of city, the easier it is for independents to compete with chains, especially in regard to advertising and other forms of promotional activity.

Mergers and Acquisitions

The economic power of certain large chains has been considerably enlarged by the acquisition of other organizations in the same or similar lines of trade. For example, in the period 1949-58, ten large food chains were particularly active in acquiring other companies. These ten corporations acquired 107 other food chains which together, in the year prior to acquisition, operated 1,474 stores with aggregate annual sales volume of $1.2 billion, 42 manufacturing establishments, and 64 wholesale distribution warehouses.

Similarly compreh- ensive data are not available for other lines of trade, but noteworthy examples were numerous in the trade press of the late 1950's. Through a series of mergers and stock purchases, a surviving firm, McCrory Corporation, obtained ownership or control of the following companies: McCrory Stores Corporation (215 variety stores), McClelland Stores Corporation (236 variety stores), H. L. Green Company, Inc. (372 variety stores), Cassels United Stores, Inc. (18 variety stores), Oklahoma Tire and Supply Company (86 companyo-wned automotive accessory stores and 167 independent franchised outlets), and National Shirt Shops of Delaware, Inc. (146 men's wear stores).

Two large department store ownership groups, Federated Department Stores, Inc. and May Department Stores Co., expanded substantially by acquiring other large department store organizations. Merger activity was also conspicuous in the shoe trade, the automotive accessory field, and the apparel trades. Since most acquisitions involved mergers of chains with chains, they did not substantially affect the total competitive position of multiunit organizations, except in the department store field where some acquired firms were large single-unit stores.

The general tendency was greater concentration of ownership among the very largest firms in the trades affected. The number of such mergers would doubtless have been greater except for the fact that some were forestalled in their incipiency or dissolved through action of the Federal Trade Commission or the U.S. Department of Justice under the terms of the Clayton Act on the grounds that "the effect of such acquisition may be substantially to lessen competition, or tend to create a monopoly.

COMPETITIVE POSITION OF LARGE, CENTRALLY MANAGED CHAINS

Since some chains operate in almost every kind of business and since almost every method of store operation or merchandising technique is used by them, no competitive advantages or disadvantages are common to all multiunit organizations. Certain competitive circumstances are, however, so widespread among large, centrally managed chains that they are characteristic of this segment of trade.

Advantages

Most chain store advantages are basically those of large-scale retailing. Some advantages of scale nevertheless take on a distinctive form within the chain store field, and some others are peculiar to all multiunit organizations.

Buying Power

By channeling the merchandise requirements of many retail units through a central office that negotiates with resources, the large chain is able to buy on more favorable terms than is the single-unit store in the same line of business. Since the manufacturer's selling expenses are relatively low when disposing of large quantities to one customer, the chain is able to obtain the lowest prices and to secure other allowances related to quantity buying as, for example, advertising funds, and compensation for store displays.

While this advantage is important, it can be overempha-sized. Ability to obtain lower net prices is significant only when comparing such prices with the prices paid by a competitor who performs similar functions in the channel of distribution. There is no question but that chains generally pay lower prices than independent retailers. However, most chains are integrated, at least to some extent, and must incur costs in performing wholesaling activities.

It is more meaningful, therefore, to compare the prices paid by chains with those ordinarily paid by wholesalers that serve independent merchants. Most large wholesalers operate on such a scale that they are able to take advantage of the maximum quantity discounts offered by well-known manufacturers selling branded goods. The chain's buying power may result in prices slightly more favorable than those paid by some wholesalers, but as a practical matter it is largely confined to situations where manufacturers are small and sell the entire output to the chain or produce only private brands of merchandise to the chain's specifications. There is no doubt that the larger chains have significant advantages in instances where they are able to contract for all of the output of manufacturers—something that cannot very well be done by the typical independent wholesaler.

Buying Skill

Large chains also have the benefit of considerable *buying skill,* a natural result of specialization of labour. At the central or district headquarters are to be found merchandising experts who spend all of their time maintaining market contacts, collecting and interpreting marketing information, viewing offerings of vendors, determining the suitability of merchandise for sale by the company, and conducting negotia-tions. Unlike the manager of the independent store, the chain buyer specializes in a narrow range of merchandise and becomes thoroughly acquainted with sources of supply and current supply and demand conditions. Unlike the "buyer" in a regular department store, the chain buyer spends practically all of his time performing the buying function; he does not have the problems of managing a retail department, preparing advertising, supervising salespeople, and other similar activities of the department manager in the large department store. Here, too, the chain's advantage is largely dissipated when compared with the wholesaler's buying organization and skill, which is similar to that of the chain.

Low Operating Costs

Certain economies, attributable to characteristic practices among large chains, result in relatively low operating costs. One of the most significant economies among chains with warehouses is derived from the *integration of wholesaling* with retailing. A better coordination between these functions is secured, stores are supplied from or through a single chain store warehouse, no salesmen need call upon store managers to solicit business, credit *problems* are eliminated, and deliveries can be effectively scheduled. On the other hand, chain store home office and district executives must supply more supervision and assistance than is normally given to retailers by independent wholesalers. In any event, it is often possible for the chain to save part of the wholesaler's margin, particularly in lines of business where wholesalers have appreciable costs of selling to retailers and the latter do not concentrate their purchases with a single source of supply.

Another economy is *curtailment of consumer services.* As compared with its typical independent competitor, the large, centrally managed chain tends to sell to a greater extent on a cash basis; to render delivery service only for bulky or expensive items, or to make a charge for delivery when provided; and to emphasize self-service or self-selection merchandising techniques, thus limiting the assistance the consumer receives from salespeople. All of these service limitations, while making possible operating economies, may be viewed in another light, namely, that they represent successful attempts to shift performance of some marketing functions to the consumer.

Many chains secure economies by *limiting the composition of their stocks.* By concentrating offerings on those items for which there is a widespread and ready demand, higher than typical rates of stock turnover are attained. As long as this is accomplished without risking loss of business on account of out-of-stock conditions, several advantages are realized. These include less risk due to merchandise deterioration or style obsolescence, less storage space required per unit of sales, lower capital costs for merchandise inventories, and lower insurance costs on inventories.

Price Appeal

Low merchandise costs stemming from large purchasing power and the relatively low operating costs of chains, when combined with a prevalent chain store philosophy that a small percentage of net profit will maximize sales and yield large *total* dollar profits, results in a third important competitive characteristic, namely, the ability to feature price appeal. This has been an historic advantage of chainsone which accounted for significant diversion of patronage from independent to chain store in the period of rapid early growth of chains. While chains, as a general rule, tend to continue emphasis upon "low prices," the effectiveness of this appeal as a patronage-attracting device has been limited by two major factors.

First, the buying advantages and pricing freedom of chains has been limited to some extent by the trade legislation of the 1930's. Second, and undoubtedly more important, is a tendency which became much more prominent in the latter 1950's, namely, the willingness of many different types of retailers to meet the lowest prices prevailing in a given local market, particularly in the case of easily identified, fast-selling, standard items. Thus, something approaching price uniformity is commonplace for such merchandise.

This tendency has become more pronounced with increased inter trade competi-tion, as illustrated by cut-rate drugstores, supermarkets, discount houses, and variety stores, all selling similar merchandise. While the appeal of price is commonly stressed in chain store advertising and store displays, most volume-conscious independents price their merchandise at similar levels, and both groups attempt to differentiate their establishments to a greater degree through various forms of nonprice competition, such as location, character of merchandise assortments, store atmosphere, and special promotional devices.

Advertising Advantages

Where chain stores are in competition with neighborhood unit stores, they have marked advertising advantages. For example, a grocery chain with stores in all sections of a city can afford to use newspaper advertising space or radio and television. Neighborhood unit stores, with localized markets, cannot afford newspaper or broadcast advertising since their places of business are relatively inaccessible to most readers or listeners. Where voluntary chains have been formed, independent grocers have combined their efforts and used citywide advertising effectively. In the main, however, the chain occupies a preferred position with reference to local advertising.

Experimentation

Chains can often undertake experiments which cannot be made without great risk by their competitors. For example, lines of merchandise can be added to or dropped from the stock at one retail unit, and the results can be used in formulating the practices and policies of all of the stores. Similar experiments can be made with respect to services, displays, stock arrangement, store layout, and other matters.

Risk Distribution and Competitive Superiority

The wide territorial coverage of many chains reduces their risks, since a lack of local prosperity and a decline in sales or profits in one store may be offset by profits in other areas or stores. This same width of their market enables chains to transfer slow-moving stocks from some of their stores to units in which the demand for such goods is greater.

By varying prices charged to consumers between different cities and sections of the country, the chain is able to average its profits and meet whatever competition may arise locally. This is an advantage which the voluntary chains cannot emulate, for a price war affects the total business of a retailer member which cannot be offset, as in the case of chains, by the profits earned in the other stores of the group.

Location Advantage

As a form of large-scale retailing, chains are in an enviable position with respect to their ability to command the most favorable merchandising sites in established business districts and in new shopping centers. It is adequate to note at this point that the competitive position of chains was considerably enhanced during the 1950's by the preference accorded to them as the dominant tenants in most planned centers.

Competitive Limitations

As in the case of the favorable factors discussed above, no single disadvantage applies to each and every chain in every line of trade. A number of unfavorable factors do, however, exert a restrictive influence upon most large, centrally managed chains.

Standardization of Operating Procedures

While standardization of merchandising and operating policies and procedures is a feature which makes it possible to operate a large chain from a central or regional headquarters office, it is also a factor which has limited chain development in certain fields where individualized management attention is of unusual importance. Large national chains are nonexistent in the hardware trade, for example, partly because of the great diversity of items which must be handled and the minute supervision and care necessary to maintain balanced stocks. Carelessness on the part of the local manager may result in a serious lack of necessary items or in excessive inventories of unsalable or slow-moving stocks. Further difficulties are found in the multiple price system which prevails in the sale of such lines as builders' hardware. Price concessions to builders often vary roughly with the volume of purchases and the bargaining power of buyer and seller. Under such circumstances chains find it particularly difficult to operate, since they may be unwilling or unable to entrust such responsibilities to local managers. In any trade in which contract work appears, chains are at a disadvantage, because each contract presents a particularized pricing problem and the need for outside sales promotion and installation introduce complications.

Limited Service

The common practice of restricting consumer services and the limitation of stocks to articles in large demand, while reducing expenses of operation, limits the appeal of many chains. There still are and are likely to be large numbers of consumers who insist upon and are willing to pay for the wider range of services and facilities which many independent stores offer. Limited service is not a policy inherent in chain store operation. At least some large chains provide every kind of common consumer service. Variety stores found it necessary to introduce various forms of service, such as credit, delivery, and "lay-away" plans, as they diversified their merchandise offerings by expanding into shopping goods lines. The well-managed independent store nevertheless has a distinct advantage in adjusting its own programme of services to meet the particular needs of the clientele it seeks to serve within its trading area.

Imitative Innovation

Within and between the various lines of trade in which chains are of greatest relative importance, many companies are only weakly differentiated from each other. In spite of excellent opportunities for research and experimentation in the chain store field, innovations have tended to be imitative rather than imaginative. Many chains have copied operating methods and techniques that have apparently worked well for other companies, thus contributing to a type of monotonous uniformity and a lack of exciting and dynamic merchandising. One critic has described the store units of most large chains as being characterized by bowling alley aisles with little or no interrupting note, uni-formity of display, warehouse atmosphere in interior layouts, display of specialty goods as though they were staples, absence of printed selling other than manufac-turers' package and price tags, and discouraging merchandise assortments.

Many chains have apparently assumed a role of mere "distributor" of merchandise which is in ready demand either because of its necessary character or habitual use, or because of advance intensive demand creation activity on the part of manufacturers. This tendency among many large chains, especially in their larger and newer stores, again affords the independent an excellent opportunity to do a more outstanding promotional and personal selling job and otherwise to create a distinctive and appealing store personality.

Public Opinion. Particularly during the 1920's and 1930's and, to some extent, continuing until the present time, there have been many attempts to limit the growth of chains by arousing consumer sentiment against them. Led by some so-called representative organizations of independents and by a few individuals who perhaps saw an opportunity to further their own interests, many arguments have been made to the effect that the independent merchant, who lives and does business in the home city, deserves patronage rather than the customarily "foreign-owned" chain. It has been alleged that chains take money out of town, fail to patronize local business, pay low wages, destroy opportunities for young men to enter business for themselves, do not bear their share of the local tax burden, destroy small business, resort to unethical or unfair practices, and tend toward monopoly. Some such allegations are obviously unfounded or exaggerated. All of them have nevertheless influenced public opinion to some degree and probably contributed to the passage of chain store tax laws and to other legal limitations. To some extent they have also doubtless contributed support to governmental policies that favour private enterprise of the small, local business firm type, as witnessed by the creation of the U.S. Small Business Administration. It is not likely, however, that such pressures upon public opinion have seriously restricted chain store patronage. While some consumers prefer independent merchants, the vast majority patronize retail stores for other kinds of reasons.

Legal Limitations

Most of the legal limitations, in connection with large-scale retailing, were originally enacted as an aspect of the anti-chain store movement of the late 1920's and the 1930's. The chain's ability to induce discriminatory advantages in purchasing was limited by the Robinson-Patman Act, and its freedom to engage in loss-leader pricing was curtailed to some extent by the state pricing legislation discussed at that point.

In addition, many states have taxed chain store organiza-tions in some special manner, with the intent, at least in part, of restricting the growth of chains and the multiplication of their store units. At one time chain store tax laws were in effect in 29 states. Original impetus to such laws was the Indiana statute, approved by the U.S. Supreme Court in 1931. In that decision chain stores were recognized for the first time as differing sufficiently from other types of retailing to justify a separate classification for license or occupation tax purposes. A classification for graduated license fees according to the number of stores in the state was thus held to be a valid classification based on substantial differences.

In all cases the tax is levied only on stores operated in the state in question, but the *rate of tax* is determined in two different ways. Most common is the Indiana-type law providing a graduated license fee based on a schedule of the number of stores in the same company *located within the state* and levying, for example, a fee 50 times greater for each store in a company operating more than 20 stores in the state than would apply in the case of a single unit store. Louisiana and several other states departed from this principle and based the rate on the total number of stores in the company *wherever located*—for example, a company with more than 500 stores no matter where located would pay a tax on each of its stores in Louisiana some 55 times greater than the tax applicable to a store in a company that operated not more than 10 stores.

One effect of these laws was to discourage the multiplication of chain stores in the states where rates were the highest. Another was to encourage chains to close marginal and small units, and to plan newer stores of larger sales capacity.

With the passage of time, chains tended to be regarded as better neighbors. It became more widely recogni-zed that they brought new business into many communities in which they located new and modern stores, that they employed local people, and that they purchased supplies and merchandise from all segments of the economy. As a consequence, many of the laws have been allowed to lapse or have been repealed. In 1960 there were only 12 states with chain store taxes based upon graduated license fees.

Increasing Efficiency of Independents

One of the major limits to the expansion of chains is the increasing efficiency of many of their independent competitors. Independents as a whole are carrying on their business much more efficiently than was formerly the case. This is due to at least two causes. The increased business of the chains has driven out many of the least efficient merchants. The better independents are the ones who have survived. Hence, the general level of merchandising ability is higher. A second reason is that many independents have learned much from the chains. Such merchandising practice as the use of open display in grocery, drug, and hardware stores, better lighting, and better entrances and fixtures have been copied, in part at least, from chains.

Superfluous brands, price lines, and sizes have all been reduced. Better display and advertising practices have been adopted, and in other ways the level of independent merchan-dising has been raised. All of this has been accelerated through the voluntary chain movement. This fact will make it increasingly hard for chains to displace existing independents in the future. If expansion is made it will be at the expense of the type of merchant who is too old, too indifferent, or too independent and limited in ability to learn the lessons of modern merchandising. Unfortunately, there are still many such merchants, or rather, storekeepers.

Future of Chain Stores

The chain store type of retailing had a phenomenal development in the 1920's. In this period many new chain organizations were brought into being and additional units were added to existing chains with the result that the chain had become a fairly mature form of retailing institution by 1929. Throughout the next two decades, the sales volume importance of chains was relatively stable at about 30 per cent of total retail trade. During the 1950's, however, chains expanded their share of total retail sales to about 33.7 per cent—a significant gain in relative competitive position. Moreover, this increase has come about principally by growth of large chain organizations, both through internal expansion and acquisition of other companies. Thus, within the chain store field, the tendency has been for a larger share of total business to be concentrated among a small number of very large firms.

Among the various factors that accounted for significant growth of chains in the 1950's, several stand out as being of unusual importance. First, the scale of operations in individual retail establishments has continued to increase, thus raising the capital requirements and level of managerial skill essential for effective competition. This, in turn, has made it somewhat more difficult for new independents to enter retailing on a level of competitive equality. Second, the 1950's were characterized by various newer forms of competition, including expansion of discount houses, branches of department stores, and the advent of the varietydepartment store. Such intertrade rivalry resulted in intense price competition, with a tendency toward price uniformity at low margins for most types of standard, easily identified items. Large chains, possessing the advantages of financial strength and risk distribution, have been able to withstand the onslaught of new types of rivals much better than many independents, particularly those who were weakly financed and who lacked the ability or willingness to adjust dynamically to changing times. Third, a large proportion of the total retail trade expansion in the 1950's took place in planned suburban shopping centers where chains have benefited from their status as preferred tenants. This has been especially noteworthy in the case of department stores, variety stores, apparel stores, and supermarkets—all lines in which chains have long been of high relative importance.

In the foreseeable future, it is expected that the factors just outlined will continue to favour the growth of chains. On the other hand, further expansion is restricted by a number of countervailing influences. One consists of various forms of voluntary chain and cooperative activities within the field of small scale retailing. Second, it must be remembered that the total competitive position of chains is a result of their status in specific lines of trade. In some lines, notably department stores and variety stores, chains have reached a point of near saturation. In other lines where managerial flexibility and individualized attention to customer problems is of unusual importance, the chain method of operation is not well suited. Third, loss of share of market among independent stores has been highly concentrated among the less efficient or marginal types of stores. Further inroads by chains become increasingly difficult due to a strong survival tendency among more capable independent store operators.

When such opposing tendencies are carefully weighed, it is concluded that the growth outlook for chains, while favorable, is also likely to be limited to slow and gradual expansion. Such growth as does occur is, moreover, likely to be concentrated within the lines of trade where chains are already strongly entrenched. Within most such lines, the major rivals of an individual centrally managed chain are other similarly managed companies. Thus, to an increasing degree the competition of chains is with other chains, within and between lines of trade, and to a lesser extent with independent merchants, set apart as a different class of organizations.

VOLUNTARY CHAINS

Independent merchants and their suppliers have resorted to a variety of competitive devices in combating chain store companies. Within lines of trade where chains have been of greatest importance, the outstanding instrument of survival has consisted of various forms of horizontal and vertical cooperation, with the objective of preserving independence while at the same time achieving certain advantages of chain operation.

Types of Voluntary Associations

Voluntary chains or cooperative associations of retailers assume a variety of specific forms. First, there are buying-and-advertising groups in which a small number of independent merchants combine their purchases and engage in advertising on a cooperative basis. Second, there are retailer-cooperative warehouse groups in which a number of independent merchants mutually own and buy through a common wholesaling facility. A third form consists of voluntary chains which are sponsored by a regular wholesaling organization that has assumed the initiative for cooperative action. Fourth, some of the corporate retailing chains have expanded their area of merchandising influence by licensing or franchising "associate" stores. Finally, the franchised retail outlets of certain manufacturers, who pursue an exclusive agency or selective distribution policy, often result in such a high degree of uniformity of operations on the retail level that this may be properly regarded as an aspect of the voluntary chain idea.

Pooled Buying and Advertising Groups

An early example of voluntary horizontal cooperation was the development of informal buying pools. Basing their action on the assumption that buying power was the principal if not the sole advantage of the chains, certain independent merchants, primarily grocers, druggists, and hardware dealers, developed plans for informal pooling of orders. They thus succeeded in gaining certain price concessions which, when combined with pool-cars as they often were, resulted in substantial reductions in the delivered cost of the merchandise. So long as they failed to attack the problem of effective competition with chains in other than the buying area, such groups were never very significant.

Group operations of small numbers of retailers located in the same metropolitan area became very important in the 1950's when greater emphasis was given to selling and promotion. Under the prevailing arrangement, several independent supermarket-type concerns cooperate in the use of a common name such as "Foodtown" or "Market Basket." By pooling their advertising budgets, they have been able to develop impressive advertising programs, rivaling those of major corporate chains. Such firms have also set high standards in store appearance and merchandising.

They often maintain the same prices in all stores in the cooperating group. In contrast with the forms of voluntary chains discussed below, the initiative comes from the cooperating retailers rather than from wholesalers, but the retailers do not own or operate any wholesale establishment. They usually pool certain of their buying requirements and often enter into a form of buying contract with some large independent wholesaling organization that serves them on a special cost-of-service basis.

Retailer-Cooperative Voluntary Groups

Many early informal buying groups found that a logical step in their development was to purchase an existing wholesale house or to form a new one. In other cases, groups of merchants were organized for the express purpose of operating their own wholesale house. In either case, a paid manager and paid employees conduct the house just about as they would if it were owned by a private corporation. Stocks of goods are purchased, stored, sold, and delivered.

Stores operated by members of retailer cooperative voluntary groups do not account for a large proportion of total retail trade but are especially noteworthy due to their substantial influence in the grocery trade and because of their unusual significance in certain geographic areas. Some cooperatively-owned wholesale grocery facilities were established by groups of retailers prior to 1900, but the principal impetus for the movement came from increasing competition from corporate chains at a later date.

About 150 retailer cooperative warehouses were in operation in 1958 and more than one-half of them were organized in the 1930's and 1940's. Between 1948 and 1958, the number of member retail stores in such organizations increased from 25,710 to 33,007, or from about 8 per cent to about 15 per cent of all grocery stores. Sales volume of member stores in the same period increased from about 11 per cent to about 15 per cent of all grocery store sales. In dollar amount, the sales increase of such member stores was 231 per cent over the 1948-58 period, a rate of gain far outstripping that of corporate chains or of wholesaler-sponsored voluntary groups. Retailer cooperatives are of greatest relative importance in the Pacific Coast States, with estimated sales of member stores amounting to more than 40 per cent of grocery trade sales in California and Arizona. Such organizations are, however, to be found in practically all sections.

Most grocery trade retailer cooperatives have from 50 to 500 members each, but a few have more than 1,000. The organization is usually of the corporate form with required minimum investment per member ranging from about $250 in some cases to several thousand dollars in others. Typically, such cooperatives are operated on the basis of one vote per member, regardless of the amount of stock ownership. Profits accruing from operations at the wholesale level are passed back to members in the form of patronage refunds. Members are usually expected or required to concentrate their purchases with the retailer-owned warehouse, thus making possible the elimination of salesmen. In some cases, individual stores are *identified* as members of a voluntary group and carry on cooperative advertising; in many instances, however, members retain a strong individual identity, engaging in no group promotional efforts, thus using the cooperative facilities solely as an economical source of supply.

In former years retailer cooperatives limited their offerings largely to staple grocery products and performed few other services for members. During the 1950's many organizations expanded their procurement services and provided a more complete source of supply. It is common for such cooperatives to supply nonfood items, frozen foods, dairy items, and in numerous instances, even perishable produce and meats. Retailer cooperatives are stronger in this regard than wholesalers who sponsor voluntary chains, but they do not engage in as extensive a range of promotional, record keeping, and management advisory services as do members of the latter type. While retailer-cooperative warehouses are predomina-ntly associated with the grocery trade, some such organizations are encountered occasionally in other lines, notably drugs, hardware, and office supplies and stationery. In most such cases, the emphasis is primarily upon the presumed economies of group buying through an owned wholesaling facility. Outside the grocery trade, such organizations have made little effort to operate according to the voluntary chain principle by common store identification or group advertising.

Wholesaler Sponsored Voluntary Chains

Many wholesalers attempted to offset declines in their sales volume incident to the growth of corporate chains by organizing groups of independent merchants who, in return for special services rendered to them by the sponsoring wholesaler, agree to buy a major part of their merchandise requirements from him. Such groups constitute what are known as *wholesaler-*

sponsored voluntary chains. They differ from retailer-cooperatives in two ways. First, the initiative for organizing comes from the wholesaler rather than from the retailers themselves. Second, the wholesale house remains under private rather than cooperative ownership.

Although wholesaler-sponsored chains vary in many details, the essential basis of operation is one of mutual cooperation. Retailers agree to concentrate their purchases with the sponsoring wholesaler. While not all retail prices are uniform, advertised articles must be sold at the same price in every member store. The wholesaler in turn agrees to furnish certain merchandising advice and to be alert in his search for favorable opportunities to buy merchandise, the sale of which can be promoted by the group. Moreover, because there is some degree of concentration, the buying power of the wholesaler is usually increased through the sponsorship of a voluntary chain. Resulting savings are passed on to member stores as an aid to them in meeting the competition of the corporate chain.

In 1958 some 330 grocery wholesaling companies were reported as sponsoring voluntary chains. Member stores are estimated at about 36,000 and account for some 15 per cent of total grocery trade sales. Between 1948 and 1958 the rate of sales increase for such member stores was considerably less than for retailer cooperatives, but it was just about the same as that for corporate chains in the food trade. The importance of wholesaler-sponsored groups varies considerably in different geo- graphic areas, with approximately one-half of the affiliated stores located in a group of eight contiguous states in the Middle Atlantic and East North Central divisions of the country.

Operating costs of voluntary group wholesalers have been traditionally somewhat higher than those incurred by retailer-owned warehouses because a larger part of total sales volume is made to small independent stores not members of the sponsored voluntary group, regular salesmen or "store supervisors" are employed to call on and assist members with operational and merchandising problems, credit accommodations are sometimes provided, and because a wider range of advertising, display, store planning, and managerial services is offered to members of the voluntaries than is received from retailer cooperative warehouses by their owners. While wholesaler-sponsored voluntary chains have attained the highest form of development in the grocery business, they are not limited to this field. Butler Brothers, the leading wholesaler of variety goods, sponsors a voluntary chain of Ben Franklin variety stores located in all sections of the United States. Such stores are operated under a franchise agreement which calls for a payment by the retailer of a yearly fee which depends on store size.

In return for this fee, the wholesaler provides: a complete warehouse service for all merchandise items needed to operate a variety store; a detailed stock control system; automatic store shipments of new merchandise items; a planned promotional programme tied to the seasonal requirements of each month of the year; professionally prepared sales plans, display signs, price tags, and store decorations; assistance from specially trained field advisors; cooperative rebates on store purchases based on the annual volume of buying from the wholesaler; and permission to use the Ben Franklin name.

Another example of a wholesaler-sponsored voluntary consists of Rexall Drug Stores that are to be found in almost all communities. They are supplied with merchandise items from wholesale warehouses operated by the Rexall Drug and Chemical Company, are identified to the public as Rexall stores by the familiar orange and blue signs of the company, and participate in a variety of special promotional events, including the nationally advertised Rexall 1-cent sales. Through a subsidiary corporation, Rexall Realty Corp., assistance is given to franchise Rexall merchants in obtaining leases in planned shopping centers.

In the restaurant and motel field, another application of the same idea consists of Howard Johnson establishments. Such units are predominately independently owned, have a uniform appearance, and are under franchise to a central wholesaling organization which furnishes equipment, supplies, and food to individual operators who agree to maintain uniform standards of quality and service.

Coordinated Groups of Voluntaries

A majority of the wholesale grocers who sponsor voluntary chains are members of a national federation of such wholesalers. In order to secure certain advantages of group action, such as large-scale buying and promotion of private brands, it became necessary for voluntary group wholesalers to operate jointly. One of the best known of these central organizations is the Independent Grocers Alliance of Chicago. More than 50 wholesaler members serve about 4,500 stores in all parts of the country. It assigns a franchise to a wholesaler who in turn grants the retailer the right to display the I.G.A. sign, carry the private brands of the organization, and receive merchandising aids. The central office buys goods to be packed under the I.G.A. labels and advertises such brands nationally. Red and White Stores, Clover Farm Stores, Food Merchandisers of America, and United Buyers Corp. are other well-known groups providing similar services.

Some 85 retailer cooperative groups are linked together through indirect ownership of National Retailer-Owned Grocers, Inc. (NROG). Three large regional affiliates of this organization carry on large-scale buying and promotional activities. Another affiliate, Shurfine, Inc., owns some 30 registered trademarks for various food product lines which are purchased by the three regional affiliates for exclusive sale in member stores.

Voluntary Affiliates of Corporate Chains

The forms of voluntary chains discussed up to this point may be viewed as defensive measures undertaken by independent merchants or their suppliers in order to compete with corporate chains more effectively. A third form consists of companies that own and operate chains of retail stores and also serve as headquarters for a similarly identified group of independent "associate" stores. When a corporate chain undertakes such action, its motive is not to promote competition with itself. Quite to the contrary, independent affiliates are usually selected from merchants located in places that do not offer sufficient volume potential to be attractive from the standpoint of chain ownership. By selling through associate stores, the chain can add substantially to its purchasing power, increase the volume of its wholesaling facilities, reduce costs or expand the extent of advertising, spread the costs of corporate administration over a broader base, and realise a profit on wholesale sales to affiliated stores.

Probably the best known example is the Western Auto Supply Company which operates 16 wholesale houses, a chain of 376 completely owned retail stores located in medium-sized and large cities, and has some 3,600 affiliated independent merchants who are identified to the public as "Western Auto Associate Stores." For the most part these independents are located in smaller communities, and the typical establishment is considerably smaller than that of the company-owned stores. The independents concentrate their purchases with Western Auto wholesale houses, participate in company advertising, and benefit from the company's merchandising advice and physical assistance in store operation. Additional examples of the same method of operation in the automotive accessory business are provided by numerous independent merchants affiliated with tire manufacturers, such as Firestone, Goodyear, and Goodrich. Each of these companies operates a chain of company-owned stores, performs wholesaling functions, buys and resells merchandise that it does not manufacture, and engages in voluntary chain activities with independent merchants whose stores resemble the company-owned retail outlets insofar as appearance, layout, operating policies, and advertising are concerned.

Examples in other lines of trade include some 1,800 "Walgreen Agencies" which supplement over 400 company-owned stores operated by the Walgreen Drug Company, and some 30 small-town men's clothing merchants who have been licensed by Bond Stores, Inc. to sell suits and coats merchandised in that company's chain of about 100 stores which are located, for the most part, in large cities.

Franchised Retail Outlets of Manufacturers

The similarity among the operations of individual retail outlets that are franchised by certain manufacturing companies places them at least on the fringe of the voluntary chain movement. The merchandising advice and assistance provided by some of the large shoe manufacturing companies, such as the Brown Shoe Company, Inc. and the various divisions of the International

Shoe Company, together with the close working relationship maintained with merchants who buy substantially from one source is one good illustration. Certain paint manufacturing companies, especially those that are local or regional in character, distribute through carefully selected retail paint stores, provide them with store signs and other store equipment, plan and carry out sales promotion programs for the whole group of such dealers, and in general function in accordance with the procedures followed by other classes of voluntary chains. Some manufacturers of men's clothing and men's furnishings enjoy similarly close working relationships with many of their dealers who are identified to the public primarily as outlets for the manufacturer's line of goods.

Similar arrangements are to be found in the gasoline service station trade. It is common for major petroleum refining companies to develop new locations under lease arrangements with property owners, thus permitting the construction and equipping of station facilities. Stations are then commonly subleased to independent businessmen who operate their stations in accordance with the terms of a franchise. This affords the petroleum company a "chain" of independently owned outlets for its products. All gasoline service stations, of course, are not operated in this manner, as some are company-owned stations and some are owned outright by the operator or by a wholesale distributor.

Appraisal of Voluntary Associations

That the various forms of voluntary chains or franchise systems have inherent strength is indicated by a long period of experience, considerable recent growth of many well-established organizations, and the emergence of new voluntary groups and franchising organizations. Enough has been accomplished to establish the principle that groups of merchants working together and with their suppliers can effectively attain many of the buying, advertising, and merchandising advantages of regular chains. Perhaps the strongest advantage is the fact that the superior planning of the sponsoring organization has raised the level of merchandising in member stores.

Reference has been made to the establishment of physical standards of store operation. Some plans allow the sponsor to cancel the membership of any retailer who fails to operate his store in such a manner as to reflect credit upon the group as a whole. Possibility of such action stimulates indifferent merchants to greater endeavor.

Certain weaknesses exist, however. Lack of strong central control is perhaps most important. The sponsor or a committee of the members can go only so far in encouragement or instruction in better merchandising methods. In many voluntary plans, the sponsor has field supervisors who work with and provide counsel for affiliated retailers, thus performing essentially the same functions as a district supervisor in a regular chain. Two fundamental differences are, however, especially significant. First, the supervisor in a corporate chain has disciplinary powers whereas his counterpart in the voluntary group lacks authority to alter undesirable situations in member stores. Second, the chain store supervisor has higher organizational status and rank than the store managers working under his direction whereas the successful operator of an independent retail store often regards the supervisor as a person of inferior status. Whereas the chain company supervisor has but one loyalty, to the firm that employs him, the voluntary group counselor has two—the group sponsor and the retailer—and must devote considerable time and energy to winning and maintaining acceptance of merchandising programs by the latter.

Such weaknesses have not seriously handicapped the expansion of voluntary groups. As previously indicated, voluntary chains in the grocery trade account for a majority of the business done by independent stores and the growth of retailer cooperatives, in particular, outstripped that of corporate chains in the 1950's. Significant expansions have occurred in other lines of trade as well.Voluntary cooperation within the framework of a franchising system is attractive to a sponsor because it provides a semicontrolled network of outlets for his products or services and because administrative problems and capital investment are substantially less than would be the case if the franchiser owned and operated all outlets. It is attractive to the retailer since it gives him a national or regional identity, provides him with training and guidance in business management, supplies a merchandising programme based on the successful experience of similar stores, and often affords him an opportunity to establish an enterprise which could hardly be started without the sponsor's aid.

It appears that the concept of voluntary association has wide application, that it has strengthened the position of independent merchants who have taken advantage of the opportunities thus offered, and that future expansion is limited almost solely by the number of qualified leaders and merchants who develop an appreciation for the benefits that such group activities may hold for them. As is evident from the context of this discussion, voluntary chains have developed primarily in lines of merchandise where merchants can utilize one principal source of supply on the wholesale level. Up to this time, little voluntary chain activity, other than group buying, has been observed in the case of fashion merchandising which involves assembling from numerous sources located in markets at a distance from the typical dealer.

11

Transportation and Assignment Models

The analysis of trade-offs among transportation and inventory elements is basic to logistics planning. This task is relatively simple when both demand and lead time elements are known with certainty. By contrast, uncertain sales and lead times create complex relationships among transportation performance elements, customer service requirements, safety stock levels, order sizes, and logistics costs. The mainstream method of analyzing these relationships in a stochastic setting follows what may be termed the "inventory theoretic paradigm."

This paradigm formulates the theoretical constructs and establishes the standard solution procedures. Although the constructs represent important elements of logistics theory. The solution procedures have important conceptual and technical limitations. This chapter contributes to the literature on joint transportation-inventory decision making by introducing a paradigm shift for determining the effects of lead time performance on the safety stock.

This alteration retains the theoretical constructs of the classic inventory theoretic approach but introduces a different solution framework. This framework builds on the work of Banks and Fabrycky and of Eppen and Martin, and offers new solution procedures that are theoretically and technically more satisfying than traditional methods. Although the primary focus of the paper is linked directly to the inventory theoretic approach for joint transportation-inventory decision making, the proposed procedures also can be used in the inventory setting alone.

CURRENT PARADIGM

The inventory-theoretic paradigm furnishes the theoretical framework and the methodology for jointly evaluating transportation and inventory decisions in the presence of uncertain sales and delivery performance. Although this paradigm is well-established in the logistics management literature.

A brief review will provide a convenient frame of reference for examining important differences between the current and proposed approaches.

THEORETICAL CONSTRUCTS

The inventory-theoretic framework encompasses three theoretical constructs. The transportation construct uses the freight rate and the speed and consistency of delivery to define each mode, or carrier, option.

The inventory construct represents inventory with two basic functions:

- Ordering replenishments and
- Holding (cycle, safety, and in-transit) stock.

The transportation service elements link these two constructs. Specifically, the speed of delivery directly affects both safety and in-transit stock, while the consistency directly affects only safety stock.

The product construct synthesizes the transportation and inventory elements to define an item by its logistics (direct shipping, ordering, and holding) costs and by either a pre-set level of item availability or the cost of shortages.

METHODOLOGY

SETTING

The standard setting focuses on a single lane (supplier-customer pair) having several transportation options for the shipment of an independent-demand item. The single supplier is either a company plant or distribution centre or a channel ally. The problem embraces a probabilistic (s,T,Q) continuous review inventory system, in which the task is to determine transportation option T, the replenishment level s, and the order quantity Q that will minimise the expected sum of annual transportation and inventory costs for a pre-specified level of service.

From an inventory management perspective, this system is an extension of the well-known (s,Q) model framework, as well as a variation of the single-item multiple-source scenario. To solve this problem, one must evaluate the impact of transport speed and consistency on inventory holding costs.

CONVENTIONAL PROCEDURES

The approach for evaluating the effects of transit time performance on inventory, as well as for determining the safety stock in a probabilistic (s,Q) inventory system, is to treat lead-time demand as a compound distribution. Since the lead-time demand L also is a random variable, the distribution of L will determine safety stock. In the logistics management literature, most writers by-pass the convolution of d and t to obtain L and simply posit that L has a common statistical form—most often, a normal distribution. They also assume that the mean and standard deviation of the d and t are either known or can be estimated, and then use equations to compute the mean and variance of L. Basic inventory theory can now be applied to evaluate L to determine the safety stock multiplier k, or equivalently the replenishment level s, that is required to realise a pre-specified level of service—usually, the fraction of replenishment cycles without a stockout. Consistent with the theoretical constructs previously described, captures the effects of speed (mu sub t) and consistency (sigma sub t) on the standard deviation of lead-time demand (sigma sub L) and, in turn, on safety stock (k-sigma sub L).

Meanwhile, equation registers the speed dimension of transportation service (mu sub t) in the calculation of expected in-transit stock (mu sub t X mu sub d). If positing a normal (or some other theoretical) distribution for L is eschewed, the analyst has to model d and t individually to construct a compound distribution of L. If the resulting distribution is analytically tractable, the analyst can proceed with the standard numerical analysis. Otherwise, simulation methods are necessary.

LIMITATIONS

The principal limitation of the compounding approach is that accurately modeling the true form of lead-time demand as a compound distribution is difficult. On one hand, no common statistical form is likely to provide a good fit for L in general, for the distribution of L will assume different shapes in different circumstances.

On the other, the convolution approach is essentially untenable. Despite extensive research to identify analytically tractable forms of when various theoretical density functions characterise 1 and d, an exact solution is possible only in a few special cases. None of these cases, moreover, is suitable in general.

Further, the mathematical derivation of a compound distribution is often a challenging analytical problem. Thus the use of the normal distribution to characterise L is a matter of both convenience and necessity—although Eppen and Martin have noted that often a central limit theorem justification is inappropriately given as support for the general use of the normal distribution.

The normal assumption eliminates the need to model the functional form of t and d to construct L and enables the analyst to evaluate L easily, while the difficulties involved in evaluating non-normal shapes of L through the use of convolution procedures makes the normal distribution assumption a convenient refuge. Yet the lead-time demand distribution (L) is prone to have a non-normal shape. Studies show, for example, that the distributions of transit time are often positively skewed and are subject to systematic "weekend" effects—two characteristics that undermine the normality assumption for L. Meanwhile, the misspecification of L can be costly. Writers have demonstrated how wrongly characterizing the distribution of L as normal can produce serious errors in the estimate of s, which will inflate either inventory or stock-out costs. Some critics cite the limitations of the compounding approach as the reason inventory practitioners rarely use it, while other commentators cite those limitations as the reason to use simulation methods. Further, such weaknesses have inspired two researchers to refine the current paradigm.

FIRST-FOUR-MOMENTS REFINEMENT

Kottas and Lau have developed a "first-four-moments" (ffm) system to enhance the current paradigm in two areas. First, their system refines the conditions by relying on the use of a four-parameter distribution that is conveniently evaluated instead of positing that the (two-parameter) normal distribution characterises L.

Since the ffm of a distribution (mean, variance, skewness, and kurtosis) summarises the general shape of a statistical distribution, a four-parameter distribution has more capability to fit diverse non-normal shapes than distributions with fewer parameters. Consequently, Kottas and Lau recommended the use of the four-parameter Schmeiser-Deutsch family of curves for modeling lead-time demand.

Second, Kottas and Lau expanded the numerical analysis to include two new formulas that use the estimates of the ffm of d and t to determine the third and fourth moments of L. These two formulas combined with equations (2) and (3) which determine the mean and variance of L, generate the ffm of the compound lead-time demand distribution. This information is then used to fit a four-parameter Schmeiser-Deutsch curve, which can be evaluated to determine the value of s that will achieve a certain stockout risk (1-P sub 1).

More recently, however, Lau presented the same framework but recommended using the Pearson family of distributions (types I, IV, and VI). The Pearson curves are not necessarily more accurate than other four-parameter distributions, but they now apparently offer a more convenient procedure for determining safety stock requirements than the Schmeiser-Deutsch curves. Although the ffm system can produce more accurate results than the traditional approach, Kottas and Lau recognised that "it is always possible that an empirical distribution is such that the corresponding Pearson's curve provides a very poor fit."

Such a result, for example, will generally occur when lead-time demand is bimodal. Besides this fit limitation, Banks and Spoerer have expressed concerns about the practicality of a ffm approach. They noted that "it is doubtful that a practitioner would use distributions with more than two parameters for representing the distribution shape" or "would go beyond the approximate treatment for a model where the ltd distribution is assumed to be known."

SERVICE FUNCTIONS

The traditional use of the P sub 1 service function limits stochastic (s,T,Q) and (s,Q) models in several ways. First, the replenishment level (s) decision is made independently of the replenishment quantity (Q). Thus, although freight rate structures reflect important economies of density in transportation operations, P sub 1 models cannot directly evaluate the relationships among volume rate structures, order sizes, and safety stock levels.

Second, the realized P sub 1 will differ from its target as Q increases, because larger replenishments will produce fewer cycles per year and fewer chances to stock-out. Thus any income effect related to the service function will be uneven among the transportation options (T) tested. Third, this service criterion reflects stockout occurrences and does not convey information about the expected number of units short.

PARADIGM SHIFT

The proposed paradigm shift encompasses procedures that can produce the correct results when certain conditions involving ordinary circumstances are met. Unlike the conventional approach, these procedures embrace the fill-rate (P sub 2) criterion. This measure of service is preferable to other service or shortage-cost criteria in joint transportation-inventory modeling, because it has the capability to calibrate safety stock levels to achieve the same expected annual shortages (service levels) for each transportation option tested.

Thus the fill-rate model permits consistent comparisons among the options evaluated. From a practical standpoint, moreover, the most recent study of customer service sponsored by the Council of Logistics Management indicates that firms prefer an order-fill service measure.

APPROACH AND ASSUMPTIONS

Although the proposed approach relies on the conventional assumptions about stationarity and independence of random variables for both period demand and lead time, it assumes a different view of lead-time demand. Specifically, the approach adopts the perspective developed by Banks and Fabrycky and by Eppen and Martin that lead-time demand comprises a convex combination of conditional probability distributions of demand erected over the range of lead time values.

This distinction is important because a special property surfaces in the "convex combination" when period demand follows either a normal (mu, sigma) or a Poisson (iota) distribution and lead time t takes on values j=1...,n with probability p sub j. The property is that each conditional probability distribution of lead-time demand (the period demand given lead time t equals j periods) is also either normal with mean and variance j-sigma sub d sup 2 or Poisson with both the mean and variance equal to j-iota. This property enables one to estimate the effects of speed and consistency on safety stock levels accurately without knowledge of the shape of L. Furthermore, one can use any discrete probability distribution of lead time, including discrete approximations of common continuous probability distributions.

CONDITIONS

The key condition of the paradigm shift is that period demand forecast errors (or period demands) are normally distributed. Fortunately, in contrast to the research about compound lead-time demand distributions, studies of period demand provide strong evidence warranting the general use of the normal distribution for the fast-moving "A" inventory items, and perhaps some "B" items, where inventory systems group items into three categories (A, B and C) by an annual dollar usage. These items should have a mean period demand rate of at least ten units.

Such high-demand items are especially appropriate for joint transportation-inventory planning, because they typically represent a high per centage of inventory assets and require relatively frequent shipments. A secondary condition considers whether period demand is Poisson distributed. Satisfying this condition permits the use of direct mathematical procedures, which Banks and Fabrycky illustrate elsewhere and are conveniently executed when the mean of the Poisson distribution is relatively small. Since the Poisson distribution is likely to characterize slow-moving "C" inventory items with low period demands, the constraint on the size of the mean is not liable to be a serious technical limitation.

The focus on period-demand forecast errors, rather than actual period demand, is important for several reasons. First, forecast systems can generate more reliable estimates of demand variability than actual demand systems. Second, the better estimates enable logistics managers to reduce safety stock requirements by as much as 15 per cent. Third, if the period forecast errors follow a normal distribution, one can develop a solution without knowledge of the lead-time demand forecast errors, or the shape of L. Fourth, as a practical matter, many firms have computer-based forecasting systems for inventory control.

NUMERICAL ANALYSIS

As stated previously, the proposed numerical analysis adopts the fill-rate (P sup 2) service criterion. For extra flexibility, however, the discussion that follows includes a brief description of the changes necessary to use the fraction-of-cycles- without-a-stockout (P sub 1) criterion. Although the conventional procedures are well-known, the proposed numerical procedures probably are best explained with the help of a step-by-step illustration contrasting both approaches. Assume, for example, that (1) the goal is a 98% order-fill rate, (2) a high-demand item (d) is normally distributed with mu sub d = 100 and sigma sub fe or sigma sub d = 10, and (3) the lead time (t) has a non-normal (positively-skewed, leptokurtic, and slightly bimodal) shape defined by a discrete empirical distribution that takes on values j = 2, 3, 4, 5, 8 with probabilities p sub j =.20.65.10.03.02, producing a mean (mu sub t) Of 3.06 and standard deviation (sigma sub t) of.957.

In effect, this lead-time distribution shows a high proportion of deliveries arriving on a certain day (j=3), as well as during a two-to-three day period (j=2 to 4), with a small proportion of shipments arriving late (j=5, 8).

Thus, it is representative of the kind of delivery performance that often materializes in the field, while the hypothetical values for the parameters of demand seem to be popular for illustrative applications in the logistics management literature.

CONVENTIONAL APPROACH

For the conventional approach, the problem is to determine the replenishment level s that fulfills the service target by using one of two functions of the unit normal variable (u) to find the value of safety stock multiplier k. The function p sub u> = (k) determines the area beyond s in the upper tail and represents the risk (alpha) of experiencing a stockout during a replenishment cycle.

The special function G sub u (k) is the partial expectation and represents the expected shortages per replenishment cycle per standard deviation.(32) A knowledge of the p sub u> = (k) or G sub u (k) permits one to find k conveniently from either tables or formulas and vice versa.

Given a fill-rate target (P sub 2), the standard procedures are as follows:

1. Compute mu sub L and sigma sub L from equations (2) and (3), which produce 3.06 and 97, respectively.
2. Determine the G sub u (k) by setting equation equal to equation and then solving for G sub u (k).

NEW APPROACH

Like the conventional approach, the proposed procedures also rely on the partial expectation function G sub u (k)! to determine the level of s that meets the P sub 2 criterion. The focus now, however, is on the convex combination of conditional period demand distributions (d sub:t=j), rather than on the compound distribution L. These equations, in turn, provide one way to determine the expected shortage per replenishment cycle (ESPRC), which is to combine (4) and (5) and then rearrange terms as follows:

Another way to determine ESPRC for a given level of s is to compute the sum of the expected units short per replenishment cycle (ESPRC sub j) for each conditional distribution of period demand (d sub:t=j) weighted by the probability (p sub j) that lead time t equals j. Thus Since the period demand when lead time t equals j is normally distributed, the conditional expected shortage per cycle is defined in the conventional manner as

For pre-specified values of P sub 2 and e, the problem is to determine the replenishment level s so the expected shortage derived from equation is equal to the result of (10), or 7.52 units in the example. Since the G sub u (k sub j) is a composite rational function G sub u (u(s)), determining s involves finding the zeroes of a polynomial function of degree four—a task that encompasses nonlinear solution procedures such as the Newton-Raphson and Lehmer-Schur methods.

One has to evaluate each one of these distributions for ESPRC sub j, or equivalently G sub u (k sub j) sigma sub j, based on some value of s, which is assumed to be 470 units for the moment.

For example, such an evaluation of period demand for a lead time of five days would indicate that the mean (mu sub j =j-mu sub d) and standard deviation. Thus the conditional expected shortage per replenishment cycle. The last row of figures identifies the ESPRC sub j for each d sub:t=j weighted by the probability p sub j that t equals j. In the problem example, therefore, the task is to find the value of s that will produce values in the last row having a sum of 7.52 units. Nonlinear methods generated the 470 units solution. Although the foregoing procedures involve complex numerical methods, "user friendly" software for microcomputers is available to help automate such methods. Such software moreover can easily accommodate the changes needed to run a P sub 1 model, which focuses on the risk of a stockout during a replenishment cycle.

On one hand, this risk is simply expressed as (1-P sub 1). On the other, one may visualize this risk as the weighted sum of the upper tail areas beyond s of each condition probability distribution (d sub:t=j) Mathematically, this view is expressed as By using one or more rational approximation formulas to assess the probability that k sub j > s, one can then follow a similar nonlinear solution approach to find the value of s that satisfies.

ACCURACY

If the distributions of d and t in the problem example represent the true forms of period demand and lead time, one can examine the errors in estimating safety stock by comparing the correct solutions with the approximations derived with conventional procedures. The error in safety stock requirements ranges from 43.9 to 19.48 as the level of Q rises from 306 to 596 units. Latin Hypercube simulation methods were used to convolute d and t to obtain a compound distribution of L comprising two thousand random deviates. The normal distribution, as well as three candidate distributions suggested by the first-four-moments approach, was then fitted to this lead-time demand distribution, and the critical values (s) from each were found for three levels of P sub 1.

Finally, as a validation measure, the theoretically correct solutions for s produced by the proposed procedures were matched with the solutions developed by directly evaluating the simulated distribution of L. The solutions were the same in whole numbers, indicating that the simulation methods created a reasonably accurate representation of L.

CONCLUSIONS AND MANAGERIAL IMPLICATIONS

Determining the correct reorder points and fixed order quantities in a stochastic setting is a complex task, especially for the integrated (s,T,Q) decision framework. The inventory theoretic paradigm comprises the theory and mainstream procedures for quantifying the effects of shipping time performance on inventory holding costs in a single-item, single-lane setting.

Although companies can easily tally period demand and lead-time data, the problem with the traditional compounding approach is that an analyst must estimate, as well as be able to evaluate, the distribution of lead-time demand. The difficulties involved in obtaining the compound distribution by convolution make such efforts impractical for routine use. Additionally, such complications have nurtured the tradition of positing that lead-time demand follows a normal distribution and then obtaining the parameters of lead-time demand from the mean and variance of the independent demand and lead-time distributions.

The casual use of the normal distribution, however, creates an approximate model that is liable to produce operationally incorrect solutions, which will inflate either stockout costs or safety stock holding costs. The Kottas and Lau first-four-moments approach addressed this problem by replacing the normal distribution with the four-parameter Pearson family of curves in the current paradigm and by presenting a way to calculate the additional parameters.

Although a Pearson curve provides an approximate model that is generally more sensitive to non-normal shapes than other theoretical statistical distributions with fewer parameters, that model does not necessarily generate correct solutions. Further, its practicality is unclear. When a key condition is met, the paradigm shift proposed in this chapter encompasses procedures that produce the correct results regardless of the shape of the compound distribution. The proposed approach shifts the focus from the compound distribution of demand during lead time to the convex combination of period demand distributions constructed over the range of possible lead times. The key condition for this change is that period demand forecast errors (or period demands) have a normal distribution. Although the normal distribution postulate is questionable for characterizing lead-time demand, its use is proper for modeling period demands for fast-moving inventory items. Such"A" items, moreover, are especially interesting candidates for joint transportation-inventory decision making.

The procedures also are appropriate when the period demands of an item follow a Poisson distribution, which is often the case for slow-moving"C" items. Such items, however, typically have a low priority for management resources and thus are not conducive to the use of (s,Q) continuous review systems.From a managerial perspective, the new solution framework offers important advantages over the traditional approach. First, managers should observe the elimination of the errors that are liable to appear with the use of conventional methods and the concomitant reductions in shortages or holding costs. Second, the procedures embrace the fill-rate policy, which is popular in practice and, unlike the classic stockout criterion (P sub 1), enables an assessment of the effects of order quantities on safety stocks. Third the proposed framework facilitates a dynamic analysis of the trade-offs among fill rates, shipment sizes, inventory levels, and volume freight-rate or purchase discounts. Finally, from a technical standpoint, practitioners can conveniently integrate these procedures into personal computer-based (s,Q) or (s,T,Q) models. Although some math programming software is required, it is commercially available and inexpensive. In fact, managers can adapt the proposed numerical analysis to a spreadsheet environment.

TRANSSHIPMENT PROBLEM

The transportation problem (TP) is a widely used spatial optimization procedure that minimizes interaction costs between origin and destination locations subject to capacity constraints. Applications of the TP are quite varied including its use in the wood processing industry, agriculture, school district delineation, and in modeling aspects of journey to work travel. The classical assignment problem (AP) is a similar optimization procedure also entailing matching resources or assets [supply] with tasks [demand] such that costs are minimized.

Management scientists utilize the AP to assign workers to tasks. Similarly, industrial engineers employ the AP to pair production machinery with jobs. The AP may also be considered a spatial optimization problem when used in applications where flows of goods, services, people, etc. occur between individual source [supply] and sink [demand] locations. A major feature separating these two interaction models is that the TP often deals with aggregates of entities at origin and destination locations, while the AP is concerned with individual entities at separate origin and destination locations.

In a typical TP application, agricultural production and consumption patterns are estimated by zone, and then flows between zones are optimized. The AP, in contrast, would be used in a situation to optimize assignments between individual farmers and warehouses. Researchers interested in these problems must choose between using exogenously generated aggregates input into the TP, or using totally disaggregate geographic entities input into the AP. Ideally, the level and configuration of aggregation would be a choice in such an interaction problem, rather than an exogenous input as is the case with the TP.

Previous literature, to the extent that it has examined aggregation issues, has taken several tracks. First, aggregation in location problems has been viewed as a means of reducing problem size. Geoffrion's article is an exemplar of this theme as it shows how aggregation can make otherwise unmanageable procurement models feasible, with quantifiable amounts of error. The modeling in Geoffrion, however, is focused on moving from procurement on an item-by-item basis, to the procurement of aggregates of items by origin zone. In addition to that type of aggregation, we wish to cluster both collection and destination entities.

Second, the introduction of error into solutions as a consequence of aggregation has garnered intense attention. In this regard Erkut and Bozkaya study aggregation errors in the p-median problem (PMP). They formulate the aggregation/location process as a 2-step optimization problem. Their results describe"the role of the aggregation method and level in this process, and experimentally show how the method and level affect the resulting aggregation errors." Again, this is a somewhat related problem, but in our case we not only group n demand points into p clusters (akin to facilities) but also cluster the m destinations into q clusters.

While intriguing in their coverage, these articles do not address the problem tackled here-we incorporate aggregation into a new location model by combining detailed raw data with an assignment/interaction step. Observations are clustered into hierarchical groups in such a way as to endogenously produce concentrations. Our work is motivated by the idea that aggregation is often intrinsically linked to a specific problem setting or modeling scenario. For example, in the hub-and-spoke literature, routing of flow through"special" network nodes is a type of aggregation whereby concentration occurs at a designated point and the bundling procedure is endogenous to the model.

This chapter introduces a generalized formulation that addresses the divide between spatially aggregate and disaggregate location modeling. Focusing on the AP/TP literature and making aggregation part of the problem, the new model permits different levels of spatial aggregation by both origin and destination and thus offers researchers a richer set of options in defining potential allocations and zoning schemes. The model may be considered a hybrid of the TP and the AP and is termed the hierarchical assignment problem (HAP). The HAP optimizes the spatial flow pattern between individual origin and destination locations, given that some grouping of individual origins and destinations is permitted to occur. The level of grouping is user-specified, and the final configuration of groups is endogenous to the HAP, but origins and destinations are treated separately in the HAP and need not be aggregated in the same way.

This feature is achieved through incorporating additional p-median-type constraints into the framework. The optimal flow pattern between groups is a function of the level of aggregation performed. Depending on the number of specified groupings, the model can produce flow patterns based on a partially aggregated set of vertices (i.e., not all nodes are necessarily placed in groups).

In sum, the new model deals with individual geographic entities (i.e., the AP), as well as optimal flows between aggregates of them (i.e., the TP). Substantive connections between the HAP and cluster analysis and hub-and-spoke networks are established and provide linkage to the literature. Aggregation is a well-studied problem in location theory but most often from the point of view of the error introduced by misrepresenting spatial entities or using improper zones in a given problem.

In contrast, we seek an objective way to cluster, concentrate, or batch geographical units in pursuit of solving an optimization problem such that intermediate representa-tions between fully aggregate and fully disaggregate interactions are available. With respect to the role of spatial zones and aggregation in interaction studies, it has been suggested by Masser and Brown and Openshaw, among others, that a zoning scheme ought to be designed such that the bulk of the interactions actually cross zone boundaries (i.e., avoid substantial intrazonal trips).

These articles have suggested sensible, yet arbitrary goals such as"keep interactions below x% of total flow." While there are ways to treat the intrazonal interaction costs as the mean of the internal trips, estimation is likely to be more accurate if it is based on small zones. If there are a small number of very big blocks or aggregates, it is inevitable that the zones will contain a great deal of intrazonal interaction. Such a scheme would artificially give the impression that many trips, for example, are contained"locally" because the definition of local contains too much territory, and these trips would not be properly accounted for in terms of interaction costs. We extend this notion to the present chapter and offer a way to measure the extent to which"intrazonal" aggregation is influencing total transportation costs.

This is a key focus of our article because the developed model allows a full accounting for the effects of aggregation and interaction and therefore sets a firmer conceptual basis for measurement and optimal aggregation. The new optimization approach developed in this chapter follows from three classic spatial models, namely the TP, the classical AP, and to some extent, the PMP. All these models are well known, and the TP and AP have been shown to be special cases of a generalized assignment problem (GAP). Rather than list each of these well-known location models separately, to conserve space and motivate our work we present the GAP and show how the AP and TP are connected to it. This is an important step for understanding the HAP structure as these models are closely tied together.

The objective function:

- Minimizes the total assignment costs of matching agents with tasks. Constraints
- Ensure each agent receives a task for which they have sufficient resource to complete. Constraints
- Assure each agent is assigned to only one task. constraints
- Limit the decision variable to integer binary values.

Although the GAP does provide a generalization of the TP and AP, it should be noted that it does so with certain limitations. From a spatial perspective, supply and demand are still exogenous inputs in the GAP, which implies that it is susceptible to the same difficulties (e.g., improperly accounting for aggregation effects, misrepresentation error, etc.) as the TP that is derived from it. Conversely, casting the GAP as an AP offers no means of dealing with aggregation. We will attempt to circumvent this issue in the AP/TP literature by the introduction of our new model. There has been substantial model development involving the AP. We briefly mention two efforts that provide additional contrast with our work.

The first of these is Kensington and Wang's (1992) exposition of the semi-AP. The semi-AP is a variant of the AP where aggregate demand is incorporated. However, similar to the GAP and TP, aggregation is an exogenous input in the semi-AP, accommodated through adjustment of the demand constraint. Further, that model is ideally suited for situations where the number of individual supplies substantially exceeds the number of aggregate demands.

In comparison, our work stays close to the traditional AP framework and deals with equal numbers of supplies and demands. A second article by Vander Wiel and Sahinidis effectively "spatializes" the AP in order to handle supplies, demands, and interactions that are external to a predefined configuration of internal source and sink nodes. Their base model allows for workers outside the system to handle internal tasks, as well as permits tasks from outside the system to be processed by internal workers.

Several variations of the initial model are presented, including one formulation based on aggregating the external source and sink nodes into a single external transshipment node that the internal nodes may access. Our model also deals with transshipment nodes in an AP context, but differs substantially because it is far less restrictive in terms of the way nodes serve this function.

In our effort, individual nodes are not predefined for transshipment purposes; rather this status is brokered as part of the optimization procedure. When viewed as a network flow problem, our model selects p origin nodes and q destination nodes to serve transshipment functions. A third model critical to the present effort is the well-known PMP. This model is significant because several components of the formulation are utilized in designing our new model. It is used to site p facilities in discrete space, including such facilities as hospitals, community centres, etc.. The PMP has been a well studied and diversely applied optimization approach since its inception, and is often used in planning applications. Aggregation effects in the context of the PMP problem have also been examined. Murray and Gottsegen, for instance, consider the effects of data aggregation on solutions to the PMP and find stability in model results across varied scales.

We too are interested in aggregation effects, but we take a different approach by first seeking to craft an optimization model that internalizes aggregation. Then we can examine how aggregation affects model solutions and interaction costs. This section has reviewed several well-known optimization problems with the intent of establishing the conceptual and technical basis for our new model.

As these models stand now, there is no approach that bridges disaggregate (AP) or aggregate (TP) models, which mean that aggregation must be treated as an exogenous input. Working with exogenous aggregation in models can result in substantial, often untraceable error that influences model solutions. Our new model addresses this issue, and is operationalized by incorporating components of the TP, AP, and PMP.

MODEL DEVELOPMENT

The HAP is an integer program, which while related to prior literature, has an additional set of aggregation constraints that cannot be handled in the conventional GAP. These constraints allow for a complete accounting of the costs of aggregating disaggregate geographic entities. The HAP objective minimizes total interaction costs between groupings of individual origin and destination locations.

The number of individual origin and destination locations is assumed to be the same in this formulation. The first term of the HAP objective is identical to that of the AP and the second term of tracks the costs associated with assigning individual origin locations to groups, while the third term accounts for the costs of assigning individual destination locations into groups. Constraints conserve originations, as individuals assigned to the ith origin point become its total productions. Similarly, constraints ensure destination totals, as individual locations assigned to the jth destination point become its total attractions. Individual origins are assigned to exactly one origin point and an individual point must be designated an origin point in order to receive assignments. Individual destinations are assigned to exactly one destination point and an individual point must be designated a destination point in order to receive assignments.

Constraints ensure exactly p individual origin locations become origin points where interaction with destination points takes place. Similarly, constraints require that q individual destination locations be chosen as destination points to receive interactions from origin points. Both p and q are user-specified, thus allowing flexibility in the level of grouping, and they need not be the same. The HAP is related to the optimization models that were previously described. Observe that the HAP essentially contains two sets of PMP constraints; one set for the origins and one set for the destinations.

Conceptually, the medians selected from the origin (p), and destination (q) sets become the nodes from which interactions take place. At the simplest level, the model treats the pth median (the ith origin node) and the individual locations allocated to it as the ith production. This essentially would correspond to [O.sub.i] from the TP. The destination medians, q, and their allocations operate in the same fashion. Nodes in the southwest portion of the region represent six individual origins while nodes in the northeast of the region represent six individual destinations.

In this example, two groups of origin nodes (p = 2) and two groups of destination nodes (q = 2) must be designed to interact optimally with one another. The model selects two of six individual origin nodes to become the places where interaction between origins and destinations take place, and the same is true of the individual destination nodes. Variables a and b account for the group allocations for origins and destinations, respectively, and x tracks interactions between groups of origins and destinations. Nodes with the dark centres are where cross-group interactions take place. Given the formulation of the HAP, it is readily observed in this example that x = 3 for both the upper and lower groupings. The HAP is a generalization of the AP and it can easily be shown that the AP is a special case of the HAP when no grouping (i.e., aggregation) takes place.

Therefore it can be demonstrated that the HAP is related to the GAP through the AP. Further, it should also be noted that the HAP is not the only optimization approach where characteristics of the PMP and TP are blended. The p-median transportation problem (PMTP) is one such optimization model where at most p of n supply nodes are chosen to fulfill the needs of m demand nodes, all while minimizing total transportation costs.

Thus, p in the PMTP is a user-specified maximum number of sources that may be active. Of course, the PMTP is like the TP in that it deals with aggregates at origin and destinations, so it does not address the identified need that is the focus of the present chapter. Once groupings of individual locations are performed, cross-group HAP interactions are similar to those found between supply and demand locations in a TP. However, one major difference between the HAP and TP is that the HAP is structured so that travel costs due to aggregation effects are fully accounted for.

Each of the three major terms in the objective function can be tracked and reported (these include the two intra- and one intergroup interaction terms). Our work stands in contrast to past research in spatial aggregation effects and optimal zoning which has focused on small zones rather than the individual entities utilized here. Furthermore, the aggregation procedure is endogenous to the HAP, which typically is not the case when aggregation examined in the context of spatial modeling.

Lastly, it should be pointed out that the HAP avoids two major error sources of error in location modeling. Prior research by Hillsman and Rhoda (1978) discussed aggregation issues as they apply to facility location and commented on the types of errors that can be produced during analyses. One type of error they discuss is Source A error, which occurs when the calculated travel cost between a facility and an aggregated demand point does not correctly account for the total travel cost between that facility and the set of disaggregated demand locations that the aggregated demand location is supposed to represent. Because we do not impose any a priori aggregation scheme, the HAP does not suffer from such error.

A second type identified is Source B error, which happens when the facility is located in the same spot as the aggregate demand location, thus implying that the travel costs are zero. Again, because we build up from disaggregate entities, and penalize for each leg of interaction, the HAP is unfazed by this feature. Thus, it is our contention that the HAP represents an interesting approach to accounting for aggregation effects in an interaction problem.

EMPIRICAL TESTS

We tested the HAP with several randomly generated sample point data sets as well as one publicly available data set. Results from three analyses are reported to illustrate experience with the model. The first set of trials uses a small data set (10 nodes) to demonstrate HAP properties and the graphical nature of the solutions in a highly manageable test problem.

The second set of trials continues with this theme, and reports on experience with a larger (30 nodes) data set. There, the individual cost terms composing the HAP objective are thoroughly examined. Lastly, a third set of trials explores network flow and spatial issues with the HAP based on a data set of U.S. cities. All analyses were conducted on a Pentium III/733 personal computer running Windows NT version 4 with 256 MB RAM. TransCAD GIS version 4.0 managed the model applications and was used for manipulating spatial data. Straight-line distances are used as travel costs between nodes in these initial experiments, but later analyses could easily extend to network-based metrics.

Distance estimates for origin-to-origin, destination-to-destination, and origin-to-destination are exported from TransCAD and read into a developed C++ program. This program produces a text file of the HAP in linear program format. The integer program contained therein is subsequently read into and solved optimally using CPLEX version 6.60.

10-NODE DATA RESULTS

Results for HAP analyses were run on a data set consisting of 10 origin nodes and 10 destination nodes generated in TransCAD GIS. All 10-node problems are solved to optimality in a negligible amount of computing time. For the first round of trials, our approach was to systematically increase p and q together from 1 to 10. For values of $p = q = 10$ ($p = q = n$ in general) that the HAP "collapses" into the classical AP because each of the 10 nodes becomes its own "group." For values of $p = q < 10$, aggregation is taking place. With no aggregation applied to the problem, the HAP solution for $p = q = 10$ is about

122 total miles traveled (this corresponds to the objective function value of the AP if solved with the same data). At the other extreme, with origin and destination nodes fully aggregated into a single group p = q = 1 (i.e., origin nodes and demand nodes are placed into one group each) the HAP solution is such that interaction costs have increased more than fourfold (523.09) over the fully disaggregate case. This is because travel is being routed well away from more direct paths between individual origin and destination locations.

The solution for p = q = 3 (objective = 371.13) is visualised. Interactions between groups are shown, as well as the exact groupings of origin and destination nodes. The spatial configuration of the groups and the means by which groups interact with one another suggests that the model is performing as expected in terms of minimizing interaction costs. However, what is interesting about this picture is that visually, three distinct hub-and-spoke-like network structures emerge.

Hub-and-spoke networks are characterised by an interhub link which connects hub locations. Flows traveling over this special linkage are usually awarded a discount because cost savings opportunities are believed to accrue through flow economies of scale. In the HAP, the link connecting a given group of origins and group of destinations may be thought of as an interhub link, although the present formulation of the HAP does not discount this flow. Another difference is that the nature of the"spokes" in the prototypical hub network is somewhat different than the regional groupings performed by the HAP.

Of course, the hub-model notion of single allocation of spoke node to hub node is built into the HAP through the single assignment constraints, although the final allocation of individual nodes to grouping nodes (i.e., hubs) in the HAP is visually different. Essentially the HAP requirement that origin nodes and destination nodes must be grouped separately results in spoke allocations that are longer and probably more indirect than those that would be found in a typical hub model. For trials two and three, we fixed either p or q at 3 and varied the other parameter from 1 to 10.

Both sets of solutions are similar in terms of their objective function values at a given level of aggregation. However, because either p or q is fixed at 3, the effects of aggregation and thus disaggregation are somewhat muted as reflected in the narrower range of objective function values found.

30-NODE DATA RESULTS

A second data set consisting of 30 origin nodes and 30 destination nodes were randomly generated in TransCAD GIS. The configurations of the individual points are not displayed in the interest of space, but solutions to the 30-node problems are provided. All problems were solved to optimality or quite close to optimality, although, an increase in computing time was required to solve these problems when compared with experience with the

10-node case. Thus for the 30-node problem we have 2700 variables and 1862 constraints, with integer restrictions on a and b. This is a difficult problem to solve to optimality and we recognise the increase in solution times from the 10-node to the 30-node case. Trials with the 30-node data set were structured similarly to trials with the 10-node data. One additional step taken in the 30-node analysis, however, was to explore the various cost components that are a part of the objective function. In this fashion, we can examine the costs of aggregating origin nodes, destination nodes, and the interactions between them given choices of p and q.

For the first round of trials we varied p and q jointly from 1 to 30. In the second and third rounds, p and q were fixed, respectively, while the other parameter of interest was varied. With regard to trends in the solutions, greater variations due to aggregation effects are possible with the larger 30-node data set. In fact, fully aggregating the point data (p = q = 1) results in five times the interaction costs versus when the individual points are left disaggregated (p = q = 30). Note the three curves intersect where p = q = 10.

Analysis with the HAP suggests that aggregation effects decrease at a decreasing rate with greater disaggregation of data. Or put another way, the largest increases in transport costs are paid when the last few aggregations are made. Further, the results indicate that in relative terms, modest levels of aggregation over the totally disaggregate case do not substantially affect transportation costs.

We can also examine the three principal cost components making up the total objective. The three cost components and total interaction costs in trials where p = q are graphically displayed. All of the results show that as aggregation is increased, the costs associated with that interaction are an increasingly larger proportion of interaction costs. For example, in the solution where p = q = 1, only about 116 of the total objective function value (1811) is due to cross-group interaction and not aggregation.

Some very interesting variations in interaction costs and the other two components are observed when either p or q is held constant. For instance, in the second set of trials where the destination parameter q is varied, we can see that only the cost component associated with the destination aggregation is monotonically decreasing as q [right arrow] 30. In fact, both the interaction costs and the origin aggregation costs initially begin to fall as q [right arrow] 30, but begin to increase again at about p = q = 10. This is due to the geography of the nodes, and suggests that for a given level of aggregation, interaction costs are lowest when similar levels of origin and destination aggregation are performed on each.

This is apparent based on the results as the lowest interaction costs are witnessed when q is in the range of 5 or 10. In general, total interaction costs obey the law of diminishing returns in that increased disaggregation improves the objective function (i.e., lowers it) at a decreasing rate. This phenomenon has been identified previously and discussed with respect to aggregation in PMPs by Francis et al.

EXPERIMENT

Up to this point, we have stressed the derivation of the HAP, as well as related aggregation issues. Now we view the HAP as a network flow problem and apply it to a real-world data set. Thus, we obtain stronger connections between the HAP and research on network flows and hub-and-spoke networks. We use a well-tested data set, the 1970 CAB records of air passengers flying between the 100 largest U.S. cities.

To illustrate possible network designs obtainable, we extracted 12 candidate origin and 12 candidate destination cities from this database. Our analysis focuses on the best way of linking cities, given some number of desired intermediate stops. We first solve the HAP with p = q = 1, and find that the model has chosen to route flow through Shreveport, LA in the south and Cincinnati, OH in the north. The modeled interaction pattern resembles the two-hub single-allocation hub-and-spoke network.

Such a network structure is also akin to the classic"bridge-line" network described in transport geography texts, whereby goods are brought from several cities by truck to an intermediate point and loaded onto train. Then after the train line traverses some distance, the goods are unloaded at another intermediate point and placed on trucks again, which are bound for shipment to destination cities. Clearly, because the HAP does not deal with mode of travel, we cannot claim that we have modeled the bridge-line-type network in its entirety. But we do, however, note the geographical similarities between the two structures. The network patterns become increasingly complex as the number of origin and destination groups are increased. At the same time, because we are forcing fewer nodes to take indirect paths enroute to their final destination, the objective functions will of course decrease as we increase p and q.

What the maps show is that two distinct hub-and-spoke-type networks emerge when p = q = 2; Cincinnati and Shreveport maintain their"hub" status, but now Tulsa and Toledo also act as intermediate nodes on their own separate network. If the number of destination groups is increased to 4 (i.e., q = 4), then Harrisburg emerges as an intermediate stop, and Philadelphia becomes its own destination group.

We have presented a new modeling approach termed the HAP. In the spirit of the GAP, our intent with the HAP has been to devise a generalization of the AP and TP. But a major difference between our efforts and those associated with the GAP and other optimization approaches is that we have accounted for the aggregation process in a way that is endogenous to the model. This was undertaken in light of the idea that aggregation is central to many optimization scenarios, such as in the hub-and-spoke literature.

Moreover, our focus on incorporating aggregation into the context of the model itself represents a departure from prevailing views dealing with aggregation. Most existing research has focused on the effects of aggregation rather than accommodating it directly into the modeling effort. From an applications standpoint, the HAP may be used to model several network structures that might be found in practice including regional hub-and-spoke systems, and other user-specified commodity distribution systems that are not necessarily replicable with current approaches.

Several possible network structures are recoverable from this model, including a bridge-line-type network, and variants on p-median and assignment model structures. In addition, from a more theoretical standpoint, a key aspect of the model is its ability to account for interaction costs because no zonal representation or "pre-aggregation" is imposed. Thus we may measure the exact costs of aggregation or assignment in network flow problems. The construction of the HAP lends itself to comparison with other optimization problems. One interesting thing about the HAP is in regard to the endogenous nature of grouping. That is, groupings are subject to some user-specified level, but are still found in pursuit of minimum transportation costs.

As our results have demonstrated, groupings of nodes are recoverable from an analysis. However, it is important to point out that in its present form, HAP results cannot result in a single optimal zonal system for origin and destination locations. This is because origin and destination locations are treated as separate point sets or "layers" by the HAP. So while we can recover groupings, or design zones for either origin or destination locations, only a comprehensive zoning system could result if the HAP formulation were altered to not differentiate between origin and destination candidate nodes. Another closely related methodological connection is from cluster analysis, especially in the way that clusters around hubs generalise the median/centroid idea.

The novelty of our approach here, however, is the endogeneity of cluster configuration. It is also possible that the HAP provides a better way to explore the kinds of routine rules of thumb concerning the desirable amount of interaction that crosses zonal boundaries. We hope that our use of disaggregate data, our method of defining clusters, and our system of accounting for interaction costs will spur further thought on these issues. To summarise, this analysis was a first step in introducing the HAP and its properties, and establishing connections to the broader literature on spatial interaction, network analysis, and aggregation effects in location models.

Our experience with the HAP showed that solution times increase rapidly as a function of problemsize. Therefore, subsequent work clearly could be undertaken to devise a Lagrangean relaxation for solving larger HAPs; after all, this is one of the more successful techniques for solving the closely related

PMP. Also worth consulting in this regard would be the work on metaheuristics such as tabu search and heuristic concentration, as these also have been very successful methods for solving the PMP. One insight that could aid in these implementations is that because various restrictions on the problem reduce to special cases (e.g., the HAP reduces to an AP), we might quickly devise bounds from the solution of the related models. Indeed, the TP, AP, and PMP have all been implemented in large-scale applications.

Another possible avenue of exploration might entail designing weights for individual objective terms and treating the HAP like a true multiobjective problem. Recall that the HAP objective function consists of three distinct cost terms. In our analysis each of the objective terms were essentially equally weighted with an assumed (1) preceding each. Clearly in some instances however, such as in hub-and-spoke networks, it is appropriate to weight certain network links more heavily, or actively discount links so that they might receive additional flow.

Our initial analysis suggests the propensity for hub-like networks to form when the HAP is used with city data, yet it may be worthwhile exploring how weighting or discounting the cross-group interaction term in the HAP affects the spatial patterns of groupings. For the hub-like situation, if there are large incentives for cross-group interaction, more spatially compact clusters of nodes will probably form. Such a scenario might also be desirable if the minimization of interaction costs between the origin and destination clusters relative to the cross-group interactions is needed.

However, determining an appropriate structure of these weights given a specific transport context is outside the scope of this chapter. A second possibility for additional work lies in incorporating quantities of goods at individual nodes (i.e., permitting varied supply and demand). Presently the HAP is formulated where nodes represent individual entities with no quantities to be shipped from these locations. This was done to build upon the basic idea of disaggregation and individual geographic elements inherent to the spirit of the GAP/AP. Although for a given problem setting, quantities may be needed at individual locations. If these considerations were to be incorporated into the HAP, this would move the model more in the direction of the GAP as well as afford it additional commonality with the PMP.

TRAVELING SALESMAN PROBLEM

Mathematicians and operations research specialists have been researching and writing about the Traveling Salesman Problem (TSP) for decades. One of the earliest known papers on the topic is "On the Hamiltonian Game (a traveling salesman problem)" by Robinson. Among the most prolific early researchers were Dantzig, Fulkerson and Johnson.

Their 1954 paper, "Solution of a Large-Scale Traveling-Salesman Problem", which describes a linear programming approach for a 49 city problem, is considered a classic in the field. An extensive TSP research project is supported by Rice University, Rice's Computer and Information Technology Institute; the Centre for Research on Parallel Computation; Digital Equipment Corporation; and the Keck Foundation.

TRAVELING SALESMAN PROBLEM

The objective in a Traveling Salesman Problem is to minimise the total length of a tour, entering and leaving each location once, while beginning and ending the lour with the same location. In this chapter, we will discuss both small-scale and large-scale problems which can be solved using Premium Solver Platform©. The basic procedures are identical. The small-scale problem will be used to illustrate the formulation of the problem.

There are seven cities in the TSP example. It would be considered a small-scale problem. However, the manual algorithms developed over the years to solve such a problem, combined with the high number of feasible, but not optimal solutions, make this a difficult and lengthy problem to solve.

PREMIUM SOLVER PLATFORM

Solver is an add-in optimization tool which is available with Microsoft Excel©. The software was written for Microsoft by Frontline Systems. More powerful versions of Solver are available for commercial and academic use. A web page maintained by Frontline Systems provides product information, as well as general information on optimization and linear programming.4 The version used for this chapter is Premium Solver Platform©, which will solve larger and more complex problems than the version which is standard with Microsoft Excel.

A significant addition to this software, which was released in 2000, is the inclusion of the"all different" constraint. This allows one to specify that a set of variables will have integer values from 1 to N (the number of variables), all of them different at the solution. This powerful feature has dramatically simplified the formulation of the Traveling Salesman Problem, as will be illustrated in this chapter.

FORMULATION OF TRAVELING

The first step in formulating the TSP problem using Premium Solver Platform© is to develop the direct distance matrix. Two differences should be noted compared to the initial mileage spreadsheet. First, row and column headings are included. The headings will be referenced as the model formulation is explained. Second, a column and row have been inserted between the spreadsheet heading and the city names. For example, note that Amarillo is assigned a 1, Austin a 2, etc. As discussed previously, these integer values will be used in model formulation related to the"all different" constraint. The second spreadsheet initially contains headings, integers and formulas.

A description of the cell values and formulas is shown below:

Cells B12..D12 hold descriptions of the column values. Cells B13..B19 initially contain integer values 1..7. Upon completion of the final solution, these cells will contain the integer values associated with cities and will define the final sequence for the tour. Cell B20 assures that the final solution tour returns to the city where the tour began. Cells C13.. C20 use the Excel operation VLOOKUP to find the name of the city associated with the integer values (1-7). Cell C21 hold the constant"Total" which is a description of the value held in cell D21. This instruction finds the associated mileage from the mileage table from the city associated with the integer value in cell B(N) to the next city B(N+1). For example, initially cell D14 will hold the distance (480) from the city associated with integer 1 (Amarillo) to the city associated with integer 2 (Austin). Cell D21 calculates the total mileage, which is the sum of cells D14..D20.

The next step in the formulation of the model is to define the objective and the constraints. As discussed previously, the process has been simplified by the addition of the "all different" constraint.

The Solver option is found under Tools/Add-ins in Microsoft Excel. The "Set Cell" parameter defines the spreadsheet cell which we wish to optimise. In this example we wish to minimise Cell D21, which holds the total distance of the tour. The "By Changing Variable Cells" parameter defines the cells which we wish to change, in order to minimise the total distance. In this example, these are cells B13..B19, which hold the integer values assigned to the seven cities. The "Subject to the Constraints" declares that the values in cells B13..B19 will be all different.

As discussed earlier, this option, which is currently only available with Premium Solver Platform, defines that the integer values will all be different. Thus, there will be only one entry and one exit to each city, and the tour will conclude where it began. The Standard Evolutionary option is appropriate for a TSP problem. Once the model is defined, one should select Solve.

ADDITIONAL PROBLEM

In order to test the model development approach outlined in this chapter, other problems were formulated and solved. In all cases, even those that were relatively large, model development time was minimal. For large problems, some Solver parameters need to be modified. Suggested modifications, which are made by selecting Options and Limit Options, are intended to prevent the calculations from ending prematurely. In addition to the above changes, one will need to execute multiple runs of the same problem to increase the probability of finding the optimal solution. The evolutionary solver is designed to find feasible, good and optimal solutions. While the evolutionary solver, which is based on genetic algorithms, is designed to find optimal solutions ideally the global optimal, this is not always possible.

Multiple runs for large problems, with the parameter changes discussed above, will likely yield the optimal solution. This solution was found by running the program thirty times. In the thirty runs, the suggested solution shown, which is a total distance of 9,585, was found thirteen times. The Traveling-Salesman Problem has been an important and popular operations research topic for decades.

Numerous algorithms and computer programs have been developed by researchers attempting to more efficiently solve the problems. Significant advances have been made possible with the release of Premium Solver Platform, which includes the "all different" constraint. This chapter illustrates an efficient solution approach for the successful application of this powerful new software tool. As this chapter illustrates, the approach efficiently solves both small and large scale Traveling Salesman Problems. Premium Solver Platform should increase the accessibility of Traveling Salesman applications and further advance the development of real world models. Over the past several decades, the legal impediments to the transportation industry have hindered the productivity of a firm's transportation activities. However, the passage of landmark deregulatory reforms in the Motor Carrier Act of 1980 has created more productive transportation options.

One of these options is "backhauling," an efficient way to reduce transportation costs by filling empty trucks on their way back to the home base after delivering goods to customers. The Interstate Commerce Commission News reported that the potential fuel savings as a result of loaded backhaul movements could exceed 42 million gallons a year nationally. Due to such large cost saving opportunities, backhauling has become a growing trend in the transportation industry, as evidenced by a recent NCPDM Survey that revealed that 83 per cent of transportation firms wanted to consider backhauling options.

Industries for which such savings are possible include distribution of dairy products, agricultural items, pharmaceutical goods, dry cleaning supplies, electronic appliances, automobiles, and hardware items, among others. In pursuing this strategy, one of the major questions facing transportation managers is how to construct the vehicle routes to include backhauling.

This broad question can be further classified into three specific questions:

- Wbackhauling,
- Which trucks should be allocated to which delivery and pickup points, and
- In what sequence should delivery and pickup points be served.

To answer such questions, a mathematical approach is developed for solving a new vehicle routing problem with backhauling (VRPB). The proposed model is capable of dealing with multiple vehicles and multiple depots, both of which are capacitated. Because of the computational complexity inherent in solving the VRPB, the problem is decomposed into submodels.

This procedure consists of three phases:

- Allocation of customers and vendors to capacitated clusters,
- Assignment of customers and vendors to depots and routes, and
- Individual route configuration.

This decomposition procedure allowed us to solve a real-world problem with three depots, 134 customers, and 27 vendors in 130 CPU seconds on a VAX-11/780 system. The next section reviews the literature related to the VRPB presented here. The literature review is followed by a more precise definition of the VRPB. Then, the various mathematical formulations and solution procedures for the VRPB are presented. The remaining section is devoted to model application and testing using "real-world" data. The chapter concludes with a discussion of the implications and contributions of this research effort. Transportation regulation has long prohibited trucking firms from utilizing backhauling options. After Section 8 of the Motor Carrier Act of 1980 overturned previous regulatory laws, the issue of backhauling was raised by many practitioners and academicians because of its great cost saving potential.

Since 1980, however, only a few analytical studies on backhauling have been conducted. Ballou and Chowdhury were among the first to incorporate a backhauling option into vehicle routing models. They initiated backhauling studies by including both deliveries and pickups on the same vehicle routes and by considering two different modes of vehicles, namely private and common carriers. In an effort to better utilise truck fleets, they considered the use of common carriers when restrictions on driving distances or times prevented the use of private carriers on the return trip. A computer-based conceptual model was suggested to handle carrier selection problems for backhaul routes.

Jordan and Burns developed continuous and discrete mathematical models for reducing empty truck-miles via backhauling for two terminal networks. The continuous model was designed to examine the impacts of terminal location and freight flow on total backhaul savings. The discrete model was developed to decide which loads should be backhauled to minimise empty truck-miles. These models, however, were limited to backhaul problems with only two terminals. Later, Jordan extended this earlier work by considering more than two terminals. The model did not design the delivery route but rather designed the backhaul route given that the delivery route was already determined.

In an effort to determine how private carriers should be routed to backhaul goods from vendors near customers, Yano et al. applied the "customised" route generation procedure for use on a personal computer. The customised route generation procedure was combined with an efficient set-covering procedure based on Lagrangean relaxation to construct optimal routes and assign those routes to private carriers. To reduce computational time necessary to find optimal routes, the set-covering procedure considered only a limited number of "good" feasible routes that included "many" pickups preceded by "many" deliveries. The good feasible routes were obtained by heuristically solving a constrained traveling salesman problem (with deliveries preceding pickups).

Casco et al. solved the VRP with backhauls by utilizing the Clarke and Wright Savings Method and Cheapest Insertion method originally proposed by Rosenkrantz et al. Initially, without backhauling considerations, pure delivery problems were solved by using the Clarke and Wright Savings method; next, pickup points were served by additional vehicles that were used for the pickup process only.

Finally, backhauls were inserted onto the initial feasible delivery-routes generated by the Clarke and Wright Savings method. The decision to insert backhauls was primarily based on the size of delivery loads after the pickup process. A penalty was assessed according to remaining delivery loads at a certain point. A high penalty cost was arbitrarily assigned to a backhaul insertion with a large remaining delivery load. The advantage of this load-based insertion procedure is that, if the delivery load that remains is small enough, the backhaul can be inserted prior to the completion of a delivery route. All of the studies reviewed here developed models and/or solution procedures for the backhaul problem. None of the previous analytical studies, however, have addressed the VRPB with multiple depots. In fact, all the prior studies but Jordan considered a single depot. Jordan considered multiple depots, but focused on "backhaul zoning" rather than "backhaul routing."

In other words, he was mainly concerned with separating customers into two groups: those to be served and those not to be served by backhauling. Consequently, he did not design the model to determine the sequence of deliveries and pickups on the route. Also, none of the earlier models was designed to determine vehicle fleet size. A primary purpose of the research reported in this chapter is to include these last two considerations into a VRPB model; consequently, this chapter extends earlier works by developing a method that solves the VRPB with multiple depots and simultaneously determines the fleet size.

PROBLEM STATEMENT

This study is concerned with the problem of coordinating shipments moving in opposite directions, i.e., outbound and inbound shipments, from and to several depots--consequently, it is similar to the multiple depot VRP. It is different, however, from the multiple depot VRP in that it considers both deliveries and pickups on the same vehicle route with precedence relationships between deliveries and pickups, whereas the multiple depot VRP considers only either deliveries or pickups on a route.

Throughout this chapter, the aforementioned problem will be referred to as"a multiple depot VRP with backhauling (MDVRPB)." The MDVRPB occurs when trucks return empty after delivering goods to their customers. To minimise these empty-truck-miles, i.e., deadhead travel distances, we consider the possibility that private carriers will be able to pick up goods or raw materials from multiple vendors after the delivery process has been completed. Theoretically, backhauls may include pickups prior to the end of a delivery route if the remaining delivery load is small enough to accommodate the pickup load. However, most trucks are rear-loaded and delivery after pickup requires the reshuffling of loads. Consequently, we do not consider such a case in this chapter; we consider backhauling only after all outbound deliveries have been made. In practice, of course, both vehicles and depots are assumed to have finite capacities. Vehicles can hold only a limited amount of goods, and depots are able to service only a limited number of loadings and unloadings. Subsequently, route design must not violate these restrictions. In light of these characteristics, the model developed here assumes both capacitated vehicles and depots.

Given the above problem context, the main issues to be addressed are:

- Determination of the fleet size to serve customers and vendors,
- Allocation of vehicles to depots,
- Allocation of customers and vendors to vehicles, and
- Routing of vehicles. Unfortunately, even the VRP without the consideration of backhauling belongs to the class of problems known as NP hard; consequently, it is unlikely that a computationally efficient algorithm exists to solve the MDVRPB optimally. Therefore, we present a heuristic solution procedure for this problem in the next section.

SOLUTION METHODOLOGY

The proposed heuristic for the MDVRPB decomposes the problem into three basic phases:

- Aggregation of customers and vendors to capacited clusters,
- Assignment of customer and vendor clusters to a depot and route, and
- The design of individual vehicle routes.

These phases are addressed sequentially, with the output of one phase serving the input for the next. This decomposition procedure allows us to solve the MDVRPB for real-world sized distribution problems efficiently. In the following subsections, we provide detailed descriptions of and justifications for the proposed decomposition solution procedure.

DETERMINATION OF CUSTOMER AND VENDOR

The initial phase aggregates customers and vendors into"capacitated clusters" based upon spatial proximity. The capacitated clusters are formed by grouping customers and vendors such that the total delivery size of customers or the total pickup size of vendors within each cluster does not exceed the capacity limit of the vehicle that is to be assigned to the cluster. Since each cluster will require a vehicle, this phase also determines the number of vehicles needed at each depot. The motivation for this aggregation is based on the fact that, in practice, we rarely see uniformly located customers and vendors. That is to say, most customers and vendors are concentrated in densely populated metropolitan areas or industrial complexes.

As a result, the aggregation of customers and vendors into a certain number of clusters based on their spatial proximity generally helps generate good initial tours of the vehicles. The idea of aggregating a set of nodes prior to the construction of vehicle routes is not novel. Numerous VRP studies have successfully utilised such a scheme.

None of these, however, explored the use of statistical clustering techniques proposed here to restrict the size of the clusters to be less than the capacity of the vehicles. As opposed to those earlier VRP studies, we propose a capacitated clustering procedure to aggregate customers and vendors. The resulting clusters will consist entirely of either customers or vendors and will be able to be served by a single vehicle.

The major appeal of this clustering procedure is its effectiveness in dealing with a large number of customers and vendors without severe computational difficulty, particularly when destinations (customers and vendors) are reasonably close together. However, the clustering procedure is not without potential drawbacks, since it creates routes based on the surrogate distances from depots to the centroids of destinations rather than actual distances.

For instance, clustering may result in very lengthy routes, when:

- Customer demand is lumpy,
- The volume associated with any natural clusters do not closely match vehicle capacities, and
- Vehicles capacities are not homogeneous.

Also, when deliveries and pickups need to be made within specified time windows, the clustering procedure may not effectively handle timing restrictions because the aggregation of customers and vendors is separate from the sequencing of deliveries and pickups. Nevertheless, to determine the capacitated clusters, we chose the minimum variance method for hierarchical clustering proposed by Ward for the following reasons. First, the hierarchical method is straightforward to use because it is easily accessible to powerful computer software packages such as SAS, and more importantly is based on a conceptually simple rule of how to search a similarity (proximity) matrix and when to combine different entities.

Due to this simplicity, the statistical capacitated clustering method is more computationally efficient in solving large-sized (with over 100 stops) problems than the mathematical programming based clustering method. Second, in the

VRP context, the number of clusters is equivalent to the number of vehicles required, i.e., fleet size, since one vehicle services each cluster. While the nonhierarchical (partitioning) clustering method requires the user to specify the number of clusters, the hierarchical clustering method does not.

Consequently, a hierarchical clustering method was selected over the nonhierarchical clustering methods to permit the simultaneous determinations of clusters and fleet size. Third, among various hierarchical clustering methods such as single linkage, complete linkage, average linkage, and Ward's minimum variance methods, we chose Ward's method because numerous experimental studies have shown that Ward's method generally outperforms other hierarchical methods in terms of solution accuracy.

Unlike others, Ward's method usually generates a near-optimal grouping of entities into clusters. Finally, the method tends to create clusters of relatively equal size. In the VRP context, equal sizes of clusters are desirable since we, as do most VRP studies, assume equal capacities of vehicles. None of the existing clustering methods was designed to generate capacitated clusters; thus, we have refined Ward's method to do so by aggregating customers into clusters with a restricted size that is equal to the vehicle capacity.

This is accomplished by treating each customer as if it contains as many observations as its demand requirement. For instance, if a customer demands ten units of goods, then the customer would be treated as an object or entity with ten observations. The execution of this part of phase one yields capacitated clusters of deliveries and pickup nodes. Each such cluster represents either a truck load of deliveries or pickups for backhaul.

ASSIGNMENT OF CUSTOMER AND VENDOR CLUSTERS TO DEPOTS AND ROUTES

Once the clusters of customers and vendors are determined, the next decision to be made is which depots and routes should serve which customer and vendor clusters. The routes are, in fact, aggregated routes that describe the depot, customer cluster, and vendor cluster visited by a vehicle. The first phase yields m customers and n vendor clusters. The assignment phase now assigns these clusters to depots and to routes via the following integer program. In order to solve this problem, one must define all of the possible routes X sub ijk. These include routes traveling only to customers as well as trips consisting solely of pickups at vendors.

Note, if $i = 0$, then X sub ojk represents the route from depot k to vendor j and back to depot k. That is, the route is a pickup route only. If $j = 0$, then X sub iok represents the route from depot k to customer i and back to depot k. That is, the route is a delivery route only. The variable X sub ook is not defined for any k since it includes neither a customer nor a vendor cluster.

The objective function:

- Minimizes the total distance of the aggregated routes. Constraint set

- Ensures that each vendor cluster is on exactly one route. As a result of (2) and
- Each of the clusters will be assigned to one, and only one, depot. Because the clusters are capacitated (i.e., not exceeding a truck capacity) each route from a depot will require exactly one vehicle to be assigned to that depot. Consequently, constraint set
- Serves as a capacity constraint on the number of vehicles that can be assigned to each depot.

As will be discussed later, these depot capacity constraints may take any one of several forms. The key to this formulation is the definition of the potential routes, X sub ijk. It has been assumed, because of the capacitated nature of the customer and vendor cluster, that each vehicle route may include at most, one customer and one vendor cluster.

It is also assumed that no vehicle route will include more than one depot. Consequently, the maximum number of X sub ijk potential routes that must be identified is k(m + n + mn), where k equals the number of depots, m equals the number of customer clusters, and n equals the number of vendor clusters. The problem size may be reduced if some of these potential routes may be eliminated as nonsensical or inappropriate.

The depot capacity constraint (4) may take several forms. As written, it constrains the total number of vehicles visiting a depot. It may be more appropriate to constrain the number of delivery or pickup loads that are assigned to a depot. This could be accomplished by replacing constraint set (4) with the following constraints. Constraint sets (4), (4a) and (4b) define depot capacity in terms of vehicles. Alternatively, it may be desirable to define these capacities in terms of units of goods hauled. This can be accomplished by replacing constraint set (4) with either constraint set (4c) or constraint sets (4d) and (4e), given below. Constraint set (4c) is similar to (4), and (4d) and (4e) are similar to (4a) and (4b) except that capacity is measured in truckloads in (4), (4a) and (4b), and in units of goods in (4c), (4d), and (4e).

DESIGN OR INDIVIDUAL VEHICLE ROUTES

Given the output of phase 2, one must now determine the actual vehicle tours for each aggregated route selected in the previous stage.

The original VRPB with multiple vehicles is now decomposed into a series of single traveling salesman-type sub-problems since:

- There is no longer a need to determine which vehicles should serve which demand nodes and
- The individual tours are designed not to exceed the vehicle capacity.

The remaining task, then, is to construct a tour for each vehicle through its assigned cluster(s). This disaggregate tour building procedure involves solving a series of modified traveling salesman problems (TSPs). These are similar to the standard TSP in that they require the vehicle eventually return to its home base. However, these problems, unlike the traditional TSP, require precedence restrictions that allow visits to pickup nodes only after all the delivery nodes have been visited. From now on, these problems are referred to as"individual VRPB's." The individual VRPB's can be solved by using the following procedure:

- First, the individual VRPB is converted to an asymmetric TSP by assigning an arbitrarily large number to arcs starting from a pickup node and ending at a delivery node. These arbitrary weights will prohibit the tour traversing from a pickup node to a delivery node. Since the resulting tour will collect pickups and deliveries at opposite ends of the tour and the tour is essentially undirected, we are indifferent as to whether the model puts pickups or deliveries"first" as we can always reverse the direction of the tour.
- Second, this series of asymmetric TSP's is solved by Little et al.'s branch and bound algorithm. Although any other exact branch and bound algorithm for realistic-size TSP's may be used, the Little et al.'s algorithm is chosen here because it was designed for an asymmetric TSP and the computer code based on such an exact algorithm was the only one available to us. While this step requires solving the NP-complete (inherently difficult) TSP, the number of nodes in each of these problems is generally small because their total demands are no more than twice the vehicle's capacity.

For example, in the real-world problem solved in the next section, the average number of nodes in these problems was 11.5, and the greatest number of nodes was 20.

HEURISTIC MODEL APPLICATION AND RESULTS

In this section we demonstrate the proposed heuristic procedures with a realistically sized problem. The problem is based upon actual data generously supplied by the transportation division of a large U.S. company. The data has been slightly altered to ensure confidentiality.

PROBLEM DESCRIPTION

A transportation division of a manufacturing company that produces and sells hardware items is responsible for delivering these goods from three distribution centres to 134 customers scattered among seven contiguous states. In addition to the delivery operations, the transportation division often sends its private carriers to pick up a variety of raw materials from 27 vendors located in nine states. Among these, five states contain both customers and vendors.

For simplicity, the travel distances, d sub ij, were represented by the Euclidean distance between node i and j. The supply and demand data are recorded in units of product. Vehicle capacity was set at 850 product units.

MODEL OUTPUTS AND COMPUTATIONAL RESULTS

The solution procedure described earlier for the VRPB generates the following information:

- The fleet size at each depot,
- The specific amount of each product to be delivered by each vehicle,
- The delivery routes,
- The backhaul routes, and
- The total travel distance of each vehicle.

AGGREGATION PHASE

The first step as to generate capacitated clusters of customers and vendors by conducting statistical cluster analysis. This was accomplished using Ward's minimum variance cluster analysis. A SAS program was written and executed on a Digital VAX-11/780 computer system. The execution times for generating the capacitated customer and vendor clusters were 7 and 4 CPU seconds, respectively.

AGGREGATE TOUR BUILDING PHASE

The second step of the heuristic is to design the aggregate routes. This is accomplished by solving the integer program. The possible routes, X sub ijk, were determined using the customer and vendor clusters generated in the previous stage. In total, there were 627 of these variables. The centroids of the clusters were used to determine the intercluster distances.

The centroid of each cluster was obtained using the MacQueen's k-means partitioning procedure. Although the formulation has binary integer restrictions, (5), for the decision variables, the problem yielded pure integer solutions when it was solved as a continuous linear program by relaxing these restrictions because its formulation is quite similar to an assignment problem formulation. Constraint set was employed as the depot capacity constraint with T sub k = 6, for all k. The solution of this problem required 5.22 CPU seconds using Marstern's XMP mathematical programming package on a VAX-11/780 computer system.

The aggregate tour building phase yielded 15 tours (and therefore, 15 vehicles) with 6 vehicles assigned to depots 1 and 2, and 3 vehicles assigned to depot 3. Twelve of the routes included customer and vendor clusters, two routes consisted only of customers and one route consisted only of vendors.

DISAGGREGATE TOUR BUILDING PHASE

As noted earlier, the aggregate tours were generated by considering the centroid of each customer and vendor cluster as a single node. Now, the detailed route for customers and vendors within each cluster must be determined. These routes are determined in the disaggregate tour building procedure which involves solving a series of traveling salesman problems.

Optimal solutions were obtained for all individual tour design subproblems by using the FORTRAN code in Phillips and Garcia-Diaz. We used this code because it is readily available. This package was written to solve any of several network problems. Consequently, a code written specifically for this problem and based upon a more efficient algorithm such as the one presented in Carpaneto and Toth could undoubtedly reduce solution times. As stated earlier, the number of nodes in each individual tour will generally not be very large due to the vehicle capacities. The asymmetric TSP algorithm in Carpaneto and Toth is capable of solving problems with up to 240 nodes efficiently.

In the aftermath of transportation deregulation, logisticians have been interested in reducing transportation costs by carrying freight on return trips, i.e., backhauling. Specifically, the problem of interest in this research is the routing of multiple vehicles from multiple depots to deliver goods to various customers. After a vehicle has delivered its goods, it may then pick up goods from vendors on its return to the depot. The proposed procedure determines the fleet size needed; the allocation of vehicles, customers, and vendors to the various depots; and the specific routes of the individual vehicles. All of these determinations are constrained by the vehicle and depot capacity.

A solution methodology is proposed that decomposes the problem into three main phases where the output of one phase becomes the input to the next phase. The first phase aggregates customers and vendors to capacitated clusters. During this phase, customers and vendors are combined into truck load sized groupings using a new capacitated clustering technique. The resulting customer and vendor clusters have a capacity equal to a single vehicle's capacity. Consequently, each cluster will require exactly one vehicle. The second phase designs aggregated routes and assigns customer and vendor clusters to depots via a zero-one integer program. In the example, this model solved easily in its linear programming relaxed form. Due to the capacitated nature of clusters, each route includes at most, one customer and one vendor.

Therefore, this model never produces subtours. The final phase designs the individual routes through the clusters and requires solving a series of asymmetric traveling salesman problems (ATSPs). By manipulating the distance matrix, each ATSP first routes the vehicle through the nodes in the customer cluster and then through the nodes in the vendor cluster. This subproblem can be readily solved with existing ATSP algorithms.

The reasons may be:

- We can ignore capacity constraints because no customer or vendor cluster exceeds vehicle capacity, and
- The number of customer and vendor nodes in the cluster is generally not very large because of the capacity restrictions.

The proposed methodology was demonstrated on a problem consisting of three depots, 134 customer nodes, and 24 vendor nodes. The data for this problem came from an actual distribution system. The solution for the entire problem required a total of 130.22 CPU seconds on a VAX-11/780 computer system. The capacitated depot solution consisted of a total of 15 tours from three depots. Twelve of these tours included both deliveries and pickups (backhauls), two included deliveries only, and one consisted solely of pickups. The results presented here clearly demonstrate that the proposed methodology can solve practical size multi-depot multi-vehicle routing problems that incorporate both vehicle and distribution centre capacities as well as backhauling.

Obviously, however, there are additional areas for continued research. Examples of these are:

- Future study should relax the assumptions of deterministic demands and supplies, as well as uniform vehicle capacity.
- The extension of the VRPB should consider cost differentials associated with the employment of private versus common carriers.
- Temporal factors can be added to the current study by including timing constraints in the form of both soft and hard time windows.
- To broaden the applicability of the model to more practical settings, future backhauling research should consider the situation where the backhauling of certain materials is strictly restricted to certain trucks due to potential health hazards.
- The basic structure of the VRPB model can be extended to include the possibility of a simultaneous delivery and pickup at the same stop.

There has been recent interest in a class of problems, dealing with combinatorial optimization, that have been hitherto neglected in both experimental and differential psychology. In particular, attention has focused on visually presented versions of the well-known traveling salesperson problem, traditionally referred to as the traveling salesman problem (TSP). In the planar Euclidean form of the problem, there are n interconnected cities, represented by n nodes, and the task is to construct a pathway that departs from one node to visit each node exactly once, returns to the starting node, and is as short as possible.

The number of possible pathways is equal to ½(n - 1)! As a result, when n is small (e.g., 5), there are relatively few pathways to choose from (in this case, 12). However, when n becomes even moderately large (e.g., 25), the number of possible pathways becomes so great that a computer evaluating a million possibilities per second would take almost 10 billion years to evaluate them all. Such problems are of interest for a number of reasons. In the problem-solving domain, they occupy a strategic intermediate position between early research in the Gestalt tradition, in which the solution process could be described as an insightful perceptual reorganization, and recent research, in which the emphasis has been on studying the nature, acquisition, and application of expertise in knowledge-rich real-world domains. Such problems can often be stated simply and understood readily and lend themselves to systematic laboratory investigation. At the same time, they are representative of many realistic, practical problems, as evidenced by the numerous applications of mathematics and computer science dealing with combinatorial optimization. In the domain of visual perception, visually presented instances of such problems are of interest because there is some agreement that the impressive human ability to arrive at near-optimal solutions to these problems depends heavily on the use of spontaneously occurring perceptual principles. If so, an examination of performance in such tasks may throw light on the operation of these principles, as well as on their possible interaction with higher level cognitive processes.

For example, MacGregor and Ormerod propose that the TSP task "may happen to parallel what is natural for the perceptual system to do... when presented with an array of dots". More specifically, Ormerod and Chronicle and MacGregor et al. hypothesized that participants begin by processing the TSP array globally by identifying the best figure fitting the dot array and then use this figure either to construct an attempted solution or to evaluate a solution that is presented to them.

According to these authors, the best-fitting global figure is provided by the convex hull of the array. The convex hull of a set of points, S, is the polygon with the smallest area, enclosing S, that cannot be crossed by a straight line joining any two points in 5. MacGregor and Ormerod further motivate this hypothesis by suggesting that the convex hull may provide a two-dimensional illustration of the Gestalt law of Prägnanz in the same way that a soap bubble surface has been used to illustrate it in three dimensions.

According to Ormerod and Chronicle, the convex hull hypothesis makes two obvious and testable predictions. The first, which follows from the hypothesised correspondence between solution processes and spontaneous perceptual principles, is that TSP solutions that are closer to optimality should be rated more highly as having good figure. The second prediction, which follows from the hypothesis that the salient principle in arriving at solutions is the global perception of a convex hull structure, is that solutions with relatively more points on the convex hull (and hence, fewer internal points) will constitute simpler TSPs and be rated as better figures. Ormerod and Chronicle tested these predictions in an experiment in which participants rated the perceived goodness of five possible solutions to each of five 10-point TSP problem instances. The solutions were constructed in the ranges 0%, 11%-18%, 21%-28%, 32%-37%, and 41%-47% longer than the optimal solution. The five problem instances (plus a standard, 10-point Dantzig configuration) also contained between one and five internal nodes that were located inside the convex hull bounding each configuration. Ormerod and Chronicle found that the participants judged optimal solutions as being good s and progressively less optimal solutions as being progressively less good figures. They also found that the participants rated the solutions to problem instances with fewer internal nodes (and hence, relatively more nodes on the convex hull) as better figures. They interpreted these results as evidence for the hypothesis that the finding of nearoptimal solutions to visually presented TSP instances is mediated by spontaneous global perceptual organizing processes, similar to that underlying the perception of good gestalts, and based on the ready identification of the convex hull of each array.

Some support for the view that the TSP solution process is strongly influenced by the operation of spontaneous perceptual principles is provided by a study by Vickers et al. (2001). In their first experiment, these authors presented two groups of participants with six different arrays of irregularly positioned dots, each representing the nodes of a TSP instance: two 10-node, two 25-node, and two 40-node arrays. The participants in the gestali group were instructed to draw a pathway that passed through each of the points just once, that returned to the starting point, and that looked"most natural, attractive, or aesthetically pleasing."

The participants in the optimization group were instructed to draw a pathway that passed through each point just once, that returned to the starting point, and that was as short as possible. Although Vickers et al. (2001) found that there was a relatively small (but significant) difference in the average length of the pathways produced by the two groups, there was also a considerable overlap between the pathways produced by the two groups, with several participants from one group producing exactly the same pathways as those from the other. Despite this agreement, however, there are some difficulties with Ormerod and Chronicle's conclusion regarding the identification of the shortest pathway with the figure judged to have the highest degree of goodness.

There are difficulties also with their conclusion that the apparent relation between perceived goodness and number of interior points provides initial support for the view that the convex hull is an important determinant of perceived goodness. These difficulties all stem from the method used by Ormerod and Chronicle to generate their configurations, which consisted of small angular perturbations and incremental transformations of one initial, regular polygon, in which all points fell on the circumference of a circle.

As the authors themselves make clear,"it is still conceivable that TSP solutions are provided through some other set of cognitive operations, unconnected with a judgment of good figure, and that the relationship with good figure... is merely coincidental". Indeed, a number of other possibilities, besides solution optimality and number of internal nodes, readily suggest themselves as potential factors contributing to the judgments of figurai goodness observed by Ormerod and Chronicle. First, the convex hulls for these five figures describe polygons with close to perfect regularity. Thus, degree of perceived rotational symmetry is a possible contributing factor. Indeed, the circular prototype, with which MacGregor and Ormerod and Ormerod and Chronicle started, encloses a given area with a perimeter of minimum length. Circular figures have long been regarded as"ideal" figures, and it is possible that the participants in the study by Ormerod and Chronicle judged the presented solutions as aesthetically pleasing to the extent that they approximated the circular prototype used by these authors as a basis for creating successive variants.

Circularity, in this instance, correlates highly with the number of points on the convex hull (r =.96), so it is possible that circularity would also provide an equally or more predictive measure of good figure for configurations in which this correlation is less pronounced. Second, the degree of convexity of the solutions or in Ormerod and Chronicle, as conventionally measured by the ratio between the area enclosed by the solution configuration and the area enclosed by the convex hull, varies systematically. Although convexity would be expected to show a correlation with the number of nodes on the convex hull, convexity is potentially a more sensitive measure.

(For example, a six-pointed regular star figure can have six convex hull nodes only, but, depending on the depth of the indentations, can possess varying degrees of convexity.) Polivanova's participants identified convexity as one of the criteria they employed in arriving at solutions, and convexity is a factor that has long been identified with the differentiation between figure and ground, as well as, more recently, with perceptual completion and the perception of holes.

Third, the actual links making up the optimal solutions also vary in regularity, as measured by progressive increases in the standard deviation in length of the connecting edges. (From scanned versions of their figures, we estimate the standard deviations to take values proportional to 0.029, 0.039, 0.111, 0.112, and 0.141 units for the figures with one to five internal nodes, respectively.) Fourth, the arrays vary with respect to the total number of potential intersections associated with all possible pairs of links between all 10 nodes of each instance. We estimate that the total number of potential intersections, expressed as a per centage of all permissible links, took values of 29.5%, 25.9%, 21.6%, 20.2%, and 19.1% for their stimuli with 1-5 internal nodes, respectively.

Because any TSP solution must avoid intersections to be optimal, and because any solution that fails to connect the nodes of the convex hull in order of adjacency must give rise to an intersection, any solution that follows the rule of avoiding intersections must visit the nodes of the convex hull in order. Thus, number of potential intersections might have contributed to the results of Ormerod and Chronicle. Fifth, measures of path complexity also appear to vary systematically. Path complexity indexes the extent to which configurations made use of k nearest neighbours in their construction.

For each edge in the configuration, numbers (1 to k) are assigned, according to whether the nodes of that link are connected to the nearest:

- Second nearest
- Or kth nearest node.

The sum of these numbers is divided by the number of edges to give a measure of path complexity. The lower the path complexity, the more the configuration tends to connect each node to its nearer neighbours. For their stimuli, with 9 to 5 convex hull nodes, respectively, we estimate that path complexity takes values of 3.0, 3.3,4.2, 5.1, and 6.0. Thus, the data of Ormerod and Chronicle could be just as consistent with a locally based process of linking near neighbours as they appear to be with a globally based process of using the convex hull as an initial perceptual framework. Finally, judging from the minuscule standard errors in the two graphs presented, Ormerod and Chronicle, like MacGregor and Ormerod, do not appear to have found any appreciable individual differences in participants' responses.

As has been argued by Vickers et al. and by Vickers, Bovet, Lee, and Hughes, such a result is almost certainly due to the relatively sparse and highly constrained arrays employed by them. Because reliable individual differences appear when the problem arrays are less constrained and are more densely populated with nodes, it is possible that such arrays might also give rise to a more complex pattern of ratings of figurai goodness than do those obtained by Ormerod and Chronicle. In view of these difficulties, the following experiment was undertaken to differentiate between the above factors potentially underlying judgments of the figurai goodness of TSP solutions and to arbitrate between alternative hypotheses concerning the relationship between these factors and the perceived goodness or aesthetic appeal of such structures.

The principal hypotheses, with which we started, were that the figural goodness or aesthetic appeal of solution pathways is based on:

- The optimality of the solution,
- The number of nodes on the convex hull or
- The number of nodes that were linked to their nearest neighbour in a solution.

These variables were manipulated in a factorial design that restricted the regularity of the figures (as measured by the standard deviation in their edge lengths) to a very narrow range, excluded actual intersections, and held the number of potential intersections constant. However, the design of the experiment also permitted an investigation of the role of the degree of convexity, circularity, and path complexity and allowed effects of the degree of rotational symmetry (as indexed by the standard deviation in the lengths of the convex hull edges) to be assessed.

This was achieved by generating large numbers of random arrays and selecting from them those configurations with the desired characteristics. This method provides a strong contrast with that used by Ormerod and Chronicle to generate their configurations, which consisted of incremental transformations of one initial, highly regular array.

In addition, the use of more complex configurations avoided ceiling effects and allowed for the possible emergence of individual differences

METHOD

In this experiment, strict rotational symmetry was excluded by employing randomly generated solution pathways linking well populated arrays of randomly distributed dots, while approximate rotational symmetry was quantified by the standard deviation in the lengths of the convex hull edges and was allowed to vary randomly. The regularity of the figures, as measured by the standard deviation in the link lengths, was restricted to a very narrow range and was not allowed to vary systematically.

There were no actual intersections, and the number of potential intersections was held constant, whereas the number of convex hull nodes, the optimality of solutions, and the number of nodes linked to their nearest neighbours that were incorporated in these solutions were varied in a factorial design. In addition, degree of convexity was allowed to vary randomly, as was the circularity and path complexity of the configurations.

STIMULUS GENERATION

In order to obtain expectations for the number of nodes on the convex hull, the number of internal node intersections,2 and the standard deviation of the internode distance, 20,000 random 25-node arrays were generated within the unit square. For these arrays, the mean number of convex hull nodes was 8.35 (SD = 1.41), the mean per centage of internal node intersections was 23.3%, and the mean standard deviation in the internode distance was 0.245. With these statistics as a basis, we generated a number of random 25-node arrays. Of these, we selected a number that had a low (13), medium (16 or 17), or high (20) number of internal nodes.

This selection was also constrained to have a constant proportion (23.0%-23.6%) of internal node intersections and a constant (0.24-0.25) standard deviation in the internode distance. A further subset of these arrays was then chosen, in which the number of internal nodes was visually indisputable. In all, 18 different arrays were chosen: 6 from each of the three internal nodes groups. In addition, 1 from each group was chosen for practice.

For each of these 18 arrays, a benchmark (putatively optimal) closed TSP solution was calculated, using a simulated annealing heuristic. Random solutions were then generated for each array that had a low (0%-5%), medium (10%-15%), or high (20%-25%) difference from the benchmark solution. (The 0%-25% range of deviations from the benchmark was chosen because it was representative of the range found in the solutions produced by the participants in several of our previous TSP studies.) For each of these random solutions, we noted the number of nodes that were linked to their nearest neighbour in the solution path. The lowest and the highest numbers of nodes connected to their nearest neighbour that could be found in solutions corresponding to each of the nine difference from benchmark and interior node group combinations were 16 and 23, respectively. Accordingly, we determined that the three nearest neighbour linked groups should be low, medium (19-20), and high (23-24). Thus, random solutions were generated for six problem instances in each of the three internal nodes, three differences-from-benchmark, and three nearest-neighbour-linked groups. These solutions were selected to have no path crossings (and as a result, connected the convex hull nodes in sequence). More than one solution was generated for each instance in order that unrealistic tours (ones that incorporated obvious, zigzag backtracking) could be eliminated. However, no other restriction was placed on the solutions. The number of attempts required to generate a single acceptable solution for a given problem instance in a given group ranged from 100 to 1,000,000.

STIMULI

The participants rated the perceived goodness of 162 configurations, each consisting of complete tours (Hamiltonian circuits) of 25 randomly distributed nodes. The 162 configurations were made up of six instances drawn from each of three (high, medium, and low) internal nodes, differences-from-benchmark, and nearest-neighbourlinked groups (i.e., of 27 level × group combinations). The nodes were represented by black circular dots, 1.5 mm in diameter, connected by black links on a light gray background and were displayed within a 14 × 14 cm square, with no border, at the centre of a computer screen. The configurations were viewed from a distance of about 50-60 cm.

DESIGN

Each participant was presented with the 162 configurations in a different order that was random, but subject to the constraint that all 27 combinations of number of internal nodes, level of optimality, and number of nodes linked to their nearest neighbours were presented once, before being repeated.

PROCEDURE

Following a practice run of 12 configurations, in which the upper and lower values of each of the three factors were represented, the participants carried out the test run, at their own pace, in one unbroken series. As has been noted by van der Helm and Leeuwenberg (2004), figurai goodness is an intuitive Gestalt notion that has no formal definition. Because this notion can be assumed to be familiar only to those who know about research into gestalt properties in visual perception, we sought to express the same notion in more widely understandable terms.

On the basis that studies of the properties considered good by naive participants have used such terms as most pleasing and liked, the participants were asked to give a "rating of the aesthetic appeal of the figure, of how attractive they found it as an abstract configuration." This wording corresponded closely to that employed by Vickers et al. (2001), who instructed participants in their Gestalt group to draw a pathway through the nodes that "looked most natural, attractive, or aesthetically pleasing." The figures were not described as possible TSP solutions, and no mention was made of path length, optimality, or any other characteristic of the configurations.

The 3 × 3 grid of panels corresponds to the three levels of nearest neighbours (in rows) and convex hull points (in columns). Each panel shows, as a bold line, the mean aesthetic rating averaged across all subjects, with one standard error in each direction, as a function of the level of difference from optimality. Each panel also shows, in gray, the mean values for the other panels, to allow for direct visual comparison. There is also a suggestion of a consistent, but much less pronounced, pattern in relation to the number of convex hull points, with mean aesthetic appeal being greatest for those configurations with the most points on the convex hull.

Because this experiment was designed as a factorial study, our initial analysis was restricted to considering group performance. This analysis, however, makes the implicit assumption that there are no meaningful individual differences between participants. If this assumption is incorrect, as was explained long ago by Estes, the averaging of performance measures used to calculate the group data can seriously distort the way those data relate to the underlying psychological processes they are supposed to measure. As it turns out, we believe that there is evidence of significant and meaningful individual differences in the data, and so the majority of our analysis is conducted at the level of individuals.

INDIVIDUAL ANALYSIS

To examine the reliability of individual differences across the 27 problem types, Pearson correlations were calculated between the average of each participant's ratings for the six problem instances of each type and the average rating for each of the other problem types (i.e., a total of 351 correlations). Of these 351 correlations, there were 224 positive correlations that were significant at the.05 level or better and only 3 significant negative correlations (N = 40 in all cases). The average of the 351 correlations was.41. With 12,990 degrees of freedom, the probability of obtaining an average correlation of this size by chance is minuscule.

Therefore, for each participant, arithmetic mean figurai attractiveness ratings were calculated over the six instances of each of the 27 internal nodes, differencesfrom-benchmark, and nearest-neighbour-linked groups of configurations. Correlations were then calculated, for each participant, between figurai attractiveness and each one of a number of stimulus variables. Several of these variables had no strong theoretical motivation and proved to have little or no predictive value. These included the area inside the convex hull, the total length of the convex hull, the average edge length of the convex hull, and rotational symmetry as indexed by the standard deviation in the edge length of the convex hull. For these variables, arithmetic means (over participants) of the absolute (unsigned) values of their Pearson correlations with figurai attractiveness were.12.34.33, and.34, respectively.

A number of variables had a stronger theoretical motivation but provided only weak to moderate predictions of attractiveness ratings. Variables in this category included the number of interior nodes, the number of nodes that were linked to their nearest neighbour, and regularity, as indexed by the standard deviation in the lengths of the configuration edges. For these variables, arithmetic means (over participants) of the absolute values of their Pearson correlations with figurai attractiveness were.34.14, and.45, respectively. Of these, only the measure of regularity made a moderate contribution to the prediction of attractiveness ratings.

Finally, four variables possessed a strong theoretical motivation and made a moderate to strong contribution to the prediction of attractiveness ratings. These variables were the per centage by which the solution length exceeded the benchmark (putatively optimal) solution, the circularity of the configurations, convexity, and path complexity. For these variables, arithmetic means (over participants) of the absolute values of their Pearson correlations with figural attractiveness were.58.66.47, and.62, respectively.

For rated attractiveness, two sets of correlations are shown:

- Correlations between mean stimulus measures (averaged over the six instances of each of the 27 stimulus types) and mean attractiveness ratings for each stimulus type (averaged over all participants and over each of the stimulus types) and
- Averages of the absolute values of the correlations between mean stimulus measures (averaged for each of the 27 stimulus types) and mean attractiveness ratings for each participant (averaged for each of the 27 stimulus types).

The most successful predictive measure overall turned out to be circularity. Therefore, the participants have been ordered according to the strength of the correlation (over the 27 configuration types) between their ratings of figurai attractiveness and the mean circularity measures for the corresponding configuration types.

With the exception of two points, the correlations for the other three measures follow a similar pattern. In recognition of this pattern of individual differences, the four most predictive measures were examined, for different partitionings of the participants, to see which measure produced the highest positive and negative average correlations for a given partitioning. The measure that was most successful in this respect was circularity, with participants partitioned into Subgroups 1-30 (average r =.94) and 31-40 (average r = -.80). For the same partitioning, path complexity produced average correlations of r = -.93 (Participants 1-30) and r =.60 (Participants 31-40).

Convexity produced correlations of r =.58 (Participants 1-30) and r = -.90 (Participants 31-40), respectively. By exchanging the rank position of 2 participants (i.e., by ranking the participants according to the correlation between their attractiveness ratings and solution optimality), per centage above benchmark produced average correlations of r = -.89 and.43, respectively.

The results presented above do not lend themselves to easy generalizations over participants. Nevertheless, a number of general conclusions can be drawn. These concern the importance of individual differences in judgments, the possibility of polar differences in perceptual style, and the relative importance of different stimulus measures for judgments of figurai goodness or attractiveness. We shall discuss each point in turn.

INDIVIDUAL DIFFERENCES

The first point is that individual differences in ratings of figural attractiveness in the present study were highly reliable, with ratings for any one solution type being positively and significantly correlated with ratings for the great majority of the other solution types. These data are different from those in Ormerod and Chronicle's Experiment 1, which showed negligible variation across participants in their ratings of figural goodness.

On the other hand, the present result is in agreement with other findings of consistent individual differences across problem instances and across different types of problems, as well as reliable correlations with psychometric measures of intelligence. It is not possible to explain the divergence, with respect to individual differences, between our results, either here or in our other studies, and those of MacGregor and colleagues in terms of the provision or otherwise of feedback or knowledge of results. It is true that the experiments of Vickers, Bovet, et al. (2003) and of Vickers, Lee, et al. (2003) provided trial-by-trial feedback by way of correct solutions. However, neither the present experiment nor the four experiments reported by Vickers et al. (2001) and by Vickers et al. (2004) provided any feedback or knowledge of results, but all showed reliable individual differences. It is also not possible to account for this divergence in terms of a difference in the opportunities for learning in our experiments and in those of MacGregor and colleagues. There is nothing to be learned in the present experiment. Meanwhile, Experiment 1 in Vickers et al. (2001) involved six different problem instances, whereas their Experiment 2 involved only one. Similarly, Experiment 1 in Vickers et al. (2004) used five different problem instances, whereas their Experiment 2 involved only one instance of each of three different types of problems.

Although the participants in these experiments were presented with fewer problem instances and had less opportunity for learning than were those in the experiments of MacGregor and colleagues, consistent individual differences still emerged. As was suggested by Vickers, Bovet, et al. (2003), the most plausible explanation for the divergence between the two sets of results stems from the fact that the stimuli used by MacGregor and colleagues contain fewer nodes and were generated in a highly constrained way, so that the problems were simpler and variations in performance were limited by ceiling effects. Similarly, the discrepancy between the present results and those in Ormerod and Chronicle appear to be due to several potentially confounding factors in the latter study that combined to produce responses that were overdetermined by correlated information.

DIFFERENCES IN PERCEPTUAL STYLE

With the exception of one or two borderline individuals, the participants in this experiment fell into two quite distinct groups: a larger group (Participants 1-30), for whom circularity and convexity were positively related to attractiveness ratings, whereas path complexity and per centage above the benchmark were negatively correlated, and a smaller group (Participants 31-40), for whom such variables were related to rated attractiveness in the opposite way.

Although we did not anticipate this outcome, in hindsight, we should have been forewarned, because the task of producing natural, attractive, or aesthetically pleasing configurations, employed by Vickers et al. (2001) with their gestalt group of participants, resulted in a similar wide spectrum of approaches that "ranged from pathway minimization... up to one or two that seemed designed to maximise the pathway length".

At this stage, we can only speculate about the explanation for this polar opposition between the two groups. There are a number of other oppositions between individual differences in perceptual style that have been investigated under the rubrics of field dependence/independence, local versus global processing, and analytic versus holistic processing. The contrast that seems to be captured in these oppositions is one between a parallel process, in which perception is determined in an immediate way by the overall configuration of a stimulus, and a more deliberate, serial process, in which attention is focused on figurai elements.

This contrast characterises quite well the opposition between the global, convex hull approach to understanding human TSP performance developed by MacGregor and his colleagues and the locally focused approach proposed by us, which is based on relational information of the kind provided by nearest neighbours. However, although this polar opposition might conceivably have some relevance for the understanding of TSP performance, it does not seem to map onto the opposition shown in the present data.

The reason is that individual participants appear to use both global and local features of the configurations in the same way, but both global and local features seem to play opposite roles in the judgments of the two groups of participants. Thus, our results echo those of Jacobsen (2004), who found that although intra-individual judgments of aesthetic attraction were consistent, their relationships to stimulus properties could not be adequately represented by a model based on average responses.

FACTORS INFLUENCING FIGURAI ATTRACTIVENESS

Despite the problem for any model based on averages, it is still possible to make some general inferences from the data regarding the relative importance of different stimulus features in determining judgments of attractiveness or figurai goodness. For example, among the theoretically motivated variables that turned out to have little or no predictive value, the number of nodes that were connected to their nearest neighbour produced the clearest result.

The arithmetic mean (over the 40 participants) of the absolute values of the Pearson correlations between this variable and rated attractiveness was very low (r =.14); over the 162 individual configurations, this correlation dropped to.07. This suggests that figurai attractiveness is not based on the extent to which a configuration incorporates nearest neighbour links.

On the other hand, the optimality of solution pathways in this study was determined largely by the extent to which such pathways incorporated higher order nearest neighbours. This is reflected in the high correlations between optimality and path complexity (r =.93) and between judged attractiveness and path complexity (average absolute r over 27 stimulus groups =.62). This suggests that the attractiveness of TSP solutions may be influenced (positively or negatively for different participant groups) by the extent to which the solutions approach optimality and have lower values of path complexity.

Of the other measures with a strong theoretical motivation, the number of internal nodes (or conversely, the number of nodes on the convex hull) was not very successful. The arithmetic mean (over the 40 participants) of the absolute values of the Pearson correlations between this variable and rated attractiveness was low (r =.34). It appears that participants show consistent preferences between configurations for which the number of internal nodes is the same.

As was suggested earlier, the number of nodes on the convex hull may not provide a useful predictive measure of TSP performance either, once the total number of nodes exceeds about 50. It is also the case that a measure of convexity might be expected to prove a more sensitive and more successful predictor of attractiveness ratings, as was the case in this experiment (average absolute r over 27 stimulus groups =.47). Indeed, although convexity was much less successful than per centage above benchmark, circularity, or path complexity in predicting attractiveness ratings by the larger group of participants, it did provide the strongest prediction of attractiveness by the smaller group (Participants 31-40). At the same time, convexity was strongly correlated with circularity (r =.75), so that it is possible that this accounts for some of its predictive value.

The measure that provided the strongest prediction of figurai attractiveness overall for both groups was circularity (average absolute rover 27 stimulus groups =.66). For the larger group of participants, this could be explained as being due to a preference for a structure that is optimal in the sense of enclosing a given area (or volume) with the shortest perimeter (or the smallest surface area in the case of a three-dimensional object).

This optimization process may be subject to particular constraints in a given situation, which may result in more complex structures than circles or spheres. However, such structures are ubiquitous in nature as well as in human constructions and are generally regarded as both aesthetically and practically satisfying. This leaves the problem of why the smaller group responded in an opposite way to circularity, as well as to the other three most predictive measures. The most plausible explanation we can suggest is that both groups of participants have an aesthetic preference for structures that are, in some sense, optimal. However, no mention was made of optimality in this experiment, nor was there any indication of what might constitute optimality.

Besides natural and artificial structures that enclose a given area (or volume) within the shortest perimeter (or smallest surface area), there are also natural structures that are optimal in exposing a given area (or volume) to the greatest possibility of interchange with the immediate environment of that area (or volume). Examples include lung tissue and numerous branching structures, such as coral or veins and arteries that have fractal characteristics. Such structures also appear to have an aesthetic attraction, and it is possible that the smaller group of participants might have judged the configurations as more or less optimal in this sense.

Although the present results are equivocal with respect to what participants regard as optimal structure, it would be possible to investigate whether aesthetic judgments of a wide range of different two-dimensional configurations and three-dimensional forms exhibit a similar pattern of maximizing or minimizing contour or surface for a given enclosed area or volume. It would also be possible to examine the extent to which such preferences might be influenced by cognitive factors, such as participants' understanding of what such configurations or forms might represent and of what a given structure might be designed to optimise. Meanwhile, there is no information in the present experiment that supports a strong link between the individual differences found here and other differences in perceptual style or personality. However, if the account above in terms of preference for different types of optimal structure is assumed, we might interpret this as a difference in preference for forms that minimise or maximise the boundaries at which exchanges with the surrounding environment can take place. If so, we might go on to speculate that the pattern of individual differences found in the present experiment could be linked to such personality traits as openness and preference for complexity. However, only further research can decide whether such speculation may prove fruitful.

The present study identifies several confounding factors that may have contributed to the conclusion by Ormerod and Chronicle that the identification of the convex hull is important in determining an overall gestalt and that the greater the number of solution nodes that fall on the convex hull, the more attractive the solution will be judged to be.

Results from the present study show that the number of convex hull nodes was only a weak predictor (either positively or negatively) of attractiveness ratings. Taken in conjunction with Vickers, Lee, et al.'s (2003) finding that the greater the number of points on the convex hull of randomly generated arrays, the poorer were participants' solutions, the present results argue against the influence of the convex hull as an important determinant of perceptual organization, of the optimality of participants' solutions, or of the perceived goodness or attractiveness of TSP solutions.

On the other hand, the present results provide qualified support for Ormerod and Chronicle's finding that participants' ratings of the goodness of TSP solutions were correlated with their relative optimality. The important qualification is that what is defined as optimal by the experimenter (in this case, minimizing total path length) may not be what the participants regard as optimal. Instead, it appears that participants are divided as to whether the most attractive configuration is that which encloses a given area within a perimeter of minimum or of maximum length (i.e., one that is most or least circular). The results did not support the view that solutions would be judged attractive to the extent that they incorporated nearest neighbours.

On the other hand, the results were consistent with the view that good organization was determined by path complexity (i.e., the extent to which a solution incorporated near neighbours of the lowest possible order). The results were also consistent with the hypothesis that judged attractiveness is influenced by convexity, although to a lesser extent. Thus, the results are consistent with the possibility that configurations are judged attractive to the extent that they are optimal and incorporate spontaneous, locally focused, perceptual organizing principles based on nearest neighbours. Similarly, the results do not rule out the possibility that attractiveness is based (albeit less strongly) on a globally focused measure.

If so, however, the most promising measure is that of convexity, rather than the number of nodes on the convex hull. To test such hypotheses, future work would need to achieve the independent manipulation of path complexity, per centage above benchmark, circularity, and convexity. In contrast to the study of Ormerod and Chronicle, the present experiment showed consistent individual differences between participants.

Each of the configuration types was rated by the participants in much the same way as each of the other configuration types. However, the attractiveness ratings for one group of participants appeared to be related to stimulus characteristics in a way that was opposite to that of the other group. Although both groups may be construed as preferring structures that are optimal (albeit in opposing ways), it seems clear that future research in this area cannot afford to focus exclusively on group performance measures.

12

Distribution Policy

INTERNATIONAL DISTRIBUTION CHANNELS

The next aspect of the marketing mix you have to analyse is distribution. International distribution is the structure formed by the producing company along with each one of their intermediaries though which the product passes until it reaches the end consumer.

What you should take into account:

- The type of product being distributed
- The target market sector
- The market quota
- The services being provided by those on the distribution chain, both suppliers and clients. That is, warehouse facilities, after sales service, etc.

First you must decide whether to distribute the products yourself or use an intermediary. Direct international sales implies extensive logistics capacity: warehouses, control systems, order processing etc. are required.

However, it is more usual to use intermediaries. The two main figures in the distribution chain are the wholesaler and the retailer.

WHAT ARE THEIR CHARACTERISTICS?

This depends very much on the market. In more developed economies, the wholesalers are medium-to-large companies, mostly specialists in specific areas and providing support services to clients. Retailers also vary a lot from one market to another and depend on factors such as consumer habits, acquisition power, culture, political-legal framework, etc. The tendency is that less developed markets have a large number of retailers.

FUNCTIONS AND STRUCTURE OF INTERNATIONAL DISTRIBUTION CHANNELS

Their functions are to introduce the product into the export destination country and make it available to the end consumer. Depending on the intervention of more or fewer agents in the channel structure, there are two types of distribution:

- *Long distribution chain*: When there are many parties in the chain, that is, many intermediaries or when there is very little known about the market and your presence is not very consolidated, the tendency is to use a distribution channel of this type. In the initial phase of market introduction, this solution is more convenient for the exporter.
- *Short distribution chain*: When one of the intermediaries in the chain is eliminated and you get closer to the end client you have a short distribution chain. The advantages gained are a reduction in intermediary commercial margins. That is, you distribute directly to wholesalers or purchasing centres. However, be aware that this requires the capacity to get to all of them, the role played by the retailer.
- *Direct distribution*: If you get to know your market sufficiently well you can adopt direct distribution methods. Exporters dealing directly with the end client gives them absolute control over marketing. However, be aware that this also implies a great deal more work. You need to be capable, with your own means, to supply the market.

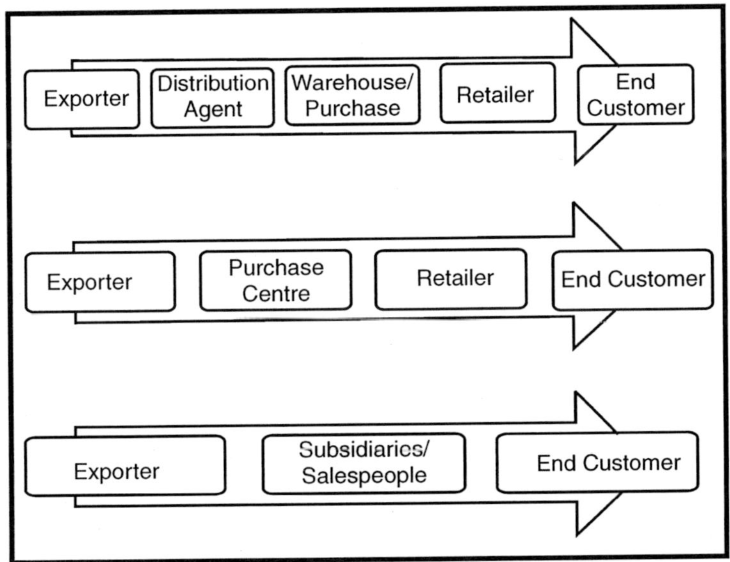

Fig. The Length of the Distribution Chain.

ROLE OF INTERNET IN INTERNATIONAL DISTRIBUTION

Information is the main drive of the Internet and how it is made available to the online masses. In fact, online businesses are now focusing on providing informative content, as well as making it accessible to the rest of the world, especially the case of online business. Webmasters are now implementing Internet marketing strategies to achieve the basic Internet requirement of quality information and accessibility.

ROLE INTERNET MARKETING

The main role of Internet marketing is simply to provide quality information to the online public, and making it accessible to them by taking into consideration the different methods used by Web surfers to collect information from the World Wide Web.

Quality information is quite easy to achieve; it only takes a little bit of advance planning regarding the layout of the Web site, as well as the range of information that you plan to put in it. Accessibility, on the other hand, requires a little more effort than coming up with informative content for your online business. You need to understand how information look-up works on the Internet and the different methods that is attributed to it.

INFORMATION MARKETING STRATEGY

Now that you have a basic idea on the role of Internet marketing strategy on your online business, you now need to learn how to assimilate it into your venture. The first step is to optimize your site for search engines; considering that this is the primary tool for information look-up on the Internet using keyword search.

SEARCH ENGINES

Search engine optimization requires keywords to be placed in specific areas of your site so that it can be picked up by search engines. The more keywords you have on your site, the higher your ranking would be on search engine results. You may want to vary the keywords according to the general content of your site for better search engine coverage.

You can also improve your page ranking for better search engine results by propagating links of your site on the World Wide Web. The more links that you have on different Web sites on the Internet pointing back to your site, the higher your page ranking would be; which in turn, will place you on the top ranks of search engine results.

LINK BUILDING

Another Internet marketing strategy to improve your site's accessibility is through the use of links. You need to expand your coverage by posting your site address on different sites on the Web through the use of links. You can publish keyword-rich substances with your link embedded into its content; or subscribed to Web directories for the self-same result.

ADVERTISING

Proper advertisement of your online venture is one of the basic stratagems of Internet marketing. Aside from increasing your online presence through search engines and links, you can take the effort to advertise your site directly to the online public, such as:

- Advertising your business on related forums and chat rooms
- Setting up banners
- Using affiliate marketers to sell of your products and services to the public, and so on.

Index

O

P

Q

R

S

U